On My 100-Year Watch

On My 100-Year Watch: Tyrants and Patriots

J. William Middendorf II
with Kenneth R. Dooley

The Naval War College Foundation, Inc.
Newport, R.I. · 2024

Copyright 2024 J. William Middendorf II and Kenneth R. Dooley

All rights reserved. No part of this book may be reproduced in any form whatsoever without permission in writing from the publisher, except for brief passages in connection with a review.

For information write:
info@jwilliammiddendorf.com
https://www.jwilliammiddendorf.com

ISBN: 979-8-218-43207-2

Typeset in Minion Pro

Printed in the United States of America
by Lakeside Book Company

Table of Contents

Foreword — Ed Feulner, Founder, Heritage Foundation … viii

1. Five Characteristics Present in Communist Takeovers and an Islamic Revolution … 3
2. Ready, Aim, Misfire: Who Gave China to the Communists … 16
3. Ready, Aim, Misfire: Redux: Who Gave Cuba to the Communists … 28
4. Ambassador to the Netherlands … 44
5. Secretary of the Navy … 60
6. Queen Elizabeth II Joins the U.S. Navy … 83
7. Iran: With Friends Like These … 96
8. The Vietnam Extraction: Operation Frequent Wind … 108
9. How 9/11 Could Have Been Prevented … 117
10. Spies Among Us … 129
11. Ambassador to the Organization of American States … 141
12. What We Must Learn From the Falklands War … 152
13. Grenada: Operation Urgent Fury: Russia Nearly Gets a Runway … 165
14. Venezuela's Young Fidel Castro … 184
15. Ambassador to the European Community … 196
16. When Russia Nearly Became a Democracy … 206
17. Project Economic Justice: Private vs. Public Ownership of Industry … 215
18. The Business of Banking … 225
19. Advisor to Presidents and a Wanna-Be … 235
20. Music, Poetry, and Art … 270
21. My Life Story … 279

Notes … 305

Index … 315

Dedication

I will always be grateful for the love and support of Isabelle, my wife of 63 years; my daughters, Frances, Martha, and Amy, and her husband, Don; my son, John and his wife Jeni, and son Roxy, and his wife Sofia.

To so many, I owe so much, starting with Secretary of the Navy Carlos Del Toro. I expressed my admiration for him by composing "The Carlos Del Toro March." Lt. David Harbuziuk, Director of the Navy Band, described the march as follows: "A number of the themes are regal and majestic; the fanfares and flourishes befit a position as important and heralded as SECNAV. The march has a strong, powerful, triumphant ending." Edward Feulner, the founder of the Heritage Foundation, who wrote the foreword of this book, stood with me as the Berlin Wall came down; U.S. Senator Jack Reed, a senior member of the Armed Services Committee, works hard to ensure that America's fighting men and women have the weapons they need to preserve our way of life; I am grateful for the sage advice of Captain George Lang, President of The Naval War College Foundation, and Philip and Patricia Bilden for their constant love and support; Ken Dooley for always asking the right questions and finding the correct answers; Dr. Patrick T. Conley, Historian Laureate of Rhode Island; Margaret Satell Stay for bringing new meaning to the title of copy editor; Frank Lennon, president of the Rhode Island Aviation Hall of Fame and Jim Carafano and Brent Sadler of the Heritage Foundation; Thomas Callender, manager of Navy Programs, General Dynamics; Chris Townsend, Navy League National President, and Mike Stevens, CEO of the Navy League. A special thanks to my friend John Duke and my assistants, Frances Coelho, Madeline Brumley, and Justin Graves.

One of the great honors of my life was serving shoulder to shoulder with Admiral James L. Holloway III, Chief of Naval Operations, while I was Secretary of the Navy. Jimmy's steady, calm, and brilliant leadership could always be counted on during difficult times.

Bill Middendorf

✶ ✶ ✶

For my brother Bob, who was always the wind beneath my wings, and my nephew Scott, who took his place.

Ken Dooley

Foreword
Ed Feulner, Founder, Heritage Foundation

J. WILLIAM MIDDENDORF II was prepared for tough decisions and leadership early in his career. He was a naval officer in World War II stationed in China, first as a member of the occupation forces and briefly as part of the security for General George Marshall, who tried to broker peace between Mao Zedong and Chiang Kai-shek. Marshall halted the shipment of weapons to the Nationalists in 1945, a decision that placed the Communists in control of China four years later. Middendorf, like many of the officers who made up the occupation team, was horrified when a writer for *The New York Times* described Mao Zedong as the "George Washington of Asia."

As a businessman in Cuba in 1958, Middendorf was among the first to identify Fidel Castro as a devoted Communist with direct connections to the Soviet Union. This was at the same time that American journalists were praising Castro for bringing freedom, free elections, and prosperity to Cuba. Middendorf escaped Havana in a small plane with bullet holes in the fuselage, placed by Castro's machine guns.

At 40, Middendorf founded a company with a seat on the New York Stock Exchange. He could have settled for business success, but he decided instead to pursue a career in public service. Making money was important, but making a difference was more meaningful to him. In 1969, he left his investment firm and accepted the role of U.S. Ambassador to The Netherlands. He became Secretary of the Navy in 1974, a time when the Soviet Navy threatened to overtake the United States' naval power. Middendorf worked to maintain America's competitive edge under presidents Richard Nixon and Gerald Ford. He supported the development of vital programs, most notably the trident missile for Ohio-class submarines, the Aegis missile defense system with its 80 Arleigh-Burke class destroyers, and the F/A-18 combat jet.

In April 1975, President Ford reached out to Middendorf to devise a plan to evacuate thousands of Americans and at-risk Vietnamese from Saigon as the Viet Cong took over the country. Admiral Holloway and Middendorf came up with "Operation Frequent Wind," in which helicopters took Americans and friendly Vietnamese to ships of the Seventh Fleet in the South China Sea. For 18 hours, 81 overloaded and crammed helicopters piloted by exhausted men ferried 1,373 Americans and 5,595 Vietnamese and third-country nationals to freedom.

As Secretary of the Navy, Middendorf had a good relationship with Mohammad Reza Pahlavi, the Shah of Iran. Middendorf's warnings about

Ayatollah Khomeini and the revolutionaries attempting to overthrow the Shah were ignored, creating a dangerous foe for the United States. Iran's abrupt transformation from a reliable U.S. security partner and hub for American investment to an anti-American regime led by an ascetic cleric confounded Washington.

In 1980, President-elect Reagan assigned Middendorf as the interim head of a transition team for the CIA. His team recommended a policy requiring information sharing between the CIA and the FBI. It also urged more stringent internal security because the Soviet Union was executing many of our spies behind the Iron Curtain. The CIA rejected all of the recommendations from Middendorf's team. If the information-sharing policy had been adopted, 9/11 might have been averted. All 19 of the terrorists involved in 9/11 were on a CIA watch list when they landed in this country for pilot training. The list was not shared with the FBI. Increased internal security might have prevented Aldrich Ames, head of the CIA's Counterterrorism group, from selling the names of dozens of our agents in the Soviet Union. Tighter controls might have uncovered turncoat FBI agent Robert Hanssen, the most dangerous spy in FBI history.

Middendorf continued to advance national security as Ambassador to the Organization of American States (OAS), where he resisted the expansion of Soviet and Cuban influence in Latin America. One of his first challenges was dealing with the Falklands War that began in April 1982 when the Argentine Military Junta invaded the islands and captured 1,000 British citizens. Middendorf had to walk a tightrope, supporting Margaret Thatcher's decision to retake the Falkland Islands without offending the pro-Argentine members of the OAS.

One year into his tour as Ambassador to the OAS, Middendorf sounded the alarm on a new runway that was being built in Granada. The small island country was under the command of Maurice Bishop, a Communist who had signed trade and military agreements with Havana and Moscow. The new runway would be long enough to handle the largest Soviet aircraft, including those with nuclear weapons. Middendorf and National Security Council staffer Constantine Menges came up with a plan that led to the invasion of Grenada and the restoration of a democratic government.

Middendorf was a tireless advocate for economic freedom in Latin America and was an intellectual force behind the North American Free Trade Agreement. As Ambassador to the OAS, Middendorf was asked about Hugo Chavez and his promises to restore freedom and economic equality to Venezuela. He urged his colleagues at the OAS and his friends in Venezuela not to support the Socialist-Marxist system Chavez proposed, including income inequality, wealth redistribution, and the other usual Communist slogans with so much initial traction. His warnings were ignored, as they had been in China and Cuba, where he had first-hand knowledge of the Communist threat. Venezuela went from the wealthiest Latin American country to the poorest, with a 93 percent poverty rate. Its humanitarian crisis has resulted in Latin America's worst refugee and migration exodus.

Bill Middendorf stood with me at the Berlin Wall in 1991, shortly after President Reagan's speech urging that the wall be taken down. That same year, as communism collapsed in the Soviet Union, President Boris Yeltsin invited a team from the Heritage Foundation to help draft a constitution for the new Russia. I was head of the team, which also included Bill Middendorf. Yelstin realized that privatization, the process of transferring state-owned facilities to private sector owners, was the only way the new Russia could survive. After many visits, we wrote the Russian Privatization Handbook, which benefited hundreds of thousands of previous state-owned small businesses. However, several critical industries such as coal, steel, and oil were turned over to a group of oligarchs who now drain huge profits and are directly under Putin's control. Economic collapse and inflation soon followed. Some of the recommendations made by the Feulner team remain in the Russian Constitution today. One of them spells out an election policy that contributed to the loss of multiple seats in Putin's ruling party in a September 2019 election.

A delegate to presidential nominating conventions as far back as Barry Goldwater in 1964, Middendorf remains active in shaping conservative foreign, defense, and economic policy through regular meetings with staff members on Capitol Hill. His decision-making, relationship building, and statesmanship on the international stage have enhanced America's security and stability during a volatile period in our history. Throughout his brilliant career, he has been devoted to his family and pursued lifelong art and music interests. He has also been a proud member of The Heritage Foundation Board of Trustees since 1989.

On My 100-Year Watch

1 | Characteristics Present in Communist Takeovers and an Islamic Revolution

NEARLY 80 YEARS AGO, I witnessed the first of six revolutions that have rocked the world. In 1945, my ship was stationed in China as part of the occupation force, and I observed first-hand the beginning of the Communist takeover. General George Marshall was sent by President Truman to China in 1945 to adjudicate between Nationalist Chiang Kai-shek and Communist Mao Zedong. Our officer contingent was enlisted for Marshall's arrival security. Marshall initially made some progress, but his decision to withhold arms shipments to Chiang Kai-shek for nine months starting in 1946 laid the groundwork for the Communist takeover in 1949. General Douglas MacArthur described Marshall's mistake as the greatest failure in diplomatic history.

In Cuba in the early 1950s, I was part owner of a business making hard board out of sugar cane waste called bagasse. We were successful, employed 400 people, and exported high-grade hardboard all over the Caribbean. Late in the 1950s, on one of my visits to our plant in Cuba, Castro forces blew up one of our buildings late one night. I escaped on a small private plane the following day to Havana. After we arrived, the pilot told me that there were bullet holes in the tail. Castro confiscated the plant without compensation in 1959 when he took power in Cuba.

When I was secretary of the navy, Iran was our most powerful and promising ally in the vast, oil-drenched region surrounding the Persian Gulf. I had several meetings with Shah Mohammad Pahlavi as secretary of the navy. Four frigates under construction were placed in limbo because of severe cuts in the defense budget. I approached the Shah and asked him to purchase the frigates for the Iranian Navy and thus keep our lines open until the next defense budget. While meeting the Shah to finalize the deal, he asked me where I was having lunch, and my aide, Bob Sims, told him. Toward the end of our lunch in Tehran, a sharply dressed official standing at attention behind me handed me a note signed by the Shah that said, "You have a deal." Before it could be finalized, the Shah came under fire from Islamic protesters in Iran, led by Khomeini, who questioned the Shah's decision to allow women to vote. It became a rallying cry for Muslim fundamentalists who opposed women's rights.

As ambassador to the Organization of American States (OAS), I was initially confronted by a regional crisis in Nicaragua that began two years before I came on board with the overthrow of Nicaraguan strongman Anastasia Somoza. Ironically and tragically for the Nicaraguans, the Sandinistas have abused the fundamental rights of their people far more. The victims number in the thousands and include journalists, business people, politicians, Catholics, Moravians, the Miskito Indian tribes, and Nicaragua's entire Jewish community.

As Ambassador to the OAS from 1981 to 1985, I was often asked about Hugo Chavez and his Communist feelings before he came to power in Venezuela. Chavez was described to me as a "young Fidel Castro with oil." I warned my friends in Venezuela not to support the Socialist-Marxist system Chavez proposed. He attracted support among the poor living in the slums of Venezuela called Barrios, where 50 percent of the population lives. Chavez was elected president in 1999 after promising to end corruption and improve living conditions for the poor.

Unfortunately, my warnings about Chavez's friendship with Fidel Castro and his admiration for people like Mao Zedong and Muammar Qaddafi were not taken seriously by some of my Venezuelan friends and OAS members. Chavez promised a peaceful social revolution that would usher in a golden age for Venezuela. He failed to deliver either prosperity or equality and immediately labeled the Venezuelan Congress and Supreme Court corrupt and expanded the military's role.

Five Characteristics

Here are the five common characteristics of each of the six countries I personally witnessed fall to Communism or a religious dictatorship.

1. **Promises of democracy, income redistribution (to themselves), agrarian reform, free elections, and all the usual Communist litany of false promises that influence the gullible until the revolutionaries' takeover**

People believed in the Chinese Communist Party because it promised to protect human rights and distribute land to the peasants. It pledged that control of industrial production would be in the hands of the working class and profits would be divided equally among its members. It used its support among workers, peasants, and a large group of intellectuals, some of whom I got to know during my tour in China. Mao referred to the intellectuals who supported his Revolution as "useful idiots," and most of them were executed or imprisoned. Mao also took away their work, homes, belongings, and freedom. Food was distributed according to merit, becoming a weapon to force people to follow the party's every dictate. As incentives to work were removed, coercion and violence were used to compel famished farmers to perform labor on poorly planned irrigation projects while fields were neglected. Millions died from starvation, while executions for offenses like stealing bread were commonplace. Mao Zedong became the greatest mass murderer in the world, whose policies led to an estimated 45 to 65 million deaths.

Fidel Castro claimed to be a freedom-fighter intent on restoring democracy in Cuba. He promised free elections and the end of dictatorships in Cuba. "Not Communism or Marxism is our idea. Our political philosophy is a representative democracy and social justice in a well-planned economy," Castro told the American public. He lied. In a televised interview in Havana a few months later, Castro declared, "I am a Marxist-Leninist and shall be one until the end of my life. Marxism, or scientific socialism, has become the revolutionary movement of the working class, and Communism will be the dominant force in Cuban politics. There cannot be three or four movements."

In the late 1970s in Iran, an extreme radical movement led by Ayatollah Khomeini was gaining strength in the underground based on Muslim opposition to allowing women to vote, a program that the Shah had implemented in 1962. Khomeini and Muslim law treated women as inferior. Supporters of the Revolution ranged from secular, left-wing nationalists to Islamists on the right, and Khomeini, who presented himself as a moderate able to bring together all the different factions leading the Revolution. As soon as he gained power, Khomeini executed or imprisoned the left-wing nationalists and established himself as the supreme leader with an unelected Guardian Council of Islamic clerics.

Daniel Ortega, leader of the Sandinistas revolution in Nicaragua, pledged to establish full observance of human rights, a peaceful and orderly transition, civil justice and to hold free and fair elections. After promising the OAS that a genuinely democratic government would be installed with free elections, the Sandinistas implemented a Cuban-style regime with a massive military building spree. The people suffer restrictions on free movement, denial of due process, lack of freedom of thought, conscience, religion, denial of the right of association, and free labor unions.

Hugo Chavez was elected president of Venezuela in 1999 after promising to end corruption and improve living conditions for the poor. He campaigned with the tired "Wealth Gap" and "Income Inequality" that Mao and Castro so effectively used before taking power in China and Cuba. Chavez promised a peaceful social revolution that would usher in a golden age for Venezuela. He failed to deliver either prosperity or equality and immediately labeled the Venezuelan Congress and Supreme Court corrupt and expanded the military's role. Free markets and human rights had no place in his utopia. He believed neighboring democratic, market-oriented nations represented a U.S. empire of sorts, though they were sovereign states.

Chavez nationalized hundreds of private businesses and foreign-owned assets, such as oil projects run by Exxon Mobil and Conoco Phillips, gutting the country of crucial technical expertise. With the international companies withdrawing from their Venezuelan operations and inexperienced, incompetent government appointees replacing company managers, engineers, and other experts, production plunged to new lows. He initiated price controls intended to make essential goods more affordable for the poor. He stacked the country's courts with political allies, passed laws restricting the ability of journalists to criticize the government, and consistently sought ways to do away with checks on his power. He expanded the power of the presidency, effectively took control of the Supreme Court, harassed the press, and jailed or eliminated political opponents.

2. Elimination of all weapons under the penalty of death

Soviet dictator Joseph Stalin's first act when he came to power in 1924 was to take all guns and freedom of thought from his enemies. He explained, "Ideas are more powerful than guns. We would not let our enemies have guns. Why should we let them have ideas," Stalin said.

"All political power comes from the barrel of a gun. The Communist Party must command all the guns; that way, no guns can ever be used to command the party." The quote was from Mao Zedong, the founder of Communist China. Mao's first act after gaining complete control of China in 1949 was to take away all guns from the population under the penalty of death. Dictators throughout much of history had disarmed their populations before they began their mass killings. Hitler took guns from the Jews in November of 1938, and Kristallnacht and the Holocaust followed almost immediately.

Everybody ought to have a gun, Fidel Castro maintained—until he took over Cuba in 1959. He changed his position, following Mao's rule that guns should not be in the hands of the people. For three weeks after the Castro government was formed, Radio Havana warned, "All citizens must turn in their combat weapons. Civilians must take arms to police stations, soldiers to military headquarters." Castro warned that anyone not doing so will face the dreaded tribunal and probably a death sentence.

In Iran, One of the first acts of the Islamic Revolution was to take all guns from citizens. They were warned to turn over all weapons at area police stations. No one can have a weapon in Iran without government approval. After gaining control in Nicaragua, Wilfred Ortega made private ownership of guns a serious crime. The country's gun control regime is one aspect of the Venezuelan crisis that does not receive much coverage. All guns were outlawed when Chavez came to power in 1999, and harsh penalties were imposed on violators. The Venezuelan Armed Forces have exclusive authority to control, register and confiscate firearms.

Two months after the victory of the Nicaraguan Revolution in July 1979, the Sandinista National Liberation Front (FSLN) leadership met in secret for three days to assess the current situation and lay plans to consolidate their power. The report, "The 72-Hour Document," was the Sandinista's basic blueprint for constructing Communism in Nicaragua and spreading subversion throughout the region. One of its early rules was to restrict gun ownership. All weapons had to be registered and approved by the local police.

3. Warm reception for Communist-Socialism in the western press and media, in each case helping the revolutionaries

Walter Duranty, of *The New York Times* described Joseph Stalin as "a quiet, unobtrusive man who saw much but said little." Duranty claimed that Russian peasants welcomed the Soviet seizure of their homes, their crops, and their farm animals. He wrote that the early 1930s famine that killed some 6 million people in Ukraine never happened.

Mao Zedong has always received favorable press from the Western media, beginning in the early days when he was an obscure revolutionary with a small following of unarmed, uneducated farmers. Today, an elaborate exhibit sits on the third floor of a building on Shanghai's waterfront. Hung on crimson walls, it celebrates foreign journalists who wrote favorably about the Communist Party's rise to power in China. The exhibit is named in honor of Edgar Snow, a journalist who covered China for *The New York Sun* and London's *Daily Herald*, and United Press International (UPI.) Snow wrote a glowing version of Mao based on a series of interviews with him in 1937. His book, *Red Star Over China*, presented a version of Mao that led many Americans to think of him as a Chinese George Washington.

William F. Buckley famously quipped that Fidel Castro could claim, "I got my job through *The New York Times*." Much of the world had been taken in by the liberal press, which made Castro a national hero in the U.S. Herbert Matthews, a reporter for *The New York Times*, described Castro in multiple articles as a freedom fighter intent on restoring democracy in Cuba, Ed Sullivan, host of a popular TV show, gave Castro a platform where he lied about being a Communist and promised free elections, ending dictatorships in Cuba. After Castro had gained control in Cuba, he said in effect, "I was just kidding about being a Communist. I've been a Communist all along and will be one until I die."

Most Iranians, the Shah included, believed that Britain supported the Revolution largely because of sympathetic coverage by BBC's journalists. In 1976, the Shah came under fire from the American press and programs like *60 Minutes*. Veteran journalist Mike Wallace, famed for his tough interviews on *60 Minutes*, asked the Shah if he endorsed torture. Increasingly hostile demonstrations in U.S. cities staged by pro-Khomeini Iranians resident in America also raised issues for the Shah and his supporters.

Newspapers in the United States hailed the Revolution in Nicaragua as a triumph for democracy. Daniel Ortega, leader of the Sandinistas, was portrayed as a great emancipator. The United States and much of the Western Hemisphere looked on with relief, anticipating a new democracy under a new government. After all, the Sandinistas pledged to establish full observance of human rights, a peaceful and orderly transition, civil justice, and free and fair elections. Ironically and tragically for the Nicaraguans, the Sandinistas continue to abuse the fundamental rights of their people.

When Hugo Chavez took control of Venezuela, he was hailed by many members of the U.S. media as a liberator. Larry Rohtor, Bureau Chief of *The New York Times* in South America, described Chavez as a liberator who would install social justice in Venezuela. According to our State Department, Venezuela went from being the wealthiest nation in Latin America to the poorest, with 93 percent of the population living below the poverty line.

4. Revolutions were not only accepted by our State Department but in many cases, they were welcomed.

Joseph E. Davies, ambassador to Moscow, claimed in 1931 that Stalin's "eye is exceedingly wise and gentle." Rexford Guy, a member of Franklin Delano Roosevelt's brain trust, became an admirer of the Soviet Union after his 1927 visit. While admitting there was "ruthlessness and a disregard for liberties and rights," Guy insisted it was worthwhile.

George Atcheson Jr., the State Department chargé d'affaire in China and advisor to General MacArthur during World War II, did not try to hide his dislike for Chiang Kai-shek and labeled his government as corrupt. He described Mao Zedong as "the George Washington of the Pacific." In 1944, the Dixie Mission, known formally as the U.S. Army Observation Group, was sent to Yunan to establish contact with the Communists. then the significant power in the country's northern area. The State Department's representative on the Mission was John S. Service, who had met earlier with Mao Zedong, Zhou Enlai, and other Chinese Communist Party (CCP) leaders.

"The impressive personal qualities of the Communist leaders, their seeming sincerity, and the coherence and logical nature of their program leads me toward general acceptance that the Communists base their policy toward the Kuomintang on a real desire for democracy in China under which there can be orderly economic growth through a stage of private enterprise to eventual socialism without the need of violent social upheaval and revolution," Service wrote. Over the next four months, Service reported back to the State Department with a series of reports praising Mao and the CCP and describing its leaders as "progressive" and "democratic." He advised that the Communists were in China to stay, and China's destiny was not Chiang's but theirs.

Patrick Hurley, the new U.S. ambassador to China, disagreed with Service. After trying to establish unity between the Communists and the Nationalists, he came to support the Nationalists exclusively. Rejecting the recommendations of Service and other State Department officers, Hurley had him, and the rest of the Dixie Mission recalled and blamed them for U.S. diplomatic failures in China. Hurley resigned in 1944, insisting that his difficulties did not come from diplomatic shortcomings or the insolubility of the conflict. He insisted it was "subterfuge " by a pro-Communist faction in the U.S. government. "The professional foreign service men sided with the Chinese Communist Party, whose policy was to keep China divided against itself," he charged.

Presidential candidate John F. Kennedy criticized what he saw as the use of U.S. government influence to advance the interest and increase the profits of private U.S. companies instead of helping Cuba to achieve economic progress, saying that Americans dominated the island's economy and had given support to one of the bloodiest and most repressive dictatorships in the history of Latin America. "We let Batista put the U.S. on the side of tyranny, and we did nothing to convince the people of Cuba and Latin America that we wanted to be on the side of freedom (Castro)." U.S. Ambassador E. I. Smith told General Batista we would no longer support his regime. Batista fled Cuba the next day, and Cuba fell to Communism.

At the opening of the U.N. General Assembly on October 3, 1978. Cyrus Vance, secretary of State, assured Iranian Foreign Minister Amir Khosrow

Afshar that it was clearly not U.S. policy to support the Shah's opposition and asked if anything further could be done to demonstrate support for Iran. President Carter's national security team met to discuss the Tehran riots and their aftermath. It had been three days since National Security Advisor Brzezinski had assured the president that Iran was not in the throes of a full-scale revolution. Brzezinski was especially critical of the CIA, which had failed to anticipate the seriousness of the unrest, and Ambassador Sullivan, whom he had learned had been in contact with the revolutionaries. Sullivan, convinced the Shah was finished, cabled Washington that the Shah's support had shrunk to the military, which was unlikely to sanction a bloodbath to keep him in power. The ideal scenario he laid out was the departure of the Shah and his top generals into exile, followed by accommodation between the Shah's military and the revolutionists.

The U.S. State Department was criticized for doing little to communicate with Tehran or discourage protest and opposition to the Shah. The intelligence community within the United States was blasted for its assessment that Iran was not in a pre-revolutionary condition. President Carter was also blamed for his lack of support for the Shah while failing to deter opposition. Bureaucratic dysfunction extended to intelligence sharing and analysis. Carter's National Security Council was unaware of CIA intelligence that documented the flow of Palestinian and Libyan money and arms to Khomeini. So, a U.S. Iran policy was set up based on hunches, flawed intelligence, grudges, and personal prejudices.

Immediately after Daniel Ortega assumed power, the United States granted emergency relief and recovery aid to Nicaragua of $118 million, five times more than we had given before the Revolution. If we were trying to buy friendships, it did not work. The government of Nicaragua treated the United States as an enemy. The incoming defense minister declared their creed Marxism-Leninism and moved quickly to consolidate power. Business leaders were jailed, and the government subjected all media to heavy censorship. It insulted and mocked the Pope, drove the indigenous Miskito Indians from their homelands, burned their villages, and destroyed their crops. To my mind, that was genocide. In July 1980, the Sandinista defense minister announced that there would be no need for elections since the people had already "voted" during the Revolution. He warned that elections could not be held until the people had been re-educated.

During my first month as ambassador to the OAS, I criticized the Nicaraguan government for not following through on its promise to hold free elections. I also helped initiate a change in policy in which the United States supported the Contras, the opposition to the Sandinistas. Unfortunately, the United States Congress passed legislation known as the Boland

Amendment for their author, Massachusetts Democratic congressman Edward P. Boland. It prohibited military appropriations between 1982 and 1984 to "overthrow Nicaragua's Government."

If our State Department had taken a more forceful role before Hugo Chavez's election in 1998, Venezuela could have been a beacon for democracy in South America. Unlike Castro, Chavez never tried to hide his Communist sentiments. He spoke with admiration about Castro and Arab leaders like Saddam Hussein and Muammar Qaddafi, even as he reached out to leaders in China, Russia, and Iran.

5. **Economic disasters always result after Communists gain control of a country. It's called "flat-lining." The economy goes from prosperity and the ability to attract foreign direct investment to a poverty level.**

"The Great Leap Forward" in the 1950s turned China into one of the most impoverished nations in the world, accompanied by an estimated 45 million deaths. Castro took his country from the most prosperous in the Caribbean down to poverty levels. Nicaragua and Venezuela followed the same pattern, with Venezuela, once the richest country in Latin America, now the poorest, with 93 percent living below the poverty line, according to our State Department. There are reports of people eating their dogs and some living on between $3 to $10 monthly.

After the collapse of the Soviet Union's controlled economy in 1991, a new Russian Federation was created by Boris Yeltsin. I was part of a group from the Heritage Foundation that President Yeltsin invited to Russia to help write a new constitution and privatization program. We saw fertile ground upon which to plant free-market seeds, which we discussed with Yeltsin and other government officials. We were asked to draw up a privatization program to encompass th7e hundreds of thousands of businesses, restaurants, factories, and construction companies that were now under the control of the government and, therefore, long waiting lines. I was one of the main architects of this particular document. Yeltsin's team proudly presented me with a marked-up copy of the document that was later approved by the Duma. Hundreds of thousands of small businesses could now deal directly with the public as opposed to the long lines waiting for service from government-owned small businesses. It is now an integral part of Russian law. Unfortunately, critical industries such as coal, iron, steel, and energy fell under the control of Communist leaders, oligarchs later beholden to Putin. We won the constitutional agreement with Yeltsin but not the Russian Parliament, the Duma, on that issue.

Some months later, I was in the guest gallery with my Heritage comrades when the Duma considered the proposed constitution. The Russian Parliament was like much of Russia: the labels had changed, but not the players. At that point, there was still a large block of Communists in the Duma, and the private property clause might keep them from stealing everything in sight as they moved to privatize the oil companies and coal, iron, steel, and energy for themselves. "Private," in this case, meant in their pockets. Many of the Communists moved from being powerful but poor to being powerful and rich. Some of them are billionaires today.

I said that to attract foreign capital, Russia needed to make an explicit declaration affirming the rights of private property and the sanctity of contracts, all to be strengthened by an independent court system that enforced both. Do these things, I emphasized, and after some 73 years of Communist misrule and with an enormous pent-up demand for everything, all else would quickly flow. Success. Employment. New markets. I suggested that privatization should be done "cold turkey" across the board, the same argument we had used successfully with Lech Walesa of Poland. I argued that some 44,000 state-owned businesses should shift from making useless things like tanks and submarines to meeting consumer needs—or shut down.

As I had in my work with Latin America, I continued to press for free market reforms and, as with my efforts in the Netherlands, to look for joint business opportunities. I helped set up a Russian-American Business Council. We easily signed up many leading American businesses to whom investment seemed like a good idea, and why not? Russia had by then declared itself open to foreign direct capital, and our corporations had checkbooks ready. There were two problems: corruption and blackmail, including threats of harm to local facilities and employees unless "protection" was purchased from some willing vendor. It was like the 19th-century Wild West (or some mob-controlled industries in 20th-century America). Promised contracts evaporated unless under-the-table payments were forthcoming. This was not a practical move for our companies. They were subject to the U.S. Foreign Corrupt Practices Act, which provides draconian remedies against individuals who offer bribes, however, defined. And, even when contracts were solid and legal, other problems arose. For example, one of our drug company members sold $150 million worth of products to the Russian Ministry of Health for distribution to hospitals nationwide. A thoroughly above-board transaction—except the bill was never paid. Upon frequent inquiry, the response was always along the lines, "You're on the list. . . ."

The Russian American Business Council staggered for about five years until many of our members grew tired of dealing with the corrupt Russian bureaucracy. Russia seemed to prosper for a while, aided by massive loans, when the economy had nowhere to go but up. However, without a firm free-market foundation, any attempt at economic restructuring was doomed to fail. If Russia had early on followed the lead of Poland or Chile, or the Czech Republic, countries that exchanged state-controlled economies for the unseen hand of the marketplace, it would have attracted the one thing developing economies need most: substantial foreign direct investment. Instead, Russia got loans the oligarchs could (and did) transfer into Swiss bank accounts and paid off Putin.

Cuba's economy had grown rapidly in the early part of the century, fueled by the sale of sugar to the United States. In 1958, Cuba had a per-capita GDP of $2,363, which placed it in the middle of Latin American countries. In 1959 when Castro took power, GDP per capita for Cuba was $2,067 a year. By 1992, the Cuban economy had declined by over 40 percent, with major food shortages, widespread malnutrition, and a lack of essential goods. Castro strangled the economy, leaving most Cubans scrambling for decent food and desperate for better living standards. The Heritage Foundation 2022 Report of Economic Development ranks Cuba 31st among 32 countries in the Americas region, and its overall score is one of the lowest in the world.

Iran was ruled by Shah Mohammad Pahlavi beginning in 1941. He initiated economic plans that improved the economy, redistributed land, and built new schools and hospitals. He also announced plans to allow women to vote, a decision that led to demonstrations from the religious right. The Shah looked for support from the United States, which never came. Some blamed the State Department, which discouraged U.S. diplomats from engaging with opponents of the Shah. Others blamed a CIA study that infamously reported to President Jimmy Carter in August 1978 that "Iran is not in a revolutionary or even a 'pre-revolutionary' situation."

In 1979, the Shah was overthrown by an Islamic Revolution and is now a theocratic republic. In terms of suppressing its people with "Morality Police," it is no different than the most brutal Communist regime. Iran is the world's foremost state sponsor of terrorism and has made extensive efforts to export its radical Shia brand of Islamist Revolution.

In addition to the humanitarian fallout and the political unraveling, the economic downturn has left cash-strapped Nicaragua in dire straits. It is the Western Hemisphere's second-poorest country (after Haiti), with a gross domestic product (GDP) per capita of $2,162 in 2017. Unlike its regional counterparts in Central America's northern triangle, Nicaraguan emigration was typically low because, despite its poverty, it was relatively safe. In fact, the country was a central hub for tourists and American retirees, capitalizing on its competitive prices.

Ortega maintained a close relationship with powerful private-sector officials because they allowed him to govern as he saw fit. With more than 82,000 Nicaraguans fleeing, the country lost 10 percent of its labor force. The 2018 and 2019 GDP contracted by nearly 4 percent. Fearing the instability and political uncertainty, foreign direct investment declined by an estimated 53 percent, and domestic investment fell by 25 percent, according to Nicaragua's leading business association. Even Ortega's former business allies, leading private-sector representatives, and the economic backbone of Nicaragua have come out against the Ortega regime. Economic recovery cannot occur without the government regaining the confidence of these industries.

According to the U.S. Department of the Treasury, large sums were embezzled from Nicaragua's state-run oil company and joint ventures with Venezuela (companies run by Ortega relatives). The Ortega family and their business allies have amassed considerable wealth as leaders of the Sandinista government in Nicaragua. Meanwhile, efforts to improve economic growth and stability have been modest. Nicaragua is ranked 25th out of 32 countries in the region, and its overall score is below the world and regional averages in the Heritage Foundation's 2023 Economic Development Index. Scores in property rights, judicial effectiveness, and government integrity are all below the world average.

Venezuela, also a member of the OAS, is a failed state by all measures. It is a classic case of Communist Flat-Lining. Venezuela went from the wealthiest nation in Latin America to the poorest, with 93 percent of the population living beneath the poverty level. The economy is in ruins, and the humanitarian crisis has resulted in Latin America's worst refugee and migration exodus. Venezuela's instability is spilling over into many countries in Latin America, Mexico, and the United States. Much of the crisis at the U.S. borders is the result of millions of Venezuelan refugees. An estimated 5,000 Venezuelans flee the country daily to Argentina, Brazil, Chile, Ecuador, Peru, Mexico, and the United States, Many of these individuals and families, lack the means to support themselves and rely heavily on their host countries. It is Latin America's worst refugee and migration crisis to date.

Hyperinflation set off the most recent and precipitous descent in Venezuela. Recently, the peso, which had traded parity of the U.S. dollar 30 years ago, is today a millionth to a dollar. Unbridled government spending and uncontrolled monetary expansion have left Venezuela in economic free fall. Twenty percent of the population has left the country because of these impoverished conditions and tyrannical power. Water shortages are endemic, blackouts are common, and the healthcare system has collapsed.

Diseases such as diphtheria and malaria, which were all but eradicated decades ago, are back.

Venezuela has been one of the world's least economically free nations since 1999, the year Chavez came to power. Its economic freedom score is 24.8, making its economy the 176th freest in the 2022 Index of the Heritage Foundation. Venezuela is ranked 32nd among 32 countries in the Americas region.

History of Communism

Harvard University's mammoth *Black Book of Communism* details the ideological roots of Communism's use of the firing squad, the Gulag, the KGB, forced famine, mass deportation, and suppression of fundamental human rights to stamp out any opposition to its tyranny. Lenin, Communism's founding father, relied on violence to further his ideological goal of a Communist world. The government during Mao's rule was responsible for vast numbers of deaths, with estimates ranging from 45 to 80 million victims through starvation, persecution, prison labor, and mass executions.

The Victims of Communism Museum opened in Washington, D.C., in June 2022 and is dedicated to an estimated 100 million human beings slaughtered, massacred, and killed by Marxist Communist regimes in the past 100 years. An additional 1.5 billion people still suffer under oppressive, tyrannical Communist regimes today. The museum has been more than 30 years in the making, starting with an idea from Anne Edwards, the wife of Lee Edwards, the prolific author, historian, biographer, and scholar at the Heritage Foundation, who was the driving force behind the creation of the museum.

Every student in every college and university who thinks Marxism, Communism, and socialism (which is just Communism under a deodorized name) is a wonderful idea should pay a visit to this museum.

2 | Ready, Aim, Misfire: Who Gave China to the Communists

Mao Zedong's first act after gaining complete control of the country in 1949 was to take away all guns from the population. It was a policy he began in 1935 as he took over each province. Anyone found with a gun was executed. Mao's most famous quote was not published in the press at that time: "All political power comes from the barrel of a gun. The Communist Party must command all the guns; that way, no guns can ever be used to command the party."

Mao also took away their work, homes, belongings, and freedom. Food was distributed according to merit, and it became a weapon to force people to follow the party's every dictate. As incentives to work were removed, coercion and violence were used to compel famished farmers to perform labor on poorly planned irrigation projects while fields were neglected. Millions died from starvation, while executions for offenses like stealing bread were commonplace. Mao Zedong became the greatest mass murderer in the world, whose policies led to the deaths of 45 million people. He executed more people than either Hitler or Stalin during World War II.

"Who lost China?" Americans have been asking this question since 1949, when Mao Zedong turned China into a Communist country. The media deserves some of the blame. Brooks Atkinson, reporting for *The New York Times* in 1930, claimed that "the Chinese Communists are not Communists. Their system now might be described as agrarian or peasant democracy." Theodore H. White, later best-known for his books about presidential elections, was among *Time Magazine* staffers who viewed Communists as "agrarian liberals," in a 1931 article. John K. Fairbank, a Harvard historian of China, declared in 1932, "The Maoist revolution is, on the whole, the best thing that happened to the Chinese people in centuries."

Mao had always received favorable press from the Western media, beginning in the early days when he was an obscure revolutionary with a small following of unarmed, uneducated farmers. An elaborate exhibit sits on the third floor of a building on Shanghai's waterfront. Hung on crimson walls, it celebrates foreign journalists who wrote about the Communist Party's rise to power in China in the 1930s. A sign reads, "With their pens and their cameras, these journalists presented to the world a fair and true image of the Chinese Communists and the People's Army, who, though equipped with inferior arms, were fighting heroically at the forefront in the struggle for national liberation."

The exhibit is named in honor of Edgar Snow, a journalist who covered China for *The New York Sun* and London's *Daily Herald*, and United Press International (UPI.) Snow wrote a glowing version of Mao based on a series of interviews with him in 1937. His book, *Red Star Over China*, presented a version of Mao that led many Americans to think of him as a Chinese George Washington. Snow claimed that peasants embraced Mao because he offered agrarian democracy. Again and again, Snow portrayed Chinese Communist leaders in glowing colors.

"Because they achieved everything against great odds, it seemed natural to the Communist veterans that a whole nation should follow in the same paths with discipline and faith matched by high fortitude, and distant glory as the ultimate reward," Snow wrote, oblivious to the fact he was describing a mass murderer.

"It is impossible not to recognize the Long March as one of the great triumphs of men against odds and men against nature," Snow wrote in the book. "While the Red Army was unquestionably in forced retreat, its toughened veterans reached their planned objective with moral and political will as strong as ever. Their conviction had helped turn what might have been a terrible defeat into an arrival in triumph."

Another quote from Snow gave a more accurate description of Mao: "Mao appears to be quite free from symptoms of megalomania, but he has a deep sense of personal dignity, and something about him suggests a power of ruthless decisions when he deems it necessary."

Although the exhibit's introduction claims that the reporters presented a fair and true image of Chinese Communists, their work was selected carefully to represent only positive portrayals of the Communist rise. "The Celestial Reds won the people to their cause not by any process of reasoning, but by arousing the hope, trust, and affection of the people," wrote Jack Belden, an American correspondent for United Press International (UPI.) "What I have done as a correspondent is to convey to the people of the world the righteous war waged by the Chinese people under the leadership of the great Chinese Communist Party in a truthful way, without exaggeration or deprecation," wrote Agnes Smedly, a reporter for Britain's *The Manchester Guardian*. Smedly was a known Communist sympathizer who served as a spy for China and the Soviet Union in the 1930s. The reporting reflects a time before perceptions turned decisively against Mao Zedong's Communists.

I was in China as an officer in the U.S. Navy in December 1945, a member of the occupation forces stationed in Shanghai. General George C. Marshall arrived in China that same month, assigned by President Harry Truman to somehow unify the battling Nationalists and Communists into a strong non-Communist government that could serve as a bulwark against the Soviet Union. Like my fellow officers, I became part of the security force for General Marshall. After a grueling six-year tenure as Army chief of staff, which began the day Hitler invaded Poland in 1939, Marshall wanted to retire. However, the risk of a Communist victory in China forced Truman to ask Marshall to go to China and broker peace.

The objective of Marshall's mission, detailed by the State Department, was to guarantee China's unity, secure Chiang's leadership, and simultaneously encourage enough reform and compromise to reduce the force of the revolution and avert the resumption of the Civil War. A principal aim was to remove China as a source of United States-Soviet tension and as a target of Soviet subterfuge.

"Without a strong, unified China, we could expect Russia to ultimately take control of Manchuria and maintain a dominant influence in North China," secretary of State James Byrnes told Marshall. Initially, it looked like Marshall was going to be successful. The Nationalists and the Communists agreed to a ceasefire in a civil war that had raged on and off for two decades. They appeared to listen as Marshall explained the Bill of Rights and read aloud from Benjamin Franklin's speeches. Later, they agreed on a plan to merge their troops into one army.

How shall I describe the Shanghai of 1945? Shanghai was war-torn, filled with what must have been millions of starving people, most with nowhere to go and nothing to do except, perhaps, to die in the streets. Many did so, and the smells were far from sweet. At any hour of the day or night, thousands of destitute people wandered about, looking for food, work, and solace, but they always seemed to be moving. When I went ashore, I quickly became a target, I thought, of curiosity. I was tall, well-dressed, and polite; real crowds would follow anywhere I went. Some people just stared; some asked for money; some would reach out and pat my arms or legs or buttocks in a manifestation of a different sort of curiosity: they were trying to locate my wallet. I quickly learned to stay alert and to keep moving.

At first, catching a ride in a rickshaw seemed like a good way to avoid the crowds; yes, but not the danger. The driver might maneuver the rig into a back alley where his confederates would be waiting and then suddenly tip the rickshaw up, throwing the passenger backward. If smashing the back of his head into the pavement didn't knock him out, the driver's cronies did. A number of sailors were thus robbed, and several killed before the word got around. The city was put off-limits for a short time, and the pace of the armed shore patrol was increased. I must admit, I have never felt so powerful in my life as when taking my turn at shore patrol, driving around in a Jeep with a Colt .45 automatic on my hip.

Inflation was rampant. When I arrived in China, the exchange rate was something like one hundred CNC (Chinese National Currency) to the dollar; in two months, the rate hit four thousand, and, within another month or two, it had topped out (or more precisely, bottomed out) at hundreds of thousands to the dollar. Americans were about the only source of fresh money: "Hey, Yankee sailor. Buy souvenir?" Some of the merchandise was legitimate, especially embroidered women's and children's clothing, great gifts for the family back home. Some were highly questionable: Japanese "battle flags" and "samurai" swords—I think practically every Yankee sailor in Shanghai came home from the War with at least one or the other.

I remember these old trucks would emerge from Shanghai in the early dawn and go up in the north. Then a few hours later, you would hear distant gunfire in the hills above Shanghai. You knew there was something going on. It really didn't sink into me that this was anything serious. And then, towards sunset, these drab trucks and soldiers would return to Shanghai, and a few years later, the whole area would be engulfed by the Mao forces.

Marshall made a decision that some say led to the collapse of the Nationalist government. After more than a year of negotiations, Marshall achieved no significant agreements. Still, the net effect was to weaken the Nationalists when, in an attempt to broker a ceasefire, he recommended that the sale of weapons and ammunition the United States had been making to the Nationalists be suspended between July 1946 and May 1947. I still remember the shock I shared with fellow officers when the arms embargo was announced. A year later, Congress recognized the mistake and rushed aid to the Nationals, but it was too late, and China fell to the Communists in 1949.

Marshall's decision might have been influenced by General Joseph W. Stillwell, who was assigned to China three years before Marshall arrived to represent U.S. interests. Stillwell had served three tours of duty in China and was the army's foremost Chinese expert. Stillwell loved China and its people, but he had no illusions or respect for its leaders, especially Chiang Kai-shek. The posting carried with it three jobs: chief of staff to Nationalist leader Chiang Kai-shek, commanding officer of American forces in China, and Lend Lease Administrator. It required an individual with tact, patience, and diplomatic skills. Stillwell lacked all three, which earned him the nickname "Vinegar Joe." Stillwell and Chiang Kai-shek repeatedly clashed about military strategy and the best use of military resources. Chiang was reluctant to fight the Japanese but was eager to get Lend-Lease supplies to fight the

Chinese Communists under Mao Zedong. Stillwell tried to get Chiang committed to fighting the Japanese. He refused to give Chiang anything without assurance that the Chinese armies would fight the Japanese.

On July 19, 1942, Stillwell's diary entry began: "Got Shang Chen (Director of the Foreign Affairs Bureau of the Chinese General Staff) in and gave him the memo on Burma for transmittal to Peanut. This is an attempt to give Peanut an out on his big demands and show his willingness to cooperate." The name "Peanut" stood for Chiang Kai-shek, a nickname Stillwell created to show his contempt for the nationalist leader. Chiang went around Stillwell's back to petition for increased Lend-Lease aid. Before Stillwell was replaced in 1944, he had shared much of his criticism of Chiang Kai-shek with his good friend, General Marshall.

George Atcheson Jr., the State Department chargé d'affaire in China and advisor to General MacArthur during World War II, tried to mediate the conflicts between the Chinese Communist Party and the Kuomintang, led by General Chiang Kai-shek. Atcheson did not try to hide his dislike for Chiang Kai-shek and labeled his government as corrupt. He described Mao Zedong as "the George Washington of the Pacific."

In 1944, the Dixie Mission, known formally as the United States Army Observation Group, was sent to Yunan to establish contact with the Communists, then the significant power in the country's northern area. They aimed to encourage cooperation and eventual unity with Chiang Kai-shek's nationalist party, the Kuomintang (KMG). The State Department's representative on the Mission was John S. Service, who had met earlier with Mao Zedong, Zhou Enlai, and other Chinese Communist Party (CCP) leaders.

"The impressive personal qualities of the Communist leaders, their seeming sincerity, and the coherence and logical nature of their program leads me toward general acceptance that the Communists base their policy toward the Kuomintang on a real desire for democracy in China under which there can be orderly economic growth through a stage of private enterprise to eventual socialism without the need of violent social upheaval and revolution," Service wrote. Over the next four months, Service prepared a series of reports, all praising Mao and the CCP and describing its leaders as "progressive" and "democratic." He advised that the Communists were in China to stay, and China's destiny was not Chiang's but theirs.

A decade-long civil war between the Communists and the Nationalists had been suspended in 1937 when they formed the Second United Front to battle the invading Japanese. But now, seven years later, Service contended that the Nationalists were "corrupt and incompetent." He and other American political officers believed the resumption of the Civil War was inevitable and that the CCP would win. But, if the United States supported the CCP in a coalition with the Nationalists, they insisted, the United States could steer the Communists out of the Soviet orbit, where they might be pushed if antagonized by the United States

Patrick Hurley, the new U.S. ambassador to China, disagreed with Service. After trying to establish unity between the Communists and the Nationalists, he came to support the Nationalists exclusively. Rejecting the recommendations of Service and other State Department officers, Hurley had him and the rest of the Dixie Mission recalled and blamed them for U.S. diplomatic failures in China.

Back in Washington, Service was arrested on suspicion of divulging confidential U.S. materials to the Communists. A grand jury declined to indict him, finding that the evidence was inadequate. He was dismissed by the State Department, where supporters contended that the lack of evidence erased doubts about Service's true position turned up by FBI surveillance. They argued that if he had been a secret Communist, much less a spy, better evidence would indeed have surfaced. Shortly before he died in 2009, Service confessed that he had given secret plans to the Communists during the Civil War.

Not every member of the Dixie Mission was taken in by Mao and Zhou Enlai. The military commander, Army Colonel David Barrett, also sent home by Hurley, wrote, "I had fallen, to some extent but not as much perhaps as did some others, for the 'agrarian reformer' guff. I should have known better, particularly since the Chinese Communists themselves never at any time claimed to be anything but revolutionaries—period."

In Washington for a meeting in November 1944, Hurley was encouraged by Administration officials to keep trying. Still, he abruptly resigned, insisting that his difficulties did not come from diplomatic shortcomings or the insolubility of the conflict. He insisted it was "subterfuge" by a pro-Communist faction in the U.S. government. "The professional foreign service men sided with the Chinese Communist Party, whose policy was to keep China divided against itself," he charged.

"The vital importance of saving China cannot be exaggerated," Senator Arthur Vandenberg said in 1948 as Civil War raged between the Nationalists and Communist China. "But there are limits to our resources and boundaries to our miracles," he added. His position reflected the thinking of many Washington, D.C., politicians.

Marshall found plenty to criticize about the conduct of the Nationalists. He complained that their "narrow-minded and bigoted militarists, and a small nucleus of political irreconcilables were only helping the Communists and were pursuing open civil war." This, he argued, was squandering Chiang's prestige, and inviting prolonged chaos that would create a "fruitful breeding ground for Communism and an exceptional opportunity for Soviet Russia to intervene." Truman backed Marshall in a letter to Chiang, stressing that Marshall spoke for the entire U.S. government and should be taken accordingly. Truman noted that recent events in China had driven the United States to the conclusion "that the selfish interests for extremist elements, equally with the Communists and the Nationalists, were hindering the aspirations of the Chinese people."

Truman concluded with an ultimatum to Chiang: "Unless convincing proof is shortly forthcoming that genuine progress is being made toward a peaceful settlement of China's internal problems, it must be expected that American opinion will not continue in its generous attitude toward your nation."

On August 6, 1945, U.S. bomber *Enola Gay* dropped the uranium bomb known as "Little Boy" on the Japanese city of Hiroshima. Two days later, the Soviet Union declared war on Japan, and more than 1 million Soviet soldiers invaded Manchuria. On August 9, U.S. forces dropped "Fat Man," a plutonium bomb, on Nagasaki. Emperor Hirohito unannounced Japan's unconditional surrender on August 15, 1945.

More than 700,000 Japanese soldiers surrendered to the Soviets in Manchuria. The Soviet occupation of Manchuria allowed the region to be transferred into the control of local Communists. Japanese guns, artillery pieces, 400 tanks, 2,000 anti-tank guns, and more than 800 aircraft were confiscated by the Soviets. All of these weapons were turned over to Mao and played a significant role in his success against the Nationalists.

The Communists restated their demands for a return to the military positions of January 13, 1946, and for nullifying the new constitution, terms previously rejected by the government. On January 21, 1946, the government offered four points as the basis for a resumption of peace talks: cessation of hostilities, with troops retaining their existing positions; army reorganization; reopening of communications; and a just and equitable solution to the problem of the regional administration.

In the meantime, the Communists resumed their offensive in Manchuria while government troops launched major drives on Communist positions in Shantung and Shensi. Early in March 1947, the government ordered all Communist personnel to leave government territory, and on March 15, 1947, Chiang charged the Communists with armed rebellion.

China's internal strife was closely linked to its diplomatic relations with the United States and the Soviet Union. After more than a year of a continuous effort to bring the national government and Communists together, the United States abandoned its task as a mediator. U.S. policy had become unpopular in China. To avoid further complications in China's affairs, the U.S.

government informed the Soviet Union that its forces in China would be reduced to 6,180 men by June 1, 1947.

The deterioration of China's economic and military situation and the spread of communism in East Asia led to the appointment of a U.S. fact-finding mission to China and Korea headed by Lt. General Albert C. Wedemeyer, who arrived in Nanking on July 22, 1947. His mission was welcomed by the Chinese government but attacked by the Communists as imperialistic. Upon his departure from China on August 24, Wedemeyer said, "If the Chinese Communists are truly patriotic, they will halt voluntary employment of force. To regain and maintain the people's confidence, the Central Government will have to effect immediately drastic, far-reaching political and economic reforms." The latter statement displeased the Chinese government, and Nationalist Premier Chang Chun declared on September 2, 1947, that China would not alter either its domestic or foreign policy due to Wedemeyer's mission. Wedemeyer's full report warned of an imminent Communist victory unless the United States dramatically increased its support for the Nationalist government. On November 11, 1947, Marshall, now secretary of state, submitted a program to Congress calling for $300 million in new aid for China.

As the Nationalist war effort shifted to the defensive, the government's strategy was to stabilize the situation in Manchuria by holding the four isolated areas of Changchun, Kirin, Mukden, and Chin Hsien, primarily through airborne resupply. The aim was also to maintain the Nationalist position in the important cities in the north and to prevent Communist expansion in northwestern, central, and eastern China. Communist-held territory had increased from about one-tenth of China in early 1946 to one-third in late 1948—an area of some 1 million square miles with 200 million inhabitants. The Communists had gained complete control of Manchuria, about half of Inner Mongolia, and large portions of several provinces.

The Nationalists' last remaining line of defense against a Communist attack on Shanghai and Nanking was the Yangtze River. Communist troop strength now exceeded that of the Nationalists, and the Communists, having captured huge stocks of artillery and armor, were now better equipped than the Nationalists. On September 1, 1948, the Communists proclaimed the North China People's Government as a forerunner to a People's Republic that would include all of China.

In 1948, the National Beijing Palace Museum and five other institutions sent their most prized artworks and artifacts to Taiwan. The extensive collection was built on the imperial collections of the Ming and Qing dynasties. The significance of that decision is illustrated by a story Edward Feulner, founder of the Heritage Foundation, told me about his recent visit to the Taiwan National Palace, where the treasures are displayed. One of the curates told Ed that he had helped pack the collection for its journey to Taiwan. "All of the artwork and artifacts would have been destroyed by the Red Guard during the cultural revolution if they had remained in Beijing," the curate said. More than 8,000 years of Chinese history, from the Neolithic age to the modern period, would have disappeared.

Chiang concluded the year by indicating his willingness to negotiate peace acceptable to all parties. The Communists marked the end of 1948 by publishing a list of 25 "war criminals." The first name on the list was Chiang's. The struggle ended in 1949 with a Nationalist appeal to the "Big Four" (the United States, the United Kingdom, France, and the Soviet Union) to mediate a settlement. The United States, which had long supported the Nationalist cause, immediately replied that such an effort would not serve any useful purpose. On January 14, 1949, Mao declared his willingness to negotiate on a lengthy list of terms, including punishment of war criminals, abrogation of the 1946 constitution, abolition of the existing form of government, reorganization of Nationalist armies, confiscation of "bureaucratic" capital from Nationalist Party elites and functionaries, land reform and the establishment of a democratic coalition government without the participation of "reactionary" Nationalist elements.

By December 10, 1949, when Chiang left, the departure of people, goods, and institutions was essentially complete. The Nationalist Air Force had begun relocating planes and other equipment as early as August 1948 and was soon followed by the Navy and the government's gold reserves. The governor of mainland provinces had all switched their allegiances to the Communists, and, by the end of 1949, virtually the entire mainland was under their control.

The ability of the People's Republic of China (PRC) and the United States to find common ground in the wake of the establishment of the new Chinese state was hampered by both domestic politics and global tensions. In August 1949, the Truman administration published the "China White Paper," which explained past U.S. policy toward China based upon the principle that only Chinese forces could determine the outcome of their Civil War. Unfortunately for Truman, this step failed to protect his Administration from charges of having "lost" China. The unfinished nature of the revolution, leaving a broken and exiled but still vocal Nationalist Government and Army in Taiwan, only heightened the sense among U.S. anti-Communists that the outcome of the struggle could be reversed.

The outbreak of the Korean War in 1950, pitted the PRC and the United States on opposite sides of an international conflict, ending any opportunity for accommodation between the PRC and the United States.

Truman's desire to prevent the Korean conflict from spreading south led to the U.S. policy of protecting the Chiang Kai-shek government in Taiwan.

The 1960s saw Mao's so-called "Great Leap Forward" in mainland China which led to catastrophic famine and millions of deaths. When Mao sensed that revolutionary fervor in China was waning in 1954, he proclaimed the Cultural Revolution. Gangs of Red Guards—young men and women between 14 and 21—roamed the cities targeting revisionists and other enemies of the state, especially teachers. Professors were dressed in grotesque clothes and dunce caps, their faces smeared with ink. They were then forced to get down on all fours and bark like dogs. Some were beaten to death —all for the promulgation of Maoism. A reluctant Mao finally called the Red Army to put down the marauding Red Guards when they began attacking Communist Party members, but not before 1 million Chinese died.

Vladimir Lenin, the founding head of the Soviet Union in 1917, used the term "useful idiots" to describe the gullible intellectuals who supported the Russian revolution. He reasoned that the same independent thinking they exhibited in supporting the revolution might make them dangerous counterrevolutionaries. Lenin shared distrust for intellectuals with Joseph Stalin, his successor. In the 1930s, Stalin began a purge of writers, intellectuals, and artists. Thousands of them died in concentration camps or were executed. Many of these gullible intellectuals had supported Stalin during the revolution. In Stalin's view, intellectuals could bring revolutionary consciousness to the working class. Fidel Castro also executed thousands of gullible "useful idiots" after taking over Cuba. Mao recognized that his No. 1 enemy was the intellectual. The so-called Great Helmsman reveled in his bloodletting, boasting, "What's so unusual about Emperor Shih Huang of the China Dynasty? He had buried alive only 460 scholars, but we have buried alive 46,000 scholars."

The Great Cultural Revolution transformed China into a great House of Fear. Deaths from hunger reached more than 50 percent in some Chinese villages. The total number of deaths was between 30 million and 40 million—the population of California. Mao kept expanding a system of 1,000 forced labor camps throughout China. And yet Mao Zedong remains the most honored figure in the Chinese Communist Party. At one end of historic Tiananmen Square is Mao's mausoleum, visited daily by large, respectful crowds. At the other end of the square is a giant portrait of Mao above the entrance to the Forbidden City, the favorite site of visitors, Chinese and foreign.

Here is how *The New York Times* described Mao—at the time of his death on September 9, 1976:

Mao Zedong, who began as an obscure peasant, died as one of history's great revolutionary figures. Born at a time when China was wracked by civil strife, beset with terrible poverty, and encroached on by more advanced foreign powers, he lived to fulfill his boyhood dream of restoring China to its traditional place as a great nation. With incredible perseverance, he harnessed the forces of agrarian discontent and nationalism to turn a tiny band of peasants into an army of millions, which led to victory throughout China in 1949 after 20 years of fighting. Then, after establishing the Chinese People's Republic, Mao launched a series of sweeping campaigns to transform a semi-feudal, largely illiterate, and predominantly agricultural country into a modern, industrialized socialist state.

With China's resurgence, Mao also charted a new course in foreign affairs, putting an end to a century of humiliation under the unequal treaties imposed by the West and winning new recognition and respect. Finally, in 1972, the United States abandoned its 20 years of implacable hostility when Richard M. Nixon journeyed to Peking, where a smiling Mao received him.

Justin Trudeau, prime minister of Canada, said in 2013, "There is a level of admiration I actually have for China because their basic dictatorship is allowing them to actually turn their economy around on a dime." His prime minister father, the late Pierre Trudeau, was complimentary toward several leftist regimes in his day, including Soviet Russia, Castro's Cuba, and China under Mao.

Who lost China to the Communists? Marshall's decision to withhold arms shipments from the Nationalists during a critical junction of the War played a major role. President Truman and a Congress that turned its back on the Nationalists must also share in the blame. General Stillwell never tried to hide his dislike for Chiang Kai-shek, and he shared his views with General Marshall. George Atcheson Jr., head of our State Department in China, described Mao as "the George Washington of the Pacific." Another State Department employee, John Servant, admitted to giving critical battle plans to the Communists.

The media helped turn China into a Communist country, with *The New York Times* describing the Communists as "agrarian liberals." Jack Belden, a United Press International (UPI) correspondent, described "the righteous war being waged by the Communists." Agnes Smedly, a known Communist who served as a spy for both China and the Soviet Union in the 1930s, described the Communists in heroic terms in *The Manchester Guardian*. No writer did more to support Mao than Edgar Snow, a journalist for *The New*

York Sun and the UPI. He wrote glowing reports about Mao in his book, *Red Star Over China*.

My friend General Douglas MacArthur said it best when he described the loss of China to the Communists as "one of the greatest blunders in American diplomatic history for which the free world is now paying in blood and disaster."

3 | Ready, Aim, Misfire: Redux—Who Gave Cuba to the Communists

EVERYBODY OUGHT TO HAVE A GUN, Fidel Castro maintained—until he took over Cuba in 1959. At a rally in Havana, before he assumed power, he explained that "This is how democracy works: it gives rifles to farmers, to students, to women, to Negroes, to the poor, and to every citizen who is ready to defend a just cause." Weapons ranging from Czech submachine guns to Belgian F.N. automatic rifles were handed out to 50,000 soldiers, 400,000 militiamen, 100,000 members of the factory-guarding popular defense force, and to many men, women, and children in Cuba's 1,000,000-strong "neighborhood vigilance committees."

Immediately after assuming power in 1959, Castro changed his position, following Mao's rule that guns should not be in the hands of the people. For three weeks after the Castro government was formed, Radio Havana warned: "All citizens must turn in their combat weapons. Civilians must take arms to police stations and soldiers to military headquarters. There was a touch of urgency about the new policy that suggested serious concern. Failure to turn in military weapons by September 1, 1959, warned Radio Havana would be punished not by criminal courts but by the dreaded Revolutionary Tribunals. Those kangaroo courts sentenced thousands of Cubans to death after Castro took over.

Vladimir Lenin, the founding head of the Soviet Union in 1917, used the term "useful idiots" to describe the gullible intellectuals who supported the Russian Revolution. He reasoned that the same independent thinking they exhibited in supporting the revolution might make them dangerous counter-revolutionaries. Castro shared this same distrust for the useful idiots who supported his revolution. Many of them were imprisoned, executed, or exiled.

Not all of the "useful idiots" were in Cuba. One of them, Herbert Matthews, a reporter for *The New York Times*, described Castro as a freedom-fighter intent on restoring democracy in Cuba. Ed Sullivan, a host of a highly rated TV show, gave Castro a platform where he promised free elections and the end of dictatorships in Cuba. "Not Communism or Marxism is our idea. Our political philosophy is a representative democracy and social justice in a well-planned economy," Castro told the American public. He lied. In a televised interview in Havana a few months later, Castro declared, "I am a Marxist-Leninist and shall be one until the end of my life. Marxism, or scientific socialism, has become the revolutionary Movement of the working class, and Communism will be the dominant force in Cuban politics. There cannot be three or four movements."

In the late 1950s, I had my personal run-in with Fidel Castro. Six years before, working for Wood, Struthers, and Company, I had negotiated a license with W.R. Grace Company to use their patent for producing hardboard from bagasse, which is processed from sugar cane stalks. Usually, these stalks are just burned, but the hardboard that can be made from them is extremely useful and valuable.

W. R. Grace's hardboard plant was in Chile, and I had to make the decision whether to establish our plant in either Puerto Rico or Cuba. Cuba had the strongest currency and the most stable economy at that time. For decades it had been one of the most prosperous countries in the Caribbean. But choosing Cuba for our plant was the worst economic decision I ever made.

At first, however, things went very well. Hardboard, used in both building construction and furniture manufacturing, was in huge demand throughout the Caribbean. The plant was busy with over 400 employees. I was there on a routine visit and had no idea what was coming until I heard an explosion. Our utility had been blown up. Bill Miller, our plant manager, warned me that I should leave immediately. Fidel Castro was in the nearby countryside, burning and looting everything in his path.

Hearing gunfire in the distance and seeing one of our warehouses set on fire, we took off from Camaguey Airport in a small plane. When we landed in Havana, the pilot told me there were bullet holes in the tail. It was a little disturbing for me to listen to members of the Havana Garden Club boast about contributing to "darling Fidel." Castro and his enforcers confiscated the plant, putting more than 400 Cubans out of work.

I had one more personal experience with Castro. When Belize celebrated independence from Great Britain in September 1981, the members of the Cuban delegation were in premium seats in front. The American delegation of Assistant Secretary of State Tom Ender and I, as ambassador to the Organization of American States (OAS), were relegated to the back. As the British flag was being lowered in the sunset, the band played the brand new "Belize Independent March," which I had been asked to write for the occasion. I had to spend a very uncomfortable two hours staring at the back of

Castro's head, the man who, 22 years earlier, at gunpoint, expropriated without compensation, our company. To my knowledge, the plant, Cubana Primadora, never reopened, nor did many other businesses that had been established in Cuba in the 1950s.

William F. Buckley Jr. famously quipped that Castro could claim, "I got my job through *The New York Times*." Much of the world had been taken in by the "freedom fighter" propaganda of the American Left, which made Fidel Castro a national hero in the United States. The then-senator John F. Kennedy said that Castro was following in the footsteps of Bolivar, the great liberator of South America. Castro's big lie about creating a democracy in Cuba began in February 1957, a low point in his decade-long revolutionary career. He was hiding out with a small group of lightly armed, poorly supplied supporters in the rugged Sierra Maestra mountains with thousands of government troops searching for them. In mid-December, he led a force of supporters organized in Mexico to attack government posts in Santiago de Cuba. Like a similar attack he had shown on the Moncada Barracks in Santiago de Cuba four years before, on July 26, 1953, they had been repulsed with high casualties on both sides.

However, after the July 26 attack, he was captured, tried, and sentenced to 15 years in prison. But after less than two years, he was released, the Government deciding that he was not a serious threat and that granting him amnesty would please the public. This time, he realized that he would be unlikely to survive another capture, so he came up with a plan. A supporter approached Ruby Phillips, *The New York Times* correspondent in Havana, offering to arrange an interview. Castro's publicity plan quickly began working out even better than he had hoped. Eager as Phillips was for this scoop, she worried she would be expelled from the island when the article appeared. So, she did not protest when *Times* editorial management decided that trekking in the Sierra Maestra was no job for a woman and a male reporter should handle the assignment.

That reporter was Herbert Matthews. Tall and slender, he was a logical, physical choice for getting through the mountain wilderness. Left unsaid was that he was also an obvious choice for political bias—his views identical to those of the *Times* editorial page. In the 1930s, his first foreign assignment covered the Spanish Civil War. In three years of observing and reporting on the fighting, he had become a passionate supporter of the Communist-leaning Popular Front government of the Second Spanish Republic in their battle against the Nationalists, an alliance of monarchists, conservatives, and traditionalists. Germany, Italy, and the Popular Front by the Soviet Union and Mexico openly supported the Nationalists. In the first of three articles based on his interview with Castro, Matthews dramatically describes the preparations for hiking into the hideout area. "To arrange for me to penetrate the Sierra Maestra and meet Fidel Castro, dozens of men and women in Havana and Oriente Province ran a truly terrible risk," he wrote in the first of three articles. "They must, of course, be protected with the utmost care in these articles, for their lives would be forfeit after the customary torture. Consequently, no names are used here, the places are disguised, and many details of the elaborate, dangerous trail in and out of the Sierra Maestra must be omitted. Why would this pitiful remnant of the "invasion" force be such a threat to the Batista Government?"

Curiously, after that anxious introduction, Matthews wrote that Castro's impending takeover of Cuba would be a slam dunk. "From the look of things, General Batista cannot possibly hope to suppress the Castro revolt." Castro, he wrote, was "already, in a measure, a hero of the Cuban youth" for the failed attack on the Moncada Barracks, where 100 students and soldiers were killed. He acknowledged that in the badly bungled second attack on December 2, 1956, Castro's force "lost their food and most of their arms and supplies and soon were being attacked by army units. They scattered and took to the hills. Many were killed. Of the 82 who had arrived on the *Gramma*, the broken-down yacht that served as the invasion ship from Mexico. No more than 15 or 20 were left after a few days.

Matthews also noted that President Batista was remarkably successful in concealing what happened. Because of the complete censorship, Havana and the other Cuban cities crackled with the most astonishing rumors constantly encouraged by the Government that Fidel Castro was dead. So it was that only those fighting with him and those who had faith and hope knew or thought he was alive. Those who knew were very few and in the utmost peril of their lives if their knowledge was traced.

Matthews explained the situation when he got to Havana on February 9, 1957, to find out what was happening. "The censorship has been applied to foreign correspondents as well as Cubans. What everybody, even those who wanted to believe, kept asking was: 'If Fidel is alive, why does he not do or say something to show that he is?' Since December 2, 1956, he had kept absolutely quiet—or he was dead."

The reality, Matthews wrote, was that Castro was waiting until he had his forces reorganized and strengthened and had mastery of the Sierra Maestra. "This, fortunately, coincided with my arrival, and he had sent word out to a trusted source in Havana that he wanted a foreign correspondent to come in. As soon as I arrived, the contact knew and contacted me. Because of the state of siege, it had to be someone who would get the story and go out of Cuba to write it."

Then came a week of organization. A rendezvous point and a time had to be fixed, and arrangements made to get through the government lines into the Sierra Maestra. After the first few weeks, the Army had reported that the remnants of Castro's forces were being starved out in the Sierra. "In reality, the Army had ringed the Sierra with fortified posts and columns of troops and had every road under heavy guard. Reports were reaching Havana that frequent clashes were taking place and that the Government troops were losing heavily proved true." After a dramatic account of their hike into the mountains to Castro's camp, he described meeting Fidel's younger brother, "slight and pleasant" and Fidel himself a few minutes later.

"Taking him, as one would at first, by physique and personality, this was quite a man—a powerful six-footer, olive-skinned, full-faced, with a straggly beard. He was dressed in an olive-gray fatigue uniform and carried a rifle with a telescopic sight, of which he was very proud. It seems his men have more than fifty of these, and he said the soldiers feared them. "We can pick them off at a thousand yards with these guns," he said.

After some general conversation, they sat down. In honor of the occasion, Castro broke open a box of Havana cigars, and for the next three hours, they sat there while he talked, never above a whisper at any time since there were columns of Government troops all around them. "The personality of the man is overpowering," Matthews wrote. "It was easy to see that his men adored him and also to see why he had caught the imagination of the youth of Cuba all over the island. Here was an educated, dedicated fanatic, a man of ideas, courage, and remarkable leadership qualities."

"As the story unfolded of how he had at first gathered the few remnants of supporters around him; kept the Government troops at bay while youths came in from other parts of Oriente as General Batista's counter terrorism aroused them; got arms and supplies, and then began the series of raids and counter attacks of guerrilla warfare, one got a feeling that he is now invincible," Matthews wrote. "Perhaps he isn't, but that is the faith he inspires in his followers. They have had many fights and inflicted many losses. Government planes came over and bombed every day. At 9 a.m. sharp, an airplane did fly over. The troops took up positions; a man in a white shirt was hastily covered up. But the plane went on to bomb higher in the mountains.

"Castro is a great talker. His brown eyes flash: his intense face is pushed close to the listener, and the whispering voice, as in a stage play, lends a vivid sense of drama," Matthews wrote. "'We have been fighting for seventy-nine days now and are stronger than ever," Castro said. "The soldiers are fighting badly; their morale is low, and ours could not be higher. We are killing many, but when we take prisoners, they are never shot. We question them, talk kindly to them, take their arms and equipment, and then set them free. I know that they are always arrested afterward, and we heard some were shot as examples to the others, but they don't want to fight, and they don't know how to fight this mountain warfare. We do. The Cuban people hear on the radio all about Algeria, but they never hear a word about us or read a word, thanks to the censorship. You will be the first to tell them. I have followers all over the island. All the best elements, especially all the youth, are with us. The Cuban people will stand anything but oppression.'"

Matthews asked Castro about the report that he would declare a revolutionary government in the Sierra. "Not yet" he replied. "The time is not ripe. I will make myself known at the opportune moment. It will have more effect on the delay. For now, everybody is talking about us. We are sure of ourselves. There is no hurry. Cuba is in a state of war, but Batista is hiding it. A dictatorship must show that it is omnipotent, or it will fall; we are showing that it is impotent." He said with some bitterness that the Government is using arms furnished by the United States, not only against him but against all the Cuban people. "They have bazookas, mortars, machine guns, planes, and bombs," he said, "but we are safe here in the Sierra; they must come and get us, and they cannot."

Castro has a political mind rather than a military one, Matthews said. "He has strong ideas about liberty, democracy, social justice, and restoring the Constitution to hold elections. He also has strong economic ideas, but an economist would consider them weak. The July 26 Movement talks of nationalism, anti-colonialism, and anti-imperialism. I asked Castro about that. He answered, 'You can be sure we have no animosity toward the United States and the American people.'"

Matthews noted that Castro speaks some English, but he preferred to talk in Spanish, which he did with extraordinary eloquence. "Above all," Castro said, "we are fighting for a democratic Cuba and ending the dictatorship. We are not anti-military, so we let the soldier prisoners go. There is no hatred of the Army, for we know the men are good, as are so many of the officers."

What also got out of Cuba safely was Matthews' belief that Fidel Castro would soon be in charge, leading his nation into peaceful prosperity and an ever more harmonious relationship with the United States. This belief could not have been more wrong. How much did Matthew's "reporting" contribute to this blunder, with hemispheric and even global consequences? Nearly five decades later, *New York Times* reporter Anthony DePalma wrote that ever since Matthews' initial encounter with Castro in the mountains of southeastern Cuba in 1957, there has been a debate—both journalistic and political—about his motives, his biases, and his inadequacies as a neutral observer. "There have been questions about how his writing may have influenced American foreign policy by creating popular, though inaccurate, images of Castro and his Movement for the American public. And there has been lingering uncertainty about whether Matthews had been duped by Castro or was simply a hopeless romantic caught up in an extraordinary moment of history.

Publishing Matthews' interview with Castro introduced a new dynamic to the impending rebellion, significantly increasing awareness of Castro in the United States, broadly across the population and specifically in Washington, where the Cold War was in high gear. Latin dictators in Argentina, Colombia, and elsewhere were being toppled. The impact of the articles in Cuba was different because Castro was already so well known. By raising the ire of Batista and focusing the efforts of the Army on eradicating the remnants of Castro's small landing group, Batista, in effect, signaled Castro's growing importance to the rebellion. Castro's group used the articles as proof of their growing strength, and in time, fundraising and recruitment benefited substantially from them. Ernesto "Che" Guevara said that Matthews's work was more important to the rebels than a victory on the battlefield. Matthews added to the initial impact of the articles with sharp attacks on Batista in the editorial pages, where he wrote nearly all of the Times' opinion pieces on Latin America. Matthews' writing on Cuba had a decisive impact on Cuba's relationship with the United States.

"Seldom has a single writer so influentially set the tone—at least as perceived by a broad cross-section of its interested readership—toward a person, movement, or historical phenomenon," wrote political scientist William E. Ratliff in *The Selling of Fidel Castro*. The British historian Hugh Thomas declared that Matthews writing had "immediately made Castro an international figure." In 1960, *El Tiempo of Bogotá* referred to Castro's victory as "the Herbert Matthews revolution." Documents show that members of the American embassy in Cuba were convinced that Castro's group was powerful enough to threaten the regime. Matthews had gone to the embassy for a briefing before heading into the mountains.

Matthews and *The New York Times* were sharply criticized for the way Castro was covered. Matthews' closeness to Castro became as much a liability as an advantage. Rather than represent the sensational peak of a long and distinguished career, his interview with Castro became a black hole in his life, drawing in his reputation and vitality. Matthews' name was ruined, and *The Times*, which had initially played up his coverage of Cuba, was considered guilty by association.

The State Department went from agreeing with Matthews's assessment that Castro was not a Communist to branding Castro the most dangerous foot soldier in the Communists' global conspiracy. And since Matthews had helped him gain power, he became a convenient and public scapegoat. But the damage had been done. In February 1958, Castro was quoted in

Coronet Magazine as "fighting to do away with dictatorship in Cuba and establish the foundations of genuine representative government." He disavowed any personal interest in becoming president, pointing out that under the Constitution, he was ten years too young. He insisted that his revolution's objectives were immediate freedom for all political prisoners, full and unrestrained freedom of public information, and wiping out corruption. "We have no plans for the expropriation or nationalization of foreign investment here." What is so fascinating about the *Coronet* article was that it was aimed at critics in the United States and at buying time against those he knew would advocate U.S. intervention.

By this time, most of the Cuban population had turned against the Cuban regime, and U.S. Ambassador E. T. Smith told Batista that the United States would no longer support him. The army commander secretly agreed to a ceasefire, promising Batista would be tried as a war criminal. Batista was warned and fled into exile on December 31, 1958. Supreme Court Judge Carlos Piedra was proclaimed president and appointed the new government. A furious Castro ended the ceasefire, ordering the commanding general's arrest by sympathetic figures in the Army and calling rebel leaders to prevent looting and vandalism during celebrations at the news of Batista's downfall on January 1, 1959. Traveling to Havana, where he arrived on January 9, he was greeted by cheering crowds in every town. Rebel columns entered Havana on January 2, while Castro entered Santiago and gave a speech invoking the wars of independence.

In response to popular demands that those responsible for Cuban deaths under Batista be brought to justice, Castro set up many trials, resulting in hundreds of executions. In his response to critics, particularly the U.S. press, Castro stated that revolutionary justice is based on moral conviction, not legal precepts. Acclaimed across Latin America, he went to Venezuela, where he met with President-elect Rómulo Betancourt to make an unsuccessful request for a loan and a new deal for Venezuelan oil. In Havana, he blasted senior government figures for eliminating thousands of jobs by shutting down brothels and casinos.

After being sworn in as prime minister, he visited the United States in April 1959. Snubbed by President Dwight D. Eisenhower, he met instead with Vice President Richard Nixon, whom he instantly disliked. After that meeting, Nixon told Eisenhower: "The one fact we can be sure of is that Castro has those indefinable qualities which made him a leader of men. Whatever we may think of him, he will be a great factor in the development of Cuba and possibly Latin American affairs. He seems to be sincere. He is either incredibly naive about Communism or under Communist discipline—my guess is the former. His ideas as to how to run a government or an economy are less developed than those of almost any world figure I have met in fifty countries. But because he has the power to lead, we have no choice but at least try to orient him in the right direction."

Traveling to Canada, Trinidad, Brazil, Uruguay, and Argentina, Castro attended an economic conference in Buenos Aires, where he unsuccessfully proposed a $30 billion U.S.-funded "Marshall Plan" for Latin America. Back in Cuba in May 1959, Castro signed the First Agrarian Reform into law, setting a cap for landholdings to 993 acres per owner and prohibiting foreigners from obtaining Cuban land ownership. That summer, he began nationalizing oil refinement, sugar production, and plantation lands owned by American investors and confiscating foreign landowners' property.

The world's most notorious guerrilla leader was about to invade their living rooms, and Americans were thrilled. At 8:00 p.m. on Sunday, January 11, 1959, some 50 million viewers tuned their television sets to *The Ed Sullivan Show*. Ed Sullivan, the well-known television personality, interviewed Fidel Castro in January 1959, shortly after dictator Batista had fled the country. Sullivan was hosting a Latin celebrity who had aroused intense curiosity across the United States: Fidel Castro, a charming 32-year-old lawyer-turned-revolutionary known for his unkempt beard and khaki patrol cap. For America's most beloved entertainment program, it was a rare excursion into politics.

The segment had been filmed at 2:00 a.m. on January 8, 1959, in the provincial outpost of Matanzas, 60 miles east of Havana, using the town hall as an improvised TV studio. It was the story of Che Guevara, Fidel Castro, and the scrappy band of rebel men and women who followed them. Only a few hours after the interview, Fidel would make his triumphant entrance into the Cuban capital, his men riding on the backs of captured tanks in euphoric scenes that evoked the liberation of Paris. It was the electrifying climax of history's most unlikely revolution: a scruffy handful of self-taught insurgents—many of them kids just out of college, literature majors, art students, and engineers, including many trailblazing women—had somehow defeated 40,000 professional soldiers and forced Batista to flee from the island like a thief in the night.

Castro was already a fashion icon for rebellious American youth, his olive-drab uniform, martial kepi, and raffish facial hair instantly recognizable. Clustered around the pair were a dozen equally shaggy young rebels who were known in Cuba simply as Los Barbados, "the bearded ones," all cradling weapons—"a forest of Tommy guns."

With his first breath, Sullivan assures CBS viewers that they are about to meet "a wonderful group of revolutionary youngsters," as if they are the latest pop music sensation. Despite their unwashed appearance, Fidel's followers are far from the godless Communists depicted by the Cuban military's propaganda machine, he adds; in fact, they are all wearing Catholic medals, and some are even piously carrying copies of the Bible. But Sullivan is most interested in Fidel himself. The sheer improbability of his victory over Batista had bathed him in a romantic aura. U.S. magazines openly described Castro as a new Robin Hood, robbing the rich to give to the poor.

Castro came across to the American public as earnest, sweet-natured, and eager to please, furrowing his brow with effort as he grasped his English vocabulary. Some of the interview is haunting in retrospect. "I'd like to ask you a couple of questions, Fidel," Sullivan says, serious for a moment. "In Latin American countries over and over again, dictators have stolen millions and millions of dollars, tortured and killed people. How do you propose to end that here in Cuba?" Fidel laughs. "Very easy. By not permitting any dictatorship to come again to rule our country. You can be sure that Batista will be the last dictator of Cuba."

At that time, Castro still refused to categorize his regime as socialist and repeatedly denied being a Communist, but he continued appointing Marxists to senior government and military positions. On July 23, Castro resumed his premiership and appointed Marxist Osvaldo Dorticós as president. Castro's government emphasized social projects to improve Cuba's standard of living, often to the detriment of economic development. He used radio and television to develop a "dialogue with the people," posing questions and making provocative statements. His regime remained popular with workers, peasants, and students, who constituted most of the country's population. The opposition came primarily from the middle class; thousands of doctors, engineers, and other professionals emigrated to Florida, causing an economic brain drain. Productivity decreased, and the country's financial reserves were drained within two years. Castro's government arrested hundreds of counter revolutionaries, many of whom were subjected to solitary confinement and execution. Militant anti-Castro groups, funded by exiles, the CIA, and the Dominican government, undertook armed attacks and set up guerrilla bases in Cuba's mountains.

Meeting with Soviet First Deputy Premier Anastas Mikoyan, Castro agreed to provide the Soviet Union with sugar, fruit, fibers and hides in return for crude oil, fertilizers, industrial goods, and a $100 million loan. Cuba's government ordered the country's refineries, controlled by Shell and Esso, to process Soviet oil, but under U.S. pressure, they refused. Castro responded by expropriating and nationalizing the refineries. Retaliating, the United States canceled its import of Cuban sugar, provoking Castro to nationalize most U.S.-owned assets on the island, including banks and sugar mills.

On October 13, 1960, the United States prohibited most exports to Cuba, initiating an economic embargo. In retaliation, the National Institute for Agrarian Reform (INRA) took control of 383 private-run businesses on October 14, and on October 25, a further 166 U.S. companies operating in Cuba had their premises seized and nationalized. On December 16, the United States ended its import of Cuban sugar, which, with shutting down promising industries like hardboard, cattle, and many others, had become the country's only major export.

In September 1960, Castro flew to New York City for the General Assembly of the United Nations. Having decided to show solidarity with African Americans, he stayed at the Hotel Theresa in Harlem, where he met with journalists and anti-establishment figures like Malcolm X. He also met Soviet Premier Nikita Khrushchev, with the two publicly condemning the poverty and racism, and they led applause to one another's speeches at the General Assembly.

The opening session of the United Nations General Assembly in September 1960 was highly rancorous, with Khrushchev famously banging his shoe against his desk to interrupt a speech by Filipino delegate Lorenzo Sumulong, which set the general tone for the debates and speeches. Castro was visited by Polish First Secretary Władysław Gomułka, Bulgarian First Secretary Todor Zhivkov, Egyptian President Gamal Abdel Nasser, and Indian Premier Jawaharlal Nehru, and also received an evening's reception from the Fair Play for Cuba Committee.

By early 1960 he had doubled the size of Cuba's armed forces, but, fearing counter-revolutionary elements in the Army, he created a People's Militia to arm citizens favorable to the revolution, training at least 50,000 civilians in combat techniques. Then, in September, he established the Committees for the Defense of the Revolution (CDR), a nationwide civilian organization implementing neighborhood spying to detect counter-revolutionary activities. By 1970, a third of the population would be involved in the CDR, eventually rising to 80 percent. Proclaiming his new administration a direct democracy in which Cubans could assemble at demonstrations to express their democratic will, he rejected the need for elections, contending that representative democratic systems served the interests of socio-economic elites.

"Now Cuba's stature in the world soared to new heights, and Castro's role as the adored and revered leader among ordinary Cuban people received a renewed boost," wrote Bourne. "His popularity was greater than ever. In his mind, he had done what generations of Cubans had only fantasized about: he had taken on the United States and won."

In January 1961, Castro ordered Havana's U.S. Embassy to reduce its 300-

member staff, contending that many were spies. The United States responded by ending diplomatic relations and increasing CIA funding for exiled dissidents; these militants began attacking ships that traded with Cuba and bombed factories, shops, and sugar mills. Presidents Eisenhower and Kennedy supported a CIA plan to aid a dissident militia, the Democratic Revolutionary Front, to invade Cuba and overthrow Castro; the plan resulted in the Bay of Pigs Invasion in April 1961.

On April 15, CIA-supplied B-26s bombed three Cuban military airfields; the United States announced that the perpetrators were defecting Cuban air force pilots, but Castro exposed these claims as false flag misinformation. Fearing invasion, he ordered the arrest of between 20,000 and 100,000 suspected counter revolutionaries, publicly proclaiming, "What the imperialists cannot forgive us is that we have made a Socialist revolution under their noses."

The CIA and the Democratic Revolutionary Front had based a 1,400-strong army, Brigade 2506, in Nicaragua. On the night of April 16, the Brigade landed along Cuba's Bay of Pigs and engaged in a firefight with a local revolutionary militia. The Brigade surrendered four days later after the militia was reinforced and their ships were bombed, and a panel of journalists interrogated captives on live television. A few were tried for crimes allegedly committed before the revolution, while the others were returned to the United States in exchange for medicine and food valued at $25 million.

Castro's victory reverberated worldwide, especially in Latin America. Still, it also increased internal opposition, primarily among the middle-class Cubans who had been detained in the run-up to the invasion. Although most were freed within a few days, many fled to the United States, establishing themselves in Florida. Consolidating "Socialist Cuba," Castro united the various groups that had opposed Batista into a governing party, the Integrated Revolutionary Organizations (Organizaciones Revolucionarias Integradas—ORI), renamed the United Party of the Cuban Socialist Revolution (PURSC) in 1962. Relations with the Soviets deepened. Soviet technicians arrived, and Castro was awarded the Lenin Peace Prize.

By 1962, Cuba's economy was in steep decline due to poor economic management and low productivity, coupled with the U.S. trade embargo. Food shortages led to rationing, resulting in protests in Cárdenas. Security reports indicated that many Cubans associated austerity with Communism. In March, Castro removed the most prominent of them from office, labeling them "sectarian." Khrushchev wanted to install Soviet R-12 MRBM nuclear missiles in Cuba to even the power balance of the United States. Castro agreed, believing it would guarantee Cuba's safety and enhance the cause of socialism. Upon discovering the missiles through aerial reconnaissance in October, the United States implemented an island-wide quarantine to search vessels headed to Cuba, sparking the Cuban Missile Crisis. While obviously offensive, Castro insisted the missiles were for Defense only and urged that Khrushchev launch a nuclear strike on the United States if Cuba were invaded. But Khrushchev was desperate to avoid nuclear war. He left Castro out of the negotiations and agreed to remove the missiles in exchange for a U.S. commitment not to invade Cuba and an understanding that the United States would remove their MRBMs from Turkey and Italy.

Feeling betrayed by Khrushchev, Castro was furious. Proposing a five-point plan, he demanded that the United States end its embargo, withdraw from Guantanamo Bay Naval Base, cease supporting dissidents, and stop violating Cuban air space and territorial waters. He presented these demands to U Thant, visiting secretary-general of the United Nations, but we ignored them. In turn, Castro refused to allow the U.N.'s inspection team into Cuba. In May 1963, Castro visited the Soviet Union at Khrushchev's personal invitation, touring cities, addressing a Red Square rally, and being awarded both the Order of Lenin and an honorary doctorate from Moscow State University.

He returned to Cuba with new ideas. Seeking further consolidating control, he cracked down on Protestant sects, labeling them counter-revolutionary "instruments of imperialism." He implemented measures to force perceived idle and delinquent youths to work, primarily by introducing mandatory military service. In September, he permitted emigration for anyone other than males aged between 15 and 26, thereby ridding the Government of thousands of critics, most of whom were from upper and middle-class backgrounds.

In January 1964, he returned to Moscow, officially to sign a new five-year sugar trade agreement and discuss the ramifications of the assassination of John F. Kennedy. Castro was deeply concerned about the assassination, believing the Cubans would be blamed. In October 1965, the Integrated Revolutionary Organization was officially renamed the "Cuban Communist Party" and published the membership of its Central Committee.

Despite Soviet misgivings, Castro continued to call for a global revolution, funding militant leftists and those engaged in national liberation struggles. Among them was Che Guevara's "Andean project," an unsuccessful plan to set up a guerrilla movement in the highlands of Bolivia, Peru, and Argentina. Castro allowed revolutionary groups from around the world, from the Viet Cong to the Black Panthers, to train in Cuba. He considered Western-dominated Africa ripe for revolution and sent troops and medics to aid Ahmed Ben Bella's socialist regime in Algeria during the Sand War. He also allied with Alphonse Massamba-Débat's socialist government in Congo-Brazzaville. In 1965, Castro authorized Che Guevara to travel to Congo-Kinshasa to train revolutionaries against the Western-backed government. Castro was personally devastated when CIA-backed troops killed Guevara in Bolivia.

Influenced by China's Great Leap Forward, in 1968, Castro proclaimed a Great Revolutionary Offensive, closing all remaining privately owned shops and businesses and denouncing their owners as capitalist counter revolutionaries. The severe lack of consumer goods for purchase led productivity to decline, as large population sectors felt little incentive to work hard. This was exacerbated by the perception that a revolutionary elite had emerged, consisting of those connected to the administration. They had access to better housing, private transportation, servants, and the ability to purchase luxury goods abroad. The corruption rot that afflicts virtually all Communist states was well underway.

Reagan's administration adopted a hardline approach against Castro, committed to overthrowing his regime. In late 1981, Castro publicly accused the United States of biological warfare against Cuba by orchestrating a dengue fever epidemic. Cuba's economy became even more dependent on Soviet aid, with Soviet subsidies—mainly in the form of supplies of low-cost oil and paying inflated prices for Cuban sugar. These subsidies averaged $4–5 billion a year by the late 1980s and accounted for nearly 40 percent of the country's GDP. Still, they also hobbled Cuba's long-term growth prospects by blocking diversification or sustainability.

In August 1994, Havana witnessed the largest anti-Castro demonstration in Cuban history, as hundreds of young men threw stones at police, demanding they be allowed to emigrate to Miami. Castro expressed the need for reform if Cuban socialism was to survive in a world now dominated by capitalist free markets. In October 1991, the Fourth Congress of the Cuban Communist Party was held in Santiago, at which several important changes to the government were announced. Castro would step down as head of Government, replaced by the much younger Carlos Lage, although Castro would remain the head of the Communist Party and commander-in-chief of the armed forces. Many older members of the government were to be retired and replaced by their younger counterparts. Several economic changes were proposed and subsequently put to a national referendum. Free farmers' markets and small-scale private enterprises would be legalized to stimulate economic growth, while U.S. dollars were also made legal tender. Certain restrictions on emigration were eased, allowing more discontented Cuban citizens to move to the United States. Castro's government diversified its economy into biotechnology and tourism, the latter outstripping Cuba's sugar industry as its primary source of revenue in 1995.

The election of socialist and anti-imperialist Hugo Chávez to the Venezuelan presidency in 1999 would help relieve some of Cuba's economic problems. Castro and Chávez developed a close friendship, and together they built an alliance that had repercussions throughout Latin America. In 2000, they signed an agreement that Cuba would send 20,000 medics to Venezuela, receiving 53,000 barrels of oil per day at preferential rates. In 2004, this trade was stepped up, with Cuba sending 40,000 medics and Venezuela providing 90,000 daily barrels.

In 1982, President Ronald Reagan labeled Cuba a state sponsor of terrorism for its support of leftist militant groups in Central America and Africa. Presidents George H.W. Bush and Bill Clinton signed laws—the Cuba Democracy Act of 1992 and the Cuban Liberty and Democratic Solidarity Act of 1996, also known as the Helms-Burton Act—that strengthened U.S. sanctions and stated that the embargo would remain in place until Cuba transitioned to a democracy that excludes the Castro family and upholds fundamental freedoms.

During his 2008 presidential campaign, Barack Obama said isolating Cuba had failed to advance U.S. interests and that it was time to pursue diplomacy with the Castro regime. Several weeks after taking office, he eased restrictions on remittances and travel, allowing Cuban Americans to send unlimited money to Cuba and permitting U.S. citizens to visit Cuba for religious and educational purposes. As Obama began softening U.S. policy toward Cuba, the island signaled openness to reform under the new leadership of Fidel's brother, Raul. Facing an aging population, a heavy foreign debt load, and economic hardship amid the global downturn, Raul Castro began liberalizing Cuba's state-controlled economy in 2009.

Reforms included decentralizing the agricultural sector, relaxing restrictions on small businesses, opening up real estate markets, allowing Cubans to travel abroad more freely, and expanding access to consumer goods. Cuba's private sector swelled, and the number of self-employed workers nearly tripled between 2009 and 2013—the death of Fidel Castro and the election of Trump in 2016 rekindled debates over United States-Cuba policy. The Trump administration grew increasingly wary of Cuba's close ties with the embattled socialist regime in Venezuela. In 2018, National Security Advisor John Bolton characterized Cuba, Nicaragua, and Venezuela as a "troika of tyranny," blaming their governments for massive human suffering and regional instability. The Trump administration sought to staunch the flow of oil from Venezuela to Cuba by sanctioning shipping firms and Cuba's state oil company. It also banned Cuban officials from entering the United States for their alleged complicity in Venezuela's human rights abuses. Meanwhile, Havana has made some economic reforms, including easing restrictions on private businesses, and unifying its dual currencies. It also expressed openness to Cuban American investors.

In April 2021, Díaz Canel replaced Raul Castro as the first secretary of the Communist Party, ending decades of leadership by the Castro family. However, the prospects for rapprochement faced new hurdles following the July 2021 outbreak of nationwide protests, Cuba's most significant in nearly three decades. Demonstrators said they reacted to worsening economic conditions, including power outages, food and medicine shortages, and spiking inflation. Analysts attribute these woes to a combination of U.S. restrictions, government mismanagement, and a nearly 90 percent drop in foreign currency due to a pandemic-related collapse in tourism. Cuba's leaders responded by blaming foreign provocateurs, arresting protest organizers, and clamping down on the internet and social media access across the island.

What can the last seven decades of this Cuba experience teach us? One lesson is to be skeptical of the "news" coverage of radical political movements, citing them as the necessary corrections for all of society's ills. His bitter disappointment largely shaped Herbert Matthews' coverage of Fidel Castro's rebellion in what he had seen in Spain two decades before when Communist "freedom fighters" were crushed. He met the dynamic, swaggering Castro and saw old wrongs about to be righted. And Matthews lived long enough to witness how power corrupts, and absolute power corrupts absolutely.

4 | Ambassador to the Netherlands

JUST AFTER THE 1968 ELECTION, Nixon staffer Peter Flanigan asked me, "Bill, if you were to come work in Washington, what would you like to do?" I told him only one position interested me: Secretary of the Navy. Well, word came back that President Nixon would be pleased to have me in that post. However, a few weeks later, I got another call from Flanigan. "The Boss sends his apologies, but he feels he has to give the Navy job to John Chafee." Chafee had been governor of Rhode Island but was now out of a job. He was not a Nixon loyalist—far from it—but Nixon wanted to reach out to the Rockefeller camp. And Chafee wanted the Navy job. "Would you mind stepping aside for the time being?" Flanigan asked. He said I would be next in line, but in the meantime, would I mind picking another post? Anything I wanted.

I was disappointed but not surprised and asked Peter for a day or two to think it over. But picking another post was not complicated: Ambassador to the Netherlands. I had been close to the Netherlands for many years. Austen Colgate, my Wall Street partner, and I owned the Van Waverin Tulip Bulb Company. It was the second largest in Holland and, dating from 1665—Rembrandt's time—one of the oldest in the world. Thus, I already knew many businesspeople and community leaders there. I did have some competition for the post, including the former child actress Shirley Temple Black, who was later appointed a delegate to the United Nations General Assembly.

I must say, however, that my first exposure to government service was, well, interesting. Someone passed me a copy of the State Department Official Instructions for processing ambassadorial nominees. Let one section stand for all: Initial Contact. After the President has announced either his intention to nominate a new Ambassador or has announced the appointment of a new Ambassador, the Assistant Secretary, or a Deputy Assistant Secretary for E.U.R. will telephone the new appointee to offer his congratulations. It is the responsibility of the country director to furnish the Assistant Secretary with the telephone number of the new appointee." This is an example of your friendly federal government at work.

As part of the processing, of course, I had to be acceptable to the host government, but the name Middendorf was a plus. My business ties with the

Netherlands (which, of course, I now had to sever) were certainly helpful, and my long-time interest in the paintings and accomplishments of Dutch and Flemish masters of the "Golden Age" was warmly noted in the press. In preparation, I decided with my partner to cover any contingencies that might arise. I took a Foreign Service Institute course in the Dutch language. I was briefed on Soviet techniques for gathering information and warned of bugging equipment that might be concealed in a shoe. This was not a TV-inspired joke.

Charles Tanguy, the State Department country director for France, coordinated my processing Let me say, right up front, that I was so impressed with Charles then—and later, as we worked on various trans-Atlantic issues—that I brought him over as deputy chief of mission when that post opened. Under Charles's guiding hand, I had more than 125 preparatory meetings with officials at the Departments of State, Treasury, Commerce, the CIA, USIA, scores of senior officials at the White House and other government agencies, and the leaders of such major international businesses as IBM, Chase, Citibank, and Chemical Bank. One of those White House officials was National Security Advisor, Henry Kissinger. Henry said, "Bill, stay close to me. The president and I would like to have you communicate on the major issues directly with us."

Yes, on major issues, I did, of course, report often to the president or the National Security Council (NSC), but as I quickly learned, it is impossible to operate an embassy on the other end of thirty or forty telegrams a day. Some of them were of great magnitude and on every issue imaginable—agriculture, trade, relations, military—without the support of a competent desk officer and others at the State Department. There was no way any ambassador could channel routine communications through a White House official with barely any support staff. In truth, I think Kissinger's primary focus on Russia, China, and Vietnam kept his attention, and he really didn't have much time to deal with issues concerning the Netherlands. Once in the job, I dealt more often with Kissinger's deputy, Helmut Sonnenfeldt, but only within the established chain of command.

The intensive schedule paid off. I got to know almost everyone at State, for example, with whom my office would ever likely have any dealings, and they got to know me. I was not a faceless bureaucrat at the other end of the communications chain. When I had a request or needed support, I got it. In fact, during my first year, I think I made fourteen trips back to the States so that, often as not, instead of a cable, there I was in person, standing at the desk to present and discuss my needs. Fourteen trips—all but one, I would add, at my own expense.

Finally, anointed by the Dutch and crammed full of data, it was time to demonstrate my fitness for the post, first privately to a handful of senators and then to the Senate Foreign Relations Committee. In this, I was confident. I wrote out responses to anticipated questions. Why do you want the job? What are your qualifications? How long do you intend to stay in the post? How do you see the job of ambassador? In truth, I was prepared to discuss geography, character, and size of the population, voting patterns, GNP, major imports and exports, nature of the host government, the names and background of leading government officials, and our modest military presence in the country.

Looking back at my notes, I find four items strongly underlined:

1. Answer only the question asked.
2. Do not volunteer info on matters not being asked.
3. Don't show off knowledge.
4. Do not prolong argument.

That's pretty good guidance for almost any situation. My friend, former Connecticut Governor John Lodge, was up for confirmation at the same time as ambassador to Argentina. Since we were both from Connecticut and had one sponsor in common (my neighbor, Senator Prescott Bush), we shared the same hearing. My other sponsor was a man who had been at Harvard with my father and uncle, former Massachusetts Senator Leverett Saltonstall.

The confirmation hearing should have been a breeze for John Lodge, who had been ambassador to Spain in the Eisenhower Administration. However, after some routine questions, the committee chairman invited him to make a closing comment if he wished. He did so wish and replied, along the lines, "Yes I do, Mr. Chairman, I want you to know that Mr. Franco is a fine fellow who has gotten a bum rap in the media." But Franco's unsavory connections with Hitler, before and during World War II, were not just media hype; the committee exploded with hostile questions.

Forewarned is forearmed. When the senator asked me the same question, I replied, "I am deeply honored by the president's nomination, and, if confirmed by the Senate, I look forward to serving in this challenging assignment." I was approved within minutes; Lodge's confirmation was held up for months. I was nominated in April and confirmed in June.

I enjoyed my first diplomatic success before leaving to take the post. The Dutch prime minister and the foreign minister were on a swing through the United States, and I was included in some official and social functions. As I had learned during my briefings, two long-standing Dutch requests were hanging in the air, unresolved. One was for a nuclear-powered submarine, and the other was for the national airline, KLM, to have landing rights in Chicago.

The Dutch argued that their responsibilities within NATO would better be served if they had a nuclear submarine; they believed that Eisenhower's secretary of State, John Foster Dulles, had promised them one. However, the issue was very complicated. The Department of Defense and the CIA were opposed; the infrastructure needed to support a nuclear boat was almost beyond belief, and there was some concern that Soviet spies could worm their way into the crew and steal secrets. I knew that there was no way I could engineer a deal.

But landing rights? Ah, good old American politics. I asked for a quick meeting with Nixon. "Mr. President," I said, "I have a favor to ask, something to get me off to a good start with the Dutch." Nixon sat there, his feet on the desk, writing down everything I said on a big yellow legal pad. When I finished, the president said he would take care of it. And he did. The Dutch were delighted, but I did not make any points with fellow ambassador, Ike's son John Eisenhower, over in Brussels. He got me on the phone and said, only half-joking, "Bill, you S.O.B.! Now the Belgians are on my case. They want landing rights for Sabena." I don't think they ever got them, at least not during his tenure.

I arrived at my post the first week of July 1969, taking over from a great career foreign service officer, William Tyler, who became head of the Dumbarton Oaks Foundation. I must say, as with the pre-confirmation processing back in Washington, nothing in my arrival was left to chance or imagination. A cable was sent from the deputy chief of mission giving the following advice about my arrival speech: "Suggest that last sentence arrival statement would sound more spontaneous as follows: Finally I am grateful to President Nixon for having assigned me as his personal representative to the country of my choice—*en ik zie er verlandend naar uit mijn uiterste best te doen in Nederland.*" Yes, I had studied the language, but I have little doubt that my rendition of the Dutch equivalent of "I look forward to doing my utmost in the Netherlands" did not sound very spontaneous.

My first public speech was a few days later, to some business council. I was giving it in Dutch and, despite diligent rehearsal, was stumbling all over the place. The subject matter, something about agricultural subsidies, was far from lively. Glancing around an audience desperately fighting to stay awake, I could tell they were losing the battle. At last, Foreign Minister Joseph Luns stood up and said, "Mr. Ambassador—with all due respect—we would be greatly thrilled if you would speak English here." Needless to say, it was the last time I tried discussing highly technical matters in Dutch. I did, however, use the language in general discourse for social courtesies and so forth.

The whirlwind of official contacts did not end when I left Washington. In my first few weeks in The Hague, I made 41 formal calls to Dutch officials and 55 to resident ambassadors. And, of course, I quickly became acquainted with the key members and inner workings of my post, spread over three sites—the Embassy, and consulates in Rotterdam and Amsterdam—employing some 226 people, of whom more than half were local, non-American staff.

I presented my credentials to Queen Juliana on July 14, 1969. I don't know how this is done in most countries, but at the Hague, it is done right. I was togged out in a complete formal diplomatic kit, top hat, white tie and tails, and white gloves ("not worn," I was advised by very detailed memoranda provided by the embassy staff, "but carried in the left hand"). I was picked up by an astonishingly ornate gilded carriage, pulled by four of the best-matched horses I or anyone else had ever seen.

More guidance from the Embassy: "On arrival at the Palace, the Queen's Chamberlain and the Ambassador alight and, with their top hats held at their left breasts, acknowledge the playing of the American and possibly also the Dutch National Anthem." On arrival, I was met by—and reviewed—the Queen's Guard. ("The Ambassador thanks the Commander and congratulates him on his fine guard.") The pomp and circumstance were real, not artificial. And walking into the Queen's palace, Huis Ten Bosch, was like walking into the 17th century, the walls covered with great paintings of the Golden Age. Things in The Hague don't change very much or very often; in truth, there is a Dutch saying: "When you die, try to do it in the Hague because, in the Hague, everything happens ten years later than in the rest of Europe."

The Queen was about 60 and had been the reigning monarch since 1947. ("The initial form of address is *Your Majesty*; then, *Madame* is used.") She was very gracious, of course, and our conversation, approximately ten minutes, was very general—of course—although she did drop a personal note. She told me how much she enjoyed playing the violin. She did not, however, then or later, offer a demonstration.

How can I best describe the job of ambassador for anyone who may someday wish for a similar role? I suppose it conjures visions of an international party-time for political fat cats in the public mind. A great deal of diplomacy involves breaking bread with friends and foes alike, and the average man in the street will likely not come to the attention of the president or White House staffers seeking to fill the jobs. The underlying reality is that most people who can make valuable contributions, whether in private industry, government service, or in a political campaign, are people who have been pretty successful. They understand the nuance of negotiations and the value of alliances.

I had the privilege of recommending to Presidents Nixon and Reagan: banker Shelby Davis for Switzerland and businessman/historian John Loeb for Denmark. In my Wall Street days, Davis had been Middendorf Colgate's major competitor in the specialized field of insurance stocks, but he was an honest, fair, and worthy adversary; John Loeb had worked with me on Ronald Reagan's first election campaign as a member of the International Economic Advisory Committee, where (with Julian Gingold) he wrote three brilliant papers on the status and future of the U.S. dollar.

I soon learned, as have many business types who take such an assignment, that the job of an ambassador is vastly different from running almost any kind of business. The business world is vertical: you gather and assess information from below, make your decision, and live with the results. In business, I could measure success or failure, often daily, by the movement of the securities I recommended or the health of our balance sheet. Diplomacy, by contrast, is horizontal. You are not an individual performer. You're part of a vast team where your efforts are submerged in the collective. Gray is the color of diplomacy, compromise is the common currency, and there is no daily measuring stick for success.

As ambassador, you represent the president, but you act as the extension of your State Department desk officer. A large part of your job is to gather information and forward what you have learned along with your recommendations. The desk officer passes your cable along to your region's Assistant secretary of State. He usually makes whatever decision seems indicated. The assistant secretary may, on rare occasions, consult with the secretary of State. On even more infrequent occasions, the secretary may confer with the president. Whatever guidance is generated is then passed back through the chain to you. Deliver this note. Take this position. Sign this treaty or agreement. And always, "Find out more."

I came into the job with 20-plus years' experience as a hard-fighting, no-holds-barred executive. I was accustomed to making my own decisions —yes, in consort with my partner, but making them quickly. I had to make quite an adjustment. This led to a permanent change in my personal style: now, I'm much more collegial, checking with everyone in sight before I make a decision.

Most ambassadors not from the Foreign Service come to the top posts because of political affiliation, but that does not give them a license to be political. A few months after I arrived on the scene, the new chairman of the

Republican National Committee, Roger C.B. Morton, thought to revitalize RNC operations in Europe. Morton sent a representative to an ambassadors' meeting in Italy, as I recall, looking for suggestions. Someone had a bright idea: have the Republican-appointed ambassadors spread a Republican message, especially to Americans living abroad. Use federal employees to promote partisanship? Well, no. The idea died a-borning. There was a proper "political outreach" component of the job: for example, trying to help Europeans understand matters like the U.S. two-party system. (Only two, they wondered? Why not seven or eight? Or twenty-eight, as competed in one Dutch legislative contest?)

And, of course, things only tangentially political were certainly within bounds. We held regular, three-times-a-year briefings for anyone or everyone in the American business community.

Roger Morton put his finger on one problem: the European image of Nixon was rather fuzzy. Little wonder: the presidential portrait hanging in the Rotterdam Consulate was a bit out of date; I made sure that Nixon replaced JFK. Over time, I tried hard to get the president to stop by on one of his European trips ("They're really looking forward to seeing you and Pat in the Netherlands") without success. To my knowledge, no U.S. president had ever visited the Netherlands while in office. Two of them, of course—John Adams and his son, John Quincy—had both been to Holland as Ministers Plenipotentiary before serving as president. George H.W. Bush—who had visited at least twice while I was in the Hague—later became the first man to visit the country as president.

On the surface, the Netherlands of 1969 looked like a happy fairy tale. Clean and scrubbed—the country and the people. Unfailingly friendly. Industrious. This general reputation of the Dutch is not invented. Teenager John Quincy lived in Holland when his father was posted there. Young John's mother, Abigail, in a letter sent from her home in Massachusetts, hoped "that the universal neatness and cleanliness of the people where you reside will cure you of all your slovenly tricks, and that you will learn from their industry, economy, and frugality." She was right on the mark.

Everyone, even the Queen, rode around on bicycles, and I quickly followed suit. When Barend Biesheuvel was appointed prime minister soon after my arrival, I pedaled to his office for my courtesy call. Of course, having lived and worked for so long in New York City, I wasn't quite sure about the safety of unattended bicycles, so I asked the security guard who opened the door if I might bring the bike inside.

I should not have worried about my bicycle, but there were plenty of other things of concern. Because, under the surface, the fairy tale was often dark. The Dutch economy was bedeviled by wage and price controls, rising taxes, and inflation—the cost of living in 1971 was 21 percent higher than the year before. The Dutch government was in perpetual turmoil. There were five major political parties, always forming, dissolving, and re-forming coalitions. During my four-year tenure, they went through four prime ministers and one eight or nine-month period without any prime minister at all.

When I arrived, Piet de Jong had the watch; quite literally, as he was a former submarine commander. He soon was followed by Barend Biesheuvel, then Norbert Schmeltzer—whose government may not even have been accorded full recognition, it was so tenuous—and then the hiatus, followed by the laborite (socialist) Joop den Uyl heading a coalition of all five parties. When he was merely a member of Parliament, Joop would often drop by my residence and share some of my wine and cigars. Once he became prime minister, he declined all invitations. "I can't come anymore," he said, "because of your country's criminal involvement in the Vietnam War." My country had been just as much involved in the war when he enjoyed my hospitality, but I guess he now felt obliged to make a statement.

Joop's political hero, his idol was the Social Democrat, Willy Brandt, chancellor of West Germany. "You have to understand," Joop told me, "that the only people who can deal effectively with the Communists are the Socialists. Because we understand each other. We wouldn't have all of these problems with the Soviet Union if people like Willy Brandt and I were in charge of Europe." Brandt even was awarded the 1971 Nobel Peace Prize for his efforts at improving east-west relations. Not long after I left my post to move on to another assignment, the world learned that the Stasi (the East German secret police) had an agent posted as a personal assistant to Brandt. So much for his ability to deal with the Communists.

Foreign Minister Joseph Luns (he who so graciously had acknowledged my clumsy attempts with the language) was a remarkable man. I believe he had served as a foreign minister longer than any other European since Tallyrand (who served in that capacity in France, 1792–1807). Joseph was a habitual joke-teller but always of the same 17 jokes, half of them at the expense of Charles de Gaulle. The joke-telling followed a predictable routine: He would recite them in a set order, joke number one, then number two, on to seventeen, and back again to one. Picture the scene: a dinner party, time set for eight o'clock. Everyone arrives precisely three minutes before eight. The Dutch are very punctual. At some time during the evening, Joseph begins the routine, but at eleven on the nose, the party is over. He might be in the middle of joke number seven—his audience is enthralled—but when the clock chimes the hour, Joseph checks his watch and makes a gracious exit without even finishing the joke. At the next affair, wherever, I swear he would pick right up at joke number eight. He was generally so well-liked that this bit of boorishness was accepted with a sort of amused tolerance. I must have heard and, of course, laughed at each of those jokes about 20 times. And I can't remember a single one.

I had been in the post for about two years when Joseph came to ask a favor. "I would like," he said, "to be secretary general of NATO." At that time, many of the top international agency jobs in Europe were already held by Dutchmen, and it seemed like backbreaking work to plug in another. But I was willing to try. I learned that Secretary of Defense Melvin Laird had not yet given any thought to the topic. So I called Mel and asked, would the United States consider supporting Joseph Luns as secretary general of NATO? Mel said, offhand, "I don't have a problem with that but is anyone else in the running"? I didn't know, but only half in jest, I suggested that a German, so close to the end of the War, would be fearful of his own shadow. The British don't want it, and the Italians couldn't have it because the outgoing incumbent was Italian. I told Mel that Joseph was not only a first-rate guy but was pretty much on our side. Mel called back about a week later and said he thought we could go with my man. With our support, Joseph won the appointment. He held the job for 13 years and did it superbly.

The senior Communist in the Netherlands—Soviet Ambassador Lavrov—was a pleasant fellow who followed the rules. Part of his job was to harangue me about supposed U.S. crimes in Vietnam and elsewhere. I suspect that it was vital for him to let his superiors back in Moscow know that he was doing his job. One time, he invited me over to his residence for a chat. After the usual pleasantries—would I like to join him in a vodka? No, but thank you—we sat down on the couch, and he launched into a carefully rehearsed peroration. How do I know it was carefully rehearsed? About three minutes into the rant, his chauffeur came into the room, whispered something into the ambassador's ear, and left. With no sign of shame, Lavrov reached up under an ugly painting hanging on the wall behind the couch. I heard an audible click, whereupon he started his little speech all over again, letter-perfect, from the beginning. I interrupted for a moment to ask if I might have a vodka after all.

This was a period of much diplomatic ferment for the United States, and Vietnam was the point around which everything seemed to revolve, a running undercurrent to everything we did. It was the time of the "Cambodian incursion," the shootings at Kent State, and the publication of the Pentagon Papers. Television coverage in the Netherlands was brutal, and we became targets of left-wing anger. I got an urgent call from the consul general in Amsterdam, Gene Braderman. He wanted some Marines to go up and protect his office from protesting anti-American mobs, then roaming through the streets, breaking things. "The Dutch can't help," he said. There were not many Marines on the Embassy detail, but give a Marine something to do, and he will do it. We got through that incident with some damage to his office, but none to personnel.

Another time, a small crowd had gathered outside the Embassy. However, television news was happy to participate, and whenever the TV showed placard-waving people tramping around outside the Embassy, even more people would show up. The crowd had grown to perhaps 300, all chanting "Ambassador come out," or words, some not quite so bland, to that effect. My security people wanted me to slip out through the back door, where my driver Charles would be waiting to spirit me away from the Embassy. I said, "We're going out the front," and told the driver to bring the car around.

Was I brave or foolish? Maybe I was just reacting without much thought. In any event, I said, "Open the door," and walked out, alone, into the crowd—sudden silence. People stepped back to let me pass. I got in the car, closed and locked the door, and said, "Charles, let's go!" Not a moment too soon. The crowd recovered from its momentary relapse into natural Dutch politesse and started banging on the car and shouting.

From time to time, there were personal threats. Once, an anonymous caller recited the exact itinerary of a trip later in the day and told me at which point I could expect to be killed. We didn't cancel the trip, but we changed the route. Another: after some particularly serious anti-American threats, I asked one of the Marine guards to spend a few hours at the residence. I wasn't so much worried about myself, but the house was full of my kids. The youngest was four. Babysitting was not in the security guard job description—protection of people was the responsibility of the local police, and the Marines were assigned to protect U.S. government property. Well, as far as I was concerned, the residence qualified. I felt a lot better when a Marine was close at hand.

Not every moment was given over to serious issues. One evening, we had a diverse group of friends at the Embassy, including Soviet Ambassador Lavrov and the 80-year-old Christian evangelist Corrie Ten Boom. Perhaps you have not heard of her; during the War, she and her family saved hundreds of Jews from the concentration camps—until they were betrayed by an informant, arrested, and sent to the camps where all but she died. After the War, she lectured and wrote several books, telling her story and carrying the message of "God's forgiveness." Corrie gave Lavrov a copy of her memoir, the international best-seller *The Hiding Place*, which he graciously accepted (perhaps just forgetful, he left it behind; I had it delivered to him the next day). Corrie and Isabelle became fast friends.

Shortly after the 1969 Apollo 11 landing, I hosted a visit by the astronauts, who brought two small pieces of moon rock with them. We presented these to the Dutch government, and they were put on public display. Later the Associated Press reported that a former prime minister, Willem Drees (now deceased and whom I don't remember ever meeting) had given to a museum what everyone seems to have thought was one of the moon rocks—it had been insured for half a million dollars until it turned out to be a piece of petrified wood. There was a flurry of finger-pointing, until AP checked around. No one in the Embassy or the State Department had any record of a gift to Drees, and the Dutch government verified that they still had "my" moon rocks safely under lock and key. I have no idea where the prime minister got his bit of petrified wood or why someone thought it came from the moon.

I tried to get out and around. I think I visited every major town in the Netherlands and, whenever possible, undertook some ceremonial task often with my whole family in tow. We opened the Cheese Market in Alkmaar, for example—on the first day of the new season—like the symbolic guest opening the New York Stock Exchange by banging on a bell. Cheese vendors waved their fragrant wares under the noses of passers-by, basket makers wove their baskets, and clog makers carved their clogs, all under the watchful eyes of a crowd of camera-wielding tourists.

I should tell you, however, about one of those ceremonial affairs gone awry. By tradition, the ruling monarch goes down to the port to welcome the herring fleet on the first day of the catch. By tradition, the monarch takes up a wriggling, live herring, and swallows it whole! The crowd then looks to the Honored Guest—me—to do likewise. Honored Guest screws up his courage and discovers that it is not as easy as the Queen made it look and chokes. The Queen, a wise and gracious woman, was most polite and did not join in the general laughter.

I came to the post as a businessman and was determined to add whatever value that experience might offer. At that time, top management at the State Department did not emphasize matters of trade, as if the business of statesmen did not include, well, business. By contrast, the Dutch were all business. Dutchmen headed or held key positions at such international trade organizations as the Bank of International Settlement, European Economic Community (EEC), Organization for Economic Cooperation and Development (OECD), and the International Monetary Fund (IMF). The Netherlands was the largest investor in the United States; the Dutch had more money invested in our country than we had in theirs, well over $2.2 billion, compared with a $1.7 billion U.S. investment there. Much of the Dutch investment, of course, was concentrated in a few firms—Shell, Unilever, Philips—among the world's largest non-American concerns.

The Netherlands was already one of our best customers, where about nine hundred American firms had operations of one sort or another. But I knew that there was room for many, many more. The Netherlands was a free market with minimal barriers to trade. Dutch foreign trade for 1972 was equivalent to 76 percent of G.P., compared with only 9 percent in the United States. We could help U.S. exporters explore the market and could help line up competent local agents or distributors. We would not act as salesmen but as trade facilitators. When I suggested this project to the Embassy staff, they jumped at the chance. We started by assessing the marketplace and analyzing opportunities, targeting industries for which we believed there was a large potential market. We didn't bother with computer hardware, vehicles, and aircraft because companies like IBM, Ford, and Boeing were already well-established in the marketplace. We concentrated our efforts on software, environmental controls, cargo handling systems, pumps and valves, printing and graphics, food processing, and franchising.

We appointed a staff national campaign manager for each target line, a remarkable team. Bob Jelley, in Amsterdam, concentrated on the computer and printing industries, Gene Griffiths in Rotterdam followed electronics and test equipment and encouraged Dutch companies to invest in the United States. In the Hague, Ralph Griffin took on materials handling and environmental systems; Carlos Moore worked with health care industries and ran our Visit U.S.A. program. Ben Kennedy focused on American plant investment and product manufacture in the Netherlands.

Commercial Attaché Harold C. Voorhees was in overall charge, and John Blodgett developed a clear plan of action: identify the products and producers; research the markets; identify all importers, dealers, and agents in the target industry; identify and appraise the quality of upcoming trade events (in the Netherlands and elsewhere). For instance, when we learned that American trade centers in Europe were mounting tradeshows in some of our target industries, we arranged charter flights. We invited Dutch merchants and potential customers to join us at their own expense. Over time, there were six such missions, each sold-out, which carried more than four hundred top-drawer Dutch customers to visit American exhibits in Oslo, London, Frankfurt, and Paris.

Our program incorporated all logical marketing techniques. Direct mail ("take advantage of one of the largest and fastest-growing markets for American products"), visits to potential customers, reverse trade missions, those charter flights, negotiations over trade barriers—notably, gaining favorable treatment for U.S. citrus exports. We coordinated with the American Chamber of Commerce and the "Visit-USA" offices in Paris and Brussels. The embassy staff developed and ran the program; I played cheerleader, advisor and activated my personal network in support.

On one of my home visits, May 1970, I sat down with Nixon, gave him a full briefing on our effort, and urged him to spread the word. As before, he sat there, feet propped up on the desk and a yellow legal pad in his lap. He took notes. I followed through with a letter to Maurice Stans at Commerce, in July on the same subject. Dutch businessmen were concerned over the U.S. recession; I arranged for Federal Reserve Board Chairman Arthur F. Burns to meet with investment bankers and government officials for freewheeling discussions. An innovative export tax-relief program proposed by the Administration was hung up in Congress; I became a lobbyist without portfolio for the Congressional Domestic International Sales Corporation (DISC). This would permit an American corporation to defer Federal corporate income taxes if the money was invested in new exports. My lobbying tactic? Not complicated. I easily won the support of a key chairman, Arkansas Congressman Wilbur Mills, who bragged that he had never been outside the United States, with a simple reminder that his State was a major exporter of soybeans and would be a major beneficiary of the program. The legislation did pass, although some inadvertent conflicts with international compacts had to be worked through. As a result, DISC was replaced in 1985 by the Foreign Sales Corporation (FSC) and—apparently still flawed—in 2000 by the Extraterritorial Income Exclusion (EIE) Act. Maybe we'll get it right.

The Department of Commerce was indeed involved in overseas business promotion, providing, among other services, outstanding "Buy American" exhibits at major European tradeshows and expos. We just knew that more could be done. Our small but potent Military Assistance Advisory Group, the MAAG, was pursuing opportunities in its own sphere, especially an open competition launched by the Dutch government to replace a fleet of aging Royal Dutch Air Force Lockheed F-104G Starfighters. The candidates included the Swedish Saab Viggen, the French Mirage F-1, the Northrop P-530 Cobra, the Lockheed CL1200 Lancer, and the McDonnell-Douglas F-4 Phantom.

We had a tough balancing act to put forward the interests of the U.S. competitors in general without favoring one over the other. However, I was not constrained from passing along an unclassified U.S. Air Force analysis—using sophisticated techniques perhaps not available to the Dutch—which showed that the F-1 "would be a disaster in combat" (for the Dutch, that is) with the newest-version Soviet M.I.G., and that the Viggen was not even in the same league. In this sort of international deal, one issue was the "offset." How much business would the winning company put in the Netherlands in co-production or totally unrelated business? The general manager of a Dutch electronics company told me he favored the Viggen because the Swedes were offering to buy other military hardware from his company; I told him, "You know, Northrop is offering a minimum of 350 million dollars' worth of direct aircraft work." He said, "Ahh . . ."

Lockheed pushed hard for their candidate: the CL-1200 Lancer (Air Force designator X-27). This was, essentially, an updated version of the F-104 with increased fuel capacity and a new engine. It was a cost-effective proposal for Lockheed—they already had the tooling. They hoped that the Dutch would see familiarity as an advantage. Lockheed designer Clarence "Kelley" Johnson, head of the famed Skunk Works, wrote to tell me that Secretary of Defense David Packard told him that the CL-1200 was a project he wanted to do very much. But then, noting a dark cloud on the horizon, Kelley added, "There is much talk here of the so-called 'lightweight fighter' for which there may be competition for a prototype soon. This aircraft makes use of one F-15 engine and is the size of the original XF-104." He was not enthusiastic: "Its range and endurance are very short, and the ability to carry external stores inferior in my view."

In March, 1972, I escorted Dutch Defense Minister Hans de Koster on a ten-day swing through the United States that included visits to both Lockheed and Northrop—not to mention visits to Army, Navy and Air Force bases and meetings with the secretaries of Defense and Air Force. At this point, the Norwegian Air Force bought twenty-two used F-104s from the Canadian Air Force. Dutch socialists, opposed to any major weapons purchase, were delighted and put some pressure on the government. If old F-104s were still good enough for the Norwegians, why not also the Dutch? The Dutch Air Force was not persuaded. By July, the field had been narrowed to one competitor, and an Invitation for Offer was sent to Northrop.

However, as Kelley Johnson had predicted, there indeed was a new USAF competition that, in effect, put all other competitions on hold. The Air Force issued development contracts to Northrop and General Dynamics one month after de Koster's trip. These led to a 1974 fly-off between a single-engine General Dynamics YF-16 and the twin-engine Northrop P-530 Cobra, now dubbed YF-17. Lockheed's CL-1200 had been evaluated and was not in the running. In the event, the YF-16 won. The so-called lightweight fighter is today the F-16, of which more than 4,000 have been put into service worldwide. In June 1975, a NATO consortium of the Netherlands, Belgium, Norway, and Denmark selected the F-16 in a head-to-head competition with the French Mirage. As for offset, most of the aircraft and engine components came to be manufactured in five NATO countries, with complete aircraft assembled in Belgium and the Netherlands. In a small irony, Lockheed—cut out of that competition—purchased the General Dynamics aircraft business in 1992. Thus, the grand winner is now certifiably a Lockheed product. YF-17 lived on to see another day: in fact, during my tenure as secretary of the Navy, it was transmogrified into the F/A-18 Hornet.

Outside the "target industry" envelope, but great fun nonetheless, we arranged for what I believe to have been the first California wine tasting and display in Europe. Just before he headed off to his new job in Washington, Ambassador Tyler had taken me down to the cellar of the residence and waved his hand over rows and rows of dusty bottles of wine. "I can't very well take it with me," he said, "and it may be some value to you." He offered to sell all to me for a very modest fee, which is how I came to be the proud owner of what may have been the best collection of first-rate wine in the neighborhood. I put much of it to good use, entertaining diplomats, especially after I had joined a wine tasting club that rotated events among the members' homes. I could almost pretend that I knew something about wine.

Thus emboldened, I convinced some California winemakers to bring samples of their wares to the Hague to discuss the California approach. The French community was furious; some of our friends thought the idea was hilarious—what a great joke. Everyone knew that California wines were called something like Mountain Red, came in gallon jugs, and sold for less than a buck. "Everyone" was surprised. Even some of the French (who came to the event, disdainful at the ready) admitted that you may have something here. I don't think the California wine industry made any quick killings on the European market, but it was a start.

Our greatest success, not a specific trade deal, but a confirmation, if you will, that we had been on the right track, came in the middle of my tour, when the Departments of State and Commerce launched a study on "assistance to American business overseas." I do believe that Nixon had paid attention. The Senate Commerce Committee convened a hearing in Brussels, at which I was pleased to testify. Teams of investigators were sent around the world, studying existing programs—all embassies promoted trade to some degree, of course—and gathering suggestions. The result: a state-commerce coordinated "target industry" program involving all overseas missions, beginning in FY 1974. The effort was remarkably similar to ours, although, where we had focused on eight product categories, they narrowed the field to five—which were more or less identical to five of ours. To conform, we dropped two of our lines but kept environmental controls because this seemed to be natural for the Netherlands. And the State Department made a change that I found particularly gratifying: when reporting on the fitness of the foreign service professionals, "Henceforth, all officers will be evaluated on the basis of their concerns for U.S. business."

Toward the end of my tour, *Business Week* (December 16, 1972) explained the Administration's new "business promotion" effort, in a focus on our program under the headline, "World Trade: A U.S. Ambassador's New Business Role." They went into pretty good detail: our eight product areas, the direct involvement of as many as twenty-two members of the embassy staff, our saturation bombing of Dutch business prospects, banks, and airline offices with brochures "designed to induce visiting U.S. businessmen—whether on vacation or business—into considering the Netherlands as a potential market." Tongue firmly in cheek, the author noted that "It does not appear that Middendorf's pushiness has sparked any resentment among the Dutch" and suggested that, because of my business background and this focus on trade issues, I was one of the more effective ambassadors in Europe. Another affirmation: a State Department inspection team declared the Hague "one of the most professionally run [embassies] of any in the Foreign Service." I was most proud to receive the State Department Superior Honor Award and, later, from the Netherlands, the Grand Master in Order of Orange Nassau, 1985., the highest award of the Dutch government.

I had set a limit on my ambassadorial tour. Four years was enough. Isabelle had been playing Ambassador's wife since 1969. And so, in March 1973, I submitted my letter of resignation and prepared for my return to the states. Charley Tanguy became chargé d'affairs, until Kingdon Gould, Jr., our Ambassador to Luxembourg, was shifted to the Hague.

On my last day as ambassador, June 9, I was sitting in my office. One of the Marines called on the intercom and said that a gentleman at the entrance with a bicycle wanted to come up. Well, I said, fine, and went over to wait at the elevator—and who should appear but former Prime Minister Biesheuvel, with his bicycle. I'm not certain whether he had ridden the bike for a long time, but his gesture—returning my bicycle call from four years before—was most gracious and fully representative of the best qualities of the Dutch.

5 | Secretary of the Navy

We Do Better When We Help Others Do Better

As secretary of the Navy, I participated in our early morning meetings with the admirals and my staff. I emphasized that a recommended solution should accompany every problem. To say this terrible threat is China or North Korea flexing its muscles should not be presented, "Woe is me, the sky is falling. Something should be done about it?" The best admirals discuss the threat and accompany it with a recommended solution, or better still, "I've taken care of it." I was always impressed by how professional most of the admirals and Marine Corps generals we had at the top of our navy team and, of course, the top civilian aides, all of whom had been tested over many years before they arrived at the top of the Navy. I always felt that Admiral Jimmy Holloway was a remarkable example of this quality.

Right at the start, I made a vow that I was not going to try to be a supererogatory CNO who would try to interfere with the operation of the ships. That was the job of the Chief of Naval Operations, the brilliant Admiral James Holloway. The primary job of SECNAV is to recruit, equip, train, and maintain the Navy and the Marine Corps—those things that, for the most part, require approval and funding from Congress. As Navy secretary from 1974–1977, some of the most important weapons systems in U.S. history were built and deployed. They include the Ohio-class ballistic missile submarine fleet and their Trident missiles that contain 80 percent of our nuclear arsenal. They remain for nearly a half-century as the backbone of our nuclear strategic nuclear deterrent. We also developed an advanced fleet of Aegis missile system-equipped battle cruisers that constitute the bulk of our surface combatant fleet. For aircraft carriers, we shepherded the F/A-18 warplane, which remains a staple of American power projection capabilities worldwide. These three weapon systems played a major part in winning the Cold War a decade later. Today, they still are part of the final shield of America.

Bill Gertz, editor, columnist, and author of eight books on national security issues, wrote the following words in the Foreword of my book, *The Great Nightfall*:

J. William Middendorf was among the premier 'steel benders'—as defense leaders who got things done are called—in helping build some of the most important arms while Navy Secretary from 1974 to 1977. During this period, he oversaw an increase in budgets for Naval systems by more than 60 percent at a time when other military service budgets remained static. More importantly, under his tenure, some of the most important weapons systems in U.S. history were built and deployed. They include the Ohio-class ballistic missile submarine fleet and their Trident missiles that are, nearly half a century later, the backbone of the U.S. strategic nuclear deterrent. Under his tenure, the Navy also developed its advanced fleet of Aegis battle management system-equipped warships. Today, Aegis ships constitute most of the warships in the Navy fleet, as well as its robust sea-based missile defenses. For aircraft carriers, Middendorf shepherded the F/A-18 warplane, a staple of American power projection capabilities worldwide. These weapon systems contributed to the ending of the Cold War.

Gertz was one of the first experts to warn about China's modern and powerful military. His book, *Breakdown: How America's Intelligence Failures Led to September 11*, examined the activities of our intelligence agencies before 9/11. I could not have a more knowledgeable person assess my career as secretary of the Navy.

I was busy in the Netherlands, and if this was an opportunity to call in my chips, I did not recognize it, nor would I have tried to exercise it. In May 1972, John Chafee left the job of secretary of the Navy to make an unsuccessful run for the U.S. Senate (he had better luck four years later). In the 1968 presidential campaign, John Warner headed up "Citizens for Nixon," and his reward had been assignment as undersecretary of the Navy. Now, he appropriately moved up to secretary.

However, about this same time, I got a visit from Nixon's attorney, Herb Kalmbach, with a different job offer. Herb told me that secretary of Commerce Maurice Stans had been asked to run the finance committee for the Committee to Re-Elect the President (known by the strangest acronym ever: CREEP) and wondered if I could come back to serve as treasurer. I declined. I felt as if I had done my share, and besides, I was enjoying my post and delighted to be supporting American interests in such a great country as the Netherlands.

Well, my four-year tour as Ambassador had ended, but in the rest of the world, the Cold War was still raging, and there were essential challenges to be faced. Peter Flanigan said that Nixon's "promise" of the SECNAV job could be kept. If I were still interested, they would bring me down to be Undersecretary, with every expectation that the top job would, at some point, open up and be mine. Yes, I was still interested. Undersecretary of the Navy, on its own merits, is an important job. It had been held, for example, by both Roosevelts, Theodore (1898) and Franklin D. (1913–1920), although at the time, it was called "assistant secretary of the Navy." I was sworn in on August 3, 1973.

Admiral Elmo Zumwalt, Jr. was Chief of Naval Operations (CNO). I had met Zumwalt several years earlier when I was still ambassador to the Netherlands—after he had been featured in the December 21, 1970, *Time* magazine; new CNO Zumwalt on the cover, headline: "The Military Goes Mod." Nice portrait, scary article: implied that there would be big social changes in the Navy, which some critics had summarized with the slogan, "Beer, Beards, and Broads." Beer machines in the barracks, beards for the sailors, and women eligible for almost any assignment. The article quoted a just-retired admiral: "How far can we permit absolute freedom of speech, deportment, and dress—and still hang on to the indispensable element of discipline?"

Zumwalt, at age 49, was the youngest man ever appointed CNO and jumped over the heads of some 30 senior three and four-star officers. Was he too young, too much in tune with the Beat and Hippie movements of the day? I was not opposed to changes designed to make life better for the sailors. Still, the Netherlands had just been going through what looked like a similar experiment, a relaxation of some military standards. Salutes were not required, and recruits could wear their hair long, in ponytails. You might call it the socialist approach: "We're all just people together." In my judgment, it was a dangerous approach. The salute—a custom from the Middle Ages—is a sign of recognition and mutual respect, not of slavish subordination. The liabilities of long hair should be evident to anyone who has ever worked around machinery.

I learned that Admiral Zumwalt would be in London the following week. I felt it was necessary—ego to the fore! —to warn him that he was sailing into shoal waters. I called his office at the Pentagon to request an appointment, and he got on the phone. "I'll be glad to see you," he said, and we set a time. I flew from Amsterdam to London at my own expense, went to Navy Headquarters at Grosvenor Square, was offered a cup of coffee and a chair, and immediately began feeling foolish. I had been expecting some sort of wild-eyed kook, and here was one of the most gracious men I had ever met.

Well, I was there with a purpose, so I began telling him about my concerns. He listened thoughtfully. He nodded and seemed to care about what

I had to say. But after about three minutes, I was thinking to myself, what am I doing here? He probably knows all this stuff already. And I was right. At some appropriate point, he said, "Mr. Ambassador, don't believe everything you see in the media. Sure, I'm trying to make some changes in the Navy, make it a better place for all of our sailors, but I'm not going to do any of this stuff I hear they're doing in the Netherlands." In summary, he said it would be a great Navy, and we'd all be proud of it.

Little did I realize that I'd be his boss in three years. When I came on board, Zumwalt had less than a year to go as CNO, and the personnel changes he had engineered, for good or ill, had been made. On balance, he did help make it a better Navy. But Zumwalt's tour was difficult and controversial. He started with a handicap: his elevation was not welcomed among much of the senior officer community, especially that dozen or so who might have expected to get the job themselves. He wanted to eliminate discrimination—racial, gender, and class—because he saw such issues as tearing at the fabric of morale. In so doing, he intruded on what some officers saw as the prerogatives of command, and many, including the retired community, derided or encouraged resistance to many of the changes. Some of them were happy to roll back the clock after he retired. No more beards!

Let me put Zumwalt and his famous (or infamous) "Z-gram" messages to the fleet in perspective with one example. Before Zumwalt, a commissioned officer could cash a personal check at the Navy Exchange or the Officers' Club for $50, a limit imposed as much to ensure an adequate supply of cash on hand as for any reasons of distrust. An officer's word was his bond. Before Zumwalt, an enlisted sailor could cash a check, on base, for $10 only. He might have several thousand dollars in his bank account, but the Navy chose not to believe him. Zumwalt changed that. Everyone was equal in the eyes of the cashier. This was not socialism and was not "interfering" in the chain of command. It was fairness.

Zumwalt moved the marker forward in a number of areas. The Navy accepted the idea of a Black flag officer with the promotion of my friend Sam Gravely, who retired as a vice admiral. A nurse, Alene Duerk, was promoted to Rear Admiral in 1972—the first-ever female naval officer of flag rank. The same year, the Navy experimented with a mixed-gender crew on a non-combatant ship, USS *Sanctuary*; it seemed to work. Just before I came aboard, Zumwalt announced additional efforts to "eliminate any disadvantage to women resulting from either legal or attitudinal restrictions." Women were thenceforth granted limited entry into all ratings, accepted into the NROTC program, and, for the first time, line officers were eligible for promotion to flag rank.

But the most challenging issues were yet to be resolved, perhaps more symbolic or emotional than practical. Should women be admitted to the Naval Academy? The real issue with admitting women to the service academies was not the cost of adding bathrooms but what to do with the women once they graduate. The law prohibited women from serving "in combat," which, for the Navy, meant aboard any ship (or in any aircraft) that could be placed in an environment where hostile fire was exchanged. Narrowly defined, they could serve only on tugboats or hospital ships. Therefore, more women could—in theory—fill so many shore billets that there would be no place for many men to go. Some could be stuck at sea forever. It was not a happy prospect, certainly not much of an inducement to remain in the Navy for a career.

We did begin admitting women to the U.S. Naval Academy in 1976, with 81 graduating along with 1212 men in 1980. Could they serve on warships or fly combat aircraft? Those questions eventually were answered in favor of women, although I was more of a reluctant observer than an active participant. At a hearing before one congressional committee, I admitted that I wouldn't want my daughter to be in combat. Afterward, a woman rushed up to me and said, "How dare you!" I was being honest; back in 1946, when LCS 53 stopped at Saipan for medical screening, I heard about several Army nurses who had wandered off into the night. Their bodies were found the next day, their throats slit by hold-out Japanese troops. I was not alone in my concern. Congress did not repeal the "combat exclusion" for another twenty years. I must acknowledge, however, that today's female aviators and crew members have thoroughly proven themselves.

Admiral Zumwalt's successor was announced in late March 1974: Admiral James L. Holloway III, who came in as the vice chief of Naval Operations the month after I began my tour. Then, in April, John Warner left to head up the Bicentennial Commission. I began filling in as "acting" Secretary of the Navy with every expectation of getting the job for real. But something strange happened on the way to my promotion. Because of the Watergate mess, Nixon was so preoccupied with keeping his job that he was little concerned with employment issues at the Pentagon. James Schlesinger, the Secretary of Defense, had his candidate for the Navy Department, a man in the shipping business. Some of my friends learned of this—Schlesinger certainly never told me so himself—and we quickly mounted a small counteroffensive. Having been treasurer of the Republican Party for so many years, I'd made many friends on the Hill and spoke with some people I knew would be supportive: Bob Wilson in the House, Barry Goldwater, John Tower, and John Stennis in the Senate.

I didn't play sore loser (you know, "I was promised") but let them all know that I was very much interested in the job if they would be pleased to speak on my behalf. It wasn't too many days before they sent a petition over to the president, urging my appointment. Nixon may not have been paying much attention before, but he certainly noticed this petition. He was then having problems with Congress and was likely to have a lot more if the talk of "impeachment" moved past the talking stage. The president clearly decided that if it would make some people on the Hill happy to see me as secretary of the Navy, why it was just fine with him.

Nixon later told me a story, which I found hard to believe, that Barry Goldwater was not one of the people who supported my candidacy. According to Nixon, when my name finally came to his attention, he called Goldwater: "Your guy is up for secretary of the Navy. Should I push it or let it go?" According to Nixon, Barry said, "Oh, Bill's had enough." That doesn't coordinate with Barry's generous support when the Senate Armed Services Committee held my confirmation hearing, which, according to Barry, may have been one of the shortest on record. The full Senate vote came less than two hours later. I was back in my office at the Pentagon and was meeting with legendary entertainer Bob Hope when I got the congratulatory phone call. (A staff officer later told me that when escorting Hope to my office, one of the Pentagon janitorial crew seemed to recognize him as someone important but looked puzzled. When Hope passed the same person on the way back from my office, she broke out with a big smile: "I know who you are! You're Jack Benny!" Hope, I was told, was not amused.)

I was not the first secretary of the Navy to have once been in wartime naval service. Both John Chafee and John Warner had served as enlisted men (Marines and Navy) in World War II and both as Marine Corps officers in Korea. However, I was the first to have a degree in Naval Science. Unknown to most people, I also had a matchless naval heritage: Baltimore mariner William Stone, an ancestor on my father's side, had been one of the first five or six captains appointed in the Continental Navy. In fact, in late 1775, Stone provided two merchant ships he owned—re-named *Wasp* and *Hornet*—to become warships in the cause of independence. This certainly gave me a sense of personal tradition for working with what I have always viewed as the most tradition-oriented of the armed services.

The job of secretary of the Navy perhaps lost some cachet—it indeed lost a seat in the president's Cabinet—when the Defense Department was established in 1947. However, the job still had a lot of clout. The Navy was a massive organization: $33 billion annual budget, 526,000 men and women in the Navy, 196,000 in the Marines, operating 215 major installations staffed by hundreds of thousands of civilian employees, more than five hundred ships, and seven thousand aircraft. It was a large and complex organization with in-place procedures, long-standing traditions, and strong-willed and independent-minded leadership.

I think that the Navy has always been this way from the beginning: attracting a breed of mariners who quickly could earn the trust of superiors and thrive on the ability to make difficult decisions when well out of touch (measured in months, if not years) of headquarters. This is a useful asset when faced with sudden danger, but it may be a complicating factor when required to work within the headquarters itself. Complicating, that is, for the headquarters staff. I wouldn't have it any other way. The last thing our Navy needs is a bunch of "yes" men and women.

My Holy Cross degree in Naval Science and my stint in the Navy, of course, gave me a certain level of knowledge and understanding. Still, my 1940s Navy had more in common with the Phoenicians than the Navy of nuclear engineering, computers, guided missiles, satellites, and lasers. I found my political, diplomatic, and business background more useful. I also had to re-orient my focus: the State Department tries to predict the actions of nations by divining intentions, whereas the Defense Department analyzes capabilities. If the Soviets devised a great new weapon or tactic, it didn't matter how peace-loving they might seem as guests at some Washington cocktail party. At the very least, DOD had to assume that, at some point, new capability might come under the control of someone who was not so peace-loving. And we had to plan for such an eventuality.

The primary job of SECNAV is to recruit, equip, train, and maintain the Navy and the Marine Corps—those things that, for the most part, require approval and funding from Congress and, therefore, the support of the American people. Here, at the height of the Cold War, making the case for the Navy—to the public and Congress—was important, indeed. To carry the message of "sea power" (which is just as vital today, of course). The United States is dependent on an overseas supply of 68 of 71 strategic materials, including oil, copper, zinc, lead, tin, rubber, titanium, and aluminum. Almost all of these, around 98 percent, must come by ship. By comparison, the Soviets imported only two raw materials from overseas: tin and rubber. A key U.S. Navy mission (then and now) is to keep the sea lanes open for our traffic. A key Soviet mission was to deny such transit. With enough submarines and minelayers, their goal was far easier.

The secretary of the Navy has broad opportunities to take the Navy story to the tax-paying public in public meetings, making speeches, and sitting down for media interviews. All of these were coordinated by my special assistant for public affairs, the exceptional Capt. Bob Sims. In my first ten months as SECNAV, I traveled 35,000 miles and gave more than fifty speeches. I honed my skills as a pitchman—well, such skills as I have. As a public speaker, I hope my message's importance offsets a less-than-oratorical delivery. I also added another tool to the kit and established a "Secretary of the Navy Luncheon Program" at the Pentagon. Three hundred of the nation's top business, financial, and labor leaders (including AFL-CIO leader George Meany, a champion of our shipbuilding programs) accepted my invitation, about twelve at a time, to sit down with senior Navy officials for a frank discussion of the issues of the day.

I made a special point to include our sailors and Marines in my outreach. I visited more than three hundred ships (including a few of our allies). Since I had once been an engineer officer and knew how under-appreciated the men in the bowels of a ship are, I created the "Golden Snipe" award, presented to the engine room crew of every ship—foreign or domestic—that I visited. There were only two exceptions: one, the USS *Constitution*, the oldest ship in the Navy, had no actual engine room, and two, conditions on another ship were so bad that the chief engineer had been relieved of his duties the morning before my visit.

However, the most important part of the job, the one with the greatest impact on both the present and the future, was to advocate for Navy and Marine Corps programs vital to our nation's defense. The money to fund every multi-billion-dollar program or buy every ten-cent lock nut, train, equip, and pay every sailor and marine, and create, repair, or rebuild every installation worldwide comes from Congress, the gatekeeper for the taxpayers. This is where my active political experience came into play. I knew a lot about the game, and I knew a lot of the players—and they knew me. Access is the first step.

Anyone in Congress may have his or her own idea as to what may or may not be appropriate. Members vote for or against programs based on a wide range of reasons. Some, too busy with their own committee assignments or special interests, don't study all the issues and vote the party line. Most, regardless of the party line, believe in a strong national defense. Some, regardless of the party line, take a far-left position that the United States has no business being the world's policeman and that the monies can be better spent on social programs. Some are interested in programs in direct proportion to the amount of money or jobs the programs will bring into their districts. We certainly played to each member's special interest when campaigning for support.

In this, I learned an important lesson during one of my first visits to Capitol Hill during a courtesy call on then-House Majority Leader Thomas P. "Tip" O'Neill, a Democrat. I asked, "How can I get more ships for the Navy?" He answered, "Let me tell you how this town works. Quincy Naval

Shipyard hasn't been getting any business lately, and there are a lot of unemployed citizens of Massachusetts up there." The message was clear. I managed to shift scheduled overhaul work on two destroyers from the Philadelphia Naval Shipyard to Quincy. This may have infuriated the Pennsylvania delegation, but I always got a fair hearing from Tip after that incident. A note on O'Neill: he was a rabid partisan, would go to the mat on almost every issue in which "Republicans" were somehow involved—but at the end of the day, he might happily meet me to drink beer and swap lies. One Thanksgiving, he invited Isabelle and me to join him at his home on Cape Cod for a ceremonial drink—quite a guy.

New weapons systems, new aircraft, new ship types: anytime you put the word "new" in front of a program, be prepared for heated arguments from Congress. Why do you need a "new" program? What's wrong with the "old" program, for which we recently put-up millions of dollars? Why can't the old program be upgraded at less cost? The questions are always fair; the answers must be just. In high season, Admiral Holloway and I—often joined by Marine Corps Commandant General Louis H. Wilson would average at least one weekly committee hearing.

While serving in the U.S. Navy in World War II, I brought my ship to Guam and visited the long beach and terrifying cliffs where the U.S. Marines had recently defeated the Japanese. A marine named Lew Wilson boldly led the charge up the beach, rescuing a wounded companion within 50 yards of the exposed beach. He continued up the cliff, taking out Japanese machine-gun nests, which had been firing down on our landing forces. "Where do they get such men?" I thought as I studied the site of the battle. Wilson received the Medal of Honor for his heroism. Years later, as secretary of the Navy, I had to decide concerning the next commandant of the U.S. Marine Corps. Although there were several outstanding Marine candidates, I felt honored to be able to appoint Wilson, now a general, to the post of commandant.

My team and I worked with congressional members and staff, covering the entire procurement and operational matters. We prepared for every call I made, often having a "murder board" practice session with my staff tossing me every problematic question they could think of and helping me with the answers. Just before going into a member's office, I mentally ran through the five points I wanted to cover. I took subject-area experts along when appropriate. If I promised to get back with a copy of a report or an answer to a question, get back I did as soon as possible. I always found strong support from members who represented Navy towns like San Diego, Norfolk, and Newport; members whose districts included major shipyards, like Bath, Maine, New London, Connecticut, and Pascagoula, Mississippi;

members who owed a favor to an important constituent, to whom we might be able to lend a hand.

Friends will at least listen to your argument and often give you the benefit of the doubt. Sometimes I called in old friendships, even though we had grown ideologically distant. A few of my most formidable opponents were liberal politicians from my old stomping grounds of Connecticut, New York, or Rhode Island. But they also were friends of many years standing. Sometimes we did a little horse-trading: an appropriation for the historical center at the Washington Navy Yard in exchange for sending some ship overhaul work to a repair facility. Sometimes we just stroked egos and gave a "friend of the Navy" award or an invitation to speak at a shipbuilding event (of which there were always at least three: the keel-laying, the launching, and the commissioning.) For an extra touch, we might invite a member's wife to be the ship's sponsor, an honorary appointment without responsibility beyond standing on a flag-draped platform, champagne bottle in hand, to say, "I christen thee USS *Whatever*" but an honor nonetheless, which forever would serve as a symbolic link between the lady and the ship.

Since every member's career thrives on local publicity (and withers without it), we made sure to contribute our share. And in this, please understand: I wasn't supporting Republicans over Democrats but was building support from both for our Navy programs. We might have a photographer on hand for a meeting and quickly provide a photograph that could be used in a constituent newsletter. I might go out to an Armed Services Committee member's home district, give a speech, and praise the congressman: "Greatest living American, stalwart in defense of the few precious moments of freedom we have left." My visit would usually result in a front-page item in a local newspaper, often with a photo of the member and me shaking hands. Does this seem shameless? Let me say it was effective. We usually got the vote, despite opposition from their congressional colleagues.

Years ago, I was conducting the Navy Band in a public concert of one of my new marches when I spotted a former Democrat member of the Senate Armed Services Committee, long retired, in the audience. From the podium, I said, "It is my honor to introduce a great American who helped keep the Navy as the final shield of freedom. Would you all please give him a well-deserved round of applause?" After, he came over and said, "That's the nicest thing that ever happened to me."

A committee staffer may, at times, be as important as a committee chairman. The staffer does the research, assembles documents, and arranges the testimony. If the staffer is opposed to your program, your job has become more complicated, so you want to be very sure that the key staff members at the least understand everything. I know of more than a few high-level appointees who would fight for a program if it meant trooping up Capitol Hill to beg congressional staffers for a hearing. Undignified, they might say. I say, dignity be damned, I was after results. I got them and made some good friends along the way.

Nixon resigned as president on August 9, 1974, and Vice President Gerald Ford, appointed not quite a year before to replace the disgraced Spiro Agnew, was sworn in as chief executive. Gerry quickly let me know that he was a "Navy" president. (Well, in a manner of speaking, so too were other Navy veterans Kennedy, Johnson, Nixon, Carter, and Poppy Bush. Is there a pattern here?) "Consider me your contact at the White House," he said. I certainly was happy to know that someone over there was interested in our efforts; We had been getting no help from the White House on any of the programs we were working. I think I heard from the White House only one time during this period, when Nixon was hunkered down in the bunker. I was alerted that a call would be coming through on the special secure phone. A staff officer escorted me to the secure room with the secure phone. This made me a bit nervous; were we about to go to war? Had I been put on report by some angry politician? It was a period during which Nixon's inner circle—Chuck Colson, Bob Haldeman, and John Erlichman—ran a reign of terror and no one felt safe. The call was from Erlichman. "Middendorf—you there?" "Hi, John." "I got a big request for you . . . "Big request? They wanted me to find a Navy Department job for someone they wanted to get rid of but, under Civil Service rules, couldn't fire.

I came aboard at the height of the Cold War, at a time when nuclear missile-equipped Soviet submarines, able to wipe out a third of our population in a matter of minutes, were lurking just off our coasts, and the Navy was focused on rebuilding our dangerously diminished fleet. While comparisons between the U.S. and Soviet Navies are no longer of the greatest significance, they were a vital part of our efforts in the 1970s. Much of our fleet was World War II vintage, reaching the nominal 30-year warship life, all at the same time. We were retiring obsolescent ships to free up money for new construction—but, in so doing, had reduced the fleet to a dangerously low level. We were down from 932 ships in 1968 to 587 in 1974 (of which only 325 were classified as "warships," the rest being patrol craft, mine sweepers, amphibious ships, and auxiliaries). A further overall reduction of 64 was scheduled through 1977.

The Soviets, on the other hand, never known for a blue-water fleet, were moving away from a traditional coastal defense and building a "new" navy from scratch, with almost 2000 ships in the water and gaining on the U.S. Navy at a rate of four to one. Granted, we knew that our ships and systems were better, but numbers could prove vital in any confrontation. The Soviets operated on the assumption that quantity equaled quality. Ten marginally qualified ships could overwhelm one great ship. Think of the parable of ants and elephants: the elephant is one, and the ants are many. If there are enough ants, they win. Nonetheless, the Soviets were catching up in real quality. For example, their newest operational anti-ship guided missile had twice the warhead of our planned counterpart, Harpoon, which was still in development.

The primary missions of the U.S. Navy, sea control and power projection, call for a variety of capabilities, but not all ships can always meet all mission requirements. In the face of budget realities, Zumwalt backed a concept dubbed "High-Low." Fewer high-cost, high-capability ships—90,000-ton big-deck carriers and guided-missile cruisers (nuclear powered)—as a trade-off for many more ships of lesser capability.

Key elements of the "low" program were patrol frigates to handle many destroyer missions and the Sea Control Ship (SCS)—a small, 17,000-ton aircraft carrier equipped with helicopters and some Vertical and/or Short Take-Off and Landing (VSTOL) aircraft. The SCS mission was to maintain control of sea lanes and to provide protection of replenishment groups, mercantile convoys, amphibious assault forces, and task groups. The concept had been tested through some two years of operations of a modified amphibious assault ship, USS *Guam*. The SCS was priced at about one-eighth the then-year cost of an attack carrier. Zumwalt was black-shoe Navy, a surface-warfare officer; there were senior brown-shoe (aviator) officers who saw SCS as an unacceptable compromise. The distinction between black and brown shoes grew out of the standard day-to-day uniform kit of the two factions: the traditional naval service dress blue uniform, worn by all officers on occasions of nominal ceremony and by ship drivers much of the time, came with black shoes; the day-to-day costume for aviators was green or khaki, with brown shoes.

The nuclear Navy (for which shoes were not a talisman), was represented by one man, Admiral Hyman G. Rickover, who believed that all major surface combat ships should be nuclear-powered: expensive to build but perhaps less expensive over a lifetime and free from the need for constant fuel re-supply when at sea. Many planners disagreed. They may have agreed with the cheaper-in-the-long-run arithmetic but could point out that the annual shipbuilding budget is not amortized over thirty years. There was hardly enough money in the world, let alone in the Defense Budget, to build a two-ocean nuclear Navy all at once. There wasn't much of an argument when it came to a focus on nuclear-powered submarines, which could operate submerged for months at a time. The submerged operational capability of a diesel-powered boat was measured in hours.

John Warner was lukewarm on the SCS. On the other hand, Secretary of Defense Schlesinger was a fan and made sure that the first significant funds for construction were in the proposed budget for FY 74. Well, Middendorf came along just about the time the budget cleared the Armed Services Committees and was nearing the Appropriations Committees. When we got word that the SCS was in trouble, Zumwalt asked for my help. He said, "I'll work the Democrats, you work the Republicans, and let's see what we can do." I went up the Hill, full of confidence. I was cordially welcomed but had a feeling that the road up the Hill had become very steep, indeed. I didn't know that the fix was in, that Rickover and some heavyweights in the aviation community had greased the skids to ease my way back down. I was caught in a tug-of-war between black shoes and brown. Nonetheless, I may have been of some service: while the House Appropriations Committee cut SCS, the Senate Appropriations Committee did not and left the money in the budget. The issue went to a conference, and the Senate won.

Then, near the end of the year, Rickover tried to move some money around in the next year's (FY 75) proposed budget—soon to be sent to Congress—to shift about $250 million of ship construction money from "low" ships to two nuclear-powered guided missile frigates. The Navy could have as many as ten patrol frigates for the same money. Rickover made a pitch to Schlesinger, who asked Zumwalt for comment. Zumwalt said, in effect, let's make a deal. Give Rickover 100 million dollars in new money if he would pledge support of the sea control ship and the frigates planned within the proposed budget.

Schlesinger made the proposal to Rickover. According to Zumwalt, Rickover said, "In other words, you are blackmailing me." Schlesinger said "Yes." Rickover said, "I accept." According to Zumwalt, Rickover didn't keep his end of the bargain. I certainly can attest to that. I went back on the Hill to start the next budget cycle, full of confidence; I returned with polite "thanks" for my comments but no commitments. I would note, despite the attempts to smother the program, the SCS concept survived, to a point, and a new class of amphibious assault carrier was given SCS capabilities through juggling the mix of aircraft on board—heavy emphasis on VSTOL and ASW helicopters.

Like many folks in the Navy Department, I had mixed experience with and mixed feelings about Rickover. For example, one day, I overheard Rickover berating some poor junior admiral who had piped up at one of my staff meetings in response to a question I posed on some nuclear issue. Rickover seemed incensed: "Who are you to speak to the Secretary?" I invited Rickover to come back to my office later and suggested he might exercise loyalty down as well as loyalty up. I told him I found his remark to that flag officer offensive and that I wanted to hear from people with contrary views who were not afraid to voice them. You know, the "Emperor's New Clothes" syndrome. Rickover was not amused.

We had one running disagreement about P. Takis Veliotis, the long-time chief executive of General Dynamics, the company that was building our nuclear submarines. I thought he was a very impressive guy, a good businessman, a hard but fair negotiator whose company was turning out some excellent ships for the Navy. Rickover said he was a crook. Rickover was right; in 1983, the man fled to his native Greece—where he remains to this day—to escape federal indictment under racketeering and fraud charges.

At our morning meetings, the briefer would pinpoint the location of Soviet missile subs. Thanks to our secret underwater network of sensitive listening devices, dubbed SOSUS (for Sound Surveillance System), we could detect them as they slipped through the Faeroes-Iceland gap, then track them as they hid for a while behind the Mid-Atlantic ridge before heading west to take up positions a few hundred miles off our coast. Of course, they were not alone: one of our extremely quiet submarines would be shadowing them, ready to retaliate in the event of an attack. One morning, while the grim subject of life or instant death was being discussed, I asked Rickover, "Rick, what the hell would we do if we got the word right now that they had a couple of missiles headed our way?" He said, "We should go home and pull down the curtains."

From the overall standpoint of national security, our most significant procurement was for the Ohio-class submarine to be equipped with a new, long-range Trident nuclear-tipped ballistic missile. I wanted to call it the "Michigan" class to honor President Ford's home state, but Gerry—among the most self-effacing of men—told me, "Do not!"). There was heavy opposition to this newest missile: we already had the Polaris/Poseidon missile submarines, secure and almost-undetectable, always at sea, carrying enough destructive power to obliterate the Soviet Union several times. Why must we spend vast sums of money on a new model?

Our national strategy was focused on "deterrence," having sufficient overwhelming force and capabilities to cause a potential enemy to back off. That argument did not address the rapidly growing Soviet blue-water fleet or its steadily improving submarine detection technology. If "Moscow" was the nominal target, the range of the Polaris/Poseidon missiles kept the boats on a tether that extended not too much west of Ireland and required operating bases in Scotland and Spain. A Trident submarine could be parked in New York harbor—or, more to the point, almost anywhere in the Atlantic Ocean, greatly complicating the search factor—and hit Moscow and its environs with 24 multi-warhead missiles launched within minutes of a Soviet attack on the United States.

Negotiating points in our favor, in a manner of speaking: the Soviet Union already had seventeen advanced submarines, which could send missiles even from Soviet national waters to pretty much any city in the United States. By the earliest Trident could enter service, 1979, the Soviets would have twenty-five of these submarines. Soviet defense spending was almost double ours—which, as a percentage of the Federal Budget, was the lowest since 1940.

We had the Republican votes for Trident but few among the Democrats. I went to Rhode Island Senator Claiborne Pell—a very liberal Democrat but a friend from way back. "Claiborne, I need your help. First, large portions of our new submarines are going to be built up here in Rhode Island. These submarines are the final shield of America, and I need your vote." The program won. Life is relationships—politics is compromising.

In my judgment, the second-most important ship program in development was a potent combination of ship, radar tracking, and computer-controlled anti-missile system, to be called "Aegis" (after the shield of the mythical Greek god Zeus). The Navy had known for some time that we had no defense against incoming anti-ship or land-attack missiles—but the solution was not clear or simple. Missiles do not fly in predictable trajectories but can maneuver everywhere. They can skim just above the surface to avoid traditional radar. They can be accompanied by a bunch of clever decoys intended to overwhelm defenses. The Navy had proposed various combinations of radar, warship hull, and onboard anti-missile missiles and had tested some, and a scheme was coming together when I had my first briefing on Aegis.

The radar—very large and very heavy—was to be installed in an oversized deckhouse on an existing hull design. I asked, what is the nominal metacentric height? As it turned out, in the interim scheme I was shown, it was dangerously high, but to my relief I found that the Navy was working on the problem. In fact, the Navy had determined that Aegis was such a complex and challenging project that in a departure from the usual practice where the contractors pretty much ran the show, a special Aegis office was set up in the Naval Ship Systems Command. It headed by a newly-promoted flag officer, Rear Admiral Wayne E. Meyer, who had been involved with the program for several years, knew the problems, knew the contractors, and knew—from exposure to some increasingly-contentious members of Congress—the strength of the opposition.

Aegis joined Trident as one of the vital programs of the day, equally controversial, and one that occupied much of my time when, along with Meyer and others, I began working on Congress. I'm proud to say that, despite the mind-boggling cost of about one billion dollars per ship, we got the program through Congress. Aegis has been installed on six different ship classes, all of which are known generically as "Aegis" cruisers or destroyers. This, I believe, has been the longest-running Navy shipbuilding project, ever, with upgrades and new components introduced as they become available. Aegis remains our main defense against anti-ship missiles (such as those just now being developed by the Chinese) and has been suggested by former Defense Secretary Robert Gates as an effective—and ready—alternative for the "missile shield" that President George W. Bush proposed to develop and install in Poland and Czechoslovakia. The first Aegis ship, the cruiser Ticonderoga (CG 47) went to sea in 1983. The 100th Aegis ship, a destroyer fittingly named USS *Wayne E. Meyer*, was delivered to the Navy in 2009.

I might note that our efforts to expand shipbuilding programs were given a hand by the Soviets themselves. During the Yom Kippur War (October 6, 1973)—where Egypt and Syria attacked Israel—96 Soviet ships were lurking in the area. The State Department could ponder "intent"—what, indeed, might they do with all those ships? The assembled forces included some of the Soviet Navy's most potent, which goes to capabilities, and we had to know how to deal with each one of those ships, if and when an "intention" became manifest. If the Soviet intent had been simply intimidation, it surely backfired. By thus flexing their naval muscles in a geographic area outside of their normal zone of interest, the Soviets helped make our budget negotiations with the Congress very successful.

How successful? In June 1976, a House/Senate conference approved the largest shipbuilding bill in at least 25 years, $6.6 billion for 17 new ships, including funds for nuclear carriers, modernization of a nuclear cruiser, and overall plans to bring the fleet to six hundred ships . . . and keep it there. It was about here that I found myself on opposite sides of my old friend Barry Goldwater, who saw his role with the Armed Services Committee as promoting planes for the Air Force. The Navy was getting a much bigger share of the budget than the Air Force and there wasn't too much he could do about it. As I noted earlier, I already had the votes lined up, working with the large number of Republican members whom the RNC helped get elected—along with those Democrats who represented communities where the Navy was a major force.

Another consequence of the Yom Kippur War: Egypt was ready to reopen the Suez Canal, which had been closed since 1967, but were stymied by huge quantities of un-exploded ordnance and damaged ships. The U.S. Navy trained more than 1,500 Egyptian military personnel in mine clearance and in a year-long operation ending in June 1975 helped raise ten sunken ships and clear more than two hundred tons of unexploded ordinance and 686,000 land and anti-personnel mines from the canal and its banks. In symbolic appreciation for the Navy support, Egyptian President Anwar Sadat awarded me the Order of the Arab Republic of Egypt (Rank A).

One of the more contentious issues—one for which the Air Force was on our side—was the plan for a logistics base on the British Indian Ocean Island of Diego Garcia. This would provide a strategically located refueling and replenishment stop for our carriers and long-range bombers. We had some important Democrats on our side—Congressmen Melvin Price and F. Edward Hebert and Senator John Stennis. But some Democrats were bitterly opposed. How would I define "bitterly?" At one hearing, one of them got so mad that I was certain he was about to take a swing at me. John Stennis had to intervene. We were desperate for funding, and the Congress was playing games. They gave us money to build a bowling alley and a movie theater for recreation but not to dredge the harbor so that our carriers could come in and park. Letting carriers anchor at Diego Garcia, they said, or letting long-range aircraft operate from the planned landing strip, would be violating the "Zone of Peace" of the Indian Ocean.

Whose zone of peace was that supposed to be? Diego Garcia is an island in the middle of the Indian Ocean, about as "in the middle" of an ocean any island could be: 1,800 miles from Saudi Arabia, 1,000 miles from India, 2,000 miles from Africa, distantly confronted by Soviet naval facilities arrayed all around the northern shores. Our critics argued, that if we played "good guy" and pulled back, if we just left Diego Garcia to the sea birds and land crabs, the Soviets would match our good intentions. That argument didn't hold water. When the British earlier had pulled their military out of a small garrison on Diego Garcia, the Soviets expanded, not contracted, their influence.

Senator Pell was strongly opposed and asked the CIA to review the matter. CIA director William Colby, perhaps trying to curry favor with some in Congress, gave Pell a damning estimate, along the lines of "the Soviets will respond with force." Pell ran with it, passing copies of Colby's warning to all his compatriots. We were flying blind as no one had bothered to share this bit of wisdom with the Navy. When we found out, Holloway and I went to Colby and asked for an explanation; he backed off a bit, and apologized. (I would note that, not too long after this incident, President Ford fired Colby and replaced him with George H.W. Bush.). It took great effort to get the program back on track, but we finally won. The facilities at Diego Garcia were there when we needed them, especially during Desert Shield/ Desert Storm (1990–1991) and operations in Afghanistan and Iraq.

Here is an instructive story: during my first week or so as SECNAV, I called all the inter-agency people in for an important meeting: we were about to enlarge the scope of one of our most sensitive programs. The code name was "Project Sanguine," the purpose, to communicate with our submerged submarines, out on station. This would be more than just a "bell ringer" capability, that is, more than a one-way system to send a one-word alert or a launch message to the sub. We could see the possibility of establishing more effective communications.

Project Sanguine used an extremely low frequency (ELF) radio signal with a wavelength of some 2,500 miles. The key to ELF transmissions was the antenna, a grid of cables, laid just underground over wide-spread solid granite substrate. The radio energy would be directed up, then bounce back from the stratosphere into the ocean to a depth of several hundred feet. The antenna grid would be laid over an area comparable in size to Rhode Island. The Navy had located just such an area, solid granite just below the surface, in rural, undeveloped, upstate Wisconsin. But there was a problem: the residents of rural up-state Wisconsin had been told by people who opposed the project that exposure to ELF might cause anything from human sexual impotency to dried-up milk cows.

The Navy calculated that the average energy received would be less than from lying under an electric blanket, or from sitting next to a 60-watt light bulb. The Navy did not do a very good job of convincing residents in that area. The opposition did a wonderful job, and Congress was giving the Navy a very hard time. As one of his last official acts as secretary of defense, January 1973, former Wisconsin congressman Melvin Laird directed the Navy to put the system pretty much anywhere except Wisconsin.

However, we had been granted sufficient real estate at a Navy facility at Clam Lake, Wisconsin, for a limited trial of the concept. We needed more land to make the test more effective, I explained to the inter-agency group, expecting that all attendees would appreciate the need for the improved capability. Someone asked a question: "What will we do if we don't get the extra land?" I said, with my usual optimism, "Maybe we can ooze out a bit," implying, of course, that we would be able to acquire more land and expand the antenna field. Well, the next day, I got a call from a congressman to ask, would I please explain what I meant by "oozing out?" A lesson learned: be careful about what you say and how you say it—to anyone. No damage done in this instance, but I learned that casual wishes were out of place and precise discretion had to be applied across the board. We later discovered that at least one man working in the CNO office was passing operational information along to North Vietnam. He was caught. And a final note: science marched on, the design of the antenna was changed, the size of the antenna field was reduced, safety was demonstrated, and the system became operational—now officially called ELF—in 1989.

Secretary of Defense Schlesinger, former head of the Atomic Energy Commission and former director of the CIA, was a deep-thinker sort, a pipe smoker who, when asked a question, would take a puff or two, look up at the ceiling, think about it, then give a reasoned response. Schlesinger tended to focus on strategic issues while Deputy Secretary Bill Clements worked on procurement. Clements and I went back many years; he had been state chairman of the Republican Party in Texas when I was treasurer of the RNC, and we were comfortable working together on even the most controversial issues.

Clements was appalled at the cost of the Navy's new air-superiority fighter, the F-14. Yes, it was a very effective weapon—armed with the Phoenix air-to-air missile, an F-14 could simultaneously take on six enemy aircraft, as far off as 200 miles, and hit them all. However, Clements called me and Admiral Holloway down to his office and said, in effect, twenty-two million a copy is outrageous; get those sharp-pencil boys of yours to come up with something a lot less expensive. Get me a $7.5 million airplane. Maybe one that can also drop bombs? The prototype Northrop YF-17 had been in competition for the Air Force "lightweight fighter" contract but lost out to the YF-16. With modifications—electronics, digitization, glass cockpit—and incorporating recent development in modularization, such as rapid engine changes, F-17 could take on the attributes of both a fighter and attack aircraft and meet the demanding requirements for carrier operations. VFAX explorations began in August 1974. By the following May, the go-ahead was given to turn YF-17 into the F/A-18 (originally called just plain F-18).

Here's another irrelevant but otherwise interesting footnote: YF-17 contractor Northrop, lacking experience with carrier-based aircraft, asked McDonnell-Douglas to join as the prime contractor for the Navy version (Northrop planned to build a "land" version on its own for overseas sales; after some legal wrangling, the land version was shelved, and Northrop became a subcontractor to McDonnell-Douglas). In 1997, McDonnell-Douglas was taken over by Boeing. It is now properly called the Boeing F/A-18. Sometimes, you can't tell the players without a program.

There were some compromises—the original model didn't carry enough fuel for optimum mission requirements; it wasn't yet the perfect all-around airplane, but for the money, it was a pretty good start. And it got better, as every year passed. "Here's your baby," I said as I gave Clements the package. I also handed him a list of nicknames from which he might choose. The F-14, for example, was called "Tomcat." On the list for the F/A-18 was

"Hornet," to continue the Navy's 200-year tradition with that name. I may have told him that my ancestor, Captain Stone, had provided the first of the seven warships named *Hornet* to the Navy. I was not disappointed when Clements picked "Hornet."

Except for the most senior promotions and postings—such as service chiefs and fleet and area commanders, which largely are determined by the secretaries of Navy and Defense and the president, almost every officer promotion is handled through a selection-board process. Almost. One exception was picking a new chief of chaplains, with the rank of rear admiral, which fell to me. I was presented with three outstanding candidates and sat down with each to try to discern which would be best for the job. My choice was Capt. John O'Connor. (The day after his promotion, he invited me to join him on a visit to the Pope, in Rome when the Pope was conferring sainthood on Mother Seaton—whose sons had served in the Navy.) Later, after retirement from 28 years of Navy service, Capt. O'Connor went on to become a cardinal in the Catholic Church.

Regarding personnel assignments, I must make note of my personal staff. The quality of all of our professional sailors is high. The folk assigned to work directly with the Secretary of Navy must be considered first among equals. Here's a list (also noting promotions or assignments that came after) and if I have left someone out—because there were staff changes from time to time that may have eluded my notes or escaped my aging memory—I ask forgiveness.

> EXECUTIVE ASSISTANT: Capt. (later Rear Admiral) Doug Mow
> ADMINISTRATIVE ASSISTANT: Commander (later Vice admiral) John Poindexter
> JUDGE ADVOCATE: Capt. (later Rear Admiral) John Jenkins.
> MARINE AID: Col. (later Lieutenant General) Dwayne Gray, followed by Col. Henry Vitali, followed by Col. (later Brigadier General) William A. Bloomer.
> CHIEF, OFFICE OF LEGISLATIVE AFFAIRS: Rear Admiral (later Vice Admiral) Edwin K. "Ted" Snyder, followed by Rear Admiral (later Admiral) George E. R. "Gus" Kinnear Jr.,
> SPECIAL ASSISTANT FOR PUBLIC AFFAIRS: Capt. Robert Sims (later Assistant Secretary of Defense for Public Affairs).
> SPECIAL ASSISTANT FOR THE BICENTENNIAL: Capt. Brayton Harris (later, Assistant Director of the Selective Service System).

I made so bold as to expand my staff by one, perhaps, unique addition. I wanted to have an experienced political operative close at hand, to conduct intelligence sweeps and run interference with the Congress, and the Navy Department Chief of Legislative affairs (noted above) and the House and Senate liaison officers—outstanding all, such as Capt. John McCain (who came in as Senate Liaison just as I was leaving office)—could only, by law and common sense, do only so much. Since Congress controlled everything, it was vital to track every nuance and know where key members stood on every critical issue. I certainly didn't have the time, even though I had the personal contacts, to hang around Capitol Hill every minute to tease out information.

I brought in Bob Freneau, a man I had worked with through the Republican Party organization and gave him the title "deputy undersecretary of the Navy" with the charge of keeping me informed. I'm not sure if that job title had existed, I may have created it. Technically, Bob was one of my special assistants, but I had learned long before the value of a good title. It opens doors that might otherwise remain closed by status-conscious military professionals who wear their rank, their pay grade, their status, on their sleeves and shoulders. That's useful if everyone is in a sinking boat, to identify the senior and therefore most responsible person. However, some military people are too concerned about their relative standing—some of them, perhaps, pathologically insecure—as with one relatively senior officer I know of, who, before taking a phone call from an officer of equal rank, would quickly check the "Register of Officers" that had every single officer in the Navy listed in order of seniority. If the caller was even one place on the list senior, the greeting was "Yes sir, (or ma'am) what can I do for you? To a junior—even if only by one number—it was the more casual, "Hey Charlie (or Charlene), how's it going?" This may conform with some obscure rule of protocol, but it can seem rather silly. Why not forget the "Register of Officers" and treat every caller, senior and junior alike, with the same courtesy? Even if the caller is a very junior officer, should a filter be invoked to shunt the call to someone in the bowels of the office solely based on rank? Perhaps the caller has something really important and timely to impart so why not take the call to find out?

To make my point: I had a staff assistant, Lt. Eric Berryman, a junior action officer with a PhD (along with a Purple Heart and two tours in Vietnam as an Army enlisted Military Policeman). You can bet that when Lt. Berryman called to speak with some high-ranking officer, civilian appointee, or Congressional staffer, he didn't identify himself as "lieutenant" but as "Dr." Berryman in the office of the Secretary of the Navy. Worked like a charm, he got to have the conversation, and he got things done. I do believe that at one point my admin officer, Commander John Poindexter (who had a PhD of his own) got wind of the tactic and gave Lt. Berryman a proper dressing-down. I do not believe that this had much if any effect on Lt. Berryman, certainly not on my appreciation for heads-up, good old style Navy initiative.

In 2020, former Secretary of the Navy Richard Spencer said he intended to name a ship after me but had not dedicated the name to an assigned hull number. Secretary Carlos Del Toro made it official on June 10, 2022. "I am pleased to honor Secretary's Spencer's previous decision to name a ship after Ambassador J. William Middendorf, and I am incredibly proud to announce it here, at the Naval War College, during the commencement of our future leaders," said Del Toro. "Middendorf's spirit of innovation and questioning helped champion programs that are still defending our nation today. This name ship will continue to inspire that legacy."

I thought back to my ancestor, William Stone, who was one of the first captains appointed to the Continental Navy. He would have been proud.

On October 26, 1976, just before the presidential elections, William Loeb, the idiosyncratic publisher of the *Manchester Union-Leader*, offered a compliment: "Middendorf," he wrote, has been the "most outstanding Secretary of the Navy since Teddy Roosevelt." Setting aside the questionable merit of the statement, he was slightly off on the facts; TR had been assistant secretary. However, if Loeb had hoped that this praise for a hard-working member of the administration would have some influence on the election, he was greatly wrong. We lost.

I was flattered when President-elect Carter asked me to stay on as Secretary of the Navy. But I had to tell him, in all candor, that although it was the best job in government it was an insecure post for a Republican in a Democrat administration. I might be in the job for six months, I predicted, maybe a year at most, before the job was targeted by some political supporter whose interest the president could not easily ignore. After almost eight years in government service, I prepared to go back into the world of high finance.

However, I was proud of our record. When I took office, the three-armed services had roughly equivalent budgets. By the time I left, the Army budget had remained relatively flat, the Air Force budget had risen slightly, but the Navy budget had soared by 60 percent. Most of that growth was in hardware—notably, the Trident, Aegis, and F/A 18 program. We had obtained approval for a building program that would take us back to a 600-ship Navy, sized to meet the threat. There was a plan, so many ships over so many years, most replacing older ships as they were scheduled for retirement.

Sad to tell, Carter's new Secretary of Defense—Harold Brown—cut our shipbuilding program sharply. Brown was more of a strategic than tactical type, focused on deterrent, not attack, capabilities. He didn't seem much interested in ships—except for the Ohio-class Trident missile submarines.

The Navy never recovered, and I'm sure there are reasons and villains galore. The surface warship level in 2005 was 111, the lowest since 1921 and the overall force level in 2007 was 279 ships, the lowest since the 19th century.

On January 7, 1977, winding down, clearing out my office to make way for Jimmy Carter's man, the excellent Graham Claytor, a call came in on the hot line from Admiral Rickover. "Hi, Rick. What's up?"

"I'm calling to wish you a Happy New Year. Do you want the one I give my friends or to the bastards? Are you, my friend?"

"I always thought I was."

"OK. Well, Mr. Secretary, I hope to hell you get what you deserve in 1977."

I don't know if it was meant as a blessing—or a curse.

6 | Queen Elizabeth II Joins the U.S. Navy

WE HAD NOT SEEN ANYTHING LIKE IT, and it was the only chance we would ever have to throw a 200th Birthday Party for the nation. On April 18, 1975, President Gerald Ford traveled to Boston to light a third lantern at the historic Old North Church, symbolizing America's third century. The following day, April 19, he delivered a major address in Concord, Massachusetts, at the Old North Bridge, where the "shot heard round the world" was fired, commemorating the 200th anniversary of the Battles of Lexington and Concord, which began the military aspect of the American Revolution.

On December 31, 1975, the eve of the Bicentennial Year, President Ford recorded a statement to address the American people by means of radio and television broadcasts. Presidential Proclamation 4411 was signed as an affirmation of the Founding Fathers of the United States' principles of dignity, equality, government by representation, and liberty. Festivities included elaborate fireworks in the skies above major American cities. President Ford presided over the display in Washington, D.C., which was televised nationally. It started on the anniversary of Paul Revere's ride, April 18, 1975, ran through the highpoint of July 4, 1976, and continued to the end of that year.

On July 6, 1976. Queen Elizabeth II and her husband, Prince Philip, visited the USS *Constitution* (*Old Ironsides*) as part of our country's bicentennial celebration of the American Revolution. Boston was the last stop on the Queen's 1976 USA tour, when she visited Washington, Philadelphia, New York City, Charlottesville, Virginia, and Newport, Rhode Island. As secretary of the Navy, I greeted the royal couple as they came on board, shortly after Her Majesty's Yacht *Britannia* received a 21-gun salute from *Old Ironsides*. It was the only time a sitting monarch ever stepped foot on the decks of America's Ship of State. Army helicopters, National Guard officers, local police, and Secret Service were all present to ensure the Queen's safety.

Various bands and dance ensembles entertained thousands of spectators as they eagerly waited outside. I will never forget the Queen's opening remarks. "We have been very moved by the welcome we have received in this city, particularly since it was here—in Boston—that all began, and it was not many miles from here, at Lexington and Concord, that the first shots were fired in the war between Britain and America, two hundred and one years ago," the Queen said. "If Paul Revere, Samuel Adams, and other patriots could have known that one day a British monarch would stand beneath the balcony of the Old State House, from which the Declaration of Independence was first read to the people of Boston, and be greeted so kindly, I think they would have been surprised. But perhaps they would have been pleased to know that we eventually came together again as free people and friends and defended together the very ideas for which the American Revolution was fought."

After presenting her majesty with a silver chalice made by Paul Revere, I took the royal couple on a tour of the USS *Constitution*. I had done my homework, carefully learning about the ship's armament, range, and firepower. I had also carefully studied the many knots that seamen had to master at that time. I thought I was well prepared, but the Queen, politely but firmly, corrected some of my misconceptions. I was told that she operated as a mechanic during World War II. After listening to her explain all of the nautical knots and the ship's firepower, I had no doubts about her mechanical ability. The royal visit concluded on the *Britannia*, where a private party took place before it set sail to Canada, where the Queen was slated to open the Olympics.

My impression of the royal couple: Queen Elizabeth II was a very gracious and extremely bright lady. Prince Philip was quiet, but it was apparent he provided a tremendous support system for the Queen. We exchanged a few private jokes during our tour of *Old Ironsides*. I understood why she described Prince Philip as her anchor and steading force when he died on April 9, 2021, at the age of 99. I am not at all surprised that she became the longest-ruling monarch in English history until her death on September 8, 2022, at the age of 96.

Under the general rubric of "if you're going to do something important, do it right," the Navy began serious planning for the Bicentennial early in 1973, when John Warner established a Bicentennial team in the office of one of the assistant secretaries. It was, and remained, a modest but significant effort, initially staffed by three people and coordinated by an officer in the Office of the Chief of Information: Capt. (later rear admiral) David M. Cooney. A thorough and methodical planner, Captain Cooney solicited ideas from throughout the Navy and put together a comprehensive program, which was being implemented, I believe, before most other government agencies had even begun thinking about the Bicentennial. It started on the anniversary of Paul Revere's ride, April 18, 1975, ran through the highpoint of July 4, 1976, and continued to the end of that year.

I learned of this effort when I reported aboard as undersecretary of the Navy when plans were being converted into programs and asked to have the project shifted to my office. It came with a team of two or three officers headed by Lt. Commander William Eibert, who was the glue that held it all together right through the end of the celebration. When John Warner was tapped to head up the national Bicentennial effort, and I moved up to SECNAV, I picked up program coordinator Captain Harris, with the title of special assistant to the secretary of the Navy for the Bicentennial.

The Navy Department allotted some $4 million in seed money for this effort, which was judiciously spread worldwide. "Seed money" is the correct term since many of the projects were expected to become self-supporting and thereby return the investment to the U.S. Treasury. Some of the projects were local: for example, a modest naval museum at the headquarters of the 12th Naval District in San Francisco, staffed by volunteers, and a grand mural painted by a well-known local artist. Some were global: we adopted the 1775 "Don't Tread on Me" rattlesnake flag as the Bicentennial "Navy Jack," to be flown when anchored or in port at every bow ship during the year of the celebration. We saw it as a colorful reminder to all, especially our young navy men and women, of our heritage as a fighting force. However, one timid politician thought this aggressive motto might offend our overseas allies and insisted that we clear this project with the State Department. There was no objection. After 9/11, the flag was returned to active duty to remind the world of our heritage as a fighting force.

The Bicentennial Navy Jack was one of the self-supporting programs. Each ship purchased the flags from central stores (as they would have done with the standard, white stars on the blue field version), which fully paid the cost of development and production. Another fully self-supporting program was the Navy Bicentennial commemorative medal, struck in gold, silver, and bronze by the U.S. Mint and sold through government sales outlets. My office also served as executive agent for medals honoring the Army and the Marine Corps (the Air Force, not created until 1947, was out of the running). Each service decided how it should be represented on its own medal. This seemed appropriate to me, but the District of Columbia Commission of Fine Arts chairman soon wrote an excited letter to the Director of the Mint, Mary Brooks, in which he asserted that all the medals "were unanimously disapproved." Why? Some contained "items whose precise meaning was unclear, and which did not seem particularly relevant." The three relevant services liked our designs. We certainly understood the symbolism, and the District of Columbia Fine Arts Commission did not have authority in this matter. In any event, by the time the chairman had raised his objection, the medals had already been struck.

Some projects didn't make it to the starting gate. There was a suggestion that the 1797-era USS *Constitution* be taken on tour all along the East Coast; visions of the proud old ship foundering in a gale put that idea to rest. A politically very well-connected man suggested that we paint the whole U.S. fleet white and emulate Teddy Roosevelt's 1907–1909 "Great White Fleet" world tour. He would have us also paint the words "Come Visit the USA" on the back end of each ship to help promote tourism. We didn't just say, "No," but the idea crumbled under its own weight when we worked up the probable cost, just in paint.

The Navy took the lead in assembling a Bicentennial Military Band, comprising members selected from the Army, Navy, Marine Corps, and Air Force bands and choral units, and organized a world concert tour. We also wanted to create a souvenir recording. Millions of Americans heard these bands in concert every year, but military band recordings could not be offered for commercial sale because of long-standing opposition from the musician's union. They could be given away—say to radio and television stations for celebrating patriotic events and late-night sign-off—but under the law governing military bands, the Department of Defense could not recover even the cost of production.

I did not believe this unique project would compete with any commercial endeavor. The musicians' union believed otherwise. We felt that an exception ought to be made for the once-and-forever Bicentennial, with proceeds being applied against the costs of the record and any surplus going to the Treasury.

We asked Congress for permission; the Armed Services Committee held a hearing. Rear Admiral Bill Thompson, the Chief of Information, made a case for the Department of Defense: one-time exception only, a purely commercial sale through a distributor to be selected on a competitive basis, and all net proceeds to be turned back into the Bicentennial account.

Sam Jack Kaufman, president of the American Federation of Musicians, offered his rebuttal: this would set a dangerous precedent; the livelihood of widows and orphans might be placed in jeopardy; military bands were not a good thing, anyway. If the military wanted music, it should hire union musicians. The members listened politely.

When Mr. Kaufman finished—there were no questions—the chairman realized he did not have a quorum. Thus, no vote could then be taken. "This hearing is in recess," he announced, "to meet at the chairman's call." The witnesses and their respective advisors drifted out of the Hearing Room. Mr. Kaufman's team was the first to leave; Admiral Thompson had been engaged in conversation with a committee staffer.

The moment the door had closed behind the Union team, committee members slipped back into the room, and the chairman rapped the gavel. "The chairman," he announced, "notes the presence of a quorum and calls this hearing back into session. On the matter now under consideration, all in favor signify by saying 'aye.'" There was a chorus of "ayes." "Opposed, nay.'" There were no nays. The machinations of Congress can be, at times, indeed interesting.

Several projects had a much longer shelf-life. One joint all-service effort, which we initially thought might be too difficult to bring off but continues to this day, was to open up the Pentagon for public tours. It was not as if sensitive or classified information might be compromised—the Pentagon, after all, is an office building, and offices have doors, and some offices have guards at the doors. On the other hand, there were some excellent reasons for allowing public tours. The anti-war protestors had demonized the Pentagon, and we wanted to show that it was just an office building inhabited by ordinary, hard-working Americans. Ironically, until the early 1970s, the Pentagon had been an open public building. A few quarts of pig's blood dumped into files—including some in my office—and a few smoke bombs changed everything. From then on, access has been guarded by increasingly sophisticated scanning devices and entry controls.

Two issues had to be resolved. One: the Pentagon was a pretty dull place to visit. There wasn't much to look at in most of the building except formal portraits of senior officers and civilian leaders. Two: it would be impractical to let tourists wander around independently, so we had to acquire and train tour guides. However, since "tour guide" is not a typical military specialty, how could we staff the tour? In a manner of speaking, the question was answered by a directive from Secretary of Defense Donald Rumsfeld, which said, in essence, "Just do it." So we gave each service a small quota and created a team of outgoing, pleasant, interested young men and women.

The "boring" issue was resolved by putting small exhibits, ship models, and paintings along the tour route—I contributed a nice collection of historic military recruiting posters—and the Navy's Bicentennial office drafted a well-crafted script for the guides. The tours remain among the most popular tourist activities in the D.C. area, although the ground rules for joining a tour have shifted as the threat has changed. One project aimed to locate and perhaps salvage some artifacts from *Bon Homme Richard*, the most famous warship of the Revolution. This converted, aging French merchantman, named for Benjamin Franklin's alter-ego "Poor Richard" and captained by John Paul Jones, was the first ship to carry the Stars and Stripes into battle—late on the evening of September 23, 1779, when engaged in a hard-fought duel with the brand-new British frigate, HMS *Serapis*.

Captain Jones is best remembered for the answer he gave the British captain, who called over in the gathering darkness to ask if the badly battered American had struck his colors. Jones's reply, as later reported by his first lieutenant and forever enshrined in the annals of naval lore: "I have not yet begun to fight!" He eventually won the battle and transferred what remained of his crew to *Serapis* as his own ship slowly sank into the North Sea, the tattered colors still flying.

The idea for a search came from Sydney Wignall, a professional British marine archaeologist, who offered to conduct the expedition—and to raise all necessary funds—if the Navy could give the effort status as a "Navy Bicentennial Project," which would allow the Navy to provide some support. Dr. Harold Edgerton, the inventor of the strobe flash, heard of our plans and came to my office to offer his help. Dr. Edgerton had recently perfected a "side-scan" sonar that recorded an almost-photographic profile of objects resting on the bottom. He not only offered the loan of his unit but pledged to send along a technician to ensure it was working correctly.

The sea bottom was littered with so many shipwrecks and World War II aircraft that the search was like looking for a needle in a several-hundred-square-mile haystack. Wignall identified many possible sites, but bad weather imposed too many delays; the search platform was needed on other assignments, and it could not go on forever. However, about a year later, author Clive Cussler read about Wignall's effort and offered to provide funding for a loosely organized, purely civilian search from the proceeds of his 1976 best-selling novel, *Raise the Titanic*. Cussler did not find the ship but was encouraged enough to return for another try. However good the talent and solid the financing, they were not successful.

Despite these failures, Cussler caught the maritime archeology bug. In the years since he has financed more than 60 searches for historic shipwrecks. His interest ends with the discovery; he keeps no souvenirs and turns the sites over to professional archaeologists and historians. Perhaps his most famous find is the Confederate submarine *Hunley*, which he located in 1995. *Hunley* was recovered from the bottom near Charleston, South Carolina, in August 2000. I did not, as a rule, inflict my own opinions in professional matters upon the uniformed professionals. There was, however, one notable exception: the naming of a ship. The Director of Naval History viewed the selection of ship names solely as the prerogative of his office, where lists of candidate names were always at the ready. In earlier times, the candidate names followed very traditional lines. Battleships recognized states of the union; cruisers were named after cities; aircraft carriers after historical ships or battles; destroyers after (deceased) heroes of the Navy and Marine Corps; submarines after creatures of the sea (real or mythical), and so forth. Things have changed a great deal, and "political" has long since pushed aside "traditional." Not only destroyers but also aircraft carriers, submarines, and cruisers are being named in honor of great men living and dead.

However, the practice in 1975 was pretty much traditional, and my interest in naming a U.S. Navy ship after the French hero of the American Revolution—Comte de Grasse—did not sit well with someone (a senior flag officer) in the Office of Naval History. The U.S. Navy had never named a warship after a foreigner (let alone a titled royalist). That officer had a very inexact view of our naval history: four of the first five ships commissioned by the Continental Congress were named after "foreigners": *Alfred* (as in, "the Great," about as royalist as one might imagine), *Columbus*, *Cabot*, and *Andrew Doria* (an anglicized spelling of the first name of the 16th-century Italian admiral "Andrea" Doria).

I had two reasons for pursuing this matter. First and foremost, we were celebrating an independence that would not have been possible but for the assistance of the French Navy. Second, relations with the French always seemed a bit strained, and nothing would be lost by thus honoring Comte de Grasse with a Spruance-class destroyer, DD 974.

The wife of French President Valery Giscard d'Estaing graciously accepted my invitation to be the ship's sponsor, exclaiming, "I am very pleased to be the mother of this ship!" Her primary duty at an event that would take place at the Ingalls Shipyard in Pascagoula, Mississippi, in March 1976, would be a time-honored routine: smash a bottle of champagne across the bow and proclaim, "I christen thee *Comte de Gras!*" My office assisted in arranging her travel and assigned one of our public affairs officers, Lt. Commander Jim Lois, as protocol liaison.

All was well until the party landed at the New Orleans airport, where they were to transfer to a motorcade for the two-and-a-half-hour drive to Pascagoula. The party landed, but the luggage couldn't be found. It seemed to have missed a too-tight connection in Houston. The fashion-conscious First Lady of France was disconsolate, exclaiming, "My special dress! My make-up! My shoes!" Lois told her to go ahead in the waiting motorcade while he solved the problem. He traced her luggage, which was arriving on the next flight from Houston. Then he convinced a Coast Guard helicopter unit in New Orleans to postpone the transport of the body of a drowned fisherman (already in progress) and lend a diversionary hand. The helicopter with the luggage landed at the shipyard just as the motorcade passed through the front gate. The journey of the drowned fisherman from the lakeshore to the mortuary was delayed only a few minutes.

The best-known Navy Bicentennial event—indeed, the best-known event of the Bicentennial period—was the grand parade of ships in New York

Harbor on July 4, 1976. Its official name was "Operation Sail and the International Naval Review," but most people called it "OPSAIL" or the "tall ships thing." It included most of the larger sailing ships and representation from 40 of the world's navies, including the Soviets. Most of the navies sent at least one ship; those that did not have sea-going vessels—for example, landlocked Bolivia, which operated a patrol force on Lake Titicaca—sent delegations of senior officers.

The Review was a magnificent affair, hosted by both the president and vice president, attracting a live audience of some 3 million and the world's largest television audience, 200 million. Many told us—not always as a compliment—that the Navy "stole" the Fourth of July from the other armed services. And it almost didn't happen.

Initially, there were to be two separate events in different cities on the same day. The organizers of the civilian-sponsored Operation Sail (OPSAIL) hoped to be in New York, and the International Naval Review was planned for Norfolk, Virginia. Our Navy Bicentennial office was working with OPSAIL, to arrange appropriate logistic support; many of the sailing ships were official navy training vessels and were entitled to military courtesies and assistance. (One of them demanded more than mere "assistance," or it wouldn't participate—the Romanian *Mercea* wanted fuel, food, and money for miscellaneous expenses. I mulled this over with Holloway, and we agreed to adopt *Mercea* for the duration.)

The suggestion for an International Naval Review, patterned after similar events in 1893, 1907, and 1957, had been submitted three years earlier in the preliminary round of Bicentennial planning. The suggestion had survived the initial winnowing process and was "on the books" as an official Navy project, along with a planning budget of $40,000. The actual costs—fuel, docking fees, and so forth—would come from normally-budgeted operations and training funds. Well, "on the books" certainly is not the same as "underway." The responsible office at the Pentagon had taken absolutely no action, none, and had not even worked up a list of available ships. No naval command in the field seemed to be interested. As a result, with just about a year to go, our Bicentennial office canceled the non-existent International Naval Review and released the allocated funds to the museum.

A new vice chief of naval operations, Admiral Worth Bagley, had just reported for duty. He called my special assistant for the Bicentennial—Captain Harris was an old acquaintance of the admiral's—and said, "I understand you're coordinating the Bicentennial projects for the Secretary. How about dropping by and giving me a run-down?" When the briefing was finished, the admiral seemed properly impressed but felt something was missing. "Wouldn't you think it would be a great idea to invite other navies to come and help us celebrate our big birthday?"

"Well," said my special assistant, "there was just such a proposal for an International Naval Review, but no one seemed to care. The paperwork had been on the desk of a commander on the CNO staff without action for two years. So, I canceled it, for lack of sufficient high-level interest, and gave the planning budget to another project."

"I'd like to know more about that naval review," Admiral Bagley said. That conversation took place around 3 pm on Friday. At 9 am on Monday, Captain Harris called the admiral and reported, "I think we have been able to locate sufficient high-level interest to ensure support, and we have put the review back in the plan." Harris did not need to tell Admiral Bagley that he had found that interest in the office files, in the form of a memo sent with the original search for ideas, proposing the Norfolk International Naval Review and signed by then-Rear Adm. Worth Bagley.

Putting the Review back in the mix was one thing, but the proposed location was the reason the project had so long been ignored. Norfolk and its environs are wonderful, packed with history, and host to a great naval base and shipyard area. However, Norfolk is not a center of international media activity or not easily adapted to a grand public spectacle. For security reasons, Norfolk was not a port where Soviet warships would have been welcome. Therefore, Harris redeemed his temporary lapse of judgment by resurrecting the Review and suggesting it be combined with OPSAIL, and the venue shifted to New York. This was not a decision I could make on my own; however, it was not difficult to get approvals from OPSAIL, New York City, New York and New Jersey, the State Department, and the White House.

We proposed to invite every Navy listed in the authoritative *Jane's Fighting Ships*—it was not up to my office to decide what was or was not a "navy" (as in the case of Bolivia). We did not want political distinctions to mar the time-honored tradition of the Brotherhood of the Sea. We offered to provide an aircraft carrier as the official reviewing platform. Our plans were approved, but with one caveat from the (Republican) White House: "You can use any carrier except the USS *John F. Kennedy*."

In truth, we hoped to use *America* or *Independence* or even *Saratoga*— ships with some logical Revolutionary connection—but each was irretrievably scheduled for overseas deployment or shipyard overhaul. The USS *Forrestal* was selected. I wish I could report that everything was perfect, but we could have used two—or three—carriers and many more small boats to ferry people back and forth between shore and ship. If memory serves, there were some three-thousand guests aboard Forrestal. It took some of them longer to get back ashore than it would later take them to go from New York back to Washington. As for me—since President Ford and Vice President Rockefeller had departed the area, I enjoyed a stint as a surrogate guest of honor for a tickertape parade up Broadway.

I should report three other potentially fatal issues which arose during the final stages of our planning. One is a good illustration of how rigid and inflexible some military folk can be. The senior naval officer in New York, responsible for coordinating all local arrangements, became apoplectic whenever *The New York Times* neglected to include "International Naval Review" when writing about OPSAIL. The admiral's public affairs officer (PAO) was caught in the middle—trying to curry favor with *The Times* for whatever good publicity might be generated and subject to the admiral's wrath when the coverage didn't measure up to his standards. I did not want to become directly involved in this issue—again. I tried to avoid inserting myself personally into the operational chain of command. But I did ask a staff member to try to resolve the problem. He went to New York, met with the admiral, and explained, "Secretary Middendorf doesn't care what they call it, as long as they write about it." The problem was not resolved: the admiral was a good man but could not let go of his fixation. So, the Bicentennial team thenceforth dealt directly with *The New York Times*. The public affairs officer, Commander Jay Coupe, who demonstrated an ability to work under pressure, went on to promotion and a prestigious and well-deserved assignment as PAO for the Joint Chiefs of Staff chairman.

Another issue, which had the potential to close our event before it got underway, centered on some recently enacted maritime environmental protection laws. Vessels operating on the inland waterways of the United States —which certainly included New York Harbor—were required to contain sewage in onboard holding tanks, which could later be emptied at specified pump-out stations or dumped overboard when far out at sea. The rules seem primarily to have been directed at small boat owners; the status of large ships—especially warships, none of which had been designed with sewage control systems in mind—was ambiguous. The status of many OPSAIL participants fell somewhere in between pleasure craft and warships.

At one of the New York planning sessions, someone raised the question: "What happens if a public-minded citizen tries to get an injunction stopping the whole thing on environmental grounds?" There was a long silence. Finally, a senior New York law enforcement official jokingly offered his version of an absurd idea: "We'll have him arrested and held until after July 4, then let him go and pay whatever damages he demands." The proper solution was more easily found, someone who lived on Staten Island pointed out at that very moment: the Staten Island ferries were dumping raw sewage into the harbor with every crossing. An injunction aimed at the visiting ships would have to apply to the ferries—end of discussion.

Finally, we barely escaped one colossal embarrassment. The Boy Scouts of America, Girl Scouts of America, and the Navy League Sea Cadet organization had an agreement with OPSAIL that selected groups of youngsters representing every state in the union could be on some of the big sailing ships for the last leg of the inbound journey. They would board in Newport, Rhode Island, and ride to the parade in New York Harbor. We thought the arrangements for actual embarkation had been made by OPSAIL, but a few days before the big event, we got a call from a reporter in, I think, Nebraska: "We hear that our kids can't get aboard the sail ships, as promised. Why is the U.S. Navy disappointing our kids?"

As it turned out, the managers of OPSAIL had told the youth organizations that the youngsters would be welcome but had not shared this concept with the operators of the ships—the Germans, Romanians, whatever. By the time I learned of the problem, happily chattering groups of boys and girls were assembling at Newport. The first ships had just arrived, and the rest were soon to follow. It was a bit late to engage the diplomatic machinery of Washington. Time for some more bold corrective action. I said something obvious, like, "The U.S. Navy doesn't disappoint Boy Scouts."

Germany's *Gorch Foch*, Poland's *Dar Pomorza*, Norway's *Christian Radich*, the Italian *Amerigo Vespucci*, Romania's *Mercea*, the Soviets' *Tovarisch* and *Kruzenstern*—all the captains were willing. Of course, the children could ride (although, at first, there was some hesitation about taking girls). The only real problem from this point was with the Soviets: they wanted to take all the youngsters and didn't understand why they had to share the glory. A short time later, the Soviets were so irritated by the Israeli raid to free hostages at the Entebbe airport (July 3–4) that they pulled out and went home. Of course, by the time that news reached New York, the Naval Review had ended, and the only damage was to the Soviet sailors who missed some great liberty in New York. Perhaps a few also missed an opportunity to defect, an action that I understand was enjoyed in some numbers by sailors from the obviously impoverished Romanian ship. I also understand that some crewmen from *Amerigo Vespucci* (actual number unknown) embarked on matrimonial seas with Italian American girls from Brooklyn. The "Brotherhood of the Seas" takes many forms.

Here's one non-Bicentennial event, but nonetheless linked by timing. The Smithsonian Air & Space Museum, on the mall in D.C., is the most-visited museum in the world; strange to note that its original plans did not include a Navy exhibit hall. This was remedied when a committee headed by retired

Vice Admiral William Martin persuaded the Smithsonian management to add one. This took the form of an aircraft carrier hangar deck displaying World War II–era aircraft and a replica navigation bridge where the visitors could listen to an audio replay of carrier operations. The Smithsonian had a bit of luck with the equipment for that bridge: a Hollywood movie producer was then preparing to film the movie "Midway." He asked my office if he could borrow the bridge equipment from an out-of-service vintage carrier that was being kept in the naval equivalent of "mothballs." I agreed to let him do so, provided that, when finished, he would arrange to have it all shipped, at his own expense, for installation at the Smithsonian. The Sea-Air Operations Gallery opened to the public in July 1976. And along the way, I enjoyed an invitation to socialize on the movie set during an otherwise-scheduled visit to the West Coast with Naval Reserve officers Jackie Cooper and Glenn Ford.

Another interesting but more significant non-Bicentennial project grew out of the great naval Review. Felix de Weldon, famed for his magnificent sculpture at the Marine Corp's Iwo Jima Memorial, spoke with Admiral Holloway and said he would be pleased to create a similar monument and ceremonial venue for the Navy. Holloway was intrigued and passed the offer along to my office. I thought it was an interesting idea—the Navy could benefit from a centrally-located plaza large enough for band concerts, promotion, and retirement ceremonies, and so forth—but saw an immediate problem. We could not accept de Weldon's offer, which could be valued in the high six figures. I knew that selection of an artist would have to come through an open competition, and that could best be handled by a Congressionally chartered, non-government, non-profit organization.

I was pleased to serve as the founding chairman of the Navy Memorial Foundation. Rear Admiral Bill Thompson, by then retired, became the first president and is the man who brought it all to a successful conclusion. Through fifteen years of Congressional Hearings, the often-conflicting interests of local arts and monuments commissions, against the carping from interested citizens ("Why does Washington need another monument, anyway?"), Bill was always up to his neck in the vital and endless fundraising effort.

There were many candidate sites for the Memorial, but most were out on the fringes of the central area and off the tourist path. Thompson held off on-site selection until he found the perfect spot on the land about to be reclaimed from demolishing some worn-out buildings at Pennsylvania Avenue and 8th Street, Northwest, just across from the National Archives. There was a problem, however, with one of the early designs for the site. A committee formed by several interested agencies proposed a structure that was a clone of the French Arc de Triomphe. The U.S. Commission on Fine Arts sent us back to the drawing board. And it was the best thing to have happened to the Navy Memorial.

As finally developed, the Memorial is on two levels. Below ground, there is a visitor center with a movie theater and lecture hall, meeting and function rooms, gift shop, offices, and the computerized "Navy Log," a modest fund-raising feature whereby anyone can purchase some space to note the service history or memories of anyone who has ever served in the U.S. Navy. Above ground is a wide plaza, 100 feet in diameter, with ceremonial fountains, twin flagpoles festooned with signal flags, and a series of bronze plaques celebrating various aspects of naval history.

Since we planned to use the Memorial for occasions of ceremony and to host concerts by military bands, I had hoped to include a covered band shell. This was not a matter of acoustics but protection: an open plaza of marble, concrete, and granite could, on a sunny summer day, cause the instruments to overheat and not be played. It was denied when I presented my idea before the Pennsylvania Avenue Development Corporation and my good friend, their chairman J. Carter Brown. I think they thought it would become a magnet for homeless vagrants. Perhaps, but I know that concerts have been cut short because of the heat.

The centerpiece of the Memorial, however, is indeed a statue. The contract went to Connecticut sculptor Stanley Bleifeld, in formal competition with 36 others. It is not a massive, heroic icon, but a quiet, only slightly above life-size bronze of the "Lone Sailor," hands tucked in his peacoat to ward off the chill and sea bag at his feet, as he looks out across an inlaid granite map of the world. The Lone Sailor was dedicated on the Navy Memorial on October 13, 1987, the Navy's 212th birthday. It has served as a living tribute to the men and women of the Sea Services—past, present, and future—for more than 35 years.

7 | Iran: With Friends Like These

A CONSTITUTIONAL MONARCHY after the UK model, Iran was administered by a prime minister from an elected parliament and reigned over by Shah Mohammad Pahlavi, beginning in 1941 when he replaced his tyrannical father. During the next 20 years, the Shah initiated economic plans that improved the economy and led to the development of major power-generating dams. He redistributed land to peasants on favorable terms, offering compensation to landlords. Significant investments in elementary school education were made free and mandatory, and he built new schools and hospitals.

I had several meetings with the Shah as secretary of the Navy. Four frigates under construction were placed in limbo because of severe cuts in the defense budget. I approached the Shah and asked him to purchase the frigates for the Iranian Navy and thus keep our lines open until the next defense budget. While meeting the Shah to finalize the deal, he asked me where I was having lunch, and my aide, Bob Sims, told him. Toward the end of our lunch in Tehran, a sharply dressed official standing at attention behind me handed me a note signed by the Shah, which said, "You have a deal." Before it could be finalized, the Shah came under fire from Islamic protestors in Iran, led by Khomeini, who questioned the Shah's legitimacy as the head of the country.

The Shah's first significant clash with dissident Ayatollah Khomeini occurred in 1962 when the Shah announced plans to allow women to vote. Khomeini thundered in his sermons that the fate of Iran should never be allowed to be decided by women. There were demonstrations, and Khomeini was arrested and exiled to Iraq. After the Shah publicly endorsed Iran's links with Israel, President Nasser of Egypt cut off diplomatic relations with Iran and increased propaganda attacks against him. Syria, Iraq, and other Arab states supported the Iranian revolutionaries, and Iraq began to menace Kuwait. As the Shah was opening his country to Western-style self-rule, it became more vulnerable to a take-over by rogue elements. During the Kennedy Administration, the Shah built up Iran's armed forces. Still, student demonstrations and teacher strikes, religious dissension in Qom, and disaffection in the tribal areas showed discontent. When Kennedy met with

Khrushchev in Vienna in 1963, Khrushchev told him that Iran would be going through political upheaval and would fall like rotten fruit into Soviet hands. Kennedy was alarmed, and a report on Iran he ordered from the State Department concurred with Khrushchev's assessment. The National Intelligence Estimate on Iran concluded that "profound political and social change in one form or another is virtually inevitable," and it predicted that such change would likely be revolutionary.

Encouraging the Shah to undertake reforms, Kennedy was pleased when the Shah appointed Ali Amini, Iran's former Ambassador to Washington, as prime minister. The Shah was apprehensive about the well-known and potentially popular Amini. In an April 1963 meeting, the Shah told Kennedy that his Army officers were worried that other countries received more military aid than Iran. Kennedy countered that the United States felt that Iran's main problems were internal and that improvements were being made due to recent reforms. He lectured the Shah about how successful Franklin Roosevelt had been with his social programs. The Shah did not argue but repeated that Iran needed "an honest, first-class army, as well as a decent standard of living." He insisted that, with such an army, Iran could resist Communist pressures. He added that he aimed to build the country into a showcase so that other Arabic nations could see that it was possible to work with the West and get more effective support than countries like Egypt, then being armed and underwritten by the Soviets. When Kennedy questioned the showcase notion as unrealistic, the Shah countered, "I am not by nature a dictator. But if Iran is to succeed, the government will have to act firmly for a time."

When the Shah returned to Iran, he dismissed Amini, whom Kennedy had just praised as a reformer. Amini was excluded from any positions of responsibility, as the Shah appropriated the idea of reform and launched what he called his "White Revolution"—White, meaning Bloodless. Reforms called for with this Revolution were not without opposition. Religious scholars were particularly enraged by the referendum allowing women to vote.

When Khomeini returned to Iran in 1965, he called for the Iranian government's overthrow, was arrested again, and exiled to Turkey on November 3, 1965. Department of State analysts warned that Khomeini's views were symptomatic of widespread popular opposition to government policies, recently extended to open criticism of American policy in Iran. This new attitude threatened U.S. interests in Iran and made the U.S. task there far more complex. However, department officials disagreed about the extent of popular discontent in Iran.

The Johnson administration encouraged a far-reaching political, social, and economic reform program. Policymakers remained concerned over potential threats to the long-term stability and viability of the Shah's regime. Iran was also valued as one of the most dependable U.S. allies in the region. Unlike many other Third World leaders, the Shah supported U.S. policies in Vietnam, the Dominican Republic, and other sensitive Cold War areas. Johnson's personal relationship with the Shah, which dated from his trip to Tehran as vice-president in August 1962, was closer than Kennedy's had been.

On January 7, 1964, the Shah sent President Johnson a letter pointing to an increasing Arab threat to Iran and arguing that the September 1962 U.S. Five-Year Military Plan for Iran had already proved inadequate. In his March 19 response, the president noted that, because of Iran's exposed position, the U.S. government had always taken the Shah's military concerns quite seriously, but that it had concluded that the basic factors that had led U.S. military experts to agree on the current Military Plan had not changed significantly since 1962. During subsequent discussions of a military modernization program for Iran, U.S. officials emphasized the importance of assuring that such a program would not hamper Iran's economic development program. At the same time, the Shah insisted that increased oil revenues over the foreseeable future would make it possible to pay for increased defense expenditures without impairing Iran's economic progress.

When Secretary of State Dean Rusk met with the Shah in Iran in early April 1965, the Shah told him that his "White Revolution" was supported by the nation, except for minority groups such as reactionary mullahs and dispossessed landlords. However, an assassination attempt on the Shah on April 10, 1965, highlighted for the Embassy that Iran's stability was unduly dependent on one man's life.

The Shah argued that successful economic development was useless unless Iran had adequate military security. In September 1965, Henry Meyer, ambassador to Iran, told Washington that the Shah was unhappy with his dependence on the United States for military supplies. He would almost certainly begin to buy arms from non-U.S. sources, possibly even the Soviet Union. In November, Meyer reported Shah's complaints that the U.S. government had seriously misunderstood Iran's actual military needs. The ambassador again urged approval of the long-delayed second installment of the U.S. military credit sales program. Following U.S. approval on November 29, the Shah began to push for a $200 million augmentation of Iran's military purchases.

When the Shah visited Washington in August 1967, the president assured him that the United States would do everything possible to meet his needs but warned that the mood of Congress made it difficult for him to make firm promises regarding future military aid. The Shah left Washington well pleased with his reception and the praise he had received for Iran's economic and social progress under his rule. On November 15, 1967, the Shah wrote the president concerning two new projected five-year plans for Iran—one for economic development and one for the reorganization of Iran's armed forces. He noted that a rough estimate of the requirements for military equipment to carry out this reorganization was in the order of $800 million and that Iran would like to buy this equipment in the United States if the U.S. government could offer the necessary credit arrangements.

In 1969, the United States agreed to a concession the Shah had been pursuing for ten years: severing all contact with any Iranians opposed to his regime. After that, a process of "reverse leverage" set in. Henry Kissinger would write 20 years later that because of the Vietnam War, it was not politically possible in the 1970s for the United States to fight a major war: "There was no possibility of assigning any American forces to the Indian Ocean in the midst of the Vietnam War and its attendant trauma," he noted. "Congress would have tolerated no such commitment; the public would not have supported it. Fortunately, Iran was willing to play this role."

The Shah's diplomatic foundation was the U.S. guarantee that it would protect his regime, enabling him to stand up to larger enemies. While the arrangement did block other partnerships and treaties, it helped to provide an environment stable enough for implementing his reforms. Another factor guiding his foreign policy was his quest for financial stability, which required strong diplomatic ties. Yet another was his wish to present Iran as a prosperous and powerful nation, fueling his domestic policy of Westernization and reform. A final component was his promise that, under his monarchy, communism could be halted at Iran's border. By 1977, the country's treasury, the Shah's government, and his strategic alliances seemed to form a protective layer around Iran. At this time, the Shah also believed that he no longer needed the army to protect his dynasty. Mosaddeq was dead. Khomeini was in exile, and the opposition political parties were fading away.

When President Nixon visited Tehran in 1972 and witnessed several terrorist attacks, he agreed to arms transfers—the so-called "blank check." Kissinger issued an official policy directive stating, "With regard to the question of arms sales to Iran, the President's policy is to encourage the purchase of U.S. equipment. Decisions as to the desirability of equipment acquisition should be left in the hands of the Iranian government, and the U.S. should not undertake to discourage it on economic grounds." While this did not stop the Pentagon from evaluating Iran's arms requests, it was understood that the requests were to be given sympathetic hearings. Soaring oil revenues convinced Washington that the Shah could afford both guns and butter and over the next four years, $17 billion went to military hardware.

When the Arab states embargoed oil in the aftermath of the Yom Kippur War in 1973, the Shah declared neutrality while seeking to employ the lack of crude oil supply to Iran's benefit. At a meeting of Persian Gulf oil producers, he proposed that they should double the oil price for the second time in a year. The resulting "oil shock" crippled Western economies while Iran saw a rapid growth of oil revenues. Iranian oil incomes doubled to $4.6 billion in 1973–1974 and spiked to $17.8 billion in the following year. This established the Shah as the dominant figure of OPEC (Organization of Petroleum Exporting Countries), having control over oil prices and production.

In 1975, U.S. Vice President Nelson Rockefeller declared: "We must take His Imperial Majesty to the United States for a couple of years so that he can teach us how to run a country." The economies of the Western nations were trapped in stagflation after the 1973–1974 oil shocks while Iran's soared on high oil prices, seeming to prove the greatness of the Shah, not only to the rest of the world but to the Shah himself.

A CIA report stated, "Thanks to the Shah himself and oil resources, Iran is well on its way to playing a leading role in the Middle East with a modernized elite, large economic resources, and strong forces. Succession is always a question in an authoritarian regime, even a benevolent one, but each year reinforces the social and political momentum in the direction the Shah has set. The U.S. can keep close to and benefit from this process and even influence Iran toward a positive regional and world role rather than a bid for area hegemony or other adventurism." Despite criticism from the West, the Shah was considered a master statesman through his domestic reforms, successful opposition to radical Arab neighbors, and ambitions for regional stability and prosperity.

The Shah did not enjoy the same intimate relationship with President Gerald R. Ford as he had with Nixon. Although Kissinger worked hard to defend the United States-Iran relationship and secure a nuclear agreement, the Shah's detractors were no longer sidelined as they had been under Nixon. Ford sought to appease these critics by foisting a nuclear agreement on the Shah that included safeguards that went beyond Iran's commitments under the 1968 Nuclear Nonproliferation Treaty. The Shah rejected Ford's demands, seeing them as a violation of Iran's sovereignty and a reversion by the U.S. to treating Iran as a client rather than a partner.

In 1976, the Shah came under fire from the American press and programs like *60 Minutes*. Veteran journalist Mike Wallace, famed for his tough interviews, asked the Shah if he endorsed torture. Increasingly hostile demonstrations in U.S. cities staged by pro-Khomeini Iranians resident in America also raised issues for the Shah and his supporters. Anti-Shah demonstrations of a few hundred Islamic protesters started in October 1977 after a controversial newspaper article described the death of Khomeini's son, Mostafa. The next day, local protests prompted by the article started in Qom, and nationwide protests and strikes began across Iran. Army units opened fire on protesters. The most significant instance was on September 8, 1978, later to become known as "Black Friday," when thousands of people gathered in Tehran's Jaleh Square for a religious demonstration. The protestors refused to recognize martial law, so the soldiers opened fire, killing and seriously injuring many. Black Friday reduced the chance for reconciliation, which became known as "the point of no return" for the Revolution.

The Shah attempted to calm the situation in early October by granting a general amnesty to dissidents living abroad, including Khomeini. It was too late. Throughout the month, extreme unrest grew into open opposition to the monarchy. Strikes paralyzed the country, and some nine million people marched against the Shah throughout Iran. During a massive demonstration in Tehran, the Shah accused the British Ambassador Sir Anthony Parsons and the American Ambassador William H. Sullivan of organizing the demonstrations, screaming that he was being "betrayed" by the United Kingdom and the United States.

When Khomeini began major disruptions in 1978, the Carter administration cautioned the Shah not to be oppressive. When I was secretary of the Navy (1974–1977), Iran was our most powerful and promising ally in the vast, oil-drenched region surrounding the Persian Gulf. I had several meetings with the Shah as secretary of the Navy. Four frigates under construction were placed in limbo because of severe cuts in the defense budget by the Carter administration. I approached the Shah and asked him to purchase the frigates for the Iranian Navy and thus keep our lines open until the next defense budget. While meeting the Shah to finalize the deal, he asked me where I was having lunch, and my aide, Bob Sims told him. Toward the end of our lunch in Tehran, a sharply dressed official standing at attention behind me handed me a note signed by the Shah that said, "You have a deal." Before it could be finalized, the Shah came under fire from Islamic protestors in Iran, led by Khomeini.

The Shah looked for support from the United States, which never came. Some blamed the State Department, which discouraged U.S. diplomats from engaging with opponents of the Shah. Others blamed a CIA study that infamously reported to President Carter in August 1978 that "Iran is not in a revolutionary or even a 'pre-revolutionary' situation."

Most Iranians, the Shah included, believed that Britain supported the Revolution largely because of sympathetic coverage by BBC's journalists. This impression was crucial due to their exaggerated idea about Britain's capacity to "direct events" in Iran. Working out various conspiracy theories about who was behind the Revolution, top candidates were some combination of Britain, the United States, and the Soviet Union.

At the opening of the U.N. General Assembly on October 3, 1978, Secretary of State Cyrus Vance assured Iranian Foreign Minister Amir Khosrow Afshar that it was clearly not U.S. policy to support the Shah's opposition and asked if anything further could be done to demonstrate support for Iran or to be helpful in these difficult circumstances. President Carter's national security team met to discuss the Tehran riots and their aftermath. It had been three days since National Security Advisor Brzezinski had assured the president that Iran was not in the throes of a full-scale revolution. Brzezinski was especially critical of the CIA, which had failed to anticipate the seriousness of the unrest, and of Ambassador Sullivan, whom he had learned *was* in contact with the revolutionaries. Sullivan, convinced the Shah was finished, cabled Washington that the Shah's support had shrunk to the military, which was unlikely to sanction a bloodbath to keep him in power. The ideal scenario he laid out was the departure of Shah and his top generals into exile, followed by accommodation between the Shah's military and the revolutionists.

On November 3, 1978, a plan to arrest about 1,500 people considered to be leaders of the Revolution was submitted to the Shah, who at first tentatively agreed, then changed his mind. On November 5, 1978, he went on Iranian television to say, "I have heard the voice of your revolution and promise major reforms." Shiite clerics railed against the Shah's relationship with Israel, claiming his acceptance of Jews was heretical. They also opposed the Shah's continuing support of women's suffrage as well as his opening of private universities because the clerics had once had sole dominion over Iran's educational system.

On November 7, 1978, in a major concession to the opposition, the Shah freed all political prisoners while ordering the arrest of a former prime minister and several senior officials of his regime, yet another series of mistakes that emboldened his opponents and demoralized his supporters. In late December, the Shah learned that many of his generals were making overtures to the revolutionary leaders and that the loyalty of the military could no longer be assured. In desperation, he requested that Gholam Hossein Sadeghi be appointed prime minister. Sadeghi had served as interior minister under Mosaddegh, had been imprisoned after the 1953 coup, and then pardoned by the Shah because he was a "patriot." Sadeghi remained politically active and was often harassed by the Shah's military. But he said he was willing to serve as prime minister under Mohammad Reza in order to "save" Iran, saying he feared what might come after if the Shah was overthrown. His primary demand was that the Shah not leave Iran, noting that it was essential to ensure the military's loyalty.

In January 1979, a meeting was held in Guadeloupe between President Carter, President d'Estaing of France, Chancellor Schmidt of West Germany, and Prime Minister Callaghan of the United Kingdom to discuss the crisis in Iran. The Shah was convinced they were holding the meeting to discuss how best to abandon him. On January 16, 1979, he flew out of Iran for the last time. Prime Minister Shahpur Bakhtiar dissolved the military and allowed Ayatollah Khomeini to return to Iran on February 3, 1979. As Khomeini arrived home, he announced, "Our final victory will come when all foreigners are out of the country. I beg God to cut off the hands of all evil foreigners and their helpers." He brushed aside all of Bakhtiar's requests and appointed his own interim government. The loose coalition of diverse political groups that coalesced to overthrow the Shah quickly splintered into rival factions that engaged in a bitter power struggle. A provisional government led by moderate leader Mehdi Bazargan presided over an increasingly polarized political environment in which secular nationalists steadily lost ground to leftists and radical Islamists. Khomeini presented himself as a moderate able to bring together all the different factions leading the Revolution. Like Lenin and Mao before him, Khomeini called the leftists who supported the revolution "useful idiots" and executed or imprisoned most of them. Pro-Khomeini revolutionary guerrilla and rebel soldiers gained the upper hand in street fighting, and the military announced neutrality. By February 11, the dissolution of the monarchy was complete. After gaining complete control of Iran on April 22, 1979, Khomeini immediately took away all guns from the population, following Mao's famous rules. He founded the Islamic Revolutionary Guard Corps (IRGC), which protects the Iranian political system and the country's strict adherence to Islamic laws.

The U.S. State Department was criticized for doing little to communicate with Tehran or discourage protest and opposition to the Shah, and the intelligence community within the U.S. was blasted for its assessment that Iran was not in a pre-revolutionary condition. President Carter was also blamed for his lack of support for the Shah while failing to deter opposition. Bureaucratic dysfunction extended to intelligence sharing and analysis. Carter's National Security Council was unaware of CIA intelligence that documented the flow of Palestinian and Libyan money and arms to Khomeini. A U.S. Iran policy was set up based on hunches, flawed intelligence, grudges, and personal prejudices.

Revolutionary militants stormed the U.S. embassy in Tehran on February

14, 1979, holding the mission personnel hostage for several hours and generating fear for the safety of the remaining Americans in Iran. Two Iranians were killed, and two U.S. Marines were wounded in the invasion. The weak response to the invasion by the Carter administration encouraged Khomeini to order Iranian students to demonstrate in memory of the first anniversary of a bloody November 4, 1978. During that demonstration, hundreds of militants emerged from the crowd and seized the U.S. embassy. Fifty-two Americans were held captive for 444 days in a prolonged crisis that boosted the power of Iranian hardliners, torpedoed the Carter administration's ill-conceived efforts to engage Iran's revolutionary leaders, and ushered in an era of rising terrorism and regional instability in the Middle East. The hostage crisis dramatically reshaped the politics of both countries.

When all diplomatic appeals to the Iranian government to secure the release of the American hostages failed, President Carter ordered a military mission as a last-ditch attempt to save the hostages on April 24, 1980. Three of eight helicopters failed during the operation, crippling the crucial airborne plans. The mission was then canceled at the staging area in Iran. During the withdrawal, one of the retreating helicopters collided with one of six C-130 transport planes, killing eight service members, and injuring five. The next day, President Carter gave a press conference in which he took full responsibility for the tragedy. The hostages were not released for another 270 days.

Although the militants who seized the hostages demanded the return of the Shah to stand trial, their real goal was to block any improvement in relations with the United States, which they saw as a threat to the consolidation of their power within Iran. Three days before the hostages were seized, Premier Bazargan met with President Carter's National Security adviser, Zbigniew Brzezinski, in Algeria. The Carter administration was anxious to restore good relations with Iran and had soft-pedaled its criticism of growing human rights violations after the Revolution. But for Khomeini, any attempt to improve relations with the United States was intolerable because the "Great Satan" would tempt westernized Iranian moderates to turn against his Islamist revolution.

The Carter administration, whose efforts to engage Iran's revolutionary leaders were rebuffed, badly mishandled the hostage crisis. Carter initially ruled out the use of force, which weakened his administration's bargaining power and strengthened the hand of the militants holding the hostages. Then his administration was lured into a series of negotiations with the Iranians in which it made concessions, such as agreeing to set up a U.N. commission to investigate American involvement in the crimes of the Shah, only to see the Iranians repeatedly renege on their promises.

Eventually, the hostages were released minutes after Carter left office. Former Iranian President Abolhassan Bani Sadr later attributed this to a fear of incoming President Ronald Reagan. Iran's Islamist hardliners learned a lesson from the hostage crisis: terrorism works. They later made terrorism a major part of their foreign policy and deployed Revolutionary Guards to export their violent Revolution to other Muslim countries. In Lebanon, the Revolutionary Guards helped to create, arm, and train Hezbollah ("Party of God"), which kidnapped another 15 American hostages in the 1980s, some of whom Iran traded for arms in the Iran-Contra affair.

Many Americans remember that President Carter's mishandling of the hostage crisis was a major factor that contributed to his overwhelming defeat by Ronald Reagan in 1980. But few are aware of the momentous impact that the hostage crisis played on Iran's revolutionary politics. The American hostages became pawns in Iran's internal power struggle and enabled Khomeini's followers to bring down the provisional government and gain a stranglehold on Iranian politics.

The Shah was seriously ill when he left Iran on January 16, 1979. French doctors who, four years before, had diagnosed his cancer, informed the American government that the Shah was dying. It was expected that he would quickly seek asylum in America, the nation that had been his strongest supporter and stalwart friend. Even Khomeini had "expressed no objections" to the Shah's exile in the United States. To this end, "Sunnylands," the sprawling Palms Springs estate of Walter Annenberg, was offered and readied as a place of haven for his royal friend.

Without consulting with the Americans, the Shah first made a quick one-week stopover in Cairo at the invitation of Egyptian President Anwar Sadat and then flew on to the household of another monarch, King Hassan II of Morocco, for an indefinite stay. If he had been loitering in the Near East region, hoping that there would be a reversal of fortunes in Iran which would result in an opportunity to return to the throne, he was destined for disappointment. Chances were dimming that the Provisional Government of Iran (PGOI) would collapse, nor had Khomeini's support among the masses of Iranians waned.

On October 22, 1979, the Shah arrived in New York on David Rockefeller's private jet. After a brief stay in Manhattan, the Shah drifted between Morocco, the Bahamas, Mexico, and Panama, before being given asylum on March 24, 1980, by Egyptian President Sadat. On July 27, 1980, the former Shah died of cancer while in exile in Cairo, 17 months after being driven out by his country's Islamic Revolution. No sitting head of state attended his funeral. The United States, France, Britain, Japan, Australia, and Israel sent ambassadors. Among the mourners was former U.S. president Richard Nixon. He described as "shameful" the U.S. administration's hot and then cold policy towards the Shah, "a loyal friend and ally of the United States for more than 30 years." In Tehran, the former monarch's death was announced on national radio, "The Vampire of the century is dead."

Sen. Joseph Biden, who chaired the Senate Foreign Relations Committee, said in a 2002 speech, "I believe an improved relationship with Iran is in the naked self-interest of the United States and Iran's as well." Biden called for engagement with Koumeini lawmakers, offering to meet with them wherever or whenever they wanted. After President George Bush labeled Iran an "Axis of Evil," Sen. Biden called for the U.S. to make positive overtures to Iran without expecting much in return. Biden voted against a U.S. Senate resolution in 2002 urging President Bush to label Iran's Islamic Revolutionary Guard Corps a terrorist group, saying he didn't want Bush to use it as a justification for war with Iran. His support of religious leader Ayatollah Khomeini led to his being named as 'Tehran's favorite senator.'

Iran continues to enforce a strict Islamic code in governing its people. A special section of the IRGC, the Morality Police established by Khomeini in 1979, beat to death a 22-year-old Iranian woman, Mahsa Amini, on September 16, 2022, for not wearing a hijab (head covering.) The incident led to riots throughout Iran, with thousands of women burning their hijabs in protests. They had only rocks to throw against the morality police because of the gun laws. At least 400 protestors have been killed, while thousands have been arrested. This was not the first time the IRGC stepped in to prevent a revolution. The IRGC arrested, beat, and killed thousands of protestors who claimed election irregularities in 2009 which led to the election of Mahmoud Ahmadinejad over the reformer Mirhossein Mousavi.

President Ebrahim Raisi, installed after rigged elections in June 2021, is a protégé of Khomeini. Iran has the world's second-largest reserves of natural gas and fourth-largest reserves of crude oil. Iranians have the legal right to own property and establish private businesses, but powerful institutions such as the Revolutionary Guard limit fair competition and entrepreneurial opportunities. Over the past 43 years, Iran has experienced very slow growth: an average of only 1.2 percent annually. Sinking under the weight of sharp drops in scores for fiscal health and business freedom, Iran has recorded an 8.1-point overall loss of economic freedom since 2017 and has fallen further in the "Repressed" category. Iran's economic freedom score in The Heritage Foundation's 2024 Index of Economic Freedom is 42.4, making its economy the 170th freest in the 2022 Index, near the bottom. Iran is ranked last among 14 countries in the Middle East and North Africa.

The judicial system is not independent of the supreme leader. The state's quality and availability of administrative services are constrained by mismanagement, bribery, and rampant corruption. Anticorruption efforts target opponents of the regime. The bloated state-owned sector and companies controlled by Iranian security forces disadvantaged private business owners who are often small-scale workshops, farms, manufacturers, or services. There is a shortage of skilled labor. Energy subsidies account for as much as 25 percent of GDP, and the government has increased its economically harmful price controls in the face of high inflation.

After 43 years of Islamic rule, Iran represents the most significant challenge to the United States and its allies in the greater Middle East. It continues to develop and improve a range of new military capabilities to target U.S. and allied military assets in the area. Iran is the world's foremost sponsor of terrorism and has made extensive efforts to export its radical Shia brand of Islamist Revolution. It has found success in establishing a network of powerful Shia revolutionary groups in Lebanon and Iraq. It has cultivated links with Afghan Shia and Taliban militants; and has stirred Shia unrest in Bahrain, Iraq, Lebanon, Saudi Arabia, and Yemen.

In recent years, U.S. Naval forces off the coasts of Bahrain and Yemen have intercepted Iranian arms shipments regularly, and Israel has repeatedly intercepted arms shipments, including long-range rockets, bound for Palestinian militants in Gaza. Iran relies heavily on irregular warfare against others in the region and fields more ballistic missiles than any of its neighbors. It has repeatedly played up its threat to international energy security, proclaiming that "if the Americans make a wrong move toward Iran, the shipment of energy will definitely face danger, and the Americans would not be able to protect energy supply in the region."

Iran seeks to tilt the regional balance of power in its favor by driving out the Western presence, undermining and overthrowing opposing governments, and establishing its hegemony over the oil-rich Persian Gulf region. It also seeks to radicalize Shiite communities and advance their interests against Sunni rivals. Iran has a long record of sponsoring terrorist attacks against American allies and other interests in the region. Regarding conventional threats, Iran's ground forces dwarf the relatively small armies of the other Gulf States, and its formidable ballistic missile forces pose significant threats to its neighbors.

8 | The Vietnam Extraction: Operation Frequent Wind

In March 1975, President Gerald Ford fought to save an American ally from being overrun by an implacable enemy. The North Vietnamese Army, mounting a massive conventional strike on the Army of the Republic of Vietnam, was advancing closer to Saigon. President Ford urged Congress to authorize military aid to South Vietnam. His pleas were met with intransigence and disdain. Although the United States had withdrawn its military forces from Vietnam after the signing of the Paris Peace Accords in 1973, approximately 5,000 Americans and 10,000 Vietnamese loyal to the United States remained in Saigon. By the end of 1974, United States active participation in the Vietnam War had ended, and we were working with the South Vietnamese to develop a self-sufficient and democratic Vietnam.

But by February 1975, things were not going well; two-thirds of the country was under the control of the North Vietnamese, and fighting was intensifying. By March 1975, the North Vietnamese were in South Vietnam. On April 1, the U.S. Army, Navy, Air Force, and Marine Corps camped in Saigon's Defense Attaché Office (DAO) compound to prepare for the evacuation. That was the signal for other embassies to get their citizens out.

When I made my last visit to Saigon in mid-April 1975 as secretary of the Navy, I was amazed at the rosy upbeat report offered by Ambassador Graham Martin. The Vietnamese CNO, Commodore Chan, thanked me for authorizing a million dollars to build a new dock. "This will keep our Navy's future bright for years to come," he said.

Well, as the world knows, things were not upbeat, and the future was not bright. Throughout March and April 1975, the North Vietnamese Army captured more and more Southern cities. South Vietnamese citizens fled in mass numbers. The fall of the second-largest city, Da Nang, caused even more inhabitants to depart. In Saigon, thousands of South Vietnamese loyal to the United States lined up at the embassy to seek entry to the United States. They knew remaining in Vietnam would result in imprisonment or even death under the North Vietnamese.

In April 1975, Secretary of State Henry Kissinger received a list of about

1.6 million at-risk people who needed to leave Vietnam, excluding Americans, their dependents, and other nationalists who worked for the American government, which left about 600,000 Vietnamese. As they could not evacuate 600,000 people, the South Vietnamese allocation was lowered to 8,000 people working for the U.S. embassy in Saigon. On April 25, 1975, 40 Marines from the USS *Hancock* were flown in by helicopter to augment the 18 Marine security guards assigned to defend the embassy in Saigon. Ambassador Martin remained optimistic that a negotiated settlement could be reached whereby the United States would not have to pull out of Vietnam. He instructed Major James Kean, commanding officer of the Marine Security Guard Battalion, not to remove trees and other shrubbery that would allow the use of the embassy parking lot as a helicopter landing zone.

On April 28, 1975, three former South Vietnamese pilots who had defected to the Communist People's Air Force dropped bombs on Son Nhut Airbase runways. The next day, the North began a final offensive against Saigon, with sixteen divisions pushing a wave of thousands of hopeful refugees toward the American embassy. Ambassador Martin planned to evacuate the Americans and loyal Vietnamese by fixed-wing aircraft from the Tan Son Nhut Airbase. But a new plan had to be developed when bomb craters and rocket fire from the advancing Vietcong made the runways unfit.

President Ford contacted me as secretary of the Navy to devise a new plan to evacuate Americans and loyal Vietnamese. All planning had to be conducted with the utmost discretion since Ambassador Martin was against any outward signs that the United States intended to abandon South Vietnam. Meeting in the Situation Room at the Pentagon, Admiral James Holloway, CNO, devised a helicopter evacuation of U.S. personnel and at-risk Vietnamese called "Operation Frequent Wind." Under this plan, CH-53 and CH-46 helicopters would be used to evacuate Americans and friendly Vietnamese to ships, including the Seventh Fleet in the South China Sea.

Operation Frequent Wind aimed to evacuate about 8,000 U.S. citizens and Vietnamese loyal to the United States and third-country nationals. The two major evacuation points chosen for Operation Frequent Wind were the DAOI Compound next to Tan Son Nhut Airport for American and Vietnamese civilian evacuees and the United States embassy, Saigon, for embassy staff. The resignation of South Vietnamese President Xuan Loc on April 21, 1975, brought more incredible crowds seeking evacuation to the DAO Compound as it became apparent that South Vietnam's days were numbered. With the fall of Saigon imminent, the U.S. Navy assembled ships off Tau under Commander Task Force 76.

On April 29, 1975, Major General Homer Smith, the U.S. defense attaché in Saigon, advised Ambassador Martin that fixed-wing evacuations should cease, and that Operation Frequent Wind should commence. Ambassador Martin initially refused to accept General Smith's recommendation and insisted on visiting Tan Son Nhut to survey the situation. Martin finally gave the green light for the helicopter evacuation to begin on April 30. In preparation for the evacuation, the American Embassy distributed a 15-page instruction booklet, including a map of Saigon pinpointing assembly areas for evacuation. It specified that the evacuation order would be read on Armed Forces Radio with the following code: "The temperature in Saigon is 105 degrees and rising. This will be followed by the playing of 'I'm dreaming of a White Christmas.'"

Americans were told to get to the evacuation centers as soon as possible after "White Christmas" was played on the radio, but it was too late. Thousands of panicked South Vietnamese jammed the streets to flee further south. Others clogged foreign embassies pleading for last-minute visas. Buses and cars carrying Americans or at-risk Vietnamese were mobbed as they were stuck in traffic. The weather presented the gravest danger. At the beginning of the operation, pilots in the first wave reported haze over Saigon with limited visibility. The weather conditions deteriorated as the process continued. The helicopters took evacuees out to sea, where American warships were waiting. Sea Cobra Helicopter gunships were escorting those choppers in case the North Vietnamese tried to shoot them down. They need not have bothered—the North Vietnamese wanted them gone. USS *Enterprise* and Coral Sea's air wings were ready to provide close air support and anti-aircraft suppression with their A-6 and A-7 attack aircraft. USAF aircraft operating out of Nakhon Phanom Air Base, Korat Air Base, and U-Tapao Air Base in Thailand were also overhead for the duration of the helicopter evacuation.

The original evacuation plans had not called for a large-scale helicopter operation at the U.S. embassy in Saigon. Buses were to shuttle people from the embassy to the airport, where helicopters would meet them. During the evacuation, a few thousand people, including many Vietnamese, were stranded at the embassy. Additional Vietnamese civilians gathered outside the embassy and scaled the walls, hoping to claim refugee status. One of the most iconic images from the fall of Saigon did not happen in Saigon. It happened at sea, where sailors pushed helicopters off their ships. As more helicopters arrived, the decks on all the ships became full. There was only one solution: dump choppers overboard. For the next 18 hours, 81 overloaded and crammed helicopters piloted by exhausted men ferried people out to the ships. Several US-1 Hueys, worth $10 million each, and at least one other CH-47 ended up in watery graves.

Admiral James Holloway was in control throughout the operation. He took charge, trying to gauge results and assess remaining needs. "How many are left at the embassy? How many more lifts?" It was clear to me why this man had been chosen to be CNO; with calm authority, he called for a final nineteen sorties, and that was that. Holloway was the father of four-star admiral and Chief of Naval Operations Admiral James L. Holloway III. As of 2019, they are the only father and son to serve as four-star admirals in the U.S. Navy while on active duty instead of being promoted to that rank posthumously or at retirement.

Marine pilots accumulated 1,054 flight hours and 682 sorties throughout Operation Frequent Wind. The evacuation of personnel from the DAO compound lasted nine hours and involved over 50 Marine Corps and Air Force helicopters. In the helicopter evacuation, 395 Americans and 4,475 Vietnamese and third-country nationals were evacuated from the DAO compound. An additional 978 United States and 1,120 Vietnamese and third-country citizens were evacuated from the embassy, totaling 1,373 Americans and 5,595 Vietnamese and third-country citizens. President Ford later called it "a sad and tragic period in America's history" but argued that "you couldn't help but be very proud of those pilots and others conducting the evacuation."

On April 30, 1975, President Ford ordered Ambassador Martin to evacuate only Americans from that point forward. Reluctantly, Martin announced that only Americans would be flown out due to worries that the North Vietnamese would soon take the city. President Ford ordered Ambassador Martin to board the evacuation helicopter. The helicopter's call sign was "Lady Ace 09," and the pilot carried direct orders from President Ford for Ambassador Martin to be on board. Ambassador Martin's wife, Dorothy, had already been evacuated by a previous flight and left behind her suitcase so a South Vietnamese woman could squeeze on board with her.

The Marines who had been securing the embassy followed at dawn, with the last aircraft leaving at 07:53. More than 420 Vietnamese were left behind in the embassy compound, with an additional crowd gathered outside the walls. The Americans and the refugees they flew out were generally allowed to leave without intervention from the North Vietnamese. Helicopter pilots knew North Vietnamese anti-aircraft guns were tracking them, but they refrained from firing. The Hanoi leadership, reckoning that completion of the evacuation would reduce the risk of American intervention, had instructed its army not to target the airlift itself. Meanwhile, members of the police in Saigon had been promised evacuation in exchange for protecting the American evacuation buses and controlling the city crowds during the evacuation.

Although this was the end of the American military operation, the Vietnamese continued to leave the country by boat and, where possible, by aircraft. South Vietnamese RVNAF pilots who had access to helicopters flew them offshore to the American fleet, where they could land. One enterprising South Vietnamese helicopter pilot, Major Nguyen, stole a CH-47 Chinook helicopter from his base. He flew to his neighborhood and ordered his family and neighbors to enter. He flew toward the South China Sea, where he spotted the USS *Kirk* and tried to land on it. The crew on deck waved him away. His chopper was too big, and if he tried to land, the rotors would destroy the upper deck and hurt or kill people. He hovered over the ship as the crew caught the passengers individually. Then he flew out to sea, jumped out of his chopper, and was rescued by a passing ship.

Ambassador Martin—carrying the embassy flag—and his Marine guard were the last to leave. He was flown out to the USS *Blue Ridge*, where he pleaded for helicopters to return to the embassy compound to pick up the few hundred remaining hopefuls waiting to be evacuated. Although President Ford overruled his pleas, Martin convinced the Seventh Fleet to stay on station for several days so any locals who could make their way to the sea via boat or aircraft to be rescued by the waiting Americans.

In the early hours of April 30, General Dũng received orders from the Politburo to attack. He then ordered his field commanders to advance directly to the city's key facilities and strategic points. At 11:30 a.m., North Vietnamese tanks smashed through the gates of the Presidential Palace less than 1 km from the embassy and raised the flag of the Viet Cong over the building. The Vietnam War was over. Later that day, President Minh announced unconditional surrender. He ordered all ARVN troops "to cease hostilities and to stay where they are" while inviting the Provisional Revolutionary Government to engage in "a ceremony of orderly transfer of power to avoid any unnecessary bloodshed in the population."

Many evacuated Vietnamese nationals were allowed to enter the United States under the Indochina Migration and Refugee Assistance Act. Decades later, when the United States government reestablished diplomatic relations with Vietnam, the former embassy building was returned to the United States. The historic staircase that led to the rooftop helicopter pad in the nearby apartment building used by the CIA and other U.S. government employees was salvaged and is on permanent display at the Gerald R. Ford Museum in Grand Rapids, Michigan. For an operation as large and complex as Frequent Wind, causalities were relatively light. Marine corporals McMahon and Judge, killed at the DAO compound, were the only members of U.S. forces killed in action during the operation. They were the last U.S. ground casualties in Vietnam. Captain William C. Nustul and First Lieutenant Michael J. Shea were killed when their helicopter crashed into the sea after a night-sea and air rescue mission.

While the news focused on the helicopter lift, the South Vietnamese Navy took bold corrective action: they loaded their ships with families and supplies. They set sail en masse for the Philippines and a very uncertain future. There was at least one thing our Navy could do to help those men with whom we had worked for so many years: establish a program whereby these families would be welcomed in the United States under a voluntary "sponsorship" program. The sponsors would provide a temporary home and a guarantee that the Vietnamese families would not become burdens upon the taxpayer.

There were legal issues to be resolved, of course. Still, we first had to establish a framework, a method for soliciting American volunteer families and then matching them with Vietnamese families. This great humanitarian effort, the brainchild of one of my special assistants, Captain Brayton Harris began the day that Saigon fell. Within two days, Harris had arranged seed-money funding through a Navy office created to provide in-country humanitarian assistance. Within a week, we had an ongoing task force headed by naval reserve Captain Charles Treischmann, who volunteered for a six-month temporary-duty assignment. When the Department of Defense learned of our effort—call it Johnny-come-lately—they stepped in with a program encompassing all the services. Our first "volunteer host" was retired Admiral Zumwalt, whose basement became the temporary home of a Vietnamese Navy family of five. Ed Feulner, president of the Heritage Foundation, and his wife Linda sponsored a Vietnamese family, allowing them to leave a refugee camp and come to the United States.

We had ignominiously lost a war, and our Vietnamese allies had lost a country. While Operation Frequent Wind was a success, the evacuation images symbolized the wastefulness and ultimate futility of American involvement in Vietnam. Hanoi decided to reorder South Vietnamese society in two ways. First, there was to be massive re-education of those who had been actively involved with the Thieu regime, whether civilian or military. Second, Hanoi planned to establish New Economic Zones (NEZ), which would eventually reclaim 2.5 million acres of jungle.

In October 1975, Hanoi announced that approximately 1.5 million of Saigon's four million residents would be moved to the New Economic Zones. A sign that the reconstruction of South Vietnam was going to be less than pleasant came on October 22, 1975, when the Hanoi government expelled all but four non-Communist foreign reporters. A Saigon official announced in Moscow that private enterprise would be permitted after the reunification of North and South Vietnam. In April, elections for the National

Assembly took place, and Hanoi became the official capital of Vietnam. Earlier, Saigon had been renamed Ho Chi Minh City. The North Vietnamese flag anthem, emblem, and capital were to be used by the new Socialist Republic of Vietnam.

On December 14, 1976, the Vietnamese Communist Party (Lao Dong) held its first Congress since 1960. More than 30 Communist parties from around the world sent representatives. Behind all this glitter lay some harsh realities. The general secretary of the Communist Party, Le Duan, had said in June 1976 that the Party and the people would build the material and technical base for socialism and would gradually improve the living standards of the working people.

The realities of Vietnamese life were difficult. Eighty-five percent of the population was engaged in producing, processing, and distributing food. North Vietnam had consistently failed to supply its food needs during the war and hoped the South would solve this problem. Unfortunately, there were problems in the South. Somewhere between 40,000 and 200,000, southerners were being held in re-education camps during that year. There were already 200,000 North Vietnamese soldiers in the South, and an estimated 500,000 Northerners were sent south to administer the society.

In March 1977, Prime Minister Pham Van Dong met in Paris with the U.S. assistant secretary of State for Asian and Pacific affairs, Richard Holbrooke. This was the beginning of negotiations intended to normalize relations. Despite some setbacks by December 1978, Holbrooke stated that politically and strategically, the U.S. position in Asia was "stronger than it has been at any time since World War II." The United States did not oppose Vietnam's application for U.N. membership in July 1977 as it had in 1976. On September 20, 1977, Vietnam was admitted to the United Nations, with the United States abstaining. In a speech to the General Assembly on September 21, Vietnam's delegate stated that Vietnam was ready to normalize relations with the United States.

It's been almost half a century since the end of the Vietnam War, and the relationship between the United States and Vietnam, particularly in trade and investment, has steadily improved since the normalization of relations in 1995. Bilateral trade between the two countries reached $90 billion in 2020, an increase of 17 percent from the previous year. The United States is Vietnam's second-largest trading partner, while Vietnam is the United States' 10th-largest. And unlike the E.U.–China partnership agreement—consideration of which has been "frozen" by the E.U. Parliament—the U.S.–Vietnam relationship is built on something much stronger—an understanding of the principles of economic freedom. Vietnam has shown steady growth in economic output and freedom in its transition to a more free-market economic system. Despite projections of an economic downturn because of the coronavirus pandemic, Vietnam actually was the highest-performing Asian economy in 2020, outpacing China with an estimated growth rate of 2.9 percent. Much of this growth is credited to Vietnam's booming manufacturing industry and the high international demand for exported Vietnamese goods. At the same time, Vietnam has been continuing to open its economy up to international trade and participating in bilateral and multilateral agreements with the rest of the world.

In 2019 Vietnam joined the Comprehensive and Progressive Agreement for Trans-Pacific Partnership, a free trade agreement among 11 countries in Asia, the Pacific, and North America. It signed its own bilateral trade agreement with the European Union. And in 2020, Vietnam became a founding member of the Regional Comprehensive Economic Partnership, a massive trade agreement joining together the 10 Association of Southeast Asian Nations countries, along with Australia, China, India, Japan, New Zealand, and South Korea, into the world's largest trading bloc. It encompasses over a quarter of the world's gross domestic product and half of the world's population.

These recent actions have been noticed and recognized in Vietnam's steady improvements in its ranking in the Heritage Foundation's Index of Economic Freedom. In the 2024 index, Vietnam jumped 15 places to become the 90th-freest economy in the world out of 178 countries ranked, and the 17th-freest in the Asia-Pacific. However, the country is still only considered moderately free due to lingering institutional weaknesses, such as persistent corruption and the lack of judicial independence, holding back its economic freedom. Still, Vietnam's efforts toward achieving more economic liberalization are commendable, especially given the current trajectory of similarly positioned countries in the region. The country's ongoing reforms in key pillars of economic freedom have led to measurable progress in ensuring private property rights and market openness.

In the 27 years of the index's publication, Vietnam has seen greater improvements in its score than other nations, such as Russia or China, especially in the categories of investment and financial freedom. As Vietnam continues embracing more free-market principles, it should be regarded as the United States' increasingly important strategic economic partner.

I was invited to Vietnam years after the country became Communist. Following some economic consultations, I left for the airport. I asked the driver to stop at the famous Hanoi Hilton prison camp, where American prisoners were imprisoned during the war. There had been rumors over the years that American prisoners were still being held there. I entered through an open gate and went down a long line of empty cell doors until I located the one where Senator John McCain had spent several years. The cell was empty, but it was in miserable condition and rat-infested. I had just finished taking a few pictures when two armed guards arrived and pointed their machine guns at me. After a nervous encounter, I was allowed to proceed to the airport. A few weeks later, I gave the photos to John. He stared at them quietly, then thanked me. I doubt that the image brought back many happy memories for John.

9 | How 9/11 Could Have Been Prevented

ON SEPTEMBER 11, 2001, 1,977 Americans were killed and 6,000 injured in the worst attack ever perpetrated on American soil. In the September 11 attacks, the hijackers were 19 men affiliated with the militant Islamist group al-Qaeda. They hailed from four countries; 15 of them were Saudi Arabian citizens, two were from the United Arab Emirates, one was from Lebanon, and one was from Egypt.

American victims' families demanded an investigation into what, how, and why it happened—where there had been failures and what lessons could be learned to prevent a repeat. In 2002, President George W. Bush appointed Thomas Kean, a former Republican governor of New Jersey, and Lee Hamilton, a former Democratic congressman from Indiana, to head an investigation.

The commission made 41 recommendations on homeland security, emergency response, congressional reform, and foreign policy. For Kean, perhaps the most important one mandated intelligence sharing to prevent further terrorist attacks—the most significant intelligence reform in U.S. history.

Kean explained: "If the FBI and the CIA and 14 other intelligence agencies had been talking to each other, most of us feel that the attack could have been prevented. We reorganized the whole intelligence apparatus, so instead of several agencies, there's now one head—the director of national intelligence—and then people from the various agencies meet together and share information."

Kean's comment reminded me of a temporary post I had 22 years earlier as the interim head of the CIA Transition Team. As the 1980 election campaign gained momentum, I provided policy assistance to Governor Reagan as chairman of the International Economic Advisory Committee and the Naval Advisory Committee. I also chaired the Finance Committee for the inauguration. Soon after the election, Reagan offered me a new but temporary challenge: to head the CIA Transition Team. This is one of those invisible tools of our government, where an incoming administration sends representatives to meet with the leadership and examine the current policies of federal programs and agencies and recommend changes in policy or operation.

My deputy on the transition team was Angelo Codevilla, an Italian immigrant best known for his work on the Reagan Administration's Strategic Defense Initiative. Like many immigrants, Codevilla felt a deep and enduring love for this country, which he expressed in a distinguished career and memorable writings. He authored 14 books that spanned an immense range of subjects, and many have become classics. He was killed on September 20, 2021, in a tragic automobile accident in California.

As we began our review, both Codevilla and I were troubled by worrisome signs that the nation's espionage machinery was becoming rusty and needed serious updating. One of the first problems we detected was the lack of information sharing between the CIA and the FBI. Years later, we learned the CIA had all the terrorists involved in 9/11 on a "watch" list but failed to share it with the FBI. Twenty-two years before 9/11, we urged that steps be taken immediately to ensure information sharing between the CIA and the FBI.

Many of our recommendations grew from work undertaken earlier by the Heritage Foundation, and most of our proposals had been debated for some time within the intelligence community. CIA director-designate Bill Casey (a friend of mine from Wall Street days) was on our side, which should have given our recommendations some status. However, even the hard-nosed Casey had a hard time penetrating the circled wagons of the CIA bureaucracy. Some of our recommendations for information sharing, consolidation, and cooperation were finally enacted (although we got no credit) some twenty-two years later with the creation of the National Intelligence Agency. However, the CIA rejected most of our recommendations, including policy changes that would have encouraged information sharing between the CIA and FBI and might have prevented 9/11.

This was, to my knowledge, the first time that a transition team had been assigned to the CIA. Admiral Stansfield Turner was Carter's man at the CIA. I knew Turner—he had most recently been serving as president of the Naval War College, where he had done an outstanding job. As for the changes at CIA, I don't know which may have been at his initiative or could be attributed to President Carter, but I felt that Carter was of the old Cordell Hull school, that "gentlemen don't read other people's mail."

The work of a transition team is "generally invisible" except, of course, when some insider—on one side or another—leaks information to the media. In our case, I believe the leaker to have been someone within the CIA who did not like the recommendations we were about to issue. The story played in *The New York Times* on December 8, 1980: "Reagan Urged to Reorganize U.S. Intelligence."

The "Middendorf-headed Team," *The Times* noted, "was about to recommend several sweeping changes in the organization and operations of the nation's intelligence programs." We were, indeed, about to issue a call for a return to an emphasis on covert action abroad and greater attention to counterintelligence at home. An article in *The New York Times* alluded to some tension between the Reagan advisers and the CIA, according to a spokesman for the CIA. It described meetings between transition team members and Admiral Stansfield Turner, director of Central Intelligence, as amicable sessions. But Reagan advisers called the encounters 'hostile and acrimonious.'"

The truth? It depends on which session (or "encounter") is being considered. My meetings with Turner, indeed, were amicable. The discussions between some working members of the team and some agency personnel were not friendly. For one thing, the CIA regarded itself as a professional, not political, and some in the Agency resented the imposition of a transition team. For another, perhaps more to the point, some of our recommendations may have questioned the Agency's traditional dominance in intelligence affairs.

We suggested a competitive intelligence analysis system: the CIA might have to defend its conclusions on any given issue against those offered by agencies such as the Defense Intelligence Agency or the FBI. We saw a path toward broader debate; some in the CIA saw this as a threat. We recommended creating a central records system that could be used by both the CIA, FBI, and domestic law enforcement agencies. We wanted to counter a growing threat of international terrorism. Our critics in the CIA saw this as a threat to civil liberties.

The CIA and FBI both have very different roles in combatting terrorism. As members of the U.S. Intelligence Community, they are assigned different geographical locations of the world and different tasks. The CIA's role in counterterrorism is to collect information on foreign countries and individuals that might threaten the security of the United States. The FBI, on the other hand, has law enforcement authority that can act to prevent domestic and international terrorism.

Evidence supports the theory that the perpetrators of 9/11 should have been barred from entering the country or arrested shortly after they arrived. Once an investigation started, it became clear that the hijackers' names were familiar to the U.S. intelligence community.

The United States has had 22 years to learn from the tragedy of 9/11 and strengthen U.S. defenses against another major terrorist attack. We need to remain vigilant and aggressive to counter such attacks.

The loss, sacrifice, and ways people rose to the occasion in the 9/11 crisis should never be forgotten. But we also need to heed the warnings of that attack and renew our resolve to ensure such a tragedy never happens again. Last year, Kabul fell to the Taliban following our precipitous withdrawal from Afghanistan, which unleashed chaos and violence as the U.S. scrambled to get out. One can only imagine how veterans who served in Afghanistan felt watching the chaos of that retreat and the country's collapse last year, which undid years of effort to prevent Afghanistan from becoming a terrorist safe haven once again.

That chaos has led to a much more dangerous situation in Afghanistan than existed even before 9/11, with the United States at more risk from terrorist organizations like al-Qaeda. Terrorists now have a safe haven to operate in Afghanistan again, just like they did before the attacks on 9/11, and we are in a poor position to conduct counterterrorism operations against them. "Over the horizon" capabilities, relying on space and air reconnaissance to conduct targeted strikes of terrorist targets with drone strikes, are insufficient to keep the threat at bay.

Without the large footprint of people in the country to act as the eyes and ears for strikes, the intelligence collection that relies on air and space assets is challenging, as the target can move before the strike is executed. Those operations are often constrained by airspace access.

On August 22, 2022, Ayman al-Zawahri, one of the chief architects of the 9/11 attacks, was killed by a U.S. drone strike in Kabul. That would seem to suggest this capability is effective since such a prominent terrorist was successfully targeted using the over-the-horizon strategy. Unfortunately, one terrorist killed does not an effective counterterrorism strategy make. The main issue is the support those groups receive from the Taliban, which will give them a solid base to plan terrorist acts against the West and make targeting the networks much more complicated. Since the Taliban took over Afghanistan, it has gained control of a large amount of territory, equipment, and funds. It is now more powerful and controls more of Afghanistan than it did in 2001. While its rule will be somewhat different from what the world saw in 2001, it's clear the Taliban still has ties to various terrorist groups bent on attacking the United States and its allies.

The terrorist threat to the United States will only grow with the Taliban rule of Afghanistan. When this terrorist threat is added to the numerous other threats we face from emboldened adversaries, such as Russia and Iran, and the growing military threat from China, we cannot afford to show weakness or let our resolve waver. To keep Americans safe in a dangerous world, we need to find our backbone and be ready to meet these challenges with the vigor they require. In summary, 9/11 will always be a time of somber remembrance for all the lives lost and people affected by the terrorist attacks, but Americans cannot forget how the attacks happened and the cost of complacency in the face of threats.

We should look back and reflect how Americans came together after 9/11 as an example for us today. Immediately following the terrorist attacks, there was a mighty surge in military enlistments by teens and young adults so often dismissed as spoiled and self-absorbed. Thousands of Americans lined up to give blood. Millions of dollars were donated to the American Red Cross, the Salvation Army and other welfare organizations. Attendance at churches, synagogues, and mosques doubled. Among the messages from religious leaders, the words of Pope John Paul II stand out: "Even if the forces of darkness appear to prevail, those who believe in God know that evil and death do not have the final word."

Examples of patriotism and sacrifice were everywhere. There was the quiet eloquence of an office worker explaining why he risked his life to help someone buried in the rubble at Ground Zero in lower Manhattan. A New York City fire chief choked back tears as he spoke of a priest friend who disappeared in a cloud of dust while searching for people to comfort. There were the passengers on United Airlines 93 who decided to "do something" to stop the terrorists who had seized their plane. Their heroism prevented the hijackers from plunging the jet airliner into the U.S. Capitol.

Americans did not crack and come apart. They stood strong on a foundation the Founding Fathers built two-and-a-half centuries ago—a unique mix of political and economic liberty. President Ronald Reagan declared that what united us far outweighed what divided us. Speaking beneath the Statue of Liberty in New York City Harbor, the president reaffirmed that we are one nation under God. Black and white, he said, we are one nation indivisible. Republican and Democrat, we are all Americans.

"Whatever the trial and travail," Reagan said, "let us pledge ourselves to each other and to the cause of human freedom—the cause that has given light to this land and hope to the world." Is such brotherhood possible today? It is—if we draw on the wisdom and the resolve of the past. If we abandon the rigid mindset of red and blue, black and white, rich and poor. If we reaffirm our commitment to a united America.

The lessons we draw from the Afghan War matter—to our allies, to our adversaries, and most of all to the rising generation that needs reassurance that America's best days are not behind her but yet to come. We should remember that we won the initial stage of the Afghan War but lost the peace because of the withdrawal of just a small U.S. force and air support. It is understandable, given the chaos surrounding the United States' exit from Afghanistan—especially the murder of the 13 U.S. troops—that our attention has been focused on the ending of America's longest war. The statistics are sobering. Length of the war: 20 years. Total number of U.S. fatalities: 2,461. U.S. wounded: more than 20,000. Afghan fatalities: more than 70,000. Cost of the war: $2.3 trillion. Major goal achieved: The Taliban was removed in late 2001 as the head of the Afghan government, denying a base of operations to al-Qaeda, the terrorist group responsible for the 9/11 attacks in New York City and Washington, D.C. Since 9/11, there have been no similar attacks by Islamist radicals in the United States that were planned or executed from Afghanistan.

Goal not achieved: The conversion of Afghanistan from independent tribes into a nation-state able to manage its own internal and external security without interference by outside powers. After 20 years of fighting, the Taliban returned to Kabul and control, for the time being, of this divided country.

Despite the remarkable airlift of an estimated 130,000 Americans, allies, and Afghan friends, there are between 200 and 1,000 U.S. citizens remaining in the country who want to get out and cannot. There are critical lessons to be learned from the Afghan War. "Protecting American territory, sea lanes, and air space. Preventing a major power from controlling Europe, East Asia, or the Persian Gulf. Ensuring U.S. access to world resources. Expanding free trade throughout the world. Protecting Americans against threats to their lives and well-being."

It is the last condition that justified the Afghan War—which, in fact, we won in a matter of months and with the loss of a handful of soldiers. We must accept that we live in a dangerous, violent world that requires us to maintain a strong national defense to defend our vital interests. We should remember that we won the initial stage of the Afghan War but lost the peace because of the withdrawal of just a small U.S. force and air support. This force was enough to keep the Taliban from seizing and holding a single provincial capital for almost 20 years.

Peace through Strength

In 1978, as I was leaving my post as secretary of the Navy, Lt. General Daniel Graham invited me to join him in forming a new organization called "Peace through Strength." He had served in Germany, Korea and Vietnam and received some of the highest decorations the military bestows. General Graham and I believed that weaknesses invited war and that if casualties were on both sides, no war was ever indeed won. A victorious war, therefore, was the one that was never fought.

During my entire career as secretary of the Navy, I had concentrated on building long-term weapon systems that would be ready when the Soviet Union reached its apogee in the mid-1980s. These weapons included the Ohio Class Trident missile submarines, which carried 80 percent of our nuclear arsenal. We also developed 80 Arleigh Burke–class destroyers, the backbone of our surface Navy, the F-18 advance fighter aircraft, and CH-53 heavy lift helicopters for the Marine Corps. The other services also developed advanced weapon systems, and "Peace through Strength" led to the ultimate collapse of the Soviet Union.

"Peace through Strength" is a phrase that suggests that military power can help preserve peace. It has been used by many leaders, from Roman Emperor Hadrian in the second century A.D. to former U.S. President Ronald Reagan in the 1980s. Hadrian is said to have sought "peace through strength or, failing that, peace through threat" as a symbol of the policy.

The first U.S. president, George Washington, enunciated a policy of peace through strength in his fifth annual message to Congress, the 1793 State of the Union Address. He said:

> There is a rank due to the United States among nations which will be withheld, if not absolutely lost, by the reputation of weakness. If we desire to avoid insult, we must be able to repel it; if we desire to secure peace, one of the most powerful instruments of our rising prosperity, it must be known that we are always ready for war.

In 1980, Ronald Reagan used the phrase during his election challenge against Jimmy Carter by accusing the incumbent of weak, vacillating leadership that invited enemies to attack the United States and its allies. Reagan later considered it one of the mainstays of his foreign policy as president. In 1986, he explained it thus:

> We know peace is the condition under which mankind was meant to flourish. Yet peace does not exist of its own will. It depends on us, our courage, to build it, guard it, and pass it on to future generations. George Washington's words may seem hard and cold today, but history has proven him right again and again. "To be prepared for war," he said, "is one of the most effective means of preserving peace."

The approach has been credited for forcing the Soviet Union to lose the arms race and end the first Cold War. "Peace through Strength" is the official motto of the Nimitz-class nuclear-powered aircraft carrier, USS *Ronald Reagan*.

On assuming office in January 2017, Donald Trump cited the idea of "Peace through Strength" as central to his overall "America First" foreign policy. As such, the introduction to the U.S. National Defense Strategy of 2018 states: The U.S. force posture combined with the allies will "preserve peace through strength."

Appeasement Is Never the Answer

When Russia invaded Georgia in 2008, annexed Ukraine's Crimea Peninsula in 2014, shot down a Malaysian Airliner in 2014, and interfered in a U.S. presidential election in 2016, the rest of the world did nothing. When Putin launched a full-scale invasion of Ukraine in February 2022, it looked like the strategy of non-confrontation would continue. Western leaders imposed only modest sanctions and did not send any troops to Ukraine. Western leaders decided that trying to save Ukraine was not worth the risk of a military confrontation with Russia.

Ukraine initially looked like another lost cause. Its military was far smaller and less well armed than Russia's, and Western experts predicted a quick Russian victory. Ukraine has surprised the world, demonstrating a patriotism that belied Putin's claim that it was not a real country. Its military stopped Russia's army from achieving a quick victory. The early success changed Western thinking in positive ways. The United States and the European Union have recently shown a new assertiveness toward Russia.

NATO is helping to coordinate Ukraine's requests for assistance and is supporting Allies in delivering weapons, ammunition, and other vital military equipment to Ukraine, including cyber security and protection against chemical, biological, radiological, and nuclear warfare threats. They are also imposing harsh economic sanctions on Russia. Many Allies also provide humanitarian aid to civilians and host millions of Ukrainian refugees. Allies are also supporting efforts for an international investigation of atrocities by providing legal expertise to Ukraine.

U.S. strategic information helped Ukraine's military kill Russian generals on the battlefield and sink the *Moskva*, a warship that was the flagship of Russia's Black Sea Fleet. After logistical and military failures dashed Moscow's plans to seize the Ukrainian capital, Russia shifted its focus eastward. The United States began to send long-range artillery suited for open-terrain battles. The Howitzers supplied by the United States are heavy cannons that fire artillery rounds as far as 24 miles.

Russia's invasion of Ukraine has forever changed Europe. It rekindled dormant discussions over security architecture and lent renewed importance to alliances. Finland has experienced a remarkable pivot in its security policy since the invasion—decades of stable public opinion had never exceeded 30 percent approval for NATO membership but has now doubled to 62 percent. Sweden and Finland are also expected to join NATO, abandoning a decades-long belief that peace was best kept by not publicly choosing sides.

Appeasement is never the answer to aggression. "Peace through strength" is the only response to people like Hitler and Putin. Russia is the aggressor, and Ukraine is the victim. A sovereign Ukraine is necessary for overall European stability, which is in U.S. and NATO interests. Modern Ukraine represents the idea that every country has the sovereign ability to determine its own path, to decide with whom it has relations, as well as how and by whom it is governed. In many ways, the long-term stability of the transatlantic community will be decided in Ukraine. The United States must act accordingly.

Thinking Long Term, Acting Now

It should be the priority of the United States to ensure that Russia pays a high price for its invasion of Ukraine. For Americans who believe in strong and secure national borders, the importance of national sovereignty, and the right to self-defense, support for Ukraine in the face of Russian aggression is natural. Now that Ukrainians have some success on the battlefield, it is time to double down on supporting them. To do so, the United States should:

- Ensure the unrestricted transfer of weapons, munitions, and other supplies to the Ukrainians, including a continuous flow of intelligence. Their need for weapons and munitions will only increase as the war drags on. The United States must lead efforts to develop a resilient and reliable system to deliver much-needed weapons and munitions on an enduring basis.

- Work with the Ukrainian government to allow American experts access to captured Russian equipment. Ukrainian forces have captured some of Russia's most advanced electronic warfare equipment, air defense systems, and Main Battle Tanks. The sooner that U.S. experts can analyze this equipment, the faster it might be able to help NATO allies and Ukraine to develop tactics, techniques, and procedures to counter and defeat Russian equipment.

- Lead efforts in Europe to create a clearinghouse for Ukrainian military needs. Many NATO members in Eastern Europe operate military equipment similar to Ukraine's. NATO should serve as a clearinghouse to match Ukraine's military needs with equipment that NATO members might be willing to share. This is especially true of spare parts and specialized equipment required for maintenance.

- Work behind the scenes, not in the public space, on difficult or controversial options for helping Ukraine. Such a complex issue of transferring fighter jets from one country to another should have never been played out in the public space. The same can be said of the proposal to transfer Slovakian S-300 missiles and systems to Ukraine. U.S. policymakers must work behind the scenes on complex issues and not give up until there is a satisfactory outcome.

- Expand the scope and reach of U.S. economic sanctions against Russia to maximum levels. The situation is desperate in Ukraine. This is not the time to keep more sanctions in "the back pocket." The existing unprecedented economic sanctions should be expanded to sanction in their entirety, and without any exemptions, all of Russia's major banks and energy sector.

- Replicate these sanctions for Belarus and any country helping Moscow to evade them. In this conflict, Belarus has served as an enabler, if not a belligerent actor. Without Belarus's support, Russia would not have been able to pressure Kyiv so quickly in the invasion. Belarus or any other country that offers support for Russia's aggression or succor for economic sanctions should feel the full force of U.S. sanctions.

- Seize frozen Russian assets to arm and support Ukraine. Since economic sanctions have been implemented, tens of billions of dollars of Russian assets have been frozen in G7 and other allied and partner countries. The United States should seize these assets and use them for training, funding, and equipping the Ukrainian military, alleviate the humanitarian crisis, and in the future, rebuild Ukraine.

- Work with NATO members to establish training facilities in Poland or other NATO countries to train Ukrainian troops in operating advanced Western military hardware. The United States should prepare now to train and equip the Ukrainians for the long term. The excuse often used for why more advanced military hardware cannot be given to Ukraine is that the Ukrainians do not know how to use it. The war in Ukraine is likely to be protracted. This means identifying military equipment that could help Ukraine to defend itself and then establishing a training and equipping program for Ukraine for the long term.

- Keep the Chinese–Russian connection in mind. Russia is China's junior, albeit important, partner on the global stage. As U.S. policymakers formulate America's strategy toward China, they must remember that anything that can weaken Russia on the global stage will impact China. It is in America's interest that Russia fails in Ukraine.

- Take advantage of Russia's geopolitical disequilibrium. Russia is almost solely consumed by events in Ukraine and the impact of economic sanctions. This is an opportunity for the United States to build its bilateral relations with important countries like Azerbaijan and Kazakhstan. Both countries are crying out for more Western engagement. Both are crucially important for helping Europe diversify its energy imports away from Russia. Both see Russian weakness in Ukraine and have recently taken a tougher line against the Kremlin in a way that would have been unimaginable before Russia invaded Ukraine. While the Kremlin considers Azerbaijan and Kazakhstan to be in their "sphere of influence," both want to pursue a balanced relationship with all major global powers. U.S. policymakers should not waste this geopolitical opportunity.

- Start planning a new approach to energy security now. If Europeans get every barrel of oil and cubic foot of natural gas from somewhere other than Russia, the safer the continent will be. While the immediate priority for the White House is arming Ukrainians and crippling the Russian economy, it should start developing an energy strategy for Europe. Good starting points would be (1) maximizing U.S. liquefied-natural-gas exports to Europe; (2) supporting an expanded Southern Gas Corridor connecting Caspian gas to southern Europe; (3) encouraging the construction of a Trans-Caspian Pipeline to bring natural gas from Central Asia to Europe bypassing Russia; (4) exploring energy possibilities in the Eastern Mediterranean region; and (5) bolstering the Three Seas Initiative to improve energy connectivity in Eastern Europe.

10 | Spies Among Us

THERE WERE WORRISOME SIGNS that the nation's espionage machinery was becoming rusty when I headed a transition team for the CIA in 1980. The CIA was shifting from an emphasis on human intelligence to the use of technological methods such as satellite imagery. My deputy on the transition team, Angelo Codevilla, and I were worried about leaks in the CIA. At the time, the Soviet Union was rounding up and executing our spies behind the Iron Curtain with alarming regularity. We recommended a policy calling for tighter security checks on CIA employees. I was not trying to impugn anyone's loyalty and patriotism, but you cannot get a top job in the Navy Department—maybe almost any job—without the FBI crawling all over your past and present. The CIA assured us that we need not worry, because everyone was polygraphed on a regular basis. We learned that the testing was done by in-house employees, which meant that friends were testing friends. Our strong recommendation that polygraph testing be outsourced was ignored.

The CIA also released anonymous attacks through *The Washington Post* on our attempts to strengthen security checks. I was blasted in *The Washington Post* for suggesting Big Brother should spy on the spies! Had we done so, we would have caught some of the more notorious Soviet spies in our midst, especially Aldrich Ames—the head of the Soviet branch of the CIA's counterintelligence group. His betrayal was said to have cost the lives of dozens of our agents in the Soviet Union alone. Ames was a CIA case officer who spoke Russian and specialized in Russian intelligence services, including the KGB, the Soviet Union's foreign intelligence service.

His initial overseas assignment was in Ankara, Turkey, where he targeted Russian intelligence officers for recruitment. Later, he worked in New York City and Mexico City, Mexico. On April 16, 1985, while assigned to the CIA's Soviet/ East European Division at CIA Headquarters in Langley, Virginia, he secretly volunteered with KGB officers at the Soviet embassy in Washington, D.C. Shortly after that, the KGB paid him $50,000. During the summer of 1985, Ames met several times with a Russian diplomat to whom he passed classified information about CIA and FBI human sources and technical operations targeting the Soviet Union.

In December 1985, Ames met with a Moscow-based KGB officer in Bogota, Colombia. In July 1986, Ames was transferred to Rome, Italy. He continued his meetings with the KGB in Rome, including a Russian diplomat assigned in Rome and a Moscow-based KGB officer. After his assignment in Rome, Ames received instructions from the KGB regarding clandestine contacts in the Washington, D.C. area, where he would next be assigned. In addition, the KGB wrote to Ames that they had paid him $1.88 million in the four years since he volunteered. Upon his return to Washington, D.C., Ames continued to pass classified documents to the KGB, using "dead drops" or prearranged hiding places where he would leave the documents to be picked up later by KGB officers from the Soviet embassy in Washington. In return, the KGB left money and instructions for Ames, usually in other "dead drops."

In the meantime, the CIA and FBI learned that American deep-seated spies in Moscow were being caught and executed. These human sources provided critical intelligence information about the Soviet Union, which was used by U.S. policymakers in determining U.S. foreign policy. Following analytical reviews and receipt of information about Ames's unexplained wealth, the FBI opened an investigation in May 1993. FBI special agents and investigative specialists conducted intensive physical and electronic surveillance of Ames during a 10-month investigation. Searches of Ames's residence revealed documents and other information linking Ames to the Russian foreign intelligence service. On October 13, 1993, investigative specialists observed a chalk mark Ames made on a mailbox confirming to the Russians his intention to meet them in Bogota, Colombia. On November 1, special agents followed him and his Russian handler in Bogota separately. When Ames planned foreign travel, including a trip to Moscow, as part of his official duties, a plan to arrest him was approved.

Aldrich Ames and his wife both pled guilty on April 28, 1994. Ames was sentenced to incarceration for life without the possibility of parole. Rosaria Ames was sentenced on October 20, 1994, to 63 months in prison. Ames was later debriefed by FBI agents, at which time he detailed compromising the identities of CIA and FBI human sources, some of whom were executed by Soviet authorities. Ames had passed a series of polygraphs with flying colors. In his 2009 book, *Advice to War Presidents*, Angelo Codevilla, my deputy on the transition team, provided an update. Between 1984 (four years after our warning) and 1994, all of the CIA agents in or from the Soviet Union or Russia were controlled by the KGB, thanks to Ames. So, were we so wrong to suggest that "Big Brother spy on the spies?" We ended up with all of these spies in our own house, spying on us.

In its investigation of the Ames case, the Senate Intelligence Committee found a counterintelligence disaster. Elements of this disaster included:

- a crippling lack of coordination between the CIA and the FBI.

- fundamental cultural and organizational problems in the CIA's counterintelligence organization.

- a willful disregard for Ames's obvious suitability problems.

- failure to coordinate and monitor Ames's contacts with the Soviet officials.

- failure to restrict Ames's assignments despite early indications of anomalies, deficiencies in the polygraph program, in the control of classified information, and lack of coordination between the CIA's security and counterintelligence operations.

Most disturbing was the CIA's failure to pursue an aggressive, structured, and sustained investigation of the catastrophic compromises resulting from Ames's espionage, in particular, the destruction of the CIA's Soviet human asset program because of Ames's 1985 and 1986 disclosures. By 1986, it was clear to the CIA that, as the SSCI report on the Ames matter concluded, "virtually its entire stable of Soviet assets had been imprisoned or executed." Yet, due to the failure to mount an effective counterintelligence effort, it was another eight years before Ames was arrested. The FBI, which lost two of its most essential assets following Ames's June 1985 disclosures, also bore responsibility for the failure to mount an adequate counterintelligence effort, as a 1997 Department of Justice Inspector General report made clear.

Tighter controls should also have uncovered turncoat FBI agent Robert Hanssen. On January 12, 1976, Hanssen swore an oath to enforce the law and protect the nation as a newly minted FBI special agent. Instead, he ultimately became the most damaging spy in Bureau history. On February 18, 2001, Hanssen was arrested and charged with committing espionage on behalf of Russia and the former Soviet Union. Using the alias "Ramon Garcia" with his Russian handlers, Hanssen had provided highly classified national security information to the Russians in exchange for more than $1.4 million in cash, bank funds, and diamonds.

In the 1990s, after the arrest of Aldrich Ames, the FBI and CIA realized that a mole within the intelligence community was still sharing classified information with the Russians. The agencies initially focused primarily—and incorrectly—on a veteran CIA case officer, who was investigated for nearly two years. A turning point came in 2000 when the FBI and CIA were able to secure original Russian documentation of an American spy who appeared to be Hanssen. The ensuing investigation confirmed this suspicion. Hanssen was set to retire, so investigators had to move fast. Their goal was to catch Hanssen "red-handed" in espionage. "What we wanted to do was get enough evidence to convict him, and the ultimate aim was to catch him in the act," said Debra Evans Smith, a former deputy assistant director of the Counterintelligence Division.

Hanssen's espionage activities began in 1985. He used encrypted communications, "dead drops," and other covert methods to provide information to the KGB and its successor agency, the SVR. The information he delivered compromised numerous human sources, counterintelligence techniques, investigations, dozens of classified U.S. government documents, and technical operations of extraordinary importance and value. Since he held key counterintelligence positions, he had authorized access to classified information. Because of his experience and training as a counterintelligence agent, Hanssen went undetected for years, although some of his unusual activities had aroused suspicion from time to time. Still, he was not identified as a spy.

Hanssen was serving in the Office of Foreign Missions at the Department of State when suspicions around him arose. FBI leadership decided Hanssen needed to be removed from his temporary position and brought back to FBI Headquarters. Special Agent Don Sullivan, a squad supervisor at the FBI's Washington Field Office at the time, volunteered to replace Hanssen. Before Hanssen left the position, Sullivan went to learn his new role at the Department of State. He was also tasked with observing and learning as much as possible about Hanssen's information technology setup in his office.

Hanssen had full access to the FBI's Automated Case Support (ACS) system and the State Department's computer systems. Sullivan noted that Hanssen spent a lot of time trolling ACS for information. "He had the opportunity. He could sit in his office and shut the door. It was not a very demanding job," said Sullivan. To get Hanssen back to FBI Headquarters, where he could be closely monitored, Neil Gallagher, assistant director of the National Security Division, called Hanssen to inform him of a bogus assignment to serve on his staff. Gallagher also told Hanssen that then-Director Louis Freeh had approved a two-year extension on his service and a promotion to the Senior Executive Service.

In January 2001, Hanssen moved into a small office at FBI Headquarters secretly outfitted with surveillance cameras and microphones. His assistant,

Eric O'Neill, was tasked with keeping investigators apprised of Hanssen's movements. By February 2001, about 300 personnel worked on the investigation and monitored Hanssen. He was tracked from when he left his house in Fairfax County, Virginia, to when he got home at night, and it was confirmed that he was still an active spy.

Investigators learned that Hanssen was set to make a dead drop on February 18, 2001. An FBI arrest team moved into position at Foxstone Park, where Hanssen had been spotted earlier by FBI surveillance. Hanssen parked on a residential street and walked down a wooded path to a footbridge with the classified materials wrapped in a plastic bag. As Hanssen returned to his car, the arrest team rushed up and took him into custody. Hanssen pled guilty to 15 counts of espionage on July 6, 2001. On May 10, 2002, he was sentenced to life in prison without parole.

John Anthony Walker Jr. was a U.S. Navy chief warrant officer and communications specialist convicted of spying for the Soviet Union from 1967 to 1985 and sentenced to life in prison. In late 1985, Walker made a plea bargain with federal prosecutors, which required him to provide full details of his espionage activities and testify against his coconspirator, former senior chief petty officer Jerry Whitworth. In exchange, prosecutors agreed to a lesser sentence for Walker's son, former Seaman Michael Walker, who was also involved in the spy ring. Walker warned the Soviets that their subs were too noisy, and the Soviets began a crash program to quiet the boats, which was well in hand when the Cold War ended. Walker warned how and why to quiet the loud generators that helped us track Soviet nuclear submarines.

Because of their noise, we could track them as they crossed the mid-Atlantic ridge to approach the American coast. We would have destroyed them as soon as they opened their missile tubes. Occasionally, there would be an "incident at sea" when a Soviet submarine turned unexpectedly and hit one of our submarines.

As a Soviet spy, Walker helped the Soviets decipher more than one million encrypted naval messages, organizing a spy operation that *The New York Times* reported in 1987 "is sometimes described as the most damaging Soviet spy ring in history." After Walker's arrest, Caspar Weinberger, President Ronald Reagan's secretary of Defense, concluded that the Soviet Union made significant gains in naval warfare because of Walker's spying. Weinberger stated that the information Walker gave Moscow allowed the Soviets "access to weapons and sensor data and naval tactics, terrorist threats, and surface, submarine, and airborne training, readiness, and tactics." Walker did not fall under suspicion by any internal investigations. He was betrayed by a disgruntled spouse, according to John Lehman, Secretary of the Navy during the Reagan Administration. Lehman stated in an interview that

Walker's activities enabled the Soviets to know where U.S. submarines were at all times. "His espionage would have resulted in a massive loss of American lives in the event of war," Lehman said.

In the June 2010 issue of *Naval History Magazine*, John Prados, a senior fellow with the National Security Archive in Washington, D.C., pointed out that after Walker introduced himself to Soviet officials, North Korean forces seized USS *Pueblo* to make better use of Walker's spying. Prados added that North Korea subsequently shared information obtained from the spy ship with the Soviets, enabling them to build replicas and gain access to the U.S. Naval communications system.

Walker's betrayal struck a personal note for me as I recalled my time as secretary of the Navy. U.S. ballistic missile submarines (SSBNs) have provided strategic deterrence for over five decades. These warships are virtually undetectable while submerged, forming the most survivable component of the United States strategic deterrent. This force is comprised of 14 OHIO-class SSBNs, each capable of carrying 20 Trident II missiles. At 560 feet in length and 18,700 tons displacement, these OHIO-class SSBNs are the largest U.S. nuclear-powered submarines.

The key to a submarine's survival is evading detection. One way U.S. Navy submarines evade detection is by lowering their noise profile, a program I supported during my Secretary of the Navy role. We developed new methods to quiet generators on our nuclear submarines, even as we improved our techniques of tracking Soviet submarines. The Soviets were unaware of their noise problem until Walker alerted them. He warned the Soviets that their subs were too noisy, and the Soviets began a crash program to quiet the boats, which was well underway when the Cold War ended. Not only did he pinpoint the problem; he provided them with solutions developed by our top-secret research.

Jonathan Pollard was sentenced to life in prison in 1987 after pleading guilty to working for the Israeli government and delivering large amounts of classified information to them. He was a U.S. Navy intelligence analyst at the time. He was the only American to receive a life sentence for passing classified information to an ally of the U.S. In defense of his actions, Pollard said he committed espionage only because "the American intelligence establishment collectively endangered Israel's security by withholding crucial information." Israeli officials, U.S.-Israeli activist groups, and some U.S. politicians who saw his punishment as unfair lobbied continually for the reduction or commutation of his sentence. The Israeli government acknowledged Pollard's espionage in 1987 and issued a formal apology to the United States but did not admit to paying him until 1998. Throughout his imprisonment, Israel made unsuccessful attempts to secure his release through official and unofficial channels. He was granted Israeli citizenship in 1995. While Benjamin Netanyahu argued that Pollard worked exclusively for Israel, Pollard admitted shopping his services successfully, in some cases to other countries.

Opposing any form of clemency were many active and retired U.S. officials, including Donald Rumsfeld; Dick Cheney; former CIA director George Tenet; several former U.S. secretaries of Defense; a bipartisan group of U.S. congressional leaders; and members of the United States intelligence community. They maintained that the damage to U.S. national security due to Pollard's espionage was far more severe, wide-ranging, and enduring than publicly acknowledged. Though Pollard argued that he only supplied Israel with information critical to its security, opponents stated that he had no way of knowing what the Israelis had received through legitimate exchanges and that much of the data he compromised had nothing to do with Israeli security. Pollard revealed aspects of the United States intelligence-gathering process, its sources, and methods. He sold numerous closely guarded state secrets, including the National Security Agency's ten-volume manual on how the United States gathers its signal intelligence. He also disclosed the names of thousands of people who had cooperated with U.S. intelligence agencies.

Pollard's case illustrates the consequences of a CIA policy of refusing to share information with the FBI and other intelligence agencies. He began applying for intelligence service jobs in 1978, first with the CIA and later with the U.S. Navy. Pollard was turned down for a job with the CIA after taking a polygraph test and admitting to heavy drug usage between 1974 and 1978. The Navy asked for but was denied information from the CIA regarding Pollard, including the results of their pre-employment polygraph test revealing Pollard's excessive drug use.

Pollard was released on November 20, 2015, following federal guidelines at the time of his sentencing. On November 9, 2020, his parole expired, and all restrictions were removed. On December 30, 2020, Pollard and his second wife moved to Israel and settled in Jerusalem.

A July 1997 Defense Security Service publication listed more than 120 cases of espionage or espionage-related activities against the United States from 1975 to 1997. And those are just the ones that got caught. On March 26, 1998, Peter Lee, a former nuclear physicist at Los Alamos National Laboratory, was sentenced to one year in a community corrections facility, three years of probation, 3,000 hours of community service, and a $20,000 fine. He had pleaded guilty to willfully passing national defense information to Chinese scientists during a 1985 visit to China. He also provided false information in 1997 to his then employer, TRW, Inc., regarding his contact with

Chinese officials. He also pleaded guilty to lying to a government agency after describing a May 1997 visit to China as a pleasure trip. Dr. Lee, then a researcher for an American military contractor, met extensively with Chinese scientists. Lee provided China with secrets about advanced radar technology being developed to track submarines, according to court records and government documents. He worked closely with the British military and visited Scotland as part of a secret team working on a method of tracking nuclear missile submarines. The information available to Lee as a prominent member of the U.K./U.S. Radar Ocean Imaging Program (ROIP) is almost certain to have compromised the security of Britain's Trident nuclear deterrent. Lee's story illustrates how classical Chinese espionage efforts use Chinese scientists who gather pieces of technical information from U.S. colleagues rather than relying on intelligence agents. It is a subtle system that emphasizes collegiality and exchange. It explains why it is difficult for U.S. counterintelligence investigators to catch American scientists who may have acted illegally.

In 2010, Jeffrey Sterling, another former CIA operations officer, shared information about "Operation Merlin," a covert operation under the Clinton Administration against Iran's nuclear program. He spent three years in prison. Chelsea Manning, who leaked 750,000 classified and sensitive documents, pleaded guilty to 10 charges. She was convicted at trial of 17 charges and sentenced to 35 years in prison. She served just seven years before President Obama commuted her sentence. Manning is a rare example of a leaks case that went to trial. Few cases do. Most are resolved through plea arrangements. Whether due to the government's desire to preserve secrecy or the need for expediency, plea deals, not extended court battles, are the norm.

A former NSA contractor, Harold Martin, accepted a plea agreement with a nine-year prison sentence after 20 years of hoarding classified information. A former Navy officer, Martin worked in a supporting role for multiple intelligence agencies, including the National Space Agency and the Office of the Director of National Intelligence. Investigators found that Martin removed a staggering amount of sensitive material, including documents, removable media, and computer files about internal NSA policy and cyber-operations. More than 50 terabytes of material, some marked "Top Secret," were recovered in the investigation.

However, the number of criminal prosecutions for leakers only scratches the surface of those who disclose government secrets. Some hide under the umbrella of whistleblowing; in other cases, the government is just uninterested or unable to move the case to prosecution. When it comes to whistleblower cases, it's important to remember that, just as there are official protections for whistleblowers under the law, there are also procedures for properly reporting information. Revealing classified or sensitive information to anyone without clearance or the authorization to receive it is not whistleblowing—it's leaking.

Edward Snowden, a former technical contractor for the NSA and the CIA leaked details of top-secret U.S. and British mass surveillance programs to the press. Snowden claimed he was simply a "whistleblower" who intended to reveal illegal surveillance programs by NSA and the CIA. He collected more than $1.2 million in speaker fees in addition to books since 2013. Snowden fled to Russia in 2015, and he was granted Russian citizenship on September 27, 2022.

The case of Julian Assange, Wikileaks founder, highlights the difference between leaks and whistleblowing in the spotlight. After Ecuador withdrew Assange's asylum in 2019, British authorities arrested him, and the U.S. government unsealed an indictment. The charges don't directly relate to the classified information published by Wikileaks, but rather to Assange's alleged conspiracy to bypass protocols in the Secret Internet Protocol Router Network, better known as the SIPRNet.

"On or about March 8, 2010, Assange agreed to assist Manning in cracking a password stored on Department of Defense computers connected to the SIPRNet," the indictment alleges. The decision not to prosecute Assange for espionage related to the leaking of classified information highlights how difficult enforcing those charges can be. Despite the severe ramifications of leaking classified information, securing criminal convictions remains rare, even as the number of criminally prosecuted cases increases.

On April 20, 2022, a British judge approved Julian Assange's extradition to the United States to face spying charges. The case will now go to Britain's interior minister for a decision, though the WikiLeaks founder still has legal avenues of appeal. District Judge Paul Goldspring issued the order in a brief hearing at Westminster Magistrates' Court, as Assange watched by video link from Belmarsh Prison. The move doesn't exhaust the legal options for Assange, who has sought for years to avoid a trial in the United States on charges related to WikiLeaks' publication of a massive trove of classified documents more than a decade ago.

The United States had asked British authorities to extradite Assange so he could stand trial on 17 charges of espionage and one charge of computer misuse. American prosecutors say Assange unlawfully helped U.S. Army intelligence analyst Chelsea Manning steal classified diplomatic cables and military files that WikiLeaks later published, putting lives at risk. Assange spent seven years inside the Ecuadorian Embassy in London to avoid extradition to Sweden to face rape and sexual assault allegations. Sweden dropped the sex crimes investigations in November 2019 because so much time had elapsed.

Modern microelectronics and information technology have revolutionized just about everything else, so it is not surprising they would have an impact on counterintelligence. After all, the currency of espionage is information. Therefore, the impact of evolving information technologies is particularly significant. One aspect of this is the miniaturization of information. It took Jonathan Pollard 17 months to spirit away enough classified documents to fill a 360 cubic foot room. Today, that information can fit in a pocket, dramatically diminishing the risk of detection while increasing the productivity of an agent. A laptop computer can fit into a briefcase or backpack yet yield an entire library of information. Another is the revolutionary change in the dissemination of information. Depending on the computer security measures in place, an agent can transfer or simply retype classified information into an unclassified e-mail system and send it around the world in seconds.

Or consider the "virtual dead drop." No more marks on mailboxes or hiding messages in a soda can. Classified information can be transferred or retyped into an unclassified computer with an Internet connection and left there for someone to "hack" into. The whole transaction may be difficult or impossible for security officials to detect or recreate. Even if the agent is careless and fails to delete classified information from an unclassified computer, it may be difficult if not impossible to prove anything beyond a security violation. Another challenge, in an era of extensive scientific cooperation between nations that are, if not adversaries, not exactly friends, is the difficulty of protecting sensitive, proprietary, or even classified information during scientific exchange or joint ventures. This problem was especially apparent in the interactions between American and Chinese engineers launching U.S. satellites in China that were the subject of an Intelligence Committee investigation. American satellite company engineers, who have multimillion-dollar payloads riding on primitive Chinese rockets, face a serious conflict of interest: how to ensure successful launches while not doing anything to improve Chinese rockets that are essentially identical to Chinese ICBMs in everything but the payload. Identifying sensitive, but unclassified, technical information at risk in transactions of this type, and then finding ways to protect it, will be an important focus.

Secrets and Leaks: The Costs and Consequences for National Security

On the walls of post offices and federal buildings during World War II were framed posters to remind us of the dangers of information leaks. "LOOSE LIPS SINK SHIPS," said one poster that showed a ship in flames, its crew bobbing in the water and on lifeboats with the statement, "A CARELESS WORD . . . A NEEDLESS SINKING." The ghosts of leaks past serve as potent reminders for us of the dangers of leaks today.

Dozens of leaked Defense Department classified documents posted online on March of 2023 reveal details of the United States spying on Russia's war machine in Ukraine and secret assessments of Ukraine's combat power, as well as intelligence gathering on America's allies, including South Korea and Israel. Many are labeled "Top Secret," the highest classification level. They contain repeated references to information based on secret signals intelligence—electronic eavesdropping—a crucial pillar of U.S. intelligence-gathering. Jack Teixeria, a 21-year-old member of the Massachusetts Air National Guard, was arrested by the FBI on April 13, 2023, in connection with the classified documents that were leaked on the Internet. Teixeira collected classified documents containing National Defense Information from a classified workstation at the Otis USANG Base and transcribed and transmitted the information in written paragraphs to other users on the social media platform. Why did he have access to secret military information?

It has become all too common for people in Washington to leak information. Policymakers may leak for any number of reasons, such as to bring attention to a good news story or discredit a bad story. They may also leak information to gauge public interest in a new policy or issue. But some leak sensitive information just because they can. These are the people, especially those that have access to classified information that we need to worry about. No security clearances should be given to people unless there is a need to know.

People entrusted with a security clearance must realize their clearance is not a right but a privilege and must be treated as such. Just because a person has a security clearance does not give the authority to determine what should and should not be classified. However, when it comes to deliberate disclosures of classified information, we must create a culture within the Intelligence Community where zero tolerance is the norm. We need to give the Department of Justice all the tools it needs to identify and prosecute individuals who deliberately share classified intelligence. The time has come for a comprehensive law that will make it easier for the government to prosecute wrongdoers and increase the penalties, which hopefully will act as a deterrent for people thinking about disclosing information.

11 | Ambassador to the Organization of American States

WHEN PRESIDENT REAGAN APPOINTED ME ambassador to the Organization of American States (OAS) in April 1981, I thought I was taking on a relatively sleepy post. The OAS grew from the 1890 International Conference of the American States, eventually becoming the Pan-American Union. Whatever was happening below our southern border was barely noticed by most Americans. However, my watch was marked by revolutions in Nicaragua and El Salvador, the fight between Great Britain and Argentina over the Falklands, the U.S. rescue of Grenada from the Communists, smoldering issues throughout Central America, and Mexican support for Castro and other leftist organizations. So much for a sleepy posting!

Cuba, not a voting member of the OAS, was wielding influence throughout much of the region at the time. It had been 20 years since the "understanding" that followed the Cuban Missile Crisis in which the Soviets agreed they would put no offensive weapons in Cuba. However, the Soviet influence in Central America was strong and growing. The governments of Nicaragua and Grenada were solidly in the Cuban/Soviet camp, and El Salvador, Guatemala, Costa Rica, and Honduras were facing attacks from leftwing guerrillas.

During my tour, I visited all 31 voting members of OAS member countries at least four times each to push for the privatization of industry, free markets, private property rights, and a stable, independent judiciary, a key to working democracies. More than 60 percent of economic activity in virtually all Latin countries was non-existent in those days. Poverty and unemployment rates were astronomical, corruption was endemic, and black markets flourished. The countries were deep in debt, and most were in default. To this point, foreign investors had lost billions, and few were interested in risking more.

One of my most important early contributions to OAS was the development of the Caribbean Basin Initiative (CBI), a comprehensive package of political and economic measures to stabilize the Caribbean Basin. With Jeane Kirkpatrick, the first woman to serve as the U.S. ambassador to the

United Nations, we presented the plan successfully to President Reagan and the cabinet. The CBI included a country-by-country assessment, pointing out the business and industrial areas with the highest potential. What local government policies would help or hinder? What technical assistance, management, or market training might be needed? Would the transportation infrastructure accommodate increased freight traffic? A country had to have a non-Communist government, an extradition treaty with the United States, an agreement to abide by copyright rules, and to cooperate in regional anti-narcotics efforts to participate in the CBI. The initial beneficiaries were 21 nations in the Caribbean, Central America, and the northern coast of South America.

Nicaragua

I was initially confronted by a regional crisis in Nicaragua that began two years before I came on board with the overthrow of Nicaraguan strongman Anastasio Somoza. Nicaraguan insurgents, operating under the name "Sandinistas," overthrew Somoza in July 1979. Daniel Ortega did not resemble a typical military strongman when he first caught the world's attention. Yet as the leader of Nicaragua's left-wing Sandinista revolution, he was credited with bringing down a dictator who had ruled Nicaragua since 1936.

Newspapers in the United States hailed the revolution as a triumph over the Somoza regime. The United States and much of the Western Hemisphere looked on with relief, anticipating a new democracy under a new government. After all, the Sandinistas pledged to establish full observance of human rights, a peaceful and orderly transition, civil justice, and to hold free and fair elections and income redistribution. All of these clichés were used by Lenin, Stalin, Mao, Castro, and Hugo Chavez of Venezuela for Communist takeovers.

Ironically and tragically for the Nicaraguans, the Sandinistas have proved that they surpass even Somoza in abusing the fundamental rights of their people. The victims include journalists, businesspeople, politicians, Catholics, Moravians, the Miskito Indian tribes, and Nicaragua's entire Jewish community. Most ironic was the treatment of those Ortega called "useful idiots," the intellectuals who initially supported him and whom he recognized as gullible enough to become counter-revolutionaries when they learned he had lied to them. Human rights violations affect all aspects of Nicaraguan life. The people suffer restrictions on free movement, denial of due process, lack of freedom of thought, conscience, religion, denial of the right of association, and free labor unions.

After seizing power, the Sandinistas supported Communist elements seeking to overthrow the government of El Salvador and destabilize the governments of Guatemala, Honduras, and Costa Rica. They assisted Cuba in training the guerrillas of El Salvador's Faribundo Martí National Liberation Front (FMLN) and armed guerrillas in Honduras and Guatemala. Ortega's police and paramilitary groups committed serious religious freedom violations by attacking Catholic clergy and worshipers and desecrating places of worship. Ortega ordered a "shoot to kill" crowd control strategy, leading to widespread violent clashes against human rights activists, students, and social leaders. Government officials, including members of the Supreme Court and Ortega's son, frequently harassed Monsignor Silvio Baez, former auxiliary bishop of Managua, demanding he leave the country for the Vatican. The frequent Ortega critic and defender of human rights activists was eventually recalled to Rome after many death threats. Protestors detained by police and armed pro-government groups report other serious abuses and torture, including sexual assault, nail removal, electric shock, and asphyxiation.

Two months after the victory of the Nicaraguan revolution in July 1979, the Sandinista National Liberation Front (FSLN) leadership met in secret for three days to assess the current situation and lay plans to consolidate their power. The report, "The 72-Hour Document," was the Sandinista's basic blueprint for constructing communism in Nicaragua and spreading subversion throughout the region. While the United States was trying to develop a positive relationship with the new revolutionary Government, the Sandinistas regarded the United States as their "rabid enemy."

After promising the OAS that a genuinely democratic government would be installed with free elections, the Sandinistas implemented a Cuban-style regime with a massive military building spree. The Sandinistas maintained close ties with Cuba and the Soviet Union from the onset. The new army numbered 25,000 men, supported by a militia of 50,000 supplemented by 2,000 Cuban military and security advisers. It was the largest army in Central America, equipped with dozens of Soviet-made tanks, 800 Soviet-made trucks, Soviet howitzers, antiaircraft guns, planes, and helicopters. Thousands of civilian advisers were from Cuba, the Soviet Union, North Korea, East Germany, Libya, and the Palestine Liberation Organization (PLO). Nicaragua became a willing platform for Cuban and Soviet covert military action.

Immediately after Ortega assumed power, the United States granted emergency relief and recovery aid to Nicaragua of $118 million, five times more than we had given before the revolution. If we were trying to buy friendships, it did not work. The Government of Nicaragua treated the United States as an enemy. The incoming defense minister declared their creed Marxism-Leninism and moved quickly to consolidate power. Business leaders were jailed, and the government subjected all media to heavy censorship. It insulted and mocked the Pope, drove the indigenous Miskito Indians from their homelands, burned their villages, and destroyed their crops. To my mind, that was genocide. In July 1980, the Sandinista defense minister announced there would be no need for elections since the people had already "voted" during the revolution. He warned that elections could not be held until the people had been re-educated.

Ortega's contempt for democratic norms and hostility toward the United States did not end with the Nicaraguan revolution. Under Ortega, the Russian government and private sector presence in Nicaragua and intelligence and security cooperation between the two countries expanded. Ortega's Nicaragua is also one of only five countries recognizing the Russian-occupied Georgian regions of Abkhazia and South Ossetia as independent states. Nicaragua's armed forces facilitated preferential port access for the Russian military.

During my first month as ambassador to the OAS, I criticized the Nicaraguan government for not following through on its promise to hold free elections. I also helped initiate a change in policy in which the United States supported the Contras, the opposition to the Sandinistas. Unfortunately, the U.S. Congress passed legislation known as the Boland Amendment for its author, Massachusetts Democratic congressman Edward P. Boland. It prohibited military appropriations between 1982 and 1984 to "overthrow Nicaragua's government."

Regimes hostile to American interests financially sustained Ortega. The late Venezuelan dictator Hugo Chavez also supported the former guerilla's ambitions. Following Nicaragua's 2006 presidential election, Venezuela's ambassador to Managua said of Venezuela's assistance: "Over the next five years, Nicaragua is going to feel the effects of true cooperation based on solidarity, not one of trade and speculation. We want to infect Latin America with our model." Venezuela kept like-minded allies in office by providing cheap fuel to promote economic growth and expand the welfare state artificially. From 2007 to 2016, an estimated $3.7 billion in subsidized Venezuelan oil reached Nicaragua and benefited the Ortega family and party loyalists. According to the United States Department of the Treasury, large sums were embezzled from Nicaragua's state-run oil company and joint ventures with Venezuela (companies run by Ortega relatives).

Costa Rica

Costa Rica abolished its army in 1948, placing itself under the security umbrella of the OAS. One of the immediate problems I faced as ambassador to the OAS was Nicaragua's aggressive policy against Costa Rica. Luis Alberto Monge, president of Costa Rica, a long-time vocal foe of Somoza, told me in 1983 that "in 40 years of Somocismo, we never had the threat that we have in four years of Sandinismo." More than 90 percent of Costa Ricans said they considered Nicaragua the principal military threat to their country.

It was not always so. During Somoza's final year of rule in Nicaragua, Costa Ricans admired the young Sandinista guerrillas fighting against the hated dictator. Costa Rica allowed its territory to be used as a conduit for arms and supplies for the Sandinistas. Castro also assisted his Sandinista friends via Costa Rican territory. After four years of Communist attempts to undermine Costa Rica's strong democratic traditions, Monge told me that his government supported the political ideals of the United States and other Western democracies. Costa Ricans went to the polls on February 2, 1986, and elected Oscar Arias to succeed Monge as President of Central America's most established democracy. The election showed that Costa Ricans cherished democracy and wished to maintain a democracy with individual freedom, where the rule of law prevails over the rule of the gun.

Costa Rica has a long history of democratic stability and one of Latin America's highest levels of foreign investment per capita. Its economic freedom score is 65.4, making its economy the 55th in the 2022 Index. Costa Rica is ranked 10th among 32 countries in the American region, and its overall score is above the regional and world averages.

Honduras

Honduras was facing the most challenging period in its modern history when I became agmbassador to the OAS in 1981. It was threatened by invasion from Nicaragua while armed guerrilla forces attacked the already fragile democracy from within the country. Already the poorest country in Central America, Honduras faced an economic crisis as unemployment and underemployment approached 45 percent. Honduras held Constituent Assembly elections in 1980 and presidential elections in 1981. An unprecedented 80 percent of the Honduran people went to the polls in November 1981 to elect a civilian government. Since then, Honduran democracy has survived some of the most difficult challenges any Honduran administration has ever faced.

Joseph Hoyo's presidential election marked the first time in 50 years that an elected civilian had succeeded another elected civilian, Roberto Suazo Cordoba, as president. Like his counterparts in El Salvador, Guatemala, and Costa Rica, President Azcona faced a staggering array of economic and political problems, many of them stemming from the aggressive expansion policies of his Sandinista neighbors. Honduras shares a 508-mile border with Nicaragua and a 226-mile border with El Salvador. These geographic factors made Honduras a pivotal element in Nicaraguan efforts to overthrow the government of El Salvador.

I warned President Hoyo in our first meeting that his country was being used as a conduit for arms, ammunition, and supplies from the Sandinistas to the Salvadoran guerrillas. I also told him that the Reagan Administration would provide economic and military assistance to the new democracy. Honduras was one of four Latin American nations to transition from military to civilian rule during my time as Ambassador to the OAS. The violence raging among its neighbors drove some 46,000 refugees into Honduras, creating an enormous economic burden.

Terrorist activity in Honduras had increased because of Cuba's increased involvement in the region. Since 1980, there have been kidnappings, aircraft hijackings, bank robberies, bombings of public buildings, attacks on U.S. corporations, a machine-gun attack on the U.S. embassy, the bombing of electrical power plants, and the September 17, 1982, siege of over a hundred people, mostly business leaders, in San Pedro Sula. In December 1982, a terrorist group kidnapped Honduran President Suazo Cordova's daughter while she was in Guatemala. They demanded that an article attacking relations with the United States be published in major Central American newspapers before she would be released. Suazo's daughter was released after the "story" was printed. It was later learned that the guerrillas were Argentine and Colombian terrorists working with leftists in Guatemala. The terrorists identified themselves as the People's Revolutionary Movement, a group with no known relation to any terrorist group in Guatemala or Honduras.

The increased violence in areas bordering Nicaragua along the Coco River forced the Honduran military to establish tighter security in that region. Threats from guerrilla groups based in Nicaragua, such as the Cinchonero Popular Liberation Movement and the People's Revolutionary Movement (MRP), prompted the Honduran government and the United States to reevaluate Honduran military readiness and security.

As ambassador to the OAS, I felt a fundamental requirement of my job was to back up my recommendations for democracy with financial aid from the United States. We were able to increase U.S. aid to Honduras from $1 million to $10 million while raising a military sales credit from $9 million to $19 million, giving Honduras a total of $29 million in military assistance for 1982. In the FY 1983, Congress appropriated $20.3 million, but we secured another $17 million for economic aid. For FY 1984, Honduras received $83 million in economic assistance, $40 million for the Military Assistance Program (MAP), and $1 million in International Military Education and Training (IMET). In addition, the Senate Foreign Relations Committee authorized an $8 million grant to reconstruct an airfield used for emergency purposes by the United States.

Honduras made two significant moves to demonstrate its commitment to democratic development. It joined with Costa Rica and El Salvador in a Democratic Community and presented a peace proposal before the OAS and the United Nations. This proposal called for general disarmament in Central America; termination of arms traffic in the area; reduction in the number of foreign advisors, and a multilateral agreement that will strengthen the democratic, pluralistic system, including rights of free expression of political will.

Honduras is ranked 20th among 32 countries in the Americas region, and its overall score is above the regional average but below the world average. Economic growth slowed over the past five years and turned sharply negative in 2020 before resuming in 2021. GDP per capita is $2,405.

El Salvador

Immediately after Somoza fled from Nicaragua in July 1979, a meeting was held in Managua to plan Sandinista's support for the armed struggle in El Salvador. By December 1980, the guerrillas had used weapons never before seen in El Salvador. Among them were the U.S.-made M-16 rifles and M-70 grenade launchers. They were a far cry from the handguns, hunting rifles, shotguns, and homemade explosives, which had been the basis of the guerrilla arsenal in El Salvador. Using the weapons smuggled from Nicaragua, guerrilla units struck at 40–50 locations throughout El Salvador. In the cities, buses were burned. In the countryside, guerrillas boarded buses and terrorized passengers. San Salvador, Santa Ana, Chalchuapa, Chalatyenango, and Zacatecoluca came under heavy fire.

The Sandinistas also provided training to the Salvadoran insurgents and served as a transit point to other external training locations. Nicaraguan and Cuban political and military training created the basic framework for using arms by guerrillas within El Salvador. The two countries coordinated the training efforts, with Cuba providing the most specialized training for sabotage and demolition operations. The Sandinistas trained Salvadoran guardrails in military tactics, weapons, communication, and explosives at training schools scattered around Sandinista military bases in Nicaragua and El Salvador.

As ambassador to the OAS, I protested strongly about the arms flow from Nicaragua to El Salvador in late September 1981. Fearful that continued support for the guerrillas in El Salvador would jeopardize the recently approved $75 million in economic aid from the United States, the Sandinistas held up arms shipment temporarily. Within months, Nicaragua resumed weapons deliveries by sea and air on an even larger scale than before the suspension.

The guerrillas had hoped for a popular insurrection, resulting in a total breakdown of the government and an immediate victory. It did not happen because most of El Salvador's population ignored the guerrillas' appeals. Unable to win the loyalty of El Salvador's people, the guerrillas set out to systematically deprive them of food, water, and transportation. The failure of the guerrillas to gain control in El Salvador also led to a decision to carry on a prolonged war of attrition and economic sabotage. Our embassy was rocketed twice and strafed five times in March and early April 1981. Guerrilla attacks against the economic infrastructure reached higher levels as they increasingly targeted power towers, water pumping stations, electrical generators, highways, and farms.

Some of the most fertile lands could not be cultivated because of guerrilla attacks. The guerrillas caused over 5,000 interruptions of electrical power, and the national water authority had to rebuild 112 facilities damaged by guerrilla action. The entire eastern region of the country was blacked out for over a third of the year in 1981 and 1982. The Nicaraguan aid allowed the Salvadoran guerrillas to continue their operations on a large scale.

The costs of this Nicaragua-based assault on El Salvador's society were high. They were all the more tragic in that by 1981, the Salvadoran government was addressing severe political, social, and economic problems that most concerned its people. In its commitment to reform, the Christian Democratic Forces Junta of El Salvador had the full support of the United States.

El Salvador held an election at the end of March 1982 that turned out to be a tragedy and a triumph. The guerrillas destroyed trucks and buses used to carry voters to the polling places. They also threatened to kill anyone who voted. "Vote today, die tonight," they warned." Despite the threats, 80 percent of eligible voters showed up at the polls—only 62 percent of American voters cast ballots in the 2020 presidential election. A presidential election was held on March 25, 1984, and José Napoleon Duarte, a founder of the Christian Democratic Party, became El Salvador's first freely elected civilian president in over 50 years. Álvaro Alfredo Magaña Borja, leader of the Democratic Action, was elected as head of the Nationalist Republican Alliance (ARENA) and Party of National Conciliation candidates.

After its 12-year civil war ended in 1992, El Salvador enjoyed robust growth under center-right governments until the leftist Mauricio Funes of the National Liberation Front (FMLN) took power in 2009. In his first act as the new president, Funes restored full diplomatic relations with Cuba, broken since the Cuban revolution 50 years earlier. "Diplomatic, cultural, and trade relations will be established immediately with our sister nation of Cuba," said Funes. He also vowed to renew and expand relations with the United States, with which "historically, we are bound by many ties, in particular by the presence of millions of our compatriots who live there, work there, and build their dreams there."

Funes promised that his government would be marked by "wisdom and integrity" and announced the launch of an "anti-crisis plan" to create 100,000 jobs in the next 18 months. Secretary of State Hillary Clinton hailed the "peaceful transfer of power" in El Salvador after two decades of U.S.-backed rebels fighting against Marxists. Clinton said Washington was "committed to helping this new administration continue to make progress and also have the tools it needs to address some of the pressing social issues it confronts." Referring to past strained ties, she added: "Some of the difficulties that we've had historically in forging strong and lasting relationships in our hemisphere are a result of our perhaps not listening, perhaps not paying close enough attention."

Guatemala

With a population of 17 million and a GDP of $77.6 billion, Guatemala is the most populous country in Central America and the one with the broadest economic base. Shortly after becoming ambassador to the OAS, I recognized that an economically healthy and democratic Guatemala would positively impact all of Central America. Vinicio Cerezo was inaugurated president of Guatemala on January 14, 1986. His election to the presidency accurately reflected the change in Guatemalan politics that took place when I was ambassador to the OAS. During my watch, Fidel Castro never succeeded in unifying the disparate elements of the extreme left in Guatemala as he did in El Salvador.

Cerezo faced a troubled insurgency on the left, an intransigent military on the right, an increasingly mobilized peasantry, and an economy in crisis with a declining GDP, escalating inflation, 40 percent unemployment, and increased taxes. To address these problems, Cerezi launched a program of export diversification, currency devaluation, price controls, and increased taxes. The results were generally favorable for the national economy, but living standards for most people were reduced. Cerezo survived three attempts on his life during my term as Ambassador to the OAS,

Guatemala is the largest economy in Central America and an upper-middle-income country, measured by its GDP per capita ($4,603 in 2020). Public debt and the budget deficit have been historically among the lowest and most stable globally. Low central government revenues (11 percent of GDP on average in recent years and an estimated 11.7 percent in 2021) limit capacity for public investment and restrict both the quality and coverage of essential public services, from education and health to access to water, mainly explaining the lack of developmental progress and significant social gaps, trailing behind the rest of Latin America and the Caribbean (LAC).

Democracy in Central America

The swell of democracy in Central America is not superficial. Electorates have welcomed it and have organized, campaigned, and voted in record numbers throughout the region. During my tour as ambassador to the OAS, 24 independent countries of Latin America and the Caribbean cast more than 280 million votes in more than 50 nationwide elections to select presidents, national legislatures, and constituent assemblies. In virtually every case, the number of people going to the polls reached record highs. With each election, the right to choose becomes more institutionalized, establishing a habit of pluralistic political practice that widens voter participation and broadens support for democratic government. With each peaceful transition from one civilian government to its successor, the democratic machinery is refined and improved. The essence of democracy is the right of citizens to decide regularly whether to keep or replace those who claim to represent them. Cuba did not hold a popular election for national office since Castro came to power in 1959, while Nicaraguan elections are filled with fraud.

Under the Administration of Jimmy Carter, support for human rights was the guiding principle in Central America. During the administration of President Ronald Reagan, the emphasis shifted toward a policy championing the broader values of democracy. President Reagan recognized that democracy is more than free elections. His message linked the future of democracy in Central America to economic development and pledged significant U.S. support. When I was ambassador to the OAS, living standards improved more dramatically in Latin America and the Caribbean than in any other region in the developing world. President Reagan also warned that the United States would not remain indifferent when democratic values are at risk, a pledge he fulfilled with the action in Granada.

As a former Wall Street executive, I recognized the importance of free trade and the economic stabilization of Central America. I encouraged private entrepreneurship and urged that countries in Central America reduce restrictions on foreign investments.

We must address the factors behind Central American migration to change the influx of illegal immigrants into the United States. We must do everything possible to end the pervasive gang violence that pushes many migrants out of their homelands. We need to target financial and logistical support to encourage Central American countries to address poverty and endemic corruption in Latin America. The lack of opportunities leads citizens to attempt to enter the United States illegally.

The United States has moral and strategic interests in seeing those representative democracies develop in Central America, and the spread of communism stopped. The Sandinistas have created a police state in Nicaragua armed by Russia, trained in Cuba, and kept in power significantly by intimidation of the Nicaraguan people. Russia has made a significant investment and hopes for a strategic and political return. Costa Rica, Honduras, and Guatemala participate in China's Belt and Road initiative, which may have devastating results in Central America.

It is time to send a clear message to Latin America that the United States remains part of the Americas and that stability and democratic evolution in all of the Americas is of significant concern to the United States government and its people. There is no better place to start than taking a stand for democracy and freedom in Central America.

President Reagan addressed his concerns with this statement in 1986:

> One doesn't need to be of a particular party or even privy to secret information to see what's happening in Central America. It's clear: Nicaraguan Communists are using their country against their neighbors while totally subjugating their own people. Their internal repression and external aggression campaign is being aided and abetted by the Soviet Union, Cuba, East Germany, Bulgaria, Iran, Vietnam, Libya, and other radical states, movements, and organizations."

12 | What We Must Learn from the Falklands War

THIS YEAR MARKS THE 42ND ANNIVERSARY of the British victory over Argentina in the Falklands War. British forces liberated Port Stanley on June 14, 1982, just 74 days after the invasion of the islands and the capture of 1,000 British citizens by the Argentine military Junta. Margaret Thatcher's decision to dispatch a task force to retake the Falkland Islands within a day of the invasion was an extraordinary display of leadership. The armada of over 110 ships and 28,000 men began to set sail for the South Atlantic—8,000 miles away—just three days after the Argentineans had landed on British soil. London went to war against the regime in Buenos Aires without a U.N. resolution specifically mandating the use of force.

Margaret Thatcher was prime minister of the United Kingdom from 1979 to 1990. She was the first woman to hold that office and became the longest-serving British prime minister of the 20th century. Thatcher strongly supported the Reagan administration's Cold War policies based on their shared distrust of Communism. During her first year as prime minister, she supported NATO's decision to deploy United States nuclear cruise and Pershing II missiles in Western Europe. She bought the Trident nuclear missile submarine system from the United States to replace Polaris, tripling the United Kingdom's nuclear forces.

Exactly one year into my tour as ambassador to the OAS, things were going well. I had completed a round of official visits primarily with the heads of state of Brazil, Ecuador, Peru, Chile, Argentina, Uruguay, Paraguay, Belize, Venezuela, Colombia, Jamaica, Barbados, Dominica, Costa Rica, Trinidad, and Tobago. In many areas, I was going against years of customs and traditions. Still, conditions in so many countries were so troubled and corruption so prevalent that I usually found a willing and receptive audience. My message was clear: to champion the benefits of free markets, free trade, the right to private property, the value of a robust and independent judiciary, the rights of citizens, and the ability to attract foreign investment.

With a population of 32 million in 1981, Argentina was Latin America's third most populous country and third strongest economic power after

Brazil and Mexico. It is also strategically located at the southern tip of South America, commanding the South Atlantic Sea lanes and passing a significant portion of the Western Hemisphere trade. Despite Argentina's highly educated populace, abundant mineral wealth, and some of the world's most fertile land, political conflict, and an unproductive, state-dominated economy impeded its development dramatically.

A democratic Argentina with a growing, healthy economy could not only be a force for peace and stability in Latin America but also an important trading partner. As ambassador to the OAS, I was directly interested in ensuring that Argentina's political and economic reforms would serve as a model of economic growth for the rest of Latin America. If not, Argentina would lapse into another period of military rule and economic chaos, discrediting the promise of free-market reforms for other Latin American countries.

On my first visit to Argentina in 1981, I met with General Leopoldo Galtieri, former commander-in-chief of the army appointed president that year. He was part of a military junta that seized government control in 1977. Galtieri suspended Congress, trade unions, and political parties, and between 9,000 and 30,000 people disappeared during his first months in office. Torture and mass executions were commonplace. He was supposed to turn around a bad economy, a job he failed miserably. One of his decisions led to a $6 billion loss for a state-owned petroleum company.

I thought our initial discussion would be centered on steps he could take to raise his country's falling GDP and attract foreign investment, which was down by 20 percent. Instead of taking positive steps, he spent our meeting placing blame in all directions, excluding himself. Nothing positive came out of that meeting, punctuated by rants and accusations.

On a subsequent visit, I was invited to a state dinner in honor of Galtieri. The invitation said the dinner would be held between 8 and 9 p.m., typical timing in Latin America. Galtieri showed up at midnight, stayed 20 minutes, and offered no apologies. I decided that Galtieri was rude and inept, but I should have added "dangerous" to my assessment, as I learned a few months later.

President Reagan came to the OAS in 1982 to announce the Caribbean Basin Initiative (CBI), a comprehensive package of political and economic measures to stabilize the Caribbean Basin. This was a program I created with Jeane Kirkpatrick, ambassador to the United Nations, to provide the Caribbean with one-way free trade with the United States. A strong showing in the elections in El Salvador the month before my first anniversary as ambassador to the OAS was encouraging. And then came a significant setback. On April 2, 1982, President Galtieri made a military issue of a long-smoldering dispute over ownership of the Falkland Islands, which were economically destitute and best known as a graveyard of sailing ships caught in the almost constant storms in the area.

The islands—called the "Malvinas" by the Argentines—had been occupied by the British since 1833. Argentina's economy had been run into the ground by gross mismanagement. Most outside observers assumed, absent any real economic or humanitarian need to reclaim the Malvinas, that the government was waving the flag and flexing some muscle to shift the public focus. President Galtieri decided it was time to take them back. President Reagan called Galtieri to urge restraint without success. Galtieri faced a slumping economy and increased civil opposition to military rule when he became president of Argentina in December 1981. His trump card was that he had promised his Navy ally, Vice Admiral Jorge Anaya, that he would fulfill Argentina's historical claims to the Falkland Islands by armed force. Nationalist sentiment over the Falklands had been precipitated in 1977 when Argentina's claim to another archipelago—the three Beagle Channel Islands—was refused by the International Court of Justice in favor of Chile.

What does history suggest regarding the status of the Falkland Islands? The first known landing there was made in 1690 by a British naval captain, John Strong. At that time, the islands were named after Viscount Falkland, a prominent British lawmaker. The British, French, and Spanish all had settlements on the islands at various points until the last European settlement was abandoned in 1811, leaving the Islands uninhabited. In 1833, the British re-established a settlement, which has existed ever since.

The United Kingdom's strongest argument for its claim on the Falkland Islands is the inhabitants' right to self-determination. The 3,000 residents overwhelmingly want to be British and not Argentine. Linguistically, culturally and historically, nobody can deny that they are British. The U.N. Charter and the International Covenant on Civil and Political Rights guarantee the right to self-determination—and Argentina is a signatory to both.

Argentina's claim to the Falkland Islands is based on two points: the principle of *uti possidetis juris* and the geographical contiguity of the islands in relation to Argentina. *Uti possidetis juris* is the belief that upon being granted independence, newly formed states should inherit the same borders that their former colonial masters had. It is not a universally accepted principle of international law. Even if it were, it would not apply here because when Argentina declared independence from the Spanish Empire in 1816, Spain did not have de facto control of the islands. The last Spanish settlement left the Falkland Islands in 1811.

In February 1982. Argentina increased pressure on the United Kingdom to relinquish the Falkland Islands. With widespread support at home,

Argentine troops landed on the Falklands and South Georgia Island in early April 1982, overcame the British Royal Marines stationed there, and raised the Argentine flag. By opting for military action, the Galtieri government hoped to mobilize the long-standing patriotic feelings of Argentines towards the islands, diverting public attention from the chronic economic problems and the ongoing human rights violations, bolstering the Junta's dwindling legitimacy. The newspaper *La Prensa* speculated on a step-by-step plan beginning with cutting off supplies to the islands, ending in direct actions late in 1982 if the U.N. talks were fruitless.

The ongoing tension between the two countries over the islands increased on March 19, 1982, when a group of Argentine scrap metal merchants raised the Argentine flag at South Georgia Island. This act would later be seen as the first offensive action in the war. In response, the Royal Navy ice patrol vessel HMS *Endurance* was dispatched from Stanley to South Georgia on March 25. The Argentine military junta, suspecting that the United Kingdom would reinforce its South Atlantic Forces, ordered the invasion of the Falkland Islands to proceed. The final decision to invade was made at a junta meeting in Buenos Aires on March 23, 1982.

On April 2, 1982, Argentine forces mounted amphibious landings, Operation Rosario, on the Falkland Islands. The invasion was met with a fierce but brief defense organized by the Falkland Islands Governor Sir Rex Hunt, under the command of Major Mike Norman of the Royal Marines. The garrison consisted of 68 Marines and 11 scientists dedicated to ocean research. They were assisted by 23 volunteers of the Falkland Islands Defense Force (FIDF), who had few weapons and were used as lookouts. The invasion started with the landing of Lieutenant Commander Guillermo Sanchez-Sabarots's Amphibious Commandos Group, which attacked the empty Moody Brook barracks and then moved onto the Government House in Stanley. When the 2nd Marine Infantry Battalion with Assault Amphibious Vehicles arrived, the governor ordered a cease-fire and surrendered. The governor, his family, and the British military personnel were flown to Argentina that afternoon and later repatriated to the United Kingdom.

Word of the invasion first reached the United Kingdom from Argentine sources. In London, a Ministry of Defense operative spoke briefly with Governor Hunt's telex operator, who confirmed that Argentines were on the island and in control. Later that day, BBC journalist Laurie Margolis spoke with an islander at Goose Green via amateur radio, who confirmed the presence of a sizeable Argentine fleet and that Argentine forces had taken control of the island.

The British had already acted before the April invasion. During a crisis meeting headed by Prime Minister Margaret Thatcher and the chief of the

Naval Staff, Admiral Sir Henry Leach, advised that "Britain could and should send a task force if the islands are invaded." On April 1, 1982, Leach sent orders to a Royal Navy force carrying out exercises in the Mediterranean to prepare to sail south. In response to events in South Georgia, on March 29, ministers sent the Royal Fleet Auxiliary (RFA) *Fort Austin* south from the Mediterranean to support HMS *Endurance* and the nuclear-powered fleet submarine HMS *Spartan* from Gibraltar, with HMS *Splendid*, ordered south from Scotland the following day. Following the invasion, an emergency meeting of the cabinet approved a task force to retake the islands. British military operations in the Falklands War were given the codename Operation Corporate, and the task force commander was Admiral Sir John Fieldhouse.

Within days after the Argentinian invasion, Al Haig, secretary of State, flew to London and Buenos Aires, trying to mediate a solution. Secretary of Defense Caspar Weinberger made two trips to meet with British Prime Minister Thatcher. The OAS Council was called into a special session but deferred action so as not to impede Haig's effort. A British armada set sail to retake the islands. Haig convinced the British to hold the fleet at Ascension Island, gateway to the Falklands, while diplomatic efforts continued.

Argentina called a special session of the OAS to demand that the British withdraw entirely. In a speech to the OAS, Haig pleaded for moderation, urging the members not to let their natural sympathies for Argentina impair a rational approach. Earlier that day, he received polite applause, an embarrassing contrast to the standing ovation given to Argentine Ambassador Nicanor Costa Mendez. In voting on a resolution, OAS members took a more even-handed approach and urged both sides to avoid using force. Jeane Kirkpatrick worked with the Latin countries in the United Nations, while my focus was on Mendez.

I enlisted the aid of my deputy, Alberto Piedra, who had been an official in Castro's Ministry of Commerce, saw the light in 1960, abandoned his home and possessions, and fled Cuba. Mendez was very open, and we worked out a face-saving compromise in a series of private conversations with Piedra and me. Pope John Paul II would divert from an already-scheduled trip to Latin America, visit the Falklands, and put up the Vatican, British and Argentine flags. We hoped this might defuse the passions of the moment and allow for the withdrawal of forces, pending a calmer discussion of the issues.

Events soon overtook our efforts. Galtieri thought Thatcher was bluffing and moved the cruiser *General Belgrano* into position. He sent word thanking me for my efforts but warning that he could not accept the proposed compromise. I was still with Ambassador Mendez at his residence just before midnight, April 30, when I got a call from Al Haig. "Bill, get back to the State Department immediately. No more negotiations. She's going in tomorrow."

This crisis presented the Reagan administration with a formidable foreign policy dilemma. Although the United States had proclaimed its neutrality on the question of the islands' sovereignty since the mid-nineteenth century, the clash between Argentina and the United Kingdom created conflicts among Reagan's foreign policy team. Jeane Kirkpatrick did not want to alienate the Argentines, regarded by the administration as key partners in halting the expansion of Soviet-directed Communist influence in the Western Hemisphere. Secretary of Defense Caspar Weinberger argued strongly to support the British. Weinberger feared the administration's failure to support the Thatcher government vigorously would tacitly condone the Argentines' actions and encourage other countries to employ similarly aggressive methods. Secretary of State Alexander M. Haig argued that Cuba and the Soviet Union stood poised to exploit the crisis and expand their influence in South America if the United States failed to prevent an escalation of hostilities. He advocated an even-handed "honest broker" approach toward both sides in such an environment.

Having failed to persuade Galtieri to refrain from landing on the islands, after much internal debate, Reagan dispatched Haig to the United Kingdom and Argentina for talks with Thatcher and Galtieri again on April 7. The backdrop to Haig's mission was ominous. In addition to an increasingly contentious war of words between the Argentine and British governments, Britain's mounting military buildup in the region raised the possibility of actual hostilities. Containing the crisis and preserving Washington's relationships with both governments hinged upon the conclusion of a negotiated settlement.

Haig shuttled between London and Buenos Aires for two rounds of intensive discussions over the next fortnight but failed to broker a peaceful solution. Supported by most Britons, Thatcher insisted on a return to the status quo ante. Any other result would, she believed, imply moral equivalence between the British and Argentine positions, validates Argentina's aggression, and diminishes the islanders' right to self-determination. Moreover, Thatcher stipulated that no negotiation over sovereignty could occur until Argentine forces withdrew.

The Argentine junta held its own suspicions about U.S. impartiality, refused to make concessions that might prejudice its claims to sovereignty over the islands, and viewed the dispute as a matter of national honor. A series of detailed proposals and counterproposals failed to break the diplomatic impasse. After a successful British operation to retake South Georgia and growing indications of the Thatcher government's readiness to seek a military solution, Argentina officially rejected Haig's final peace proposal on April 29.

The following day, after the National Security Council meeting, Haig announced the breakdown of negotiations, administration support for the British position, and the suspension of military and economic aid to Argentina. On May 5, Weinberger met with British Defense Secretary John Nott to finalize arrangements to fulfill British requests for military equipment as part of a broad range of political, diplomatic, and military measures undertaken by the United States to support the Thatcher government.

When Argentina refused the United States' peace overtures, Haig announced that the United States would prohibit arms sales to Argentina and provide material support for British operations. Both houses of Congress passed resolutions supporting the U.S. action siding with the United Kingdom. The United States provided the United Kingdom with 200 Sidewinder missiles for the Harrier jets, eight Stinger surface-to-air missile systems, Harpoon anti-ship missiles, and mortar bombs. On Ascension Island, the underground fuel tanks were empty when the British Task Force arrived in mid-April 1982, and the leading assault ship, HMS *Fearless*, did not have enough fuel to dock when it arrived off Ascension. The United States diverted a supertanker to replenish the fuel tanks of ships there at anchor and storage tanks on the island—approximately 2 million gallons of fuel were supplied. The Pentagon further committed to providing additional support in the event of the war dragging on into the southern hemisphere winter.

The United States allowed the United Kingdom to use U.S. communication satellites to enable secure communications between submarines in the Southern Ocean and Naval H.Q. in Britain. The United States also passed satellite imagery and weather forecast data to the British Fleet. President Ronald Reagan approved the Royal Navy's request to borrow a Sea Harrier-capable Iwo Jima-class amphibious assault ship if the British lost an aircraft carrier.

Most Latin American countries viewed U.S. support for Britain as a betrayal of the hemispheric solidarity embodied in the 1947 Inter-American Treaty of Reciprocal Assistance (the Rio Treaty). Despite this public tilt toward the British position, the Reagan administration continued its efforts to control the conflict and mitigate the fighting's impact on U.S. interests. In addition to offering broad support for peace initiatives undertaken by the Peruvian president and U.N. General Secretary Javier Pérez de Cuéllar, the administration pressed the belligerents to draw down their military engagement. Ambassador-at-Large General Vernon Walters met secretly with the Argentine junta, while Reagan attempted to intercede with Prime Minister

Thatcher personally. Over the course of two tense telephone conversations in late May, Reagan failed to persuade Thatcher to refrain from "scoring total victory" in the South Atlantic to avoid toppling the Junta.

Margaret Thatcher was famous for "handbagging" her opponents, subjecting them to verbal assault or criticism. She "handbagged" the civil and diplomatic services from 732,300 employees to 659,000, a reduction of 73,000. No one—diplomats, clergy, presidents, dictators, or ambassadors—escaped her swinging "handbag": I was "handbagged" during the Falklands War when she decided I did not offer her full support. Because of my OAS solidarity considerations, I could not provide her full support. She also told me in 1983 that she supported my decision to invade Grenada, even though she had publicly denounced it. Later we became good friends, and she appointed me co-treasurer of the International Democratic Union, an organization she founded with President Reagan to promote democracy worldwide. After she died in 2013, I bought one of her handbags for my daughter Frances.

On May 1, the British bombed the islands. The next day, the *General Belgrano* was sunk by a British nuclear submarine firing a World War II torpedo that killed 321 Argentinian sailors. On May 4, an Argentine fighter aircraft hit HMS *Sheffield* with a French-built missile, killing 22 British sailors. A territorial dispute had become a war. By the time it ended 70 days later, the British had fully controlled the islands. They had lost 255 men, six ships, and 34 aircraft. The war had cost the Argentinians about 700 men, and very quickly, Galtieri lost his job.

Argentina itself was politically backed by many countries in Latin America, though notably not Chile. At the outbreak of the war, Chile was in negotiations with Argentina for control over the Beagle Channel and feared Argentina would use similar tactics to secure the channel and refused to support the Argentine position during the war. During OAS meetings, most representatives of the OAS told me privately they felt that Galtieri created the war to divert attention from Argentina's fiscal woes.

Some members of the OAS accused the United States of violating the Rio Treaty, which required all members to come to the assistance of any American republic subjected to unlawful force from outside the alliance. Our position was clear: In this case, the illegal aggression came from within the alliance, not from outside the hemisphere, and thus neither we nor any other member was required to support Argentina. Many OAS members disagreed, offended that we would back the British in a dispute against a country on our side of the world. They had little respect for Galtieri, but he was a member of their club.

The night before an OAS vote, which might have condemned our actions for supporting Great Britain, I visited with Mexican Ambassador Don Raphael Villa Colina. Don Raphael told me many times that he was under tremendous pressure to vote against the United States in every possible dispute. I convinced him not to vote in favor of the condemnation resolution. He was able to neutralize some of the fence sitters the next day, and we received a "neutral" vote which was, in effect, a successful vote.

A *Wall Street Journal* editorial was highly complimentary about my role in heading off a negative vote from the OAS concerning our role in the Falklands War. I received my second Superior Honor Award, which I shared with my entire staff since it had been a joint effort. As for the Falklands, the fighting had ended, but not the arguing. The Argentines affirmed that the islands were theirs forever but agreed that renewed hostilities were out of the question. Margaret Thatcher authorized British banks to participate in Argentine debt rescheduling. Wounds were, perhaps, healing. In December 1983, I was honored to be a guest at the inauguration of the first president of Argentina to have been freely elected in 25 years, Raul Alfonsin. It had a significant social impact, destroying Argentina's military's image as the "moral reserve of the nation" it had maintained through most of the 20th century. At this point in history, democratization had reached about 90 percent of the population of Latin America.

The Argentine writer Jorge Luis Borges described the war as "a fight between two bald men over a comb." But the war brought many consequences for all the parties involved, besides the considerable casualty rate and significant shipping and aircraft losses. In the United Kingdom, Margaret Thatcher's popularity increased. The success of the Falklands campaign was widely regarded as a factor in the turnaround in fortunes of the Conservative government, which had been trailing behind the SDP–Liberal Alliance in the opinion polls for months before the conflict began. Following the success in the Falkland, the Conservatives returned to the top of the opinion polls by a wide margin and went on to win the following year's general election by a landslide.

The islanders had full British citizenship restored in 1983. Their quality of life was improved by investments the United Kingdom made after the war and by the economic liberalization that had been stalled through fear of angering Argentina. In 1985, a new constitution was enacted promoting self-government, which continued to give power to the islanders.

The Soviet Union described the Falklands as "a disputed territory," recognizing Argentina's ambitions over the islands and calling for restraint on all sides. The Soviet Union did mount some clandestine logistics operations in favor of the Argentinians. Soviet media frequently criticized the United Kingdom and United States during the war. Days after the invasion by the

Argentinian forces, the Soviets launched additional intelligence satellites into low Earth orbit, covering the southern Atlantic Ocean. There are conflicting reports on whether Soviet ocean surveillance data might have played a role in the sinking of British ships.

As secretary of State, Al Haig followed the concept of "linkage," the idea that Soviet actions worldwide had to be considered in any negotiations. When George Shultz succeeded him in 1982, he brought a new approach, warning that the lack of contact between the United States and the Soviet Union was dangerous. "We needed to get away from the old concept of 'linkage,' which is an obstacle to diplomacy," Schultz said.

The new policy brought Reagan and Soviet leader Mikhail Gorbachev together for a summit meeting in Reykjavik, Iceland, on October 11 and 12, 1986. Reagan and Gorbachev seriously discussed the elimination of all ballistic missiles held by their two countries. They aired the possibility of eliminating all nuclear weapons. After two days of marathon negotiations, the two leaders came close but ultimately did not arrive at an agreement that would eliminate all their strategic nuclear weapons by 2000. They failed to reach a consensus over Reagan's refusal to compromise on the Strategic Defense Initiative (SDI.)

While the summit in Reykjavik was seen by many as a failure, it gave an impetus to reduction by paving the way toward concrete agreements on intermediate-range nuclear forces and strategic nuclear weapons. In December 1987, Reagan and Gorbachev signed the Intermediate-Range Nuclear Forces Treaty (INF), the Cold War's first-ever arms reduction agreement, in Washington, D.C. It called for the complete elimination of all mid-range nuclear weapons in Europe. Reagan was unlike any other U.S. president in his revulsion against the immorality of nuclear war, his willingness to do something about it, and his ability to act on his instincts. Turning away from classical arms control, he insisted on nuclear disarmament and succeeded remarkably.

The Falklands War is a classic example of a nation-state asserting its national sovereignty and right to self-defense. With the strategic support of the United States and Chile, the British Army, Navy, and Air Force ultimately defeated a larger Argentine force. Britain's victory came at a high cost, with the loss of 255 British service members. It was a sacrifice, though, that the British nation was willing to bear to defend British territory and the cause of freedom.

The best example of unintended consequences from budget-driven defense cuts is the United Kingdom's experience in the early 1980s. Faced with a severe economic downturn, the 1981 U.K. Defense Review noted that commitments to spend money on defense were outstripped by the availability of funds. Most of the cuts fell on the Royal Navy, which was to lose 20 percent of its destroyers and frigates, one-third of its light carriers, both of its amphibious ships, and a significant part of its supporting infrastructure. Of the four Royal Dockyards, Chatham and Pembroke were to close, and Portsmouth lost its refitting capability. The cuts in the Royal Navy's force structure were based partly on the belief that any future overseas expeditionary operations would be conducted as part of NATO. Therefore, it is unsurprising that one of the ships to be cut was the HMS *Endurance*, the Antarctic patrol ship that provided the Royal Navy's presence in the Falkland Islands.

President Galtieri observed these moves in Argentina and concluded that Britain would not or could not defend the islands. On Friday, April 2, 1982, Argentina invaded the Falklands—ironically, layoff notices were handed out at the Royal Dockyards in Portsmouth on the same day. Nonetheless, the fleet was readied for deployment over the weekend, and the first ships left the following Monday. By July 1982, 44 ships were modified or repaired at Portsmouth to support the Falklands campaign.

One wonders how the Falklands battle would have played out if Galtieri had not been pressured by growing demonstrations at the end of March and had waited a few months. If the Royal Navy ships had been deactivated and the dockyards de-staffed, the results might have been quite different. The capabilities of the Royal Navy and the industrial base that supported it proved decisive in this conflict, notably since Britain fought this engagement with limited support from its allies.

While I was ambassador to the OAS, Argentina opposed Washington's support for the Contra Freedom Fighters in Nicaragua and voted against us on several other security issues. A significant problem in United States–Argentine relations was the military's domination of Argentina's government. The armed forces hand-picked thirteen of the 21 presidents since 1943, primarily from within their ranks. The undemocratic and repressive character of the military regimes made for an uneasy relationship with the United States. Military aid from the United States to Argentina ceased in 1977, when the U.S. Congress approved the Humphrey–Kennedy amendment banning the sale of arms to countries violating human rights.

Lessons from the Falklands War

The Falklands War illustrates the fundamental point that, in international affairs, one should always treat one's friends better than anyone else. But it also offers many lessons for America as it struggles to avoid the devastating effects of defense sequestration and maintain a military that provides for the common defense.

Lesson 1: Be Prepared for Surprise

The Falkland Islands had long been a minor concern for Britain, but in 1982, no one expected an Argentine invasion. Indeed, Britain had just completed a defense review that argued—sensibly, in the Cold War context of the times—that Britain's most important role in NATO was to protect the North Sea from the Soviets.

Every government tries, as it must, to forecast the future, but most governments fail most of the time. Strategic surprise is a fact of life; governments need to remember that and—especially in defense—keep enough reserve capacity and flexibility to act successfully when their predictions are wrong.

Lesson 2: Focus on Mortal Threats

Once Argentina invaded, Britain had to respond. What was remarkable was that it responded with force. No one—certainly not the Argentines—believed that Thatcher's Britain would fight back or that it could do so effectively. They were proven wrong on both counts. But once the war was won, Britain did not turn the focus of its defense effort to the Falklands. It remained committed to the defense of Western Europe from the Soviet threat. Events demand a response, but not every event is a mortal threat; Argentina was an enemy, but it was not the Soviet Union.

By the same token, the United States today has core national security interests in the safety of the homeland, the prevention of major power threats to crucial U.S. interests around the world, and maintaining the freedom of the global commons, including on the sea, in space, and cyberspace. The United States cannot afford to allow other concerns to distract from these core interests.

Lesson 3: Who Dares, Wins

Winston Churchill once noted that the chains of consequence of a great victory are very long. Once victory is won, the consequences seem inevitable. But achieving victory requires statesmanship and courage to believe they might exist. The war results were not limited to the liberation of the islands. The war discredited the Argentine military dictatorship that launched it and led to the restoration of democracy in Argentina in the 1983 election. It also helped to discredit dictatorships across South America. It played a role in the return to democracy across the entire region in the 1980s when I was Ambassador to the OAS. Finally, it showed the Soviet Union—whose experts were sure that Argentina would win—that Britain was back and proved that the resolve of the West to stand up for its values was strengthening. The lesson that standing up for principles can have enormous consequences is a lesson that Americans should always bear in mind. No one in June 1982 could have believed that a war in the remote South Atlantic could have such significant consequences or do so much for democracy. The war was fought over the islands, but it ended up being about a great deal more.

Lesson 4: There Are No Permanent Victories

The reward of victory is in a better position to face the next problem. It would be pleasant if the world were a place where problems remained settled, and victories stayed won, but the history of the Falkland Islands and Argentina disproves these notions. Thirty years later, in 2012, the Falkland Islands were again the subject of a campaign by an Argentine government in dire economic straits and used the Falklands to distract the Argentine people from the mess the government had made of their country. South America again swung back in the direction of authoritarianism. And British authorities again profess confidence that, even if Argentina wanted to act, it could not do so. Thanks to successive defense cuts since the end of the Cold War, Britain may lack the capacity to retake the islands only, making this return of history even more dangerous.

Lesson 5: Maintain Defenses and Back a Key Ally

For the United States, backing Britain was not simply a matter of taking the side of an ally, though that is essential. It is a matter of defending the rights of people everywhere to democratically choose their own form of government and the United States' recognition that sovereignty derives ultimately from the will of the people. The government must provide effectively for the common defense, and that national sovereignty in the world is based on popular sovereignty at home. Those are wise American traditions to apply to the U.S. defense budget and the world today.

13 | Grenada, Operation Urgent Fury: Russia Nearly Gets a Runway

IN 1983, ONE YEAR INTO MY TOUR as Ambassador to the Organization of American States (OAS.), I had completed a round of official visits with the heads of state of all members of the OAS. Frequently, I enhanced my visit with a piece of music I composed—a march, a nocturne, or a rhapsody—played by a local orchestra as part of the official ceremonies.

My message was clear: to champion the benefits of free markets, free trade, the right to private property, and the value of a strong independent judiciary, all of which would contribute to a strong economy, protect the rights of citizens, and attract foreign investment. In many cases, I was going against years of custom and tradition, but conditions in many countries were so troubled that I often found a willing and receptive audience.

I could not make much progress with the Communists in charge of Grenada, an island about 133 square miles in size, twice the size of Washington, DC, with a population of about one hundred thousand, primarily English-speaking descendants of enslaved Africans. Grenada belonged to France for more than a century before it was ceded to Great Britain in 1763 by the Treaty of Paris. A British dependent, Grenada was under colonial administration after 1833 before attaining home rule in 1967 and complete independence in 1974.

In March 1979, widespread dissatisfaction with economic conditions and the government of Prime Minister Sir Eric Gairy resulted in a bloodless coup in which the Marxist Maurice Bishop, leader of the New Joint Endeavor for Welfare, Education, and Liberation (JEWEL), took full power. He immediately signed trade and military agreements with Havana and Moscow. Bishop led a Communist-style government that looked to Cuba and the Soviet Union for financial support. He blamed the United States for all the island's ills, real and imagined. Bishop's regime replaced democratic institutions with Marxist ones during the next few years and deprived Her Majesty's governor-general, Sir Paul Scoon, of any influence. Under Bishop, Grenada moved into the orbit of Cuba and the Soviet Union.

With Fidel Castro in Cuba and Bishop in Grenada, Soviet influence was established in the northernmost and southernmost of the Antilles, the chain of islands that bounds the Caribbean from the Florida Keys to the coast of Venezuela. Hostile control of a portion of the Antilles by Soviet Union proxies threatened U.S. strategic interests, particularly vital air and shipping lanes throughout the Caribbean.

Bishop was spiritually and militarily allied with Cuba and the Soviet Union but vowed to lead his country to a new and better future. Toward the end of 1980, a large force of Cuban workers began constructing a 9,000-foot runway on Grenada. Bishop said the runway was to encourage tourism. However, the $71 million airport, sized to handle wide-body jet aircraft, was too big for the intended purpose: the passenger load of two 747s would fill every hotel room on the island. Grenada already had an airport with a 5,000-foot runway, and it efficiently handled aircraft from other Caribbean nations. Why such an ambitious project? Put military bases in Nicaragua, Havana, and Grenada, and you covered an area as large as the United States.

Another critical point was that Grenada was not included in the "Missile Crisis Understanding," which meant the Soviets would be free to put whatever weapons they wanted in Grenada. With a Grenada base, Soviet aircraft could interdict the vital sea lanes of the Caribbean in times of crisis. During World War II, Adolph Hitler's U-boats sank more American tonnage in the Caribbean than in the Atlantic Ocean. In the 1980s, more than half of the oil imported into the United States was carried on ships passing within a few miles of Grenada.

Cuba was the driving force behind the airfield, providing most of the equipment and materials and a couple of hundred construction workers and technicians. The United States acted by blocking loans from the European Economic Commission. Grenadian Ambassador and U.N. Representative Dessima Williams harangued the OAS Permanent Council with charges of U.S. economic hostility against Grenada. "They have started a hysteria in the international community that our airport is a Cuban base. Once again, a big, rich country like the United States has been confronted by the world, trying to destabilize a developing nation like Grenada through unprincipled, unjust, inhumane acts."

Recognizing the limited capabilities of the Organization of Eastern Caribbean States (OECS) President Reagan decided in early October 1983 to assist in defending their soil or in responding to emergencies on neighboring islands. He directed the Department of Defense to maintain military forces in the eastern Caribbean to deter aggression and provide emergency air or sealift of refugees or other groups. The President also directed frequent exercises in the Caribbean and periodic updating of contingency plans for the region.

In June 1983, Prime Minister Bishop was scheduled to visit Washington and address the OAS Permanent Council. A few days before the event, and to my great surprise, Ambassador Williams took me aside and asked if I would be willing to meet unofficially with Bishop. I asked Bill Clark, the president's National Security Advisor, to join me at the meeting with Bishop and Ambassador Williams, which we held secretly in a back room at a local hotel.

Bishop was trim, athletic, bearded, and very wary. He wanted to talk, but I distinctly remember thinking he didn't know what he wanted to say. He came across not as a rugged, tough, uncompromising revolutionary but as a worried, haunted man. In most of my dealings with the Soviets, you could see the machinery behind the conversation, like a verbal chess match. You say something, and they search their mental index and find the proper rejoinder, peppering the talk with the buzzwords of the day, such as "peace" or "harmonious relations." I did not have that impression of Bishop. He admitted that he did not have a free hand, and the Soviets dominated his government. His partner in the coup, Deputy Prime Minister Bernard Coard, was a willing slave of the Soviets. I believe that Bishop wanted to find a way to drop Coard and the Soviets but stay in power.

I was obligated to point out the issues that were impeding better relations with the United States: political prisoners held without trial; suspension of press freedom and the right of assembly; indefinite postponement of free elections, and a foreign policy parroting the Cuban-Soviet line; the growing presence of Cuban and Soviet personnel and their involvement in projects that had profound implications for security throughout the area.

I appealed to his sense of national pride to help his people. He grew up in a free country. It may have been a British colony, but it wasn't under British domination. In fact, the British legacy had been a boon—a strong judicial system and organized government. "If you move toward freedom in your country, you will gain a tremendous ally in the United States—trade, tourism, positive net cash flow to help your people, and direct investment. Right now, Grenada is a pariah in the Caribbean," I said. I warned him that promoting the Communist cause while criticizing the United States would not be helpful.

Judge Clark and I offered to find a compromise where Bishop could outline a path to democracy and allay our fears about the airport. Our conversation lasted for more than an hour without resolution. Why did he want this meeting? I have no solid answer, but from the look in his eyes, I believe he was trapped between the hardcore ideology of his fellow revolutionaries and the geometric logic of benefits sure to arise from cooperative development and growth within the Western community of nations. And he didn't know how to reconcile the two.

Judge Clark and I told the right people that there might be an opening here, but no one at the State Department got too excited. They got the information, assessed it, and filed it away. The day after our conversation, Bishop played to his militant supporters, blasted the United States, and accused us of planning an invasion. Bishop returned home and was jailed after a coup by Deputy Prime Minister Coard.

In turmoil following Bishop's arrest, I had an urgent call from National Security Council (NSC) staffer Constantine Menges to come to the White House and mull over the matter of Grenada. I had met him in 1980 during the Reagan presidential campaign, and we were both alarmed three years later by what was going on in Grenada. In 1983, Menges was a national intelligence officer for Latin American affairs at the Central Intelligence Agency under Director William Casey. He worked for the National Security Council as a special assistant to the president, specializing in Latin America. White House and State Department members dubbed him "Constant Menace," a play on his name, for his ardent support of action, covert and otherwise, against Nicaraguan Sandinistas, Salvadoran rebels, and Communists in Grenada.

Menges described me in a book he wrote about the National Security Council: "He was one of the select few Reagan supporters who had received a policy-level presidential appointment in the Department of State, and he totally supported Ronald Reagan's foreign policies in Latin America."

In October 1983, I met with Menges at his office in the Old Executive Office Building next to the White House. We discussed the overall situation in Latin America. Then he handed me a brilliant political-military plan calling for protecting U.S. citizens and restoring democracy in Grenada. An international security force of democratic Caribbean countries would carry out his plan to free Grenada. "Can you keep the Latins on our side if we invade?" he asked. "Sure, if we win," I said.

After reviewing the plan, Menges asked for my opinion. "If it could be done, it would be a great step for freedom," I said. Then he asked me a critical question: How many OAS members would oppose, and how many would support military action in Grenada? I told him I would study the plan and develop my best judgment on how OAS members would react and how they might get involved. I also told him we should meet with the NSC to present his plan. As I left his office, I said, "It's a great idea, but I wouldn't get my hopes up if I were you."

All the Latin countries were playing the odds—the free world versus the rest of the world. Many of them were hanging by a thread, hoping for support from one side or the other. Ideology was not an issue with some of them. They didn't care which if they were on the winning side. The Soviets were giving out a lot of free lunches, the United States couldn't make up its mind, and everyone was hedging their bets.

Meanwhile, Bishop escaped from jail and tried to regain control. He was recaptured and brutally murdered, together with 50 of his supporters. The island lurched into anarchy and violence, and the head of the army, Hudson Austin, pushed Coard aside, took over, and established a revolutionary military council. He imposed martial law with a shoot-on-sight curfew. Ensuring the safety of American students was no longer theoretical. The memory of the Iran hostage crisis was fresh, and we didn't want to see another.

In the wake of the murders and the resulting public furor, General Austin dissolved the civilian government and established a Revolutionary Military Council with himself as spokesman. Austin closed the airport, imposed a four-day, 24-hour curfew, and warned that violators would be shot on sight. These restrictions prevented U.S. citizens on the island from leaving and caused extraordinary hardship to the American students in the St. George's School of Medicine. The students had to violate the curfew to obtain adequate food and water supplies. Attempts to resolve the crisis peacefully met with constant roadblocks as the Communist government exploited the situation. Endeavors to arrange the departure of the American students were blocked, heightening suspicions that they were viewed as hostages or bargaining chips.

Menges and I reached out to Secretary of State George Shultz to express our alarm about what was happening in Grenada. Our efforts to meet with the National Security Council got nowhere. We shared the plan with Lt. Colonel Oliver North and got a positive reaction, although he was dubious about implementing the plan. "Nothing was done after the terrorist bombing of the United States embassy in Lebanon in April 1983, or in September 1983 after the Soviets shot down a civilian Korean Airline flight," North warned. Through his efforts, Menges and I had our first meeting with the Crisis Pre-planning Group of the National Security Council on October 20, 1983. Present were Vice President George Bush, John Poindexter from the National Security Council; John McMahon and Duane Clarridge from the CIA; Lawrence Eagleburger and Langhorne Motley from the State Department; Caspar Weinberger and Fred Ikle from Defense; Anthony Motley, assistant secretary for Latin America; General John Vessey, chairman of the Joint Chiefs of Staff; Oliver North, Constantine Menges, and me.

Menges and I described the deteriorating political situation in Grenada after the deposing and execution of its leader and fifty other citizens by its own military and the potential for 700 U.S. citizens to become hostages. In discussing the feasibility of a quick in-and-out response to rescue citizens and leave, Menges warned, "If we leave the Communists in place, it will become even more hostile. I believe it might then offer its territory as a base for Soviet-bloc forces, including nuclear weapons." At first, the plan was met with absolute silence. "I believe this plan could be carried out with regional international support," I said. "We could restore democracy while rescuing our citizens," I added.

A State Department official suggested we reach out to General Hudson Austin, one of the group leaders that had taken over, to find out what kind of person he was. "I think his killing of more than fifty people recently tells us what kind of person he is," Menges replied.

Not all members of the NSC were impressed with our arguments. General Vessey focused on the risks of using U.S. military force and the possibility of third-country military intervention on behalf of the Grenadian government. He questioned the impact a U.S. military operation in Grenada might have upon U.S. forces in Europe. He also said that a Navy task force headed for deployment in the Mediterranean could not be diverted. "The Navy can adjust," I told General Vessey.

In the meantime, we had obtained an emergency resolution from the OECS, and I must note my behind-the-scenes arm-twisting. It called upon the United States to intervene militarily in Grenada. Support for military action was strengthened when I explained that the governments of Jamaica, Barbados, and other members of the OECS offered forces to take part in the invasion. Under Article 8 of the OECS collective security treaty of 1981, the members voted to ask Barbados, Jamaica, and the United States to join them in sending a multinational peacekeeping expedition to Grenada. Sir Paul Scoon, the governor-general of Grenada, also asked the OECS to free his country from the Revolutionary Military Council.

A primary concern voiced at the meeting was how the Grenadian population would interpret an American invasion. The English-speaking Grenadians, far from harboring anti-American sentiments, were, in fact, pro-American. "Most OAS members would support an invasion," I said. I pointed out that no anti-American signs were seen during a demonstration on the Island on October 19, 1983, while many anti-Communist banners were on display.

President Ronald Reagan played golf during our meeting in Augusta, Georgia, but he joined us by a secure telephone line. One White House staffer warned the president that there would be a harsh political reaction to an American strike on a small island nation. "I know that, and I'm prepared to deal with it," the president said. Vice President Bush asked President

Reagan if he wanted to simply rescue the students or eliminate Cuban intervention on the island and restore democratic government. "Well, if we're got to go there, we might as well do all that needs to be done," the president replied.

President Reagan then ordered U.S. naval forces to be diverted toward Grenada and operational planning to proceed. Since Grenada moved into the orbit of the Soviet Union and Cuba in 1979, U.S. agencies had few opportunities to collect intelligence. Aerial photography indicated numerous sites for landing zones and parachute drops. Intelligence calculated Grenadian forces at about 1,200 regulars with more than twice that number of militia and four torpedo boats. Since the precise deployment of Grenadian forces was unknown, picking the sites to land troops was a risky business.

The presence of well-armed Cubans complicated planning. Intelligence did pick up two significant pieces of recent information. On October 6, 1983, the Cuban vessel *Vietnam Heroica* landed an undisclosed number of Cuban workers, presumably to join others already at work on the runway at Point Salines. The following week, other Cuban vessels delivered arms for transit to undisclosed locations in the island's interior.

A swift, precise strike probably would rescue most students and avert a hostage situation. Removing the pro-Cuban junta would eliminate a threat to U.S. strategic interests in the Caribbean. General Vessey recommended a surprise attack called Operation Urgent Fury. While catching the enemy off guard, it could perform rescue operations and seize key military targets vital to the enemy's command and control of defensive operations. The first decision was to recall the aircraft carrier *Independence* from its peacekeeping assignment in Lebanon and assign it to support the invasion of Grenada.

One plan called for an amphibious assault by Marines on one airfield while Rangers would seize the other. Troops from the 82nd Airborne Division would provide support. Five specifically equipped C-130s would drop the Marines and Rangers under cover of darkness at Point Salines at the southwest tip of Grenada and Pearls, midway up the east coast. From Point Salines, some of them would then move up the west coast about four miles to St. George's, the island capital, and capture the radio station and police headquarters. These forces would then move about four miles southeast to capture the Grenadian military barracks at Calivigny. Later, sixteen C-130s would land the 1st and 2d Ranger Battalions at Point Salines and Pearls. They would consolidate control of all objectives and pursue any enemy forces fleeing into the highlands.

The second plan called for an amphibious/hellebore assault by Marines with a Ranger follow-up force. SEAL teams would go ashore after midnight on October 24 to reconnoiter beach conditions at Point Salines and Pearls. By the dawn of October 25, a battalion landing team with air cover from the USS *Independence* would land on the beaches or move by helicopter to objectives at Point Salines airfield, the St. George's medical school, and the Grand Anse beach about two miles below St. George's. Once the Marines had secured their objectives, Rangers could land at Point Salines and move to St. George's to seize police headquarters, government buildings, and army headquarters.

Either option had risks. Landings by Rangers or Marines might prompt the Grenadians or Cubans to kill or hold the students hostage. The Cuban construction workers might reinforce Grenadian troops and inflict significant casualties on U.S. forces. The Soviet Union might exert pressure on U.S. forces or those of U.S. allies in Europe or the Middle East. If any of these events occurred, the Reagan Administration could expect criticism from Congress and foreign governments.

General Vessey stressed the importance of communications security. He directed that all coordination be limited to secure teleconferences and messages. In the Pentagon, these precautions were too late, for CBS had already learned of the diversion of the warships to Grenada and would break the story on the news later that evening.

The Joint Chiefs of Staff decision to plan for a large multi-service operation was based upon a thorough analysis, which envisioned the rescue and evacuation of U.S. citizens and foreign nationals from many points on an island about twice as large as the District of Columbia. The Joint Staff also considered the need to neutralize an enemy force of uncertain strength, intent, or disposition.

Intelligence analysts offered planners estimates of 1,000 to 1,200 People's Revolutionary Army (PRA) regulars, 2,000 to 5,000 militiamen, and about 250 armed Cubans. These estimates would later be shown to be much lower than the actual numbers of such forces on the island. Given the uncertainty, the JCS determined that a military operation should be a surprise attack with overwhelming force.

Donald Cruz, the United States consular officer to Barbados, traveled to Grenada to meet with Major Leon Cornwall, the titular head of the Revolutionary Military Council. Cornwall was vague and evasive about the identities of Grenada's other leaders and their intentions toward U.S. citizens. Talking with students from the medical school at St. George's, Cruz found them apprehensive about the future. A plane sent to retrieve him was temporarily denied permission to land.

Nearby in Bridgetown, Barbados, the OECS convened in an emergency session to discuss ways of ending the anarchy and violence in Grenada. Under Article 8 of the OECS collective security treaty of 1981, the members voted to ask Barbados, Jamaica, and the United States to join them in sending a multinational peacekeeping expedition to Grenada. Hours later, early in the morning of October 22, Sir Paul Scoon, the governor-general of Grenada, asked the OECS to free his country from the Revolutionary Military Council. The OECS sent its request and the governor-general's to the ranking U.S. diplomat in the Caribbean, Charles A. Gillespie, executive assistant to the assistant secretary of State for inter-American affairs. From Barbados, Gillespie dispatched the requests to the State Department on October 22.

Members of the SSG contacted Secretary Shultz and Robert C. McFarlane, assistant to the president for National Security Affairs, both of whom were vacationing with President Reagan in Atlanta. Shultz and McFarlane informed the president of the two requests, and he called a teleconference with the members of the SSG at 0900 hours. With two separate requests for intervention, the NSPG scrapped the idea of a peaceful evacuation. The NSPG tasked the Joint Chiefs of Staff to plan a military expedition to seize Grenada from local military forces.

At 2:27 on the morning of October 23, the Marine barracks in Beirut was destroyed in a suicide-bomb attack, killing 241 servicemen. In the wake of the attack, President Reagan, Secretary Shultz, and McFarlane returned to Washington for emergency sessions of the NSC and the NSPG Oliver North was pessimistic about the Grenada plan moving forward. He told Menges and me that he thought the Grenada operation would be canceled because of what happened in Lebanon.

On Sunday, October 23, the NSC held a meeting at the White House that included Bush, Shultz, Weinberger, Vessey, McMahon, Poindexter, McFarlane, Menges, and me. To begin the operation on the night of October 25, the earliest possible date, a presidential decision would be required by 2000 hours on October 23. In the wake of new intelligence that the Grenadians were mobilizing about two thousand reservists to join an estimated 1,500 regulars and approximately six hundred armed Cubans (over four thousand troops altogether), the JCS concluded that neither the JSOC/Rangers nor the Marines alone would suffice. According to General Vessey, the Joint Chiefs of Staff wanted "to go in with enough force absolutely to get the job done."

After discussing the Lebanon crisis, Secretary of Defense Caspar W. Weinberger briefed President Reagan on the plan for the proposed operation in Grenada. Having heard reports from Ambassador McNeill and Maj.

General Crist in Barbados that the violence and danger to U.S. citizens had increased. President Reagan asked, "How soon can we launch an invasion?" McFarlane said forty-eight hours. Reagan ordered, "Do it."

The presidential decision to use military action authorized Adm. McDonald to organize a joint force with the missions of evacuating U.S. citizens, disarming hostile troops, and restoring orderly government to Grenada. If danger to the United States citizens on the island had significantly increased within twenty hours of receipt of the executive order, Adm. McDonald was free to launch an immediate rescue.

On October 23, the State Department sent Ambassador Francis J. McNeill to meet with the OECS, Jamaica, and Barbados representatives in Bridgetown, Barbados, and assess their countries' willingness to join peacekeeping operations. At the secretary of State's request, Major General George B. Crist, USMC, vice director of the Joint Staff, accompanied the Ambassador to advise him concerning U.S. capabilities for military action in the Caribbean. Maj. General Crist would help the Caribbean states organize a small peacekeeping force and coordinate its activities with the United States forces, the CIA, and the State Department.

Secretary Weinberger gave General Vessey full power to conduct the operation. The chairman had the authority to call up backup forces, deploy them, and issue guidance to unified and specified commanders—without going to the secretary. Both Secretary Weinberger and General Vessey hoped to speed up responses to problems and requests from the tactical commander.

Secretary Shultz instructed Undersecretary for Political Affairs Lawrence S. Eagleburger and Assistant Secretary Langhorne A. Motley to work with Maj. General Crist to arrange and publicize the role of the Caribbean allies. The Secretary recommended that elements of the Eastern Caribbean force, known as the Caribbean Peacekeeping Force (CPF), be integrated into U.S. command arrangements, be included in the initial landings on Grenada, and be given a conspicuous role in the reconstruction of the government. Secretary Shultz envisioned a brief U.S. presence followed by the rapid drawdown of military forces.

From Barbados, the U.S. defense attaché reported that Grenadian security guards and troops at the Richmond Hill Prison, St. George's, had received orders to kill all prisoners in the event of invasion. DIA also had unconfirmed information that British subjects and other foreign businessmen had already been executed. Meanwhile, the Barbados National Radio spoke of growing dissatisfaction with the Grenadian armed forces over the brutal excesses of the regime and the failure of militia members to report to their assigned units.

Grenada, Operation Urgent Fury: Russia Nearly Gets a Runway

On October 25, 1983, President Reagan delivered the following message:

Ladies and gentlemen, on Sunday, October 23, the United States received an urgent, formal request from the five-member nations of the Organization of Eastern Caribbean States to assist in a joint effort to restore order and democracy on the island of Grenada. We acceded to the request to become part of a multinational effort with contingents from Antigua, Barbados, Dominica, Jamaica, St. Lucia, St. Vincent, and the United States. I might add that two of those, Barbados, and Jamaica, are not members of the Organization but were first approached, as we later were, by the OECS and asked to join in that undertaking. And then, all of them joined unanimously in asking us to participate.

Early this morning, forces from six Caribbean democracies and the United States began landings on the island of Grenada in the Eastern Caribbean. We have taken this decisive action for three reasons. First, and of overriding importance, protecting innocent lives, including up to a thousand Americans, whose personal safety is my paramount concern. Second, to forestall further chaos. And third, to assist in restoring conditions of law and order and of governmental institutions on the island of Grenada, where a brutal group of leftist thugs violently seized power, killing the Prime Minister, three Cabinet members, two labor leaders, and other civilians, including children.

Let there be no misunderstanding; this collective action has been forced on us by events with no precedent in the eastern Caribbean and no place in any civilized society. American lives are at stake. We've been following the situation as closely as possible. Between 800 and a thousand Americans, including many medical students and senior citizens, make up the largest single group of foreign residents in Grenada.

From the start, we have consciously sought to calm fears. We were determined not to make an already bad situation worse and increase the risks our citizens faced. But when I received reports that a large number of our citizens were seeking to escape the island, thereby exposing themselves to great danger, and after receiving a formal request for help, a unanimous request from our neighboring states, I concluded the United States had no choice but to act strongly and decisively. Let me repeat, the United States objectives are clear: to protect our citizens, facilitate the evacuation of those who want to leave, and help restore democratic institutions in Grenada. I understand that several Caribbean States are asking that the Organization of American States consider the situation in Grenada. Our diplomatic efforts will be in close cooperation with the Organization of Eastern Caribbean States and the other countries participating in this multinational effort.

On October 25, 1983, ships of the USS *Guam* amphibious ready group and C-130s from Hunter Army Airfield, Georgia, approached Grenada. Acting upon information from the SEALs' reconnaissance, nearly 400 Marines made a helicopter assault upon Pearls at 0500 hours. Although scheduled at precisely the same time, the airdrop of several hundred Rangers at Point Salines was held up for thirty-six minutes because of the loss of the inertial navigation system in the lead C-130, which required that the sequence of C-130s be adjusted in the air. It cost the JSOC forces the cover of darkness and tactical surprise and delayed the Ranger units on the landing zone.

Combat results were uneven during the first hours. The Marines encountered very light resistance at Pearls and none at Grenville. They occupied the airfield and nearby objectives within two hours. Special operations forces and the Rangers began landing on the island at 0536 hours. Helicopters tried approaching targets near St. George's, but Grenadian troops opened fire with antiaircraft and automatic weapons. As the Rangers' C-130s approached Point Salines airfield, the Cubans put up stiff resistance using antiaircraft guns and automatic weapons. Lt. Colonel Wesley B. Taylor, commanding the 1st Ranger Battalion, decided to reduce the time of descent and vulnerability to the ground fire by having his men jump from five hundred feet.

Once on the ground, a company of Rangers assembled at either end of the airfield. The two companies attacked the Cuban defenders by hot-wiring a bulldozer and using it to clear obstacles strewn on the runway. The Cubans fought back with small arms and machine guns. At one point, they sent armored personnel carriers toward the Rangers. Within the next two hours, gunships from the carrier USS *Independence* suppressed the armored personnel carriers, and the Rangers surrounded and captured about 250 Cubans. At 0900 hours, the Rangers rescued 138 American medical students at the True-Blue Campus adjacent to the airfield, only to learn that over two hundred more were still trapped at Grand Anse, a few miles to the north.

Learning almost immediately of the Cuban resistance at Salines, the JCS conferred at 0600 hours. The volume of Cuban firepower proved a tactical surprise, but General Vessey reassured his colleagues that gunships and superior ground forces would quickly suppress further resistance. To expedite a ceasefire, he recommended that the secretary of State bluntly inform Havana and St. George's regimes that there was "no point in shooting muskets at us; we are going in with overwhelming force."

The resistance encountered by the Rangers convinced the U.S. commanders that the Cuban construction workers constituted a combat force. In fact, on October 24, Cuba's Premier Castro sent an experienced officer, Colonel Pedro Tortola Comas, to direct the defense of southern Grenada. Tortola Comas's men had just begun to break out the weapons and pile up sandbags when the first battalion of Rangers attacked. Later, U.S. forces would find a thousand rifles, equipment, and barracks for a full-strength Cuban battalion. The interrogation would reveal that many of the Cubans fought for Castro in Ethiopia and Angola.

After the initial reports of Cuban resistance arrived at the Pentagon, General Vessey approved a request to send two battalions of the 82nd Airborne Division at Fort Bragg to Grenada. Commanded by Major General Trobaugh, the 1,500 paratroopers began the airlift to Point Salines at about 1000 hours. After their arrival, General Trobaugh consolidated the two airborne battalions with the Rangers and JSOC teams into Task Force 121. From the beaches at St. George's, a team of SEALs made its way east of the city to the residence of governor-general Scoon. After overwhelming the guards and rescuing the Governor-General, the SEALs came under heavy fire from armored personnel carriers. Lacking antitank weapons, the SEALs held off their attackers with grenades and automatic weapons and waited for the Rangers to rescue them. However, the lightly armed Rangers were heavily engaged north of Salines against what appeared to be a fully equipped Cuban battalion and could not move fast enough to support the SEALs. Vice Admiral Metcalf ordered Navy and Marine aircraft to fly combat sorties over the governor-general's residence and the vicinity to support the SEALs.

In mid-afternoon, squadrons of A-7 Corsairs from the USS *Independence* began attacking Fort Frederick and Fort Rupert. Heavy antiaircraft fire from Fort Frederick and Fort Rupert downed two Marine Sea Cobra helicopters and deterred others from approaching the governor-general's residence. Meanwhile, Grenadian military broadcasts indicated that Fort Frederick was probably an enemy command post. Admiral Metcalf's desire to protect the governor-general and the SEALs while destroying a Grenadian headquarters and antiaircraft site overcame his concerns about severe "collateral damage."

The resistance encountered between St. George's and Point Salines, combined with the realization that a second medical student campus existed at Grand Anse, prompted a reassessment of the tactical ground situation.

Meeting about noon, Vice Admiral Metcalf and Maj. General Schwarzkopf agreed that most, if not all, of the action, was on the southern part of the island. Schwarzkopf recommended to Vice Admiral Metcalf that Marines land at Grand Mal Bay north of St. George's to open a "second front" to the rear of the Grenadian and Cuban forces. Metcalf agreed. After sailing around Grenada, a landing force of 250 Marines, five tanks, and thirteen amphibious vehicles landed at Grand Mal at about 1900 hours. It moved south and east toward the governor-general's residence.

Combat operations continued throughout the daylight hours of October 27. Meeting scant resistance in the St. George's area, the Marines rapidly fanned out and occupied Fort Lucas, Richmond Hill Prison, and other points. Meanwhile, paratroopers advanced methodically eastward across southern Grenada. After meeting fierce Cuban resistance at Salines, Frequente, and Grand Anse, it was thought the enemy might be strong enough to resist or even counterattack. Problems with the runway at Point Salines had delayed the deployment of the paratroopers and the arrival of helicopter gunships. The paratroopers depended on fire support from naval aircraft and gunfire without the helicopters.

Translators and intelligence experts from the CIA studied captured documents confirming the presence of more than 1,600 Cuban workers and Soviet advisers within every government ministry. They also revealed the Marxist regime's dependence on Cuban support to remain in power. The analysts could substantiate earlier estimates that the Cubans were constructing the oversized runway to fly large jets from Cuba and the Soviet Union to Latin America and Africa destinations.

Assistant Secretary of State Langhorne Motley arrived in Grenada on October 27. General Crist briefed him on final preparations to move Governor-General Scoon and the CPF to St. George's, where the CPF would assume control of all critical political facilities. With Secretary Motley and the CPF now fully in charge of efforts to reconstruct a viable government on the island, Maj. General Crist viewed his mission as complete, and he returned to the Pentagon the following day.

Earlier resistance convinced the JCS that the six hundred prisoners accounted for a little more than half of the Cubans on the island. The acting chairman of the JCS, General John A. Wickham, Jr., estimated that up to five hundred Cubans might have fled to Grenada's mountainous interior to wage guerrilla warfare. He asked Admiral McDonald to submit a concept of operations for isolating and eliminating them. The paratroopers conducted sweeps of the mountains to flush out any remaining pockets of resistance. While sweeping the peninsula of Lance aux Epines near St. George's, airborne troopers located the last group of 202 US medical students, bringing the number rescued to 564. Subsequently, the troops linked up with Marines at the Ross Point Hotel near St. George's.

By October 28, the tempo of combat operations had declined significantly; units were dealing with occasional snipers, mopping up, and searching for Hudson Austin, Bernard Coard, and other members of the revolutionary junta. During the last five days of Operation Urgent Fury, the capture of Bernard Coard, Hudson Austin, Leon Cornwall, and Edward Layne and their incarceration onboard the USS *Guam* virtually ended significant organized resistance in Grenada.

Late in the afternoon of November 2, the combat phase of Urgent Fury ended. Secretary Weinberger ordered General Trobaugh to continue reconstruction to withdraw all U.S. troops as soon as the new government could stand independently. Nearly eight thousand soldiers, sailors, airmen, and Marines had participated in Urgent Fury along with 353 Caribbean allies of the CPF. U.S. forces had sustained 19 killed and 116 wounded; Cuban forces lost 25 killed, 59 wounded, and 638 personnel captured. Grenadian forces casualties were 45 killed and 358 wounded; at least 24 civilians were killed.

In Washington, President Reagan told Congress and the press the reasons for U.S. operations in Grenada. Reporting to Congress under the War Powers Resolution, the president informed Thomas P. "Tip" O'Neill, speaker of the House, and Strom Thurmond, president pro tempore of the Senate, that U.S. troops had joined the "OECS collective security forces in assisting the restoration of conditions of law and order and to facilitate the protection and evacuation of United States citizens." Then, in reference to the resolution's 60-day limitation upon such intervention without congressional approval, Reagan added, "Our forces will remain only so long as their presence is required."

When reporters asked for details about the military situation, the president replied: "We are yielding to the influence of General Vessey in that we don't think in these early hours of that landing that we should be on the horn asking the commanders to stop and give us detailed reports." On the international scene, news of U.S. military operations on Grenada aroused the government of Prime Minister Margaret Thatcher in Great Britain and the Canadian government. Public questions and criticism of the need for Operation Urgent Fury surfaced during the operation and continued well into 1984. General Vessey detailed the reasons for the invasion to the press on October 29. On November 2, Deputy Secretary of State Kenneth W. Dam and Maj. General Crist explained the operation to the House Foreign Affairs Committee, while Admiral McDonald and General Paul Gorman, commander in chief of U.S. Southern Command, provided a similar briefing to the Senate Armed Services Committee.

On November 8, members of the House Appropriations Committee questioned Secretary Weinberger and General Paul X. Kelley, USMC, Commandant of the U.S. Marine Corps, about the press embargo and joint tactical planning and execution. During an appearance on *Meet the Press* on November 6, 1983, General Vessey candidly summarized the operation in these words:

> We planned the operation in a very short period of time—in about 48 hours. We planned it with insufficient intelligence for the type of operation we wanted to conduct. As a result, we probably used more force than we needed to do the job, but the operation went reasonably well. Things did go wrong, but generally, the operation was a success. The troops did very well.

On November 3, 1983, the General Assembly of the United Nations voted 108 to 9 for a resolution deploring the "armed invasion" in Grenada. Only Israel and El Salvador joined the six Caribbean countries in voting against the resolution offered by Nicaragua and Zimbabwe. Many who abstained made public statements of opposition to the United States, including Britain, Japan, West Germany, and Canada. "The United States is proud to have participated in the liberation of the people of Grenada, Jeane Kirkpatrick, U.S. ambassador to the United Nations, told the assembly after the vote. "We are proud to have voted against a resolution that deplored this positive and constructive achievement," she said.

At a special meeting of the OAS, I assured members that U.S. forces would remain in Grenada only as long as necessary to restore order and government and evacuate Americans. Meanwhile, Nicaragua, Mexico, Peru, Bolivia, Colombia, Argentina, Venezuela, Ecuador, Panama, Brazil, the Dominican Republic, Uruguay, the Bahamas, and Trinidad-Tobago condemned the invasion as a violation of the principles of non-intervention and self-determination. But St. Lucia, Dominica, Barbados, St. Vincent, Antigua, and Jamaica justified the action saying it was a pre-emptive operation against military threats of leftist Grenada's regime.

The Bolivian ambassador introduced a resolution condemning the invasion after playing a tape recorded by Ambassador Williams, in which she attacked the United States. I was surprised that the Nicaraguan ambassador, who represented the Sandinistas, did not second the resolution. Sitting next to me was Don Rafael de la Colina, the Mexican, who usually would be the one to support such a condemnation. I had the privilege of visiting with him the night before, presenting my views and asking him how he would vote.

He kindly suggested that he would reflect on it, but he certainly created a very strong impression on me that he could remain neutral. And that was a very great encouragement to me because I knew that if he didn't second the resolution condemning the United States, no one else would, including the Nicaraguans.

The Bolivian ambassador said, "There is a motion before the chair. Do I hear a second?" All eyes turned to Don Rafael. It seemed to be a foregone conclusion that this senior representative of a nation that had fought one big and two little wars against the big bully of the North would join in the condemnation.

He did not rise. He did not speak. The Bolivian called out: "Is there a second?" Don Rafael said nothing. Finally, after a few minutes, the Bolivian backed down. "There being no second, the motion is withdrawn."

I embraced Don Rafael, and some other delegates came over and did the same. I believe the delegates realized that our action in Grenada signaled a sea change, the turning of the tide of Soviet incursions in the Western Hemisphere.

After my speech to the OAS, Pieter Von Bennekom, vice president of United Press International (UPI), wrote this article:

> At a special session of the OAS after the invasion. Prime Minister Eugenia Charles of Dominica told the group that U.S. and Caribbean forces would leave the island as soon as a provisional government was set up. Some members of the OAS believed the invasion violated the OAS Charter and the Rio Treaty, which prohibited intervention in the affairs of member states. A tape-recorded message from Grenada's ambassador to the OAS, Dessima Williams, was played to her colleagues. She said she went into hiding because of threats against her life.

Immediately after the session, Permanent Council President Fernando Salazar Paredes of Bolivia called for a special afternoon session, alluding to several delegations troubled by the military action. He did not name the nations involved, but sources said Mexico and Nicaragua requested the session. But after three hours of hearing angry voices of condemnation of the invasion by some countries and understanding by others, the afternoon session concluded without a censure resolution even being proposed. I assured my OAS colleagues, 'the presence of the collective security force will be continued for only as long as is necessary to ensure its objectives. I listed those goals as "to restore law and order, help the people of Grenada restore functioning institutions of government, and facilitate the departure of those who wish to leave." My speech was credited with the OAS decision not to even propose a censure resolution.

The right to choose and change a nation's government through the ballot box is sacred. The reality that Grenadians were being denied that right was the reason for the invasion, the first time the United States had intervened militarily in the English-speaking Caribbean. For 39 years, the people of the island nation of Grenada celebrate October 25 as their Thanksgiving, a special day to commemorate how the United States military rescued them from a Communist takeover and restored constitutional government.

The success of the Grenada campaign is inspiring evidence of long-term payoffs for removing repressive regimes in favor of democratic ones. Almost all Grenadians agree they are better off due to the American action. Today, Grenada is prosperous, peaceful, and progressive. Tourist boats that disappeared during Communist rule have returned, as have foreign investments.

Operation Urgent Fury also gave the administration a sense of momentum, propelling them to intensify U.S. support for pro-U.S. regimes in El Salvador and Guatemala and Contra rebels fighting the Sandinista government of Nicaragua. The Monroe Doctrine's concepts will remain alive as long as the American Government and people believe it is proper and necessary for the United States to act unilaterally against colonization or puppet governments in the Western Hemisphere.

Years after the Grenada invasion, in 1991, I was part of a team from the Heritage Foundation that had been invited to the Soviet Union to help write a new constitution. We stayed at the Hotel "Octobraskaya," dubbed thus in honor of the October Revolution of 1917. It was up-scale and cheap; all the extras were included in a government-subsidized fee, including a copious buffet with unlimited caviar and vodka. The top Communists lived well.

How can I ever forget one dinner meeting with a group of former Soviet (and now Russian) generals and admirals? Awash with the free vodka—I lost count at nine—they dropped all diplomatic pretense and turned boastful. Most notable was one, notable first for his appearance, not to be believed had he been portrayed in a movie or a comic strip. Medals and ribbons in profusion, pinned to his left shoulder, chest, and upper stomach in sufficient numbers to provoke a permanent list to port, and a neck—so thick—that started at his ears and went straight down. He is notable, too, for his role as one of the officers in charge of crushing the Czech uprising, the "Prague Spring."

"Crushing." Not my term, but his. Early in 1968, the Czechs began maneuvering for freedom from Moscow, led by a Communist functionary-turned-patriot, Alexander Dubček. Dubček sought, in his own words, "Socialism with a human face" to reassure Moscow that he and his government were good Communists, just working to clean up some internal problems. Moscow was neither convinced nor amused and dispatched my dinner companion to take care of the problem.

"First," he said, "We had to get Dubček out of town." The tanks were standing by, ready to move in. But—how to move him out? Offer him an honorary degree from a distant university or an invitation to an important meeting, even a bribe? The Soviets managed to get him out of the way on some pretext I am unaware of.

And then: "And then we rolled! We crushed them. We crushed them." This was a line punctuated by an upward thrust of his right fist, leaving no doubt as to his meaning. His friends burst into applause. This had been his shining moment, the high point of a career now floundering in stagnation.

A few vodkas later—a few, or many, memory fails—another general launched into the subject of Grenada. "We really had plans for that island," he said. "Cuba was off limits because they couldn't bring in any more Soviet assets, too many people were watching, but Grenada, they thought, was off the radar. "We could hardly wait for the new airport," he said. "We had high hopes, except for that shit, Reagan."

I said, "I guess you'd have to call him a 'victorious shit.' "

"Big shit!"

"Yeah," said I, "but he's our big shit!"

Captain William Stone
Painting by Charles Nelson Peale 1774

Top row:
Middendorf's great-great-great grandfather, Captain William Stone, was one of America's first Naval officers commanding the original *Hornet*. It sailed with the First Continental Fleet under Commodore Esek Hopkins. He owned and built the *Hornet* and the *Wasp*, part of the original US Navy's eight ships. c.1775.

Middendorf's mother Sara Boone Middendorf was presented to the St. James Court in England.

1914 Harvard winning crew. Middendorf's father and uncle are on far left and far right. ▶

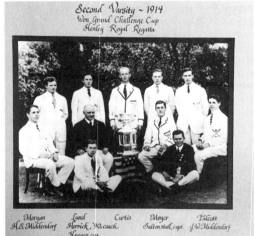

Father, H.S. Middendorf (Bow #4), and Uncle Bill (Bow #5), rowing for Harvard, won the Grand Challenge Cup for the 1914 Henley Royal Regatta in England. The 1914 Harvard crew is crossing the finish line!

JWM serving in the NROTC at Holy Cross

Ens. J.W. Middendorf II (USNR), 1945, engineer officer and navigator of LCS (L) 53.

JWM's father Henry Stump Middendorf

Uncle John William Middendorf, Jr.

The Middendorf family at their home on Husted Lane. (Seated from left) John, 8; Amy, 10; Ralph, 2, and Franny, 13. (Standing from left) Martha, 11, and Mr. and Mrs. Middendorf.

On the campaign trail with Barry, Peggy Goldwater with campaign treasurer Bill Middendorf (right). Photo by Don Dornan

USS LCS(L)(3)-53 under way in San Francisco Bay while returning home in 1944. ENS J.W. Middendorf USNR is the tall man on the bridge.

ROBERT FROST American Poet & Friend

In the late 1950's, Middendorf became friends with Robert Frost and visited him at his log cabin in Ripton, Vermont.

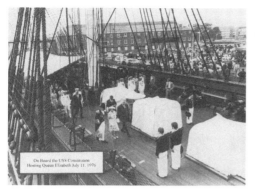

Secretary of the Navy Miiddendorf on the USS *Constitution* with Queen Elizabeth II

Queen Elizabeth was invited to the USS *Constitution* for the 1976 celebrations by Secretary of the Navy Middendorf.

J. William Middendorf II on board Air Force II with Vice President George H.W. Bush

Bottom row: Ambassador to the Netherlands J. William Middendorf II with Dutch Foreign Minister Luns

The Defense Team, 1976. From left: Secretary of Defense Donald Rumsfeld, Secretary of the Navy J. William Middendorf II, Secretary of the Air Force Thomas Reed, and Secretary of the Army Martin Hoffman. (Defense Department)

President Eisenhower and J. William Middendorf II at Goldwater Strategy Session, 1964 ▶

President Gerald Ford on Forrestal carrier with Secretary of the Navy Middendorf

President Ford and Secretary Middendorf

President Nixon and Secretary Middendorf have a walking meeting on the lawn of the White House.

Mouza with husband Admiral Zumwalt, President Ford, Secretary Navy Middendorf and wife Isabelle at Army Navy football game

J.W. Middendorf conducting his *U.S. Capitol March* on the Capitol steps. July 1978

Secretary of the Navy Bill Middendorf and immediate staff. L–R: John Jenkins, Bob Sims, Chris Coon, Bill Kelly, Bob Ferneau, Les Palmer, Henry Vitali, Jerry Burke, Secretary Middendorf, and Doug Mow.

6/20/74–At the Pentagon swearing-in ceremonies of J. William Middendorf II to be Secretary of the Navy, there was a surprise for Middendorf and his wife, Isabelle. Middendorf's hobby is music; at present, he is composing a march for Secretary of Defense James Schlesinger, so Schlesinger brought in a Marine Band drum major followed by a fife and drum corps to provide Middendorf with some inspiration.

Inspecting the Queen's honor guard the day I presented my credentials as ambassador to the Netherlands.

11/2/76 – Sporting a Marine Corps tee shirt U.S. Navy Secretary J. William Middendorf II gives the "V" sign to onlookers after defeating the U.S. Marine Corps team in a rowing race, led by famed Marine Corps Commendant General P.X. Kelly, on Rome's Tiber River.

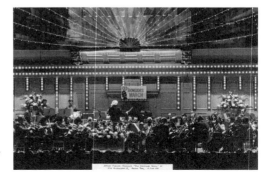

Arthur Fiedler conducts Secretary of the Navy Middendorf's "Old Ironsides March," Boston Pops Orchestra, June 1975.

To J. William Middendorf, II - With Best Wishes!
Ronald Reagan

For Ambassador J. William Middendorf
With best wishes,
Ronald Reagan

INVEST IN AMERICA
PRESENTATION
1982

On October 2, 1981, OAS Ambassador J. William Middendorf met with Army General Alfredo Stroessner. Stroessner came to power in 1954, and military rule continued until 1989, upon which the nation of Paraguay moved toward a multi-party democracy with a new constitution adopted in 1992. Paraguay in the 21st century has largely avoided the political strife and strong-man rule that characterizes much of its history.

Prime Minister Margaret Thatcher with Ambassador Middendorf at the International Democratic Union Meeting, Tokyo, September 5, 1989

OAS Caribbean Initiative President Reagan and Ambassador Middendorf

As Ambassador to the Netherlands Middendorf hosted local monthly composer evenings.
L–R: J. William Middendorf II, composer, and master pianist Arthur Rubinstein.

◄ *Thumbs Up, America!* Inaugural theme for President Ronald Reagan and his First Lady, 1981. Composed by Amb. Middendorf, with lyrics by Sammy Cahn.

Secretary of the Navy Middendorf with Bob Hope, June 6, 1974

▲ Middendorf with American painter and friend Edward Hopper

Ambassador Middendorf plays on the Netherlands baseball team.

Master stained glass maker Joep Nicolas teaches Ambassador to the Netherlands J. William Middendorf II.

OAS Meeting during Argentina-Britain Falkland Islands crisis

Shah of Iran Mohammad Reza Pahlavi

Meeting with OAS Ambassador J. William Middendorf II prior to formation of Project Economic Justice Task Force in Washington, DC, 1984. L–R: David Luft, Amb. Middendorf, Frank Gannon of CARA, Norman Kurland, Fr. William Ferree, William Schirra.

High Road to Economic Justice report to President Reagan in August 1987. In commending the task force effort, Reagan offered a kind personal comment: "Scientists say a perpetual motion machine is impossible. Considering that this task force completed its work without any appropriation from Congress, I think we should introduce Bill Middendorf to a few scientists."

Bill Middendorf sketching at a meeting

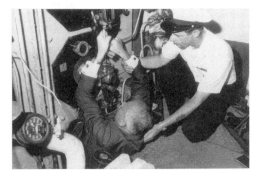
1974–1977
Navy Secretary Middendorf, a former engineering officer in WWII, inspected the engine rooms of over 325 ships from 20 different nations.

Presenting the "Order of the Golden Snipe" after a successful inspection.

To "the Father of the Marine Corps Marathon" in 1976, as the 62nd Secretary of the Navy, Amb. J. William Middendorf II approved the first MCM. He also ran in the first eight editions of the race. Each year "The Middendorf Award" is presented to the MCM male and female champions. Presented by MCM Director Alex Hetherington, on the occasion of his predecessor's retirement, 18 January 2023.

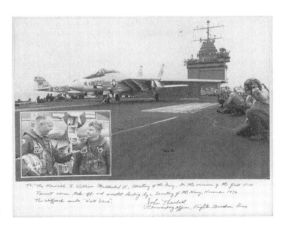

Secretary of the Navy Middendorf on the first F-14 Tomcat Carrier

Mr. Gorbachev, Tear Down This Wall!
Ronald Reagan

Mr. Gorbachev, "Tear Down This Wall"
Ed Feulner and Ambassador Middendorf experiencing a joyous moment tearing down the Berlin wall.
November 1989

As Communism was collapsing in the Soviet Union, President Boris Yeltsin invited a team from the Heritage Foundation, including Dr. Edwin J. Feulner and J. William Middendorf, to draft a constitution for the new Russia called *The Privatization Handbook*. Yeltsin realized that privatization, the process of transferring state-owned facilities to private-sector owners, was the only way the new Russia could survive. Unfortunately, Communist members of the Duma prevented many of the key recommendations from going into effect. A small group of oligarchs obtained control of a dozen central industries. Economic collapse and inflation followed.

My wife Isabelle

HENRY KISSINGER

Bill Sketching

President Ronald Reagan

My Brilliant Ride

Marine Corps Marathon (MCM). Middendorf ran the first 8 MCM 1977–84.

J.W. Middendorf and Jay Limerick of New Zealand win World Masters Doubles Rowing Championship, Toronto 1985.

Ambassador Middendorf receives his 5th (3rd from the Navy Department and 2nd from the Defense Department) Distinguished Public Service Award presented by Secretary of the Navy Carlos Del Toro on April 10, 2022, at the Naval War College. ▶

14 | Venezuela's Young Fidel Castro

VENEZUELA IS NOW PAYING THE PRICE for adopting gun control under Hugo Chavez in 2012. The shocking nature of an economic collapse that led Venezuela from one of the richest countries in Latin America to one of the poorest has been well documented. One aspect of the Venezuelan crisis that does not receive much coverage is the country's gun control regime. All guns were outlawed when Chavez came to power, and harsh penalties were imposed on violators. The Venezuelan Armed Forces have exclusive power to control, register and confiscate firearms. Many citizens regretted the repressive gun control legislation the Venezuelan government implemented in then. Naturally, this regret is warranted. The Venezuelan government is among the most oppressive in the world. It has a proven track record of violating fundamental civil liberties such as free speech, debasing its national currency, confiscating private property, and creating economic controls that destroy the country's productivity.

Once Chavez was elected president, the U.S.–Venezuelan relationship underwent radical changes. Deeply influenced by Fidel Castro as well as other anti-U.S. scholars and leaders, Chavez's bombastic, populist rhetoric leveraged against the country's elite helped him to create a base of support for his policies. Chavez hosted *Aló Presidente*, a weekly radio and television show which aired throughout his presidency and gave him an advantage over his political opponents. His presence on national broadcast media allowed him not only to connect emotionally with his followers but also to impose his narrative over the opinion of dissenting leaders who could not access mass media as easily. Elections have proven to be useless, as they've been mired with corruption and charges of government tampering. For many, taking up arms is the only option left for the country to shake off its tyrannical government. The Venezuelan government has prevented an uprising by passing draconian gun control.

As ambassador to the Organization of American States from 1981 to 1985, I was often asked about Hugo Chavez and his Communist feelings before he came to power. In 1983, Chavez was a teacher at the Military Academy of Venezuela with a reputation for rousing lectures and political criticism of the government. He began to travel the country, recruiting new members for his leftist military movement. Chavez was described to me as a "young Fidel Castro with oil." I warned my friends in Venezuela not to support the socialist-Marxist system Chavez proposed, including wealth redistribution, and other Communist tenets. He attracted support among the poor living in the slums of Venezuela called barrios, where 50 percent of the population lives.

Unfortunately, my warnings about Chavez's friendship with Fidel Castro and his admiration for people like Mao Zedong and Muammar Qaddafi were not taken seriously by some of my Venezuelan friends and OAS members. The descriptions of my relevant China and Cuban experiences fell on deaf years regarding Venezuela. I was told that Venezuela's prosperity and civil structure were too secure to be vulnerable.

Hugo Chavez was a career Army paratrooper commander dissatisfied with Venezuela's pro-U.S. government when he led a failed military coup against President Carlos Andres Perez in 1992. Chavez was subsequently captured and appeared on television asking his co-conspirators to give up the fight "for now." Although his coup attempt was unsuccessful, his television appearance endeared him to Venezuela's poor, who viewed Chavez as their hero fighting government corruption. After serving two years in jail, President Rafael Caldera pardoned Chavez and his fellow officers.

Four years later, Hugo Chavez launched an anti-corruption, anti-poverty campaign and won the 1998 election with 56 percent of the popular vote, mainly due to his near-universal support from Venezuela's poor and oppressed. Chavez's election was welcomed by many members of the U.S. media, including Larry Rohter, Bureau Chief of *The New York Times* in South America, which was widely influential in America and with policymakers. On July 28, 2000, Rohter wrote a column about Chavez, including the following:

> For the Latin American left, hungry for a homegrown hero, Mr. Chavez is a godsend, a charismatic military man who condemns capitalism and promises social justice. An orator who is by turns spellbinding and funny, Mr. Chavez has gathered the poor into a powerful force that is demanding change.

The U.S. media seemed to value coverage of conflict and novelty in ways that encourage populist movements. Chavez's rise to power was fueled by his populist rhetoric as well as his ability to monopolize U.S. press coverage. Chavez captured the focus of U.S. media coverage, indicating that conflict and novelty may be the highest news values in contemporary U.S. society.

He was nearly a media darling in his outrageous denunciations of President Bush. Chavez was the most prominent source quoted in the U.S. media. It appears that Chavez knew how to use harsh language and dramatic gestures in his speeches and his regular radio and television appearances.

This propaganda tactic was very effective for Chavez, Mao Zedong of China, and Fidel Castro of Cuba, allowing them to dominate the media and portray themselves as patriotic or morally good and their opponents as corrupt enemies. American journalist Edgar Snow described Mao as a Chinese version of George Washington in a series of interviews in 1937. Herbert Matthews, a reporter for *The New York Times* wrote in 1957 that Castro had "strong ideas of liberty, democracy, social justice, and the need to restore the Cuban Constitution and hold free elections."

If our State Department had taken a more forceful role before Chavez's election in 1998, Venezuela could have been a beacon for democracy in South America. A free press is a necessary ingredient for democracy, but with freedom comes responsibility. Stories by American journalists hailing Chavez as a representative of the poor helped him gain power. Unlike Castro, Chavez never tried to hide his Communist sentiments. He spoke with admiration about Castro and Arab leaders like Saddam Hussein and Muammar Qaddafi, even as he reached out to leaders in China, Russia, and Iran.

Upon entering office in 1998, Chavez ordered the constitution rewritten to keep himself in power. He established Cuban-style neighborhood spy committees, called "Bolivarian Circles," to inform on citizens who expressed dissident ideas. Chavez's policies provoked and sparked strikes that shut down the state oil company. Dissidents were shot or incarcerated. Chavez enacted new laws to seize private property, close commercial radio and TV stations for airing content deemed "contrary to national security," and jailed ordinary citizens for voicing criticism of public officials. He consolidated single-party rule by stacking Venezuela's courts with provisional, partisan judges and won a referendum on his leadership only after padding the electoral rolls and intimidating his opponents.

Chavez supported the Revolutionary Armed Forces of Colombia (FARC) guerrillas and allowed FARC units to camp in Venezuelan territory. His regime granted FARC commander Rodrigo Granda Venezuelan citizenship before he was captured and returned to Colombia. Chavez's regional satellite TV network, Telesur, bashed Colombia for its relations with the United States and beaming Marxist propaganda throughout South America. He proposed two cartels, Petrocaribe and Petro Sur, to integrate Latin America's state hydrocarbon industries under his dominion with the idea of choking off regional sales to the U.S. He opposed the planned Free Trade

Area of the Americas while advocating his own Bolivarian Alternative for the Americas (ALBA), a vaguely defined aid network financed by Venezuelan oil profits. He committed more than $3 billion a year in aid to Latin American neighbors without accountability to Venezuelan citizens.

Chavez also announced plans to acquire nuclear technology from Iran, fueling fears he might try to develop a bomb. He embarked on an arms buildup to scare Brazil and Colombia, planning to buy more than a million rifles, armored vehicles, attack helicopters, and fighter bombers from Russia. The new constitution changed the country's name to the Bolivarian Republic of Venezuela, re-structured the government with a weaker legislative and a stronger executive branch, and inaugurated a wide range of socioeconomic changes in line with Bolivarianism, or what Chavez deemed socialism for the 21st century. He promised a peaceful social revolution that would usher in a golden age for Venezuela. He failed to deliver either prosperity or equality and immediately labeled the Venezuelan Congress and Supreme Court corrupt and expanded the military's role.

Chavez repressed his own citizens by confiscating property, permitted thousands of Cuban officials to form a secretive shadow regime within his government, and enacted "social responsibility" laws that made it a jailable offense to criticize public officials. He opposed the United States, its prosperity, and its definition of representative democracy. Free markets and human rights had no place in his utopia. He believed neighboring democratic, and market-oriented nations represented a U.S. empire of sorts, though they were sovereign states.

Chavez nationalized hundreds of private businesses and foreign-owned assets, such as oil projects run by Exxon Mobil and Conoco Phillips, gutting the country of crucial technical expertise. With the international companies withdrawing from their Venezuelan operations and inexperienced, incompetent government appointees replacing company managers, engineers, and other experts, production plunged to new lows. He initiated price controls intended to make essential goods more affordable for the poor by capping the price of flour and cooking oil. Many Venezuelan companies stopped production because the price controls made them unprofitable, increasing costs.

Chavez stacked the country's courts with political allies, passed laws restricting the ability of journalists to criticize the government, and consistently sought ways to eliminate checks on his power. He expanded the power of the presidency, effectively took control of the Supreme Court, harassed the press, and jailed or eliminated political opponents. In speech after speech, he attacked business, opposition, and media leaders who questioned his methods and objectives, calling them degenerates. When

Catholic bishops spoke out against him, he called them "evils investments." The Human Rights Watch of the United Nations issued a report in 2008 critical of Chavez's human rights record. It claimed that he manipulated the country's courts and intimidated the media, labor unions, and civil society.

In 2000, Chavez was reelected in a landslide, but two years later, he lost the military's support after proposing harsh retaliation measures against protestors who opposed his "Cubanization of Venezuela." However, a 36-hour coup headed by Pedro Carmona, a prominent business leader who was declared interim president, ended after the public demanded Chavez's return to power. During this time, Chavez accused the U.S. of backing the short-lived coup and plotting his assassination, claims which he frequently reiterated over the course of his presidency. Moreover, after Chavez was reinstated, workers at the Petróleos de Venezuela S.A. (PDVSA), the state-owned oil company, went on strike for two months to try and force Chavez out of office. However, Chavez used this strike as an opportunity to dismiss more than 18,000 employees, replacing workers and technocrats with loyal political supporters so that his government could regain control of the country's oil industry.

In 2003 Chavez launched the Bolivarian Missions, a wide range of social programs funded by oil revenues, to strengthen his public support. These government programs provided adult literacy, health care, housing, and food services for low-income Venezuelans. The Bolivarian Missions restored Venezuelans' confidence in Chavez, which was affirmed by his 2004 recall referendum victory. Furthermore, after Chavez's allies won all 167 seats in Venezuela's National Assembly in 2005, he announced his plan to create a two-million-person civilian military to fight against foreign invasion while ending the 35-year military relationship between the United States and Venezuela.

During his presidency, *Aló Presidente* provided Chavez with a direct, unfiltered channel to communicate with the Venezuelan people, but he did not spend all his time on the show in serious policy discussions. Chavez sang, danced, told stories of his youth, explained his ideology, showcased factories and housing complexes, and confronted his domestic and international political enemies.

Chavez used the historical, socioeconomic, and religious rhetorical frames on *Aló Presidente* to build and maintain support for his Bolivarian Revolution in Venezuela. He frequently glorified historical political figures such as Cipriano Castro, a military strongman who seized the presidency in the violent Revolución Liberal Restauradora in 1899. He expressed deep admiration for Castro's refusal to repay loans to imperialist Britain, Germany, and Italy. Although Chavez downplayed Castro's violence, repression, and corruption, he openly admired Castro's nationalism and pride.

In 2006, President George Bush's Secretary of Defense, Donald Rumsfeld, compared Chavez to Adolf Hitler and accused him of authoritarianism and supporting violent acts against U.S. allies. Bush countered Chavez's anti-U.S. statements by declaring the U.S. supported the Venezuelan people in their quest for democracy and economic wellbeing in the face of Chavez's growing despotism, socialism, and corruption. While Chavez's rhetoric was framed to discredit Bush and his motives toward Venezuela and Latin America as untrustworthy, Bush seldom criticized Chavez directly, relying instead on members of his administration to undermine Chavez.

In 2006, Chavez was reelected with a 63 percent landslide victory and announced the creation of Venezuela's single political party, the United Socialist Party of Venezuela. Now that Chavez and his Chavistas controlled all three branches of government, they nationalized the energy, agriculture, and banking industries, canceling broadcast licenses for private organizations critical of their government and creating state-owned media outlets to promote their cause.

While addressing the U.N. in 2006, Chavez said: "The devil came here yesterday, and it smells of sulfur still today."

Chavez made the sign of the cross, folded his hands into prayer position, glanced upwards, and continued: "Yesterday, ladies and gentlemen, from this rostrum, the President of the United States, the gentleman to whom I refer as the devil, came here, talking as if he owned the world. I think we could call a psychiatrist to analyze yesterday's statement made by the President of the United States." His statement was received with thunderous applause at the U.N. General Assembly as well as international acclaim.

In 2007, Chavez severed ties with the International Monetary Fund (IMF) and the World Bank, denouncing them as institutions dominated by U.S. imperialism. Alternately, Chavez tried to develop a Bank of the South funded largely by Venezuela's oil revenues that would provide loans to South American countries without the free-market reforms required by the IMF or World Bank. Although leaders from Argentina, Brazil, Paraguay, Uruguay, Ecuador, and Bolivia signed an agreement pledging large deposits, the Bank of the South never became a viable institution. Chavez continued his attacks on what he deemed as imperialist U.S. policies, including the Iraq War, and cultivated relationships with U.S. enemies such as Cuba and Russia. Moreover, Chavez sought to build Venezuelan international influence through leadership in the Organization of Petroleum Exporting

Countries (OPEC), a failed attempt to gain a seat on the United Nations Security Council, and deals providing cheap oil to Latin American and Caribbean countries.

Later in 2007, Venezuela held a referendum on amendments to the 1999 constitution because Chavez wanted to abolish presidential term limits, restrict, or eliminate press freedoms, and detain disloyal citizens without habeas corpus during a state of emergency. However, this referendum failed, marking the first time Chavez lost an election in nine years and delaying his plans to transform Venezuela into a socialist state. While denying that the Bush administration was supporting regime-change efforts in Venezuela, Condoleezza Rice, President Bush's national security advisor, stated that: "We do hope that Chavez recognizes that the whole world is watching and that he takes advantage of this opportunity to right his own ship, which has been moving, frankly, in the wrong direction for quite a long time."

By 2008, U.S.–Venezuelan relations reached an all-time low after Chavez expelled the U.S. ambassador and recalled Venezuela's ambassador from Washington. In 2008, the Human Rights Watch released a 230-page report on the Chavez regime's human rights record that found he had used the judiciary for his own financial and political gain while intimidating the media, labor unions, and the public.

Chavez announced in 2011 that he was being treated for cancer. Two years later, he said his illness prevented him from serving as president and recommended Vice President Nicholas Maduro as his successor. When Chavez died on March 5, 2013, Maduro campaigned on a promise to carry on Chavez's legacy. He barely edged out opposition candidate Henrique Caprilles, taking merely 50.6 percent of the vote. Maduro was not lacking in leftist convictions. He studied in Cuba, was a super left-wing Socialist League member, and worked as a union negotiator before joining electoral politics in Venezuela.

As Venezuela's economy collapsed, Maduro's popularity has also plummeted, and protests have rocked the country. He has reacted to the chaos and dissent with authoritarian tactics. In 2016, he blocked an attempt to hold a referendum on whether he should be recalled. In March 2021, his loyalist-stacked Supreme Court dissolved the opposition-controlled legislative branch and usurped its power. He also violently cracked down on protests and imprisoned major political rivals.

Hyperinflation set off the most recent and precipitous descent. Recently, the peso, which had traded at parity of the U.S. dollar 30 years ago, is today a million to a dollar. Unbridled government spending and uncontrolled monetary expansion have left Venezuela in an economic free fall. The State

Department said that 93 percent of Venezuelans live below the poverty level, and the income of three to $10 a month is inadequate to pay for food and medicine for families. Twenty percent of the population has fled the country because of impoverished conditions and tyrannical power. Water shortages are endemic, blackouts are common, and the healthcare system has collapsed. Diseases such as diphtheria and malaria, which were all but eradicated decades ago, have returned.

Maduro is scrambling to cling to power as an unprecedented economic crisis batters his country. In recent months, he has been tossing political opponents in prison, cracking down on street protests with lethal force, with government security forces killing demonstrators. He has repeatedly postponed regional government elections to stave off his party's power threats. Venezuela's economic and political crisis reached a level of international emergency as Juan Guaido denounced Maduro in January 2019, claiming that the reelection was a sham. The United States immediately recognized Guaido as interim president. And many of Venezuela's neighbors and most Western countries have followed suit.

With Venezuela in flames, China and Russia seek claims in the rubble. For years, China and Russia have sought more influence in the Western Hemisphere and are increasingly motivated to bolster their economic and security positions in South America, Central America, and the Caribbean. China has pledged to invest $250 billion and reach half a trillion in trade, while Russia has invested billions in Venezuela. About 100 Russian troops landed outside of Caracas, Venezuela's capital, with unidentified equipment on March 16, 2019. Some U.S. officials feared they came to help Maduro fend off a U.S.-led attempt to depose him.

The U.S. recognizes Guaido, the leader of the country's opposition-controlled legislative body, as Venezuela's rightful president. Another problem is the presence of 20,000 to 25,000 Cuban security officials. Communist-run Cuba has been a key backer of the Venezuelan government since the revolution under Chavez in 1998. Right now, these Cubans represent his Praetorian Guards more so than his military that he can't entirely trust. In effect, Maduro has become a total pawn of Cuba.

Most polls indicate that over 80 percent of Venezuelans want Maduro gone. Some even encourage a civil uprising. To have a war, both sides must be armed. In the case of Venezuela, only one side—the government—has guns. As in all Communist takeovers, the first order of business is to take away the guns of the civilian population to control them totally. Maduro enjoys the full support of the armed Cuban forces, which are responsible for brutally repressing protests and terrorizing the population on motorcycles with the assistance of the police and the National Guard. In previous unrest, almost all the fatal victims have been civilians killed by the National Guard or the Cubans.

What is happening in Venezuela repeats that same old story of a country after the socialist locusts swoop in, promising to improve living conditions for the poor. Wealth is transferred to a small group of Communist leaders like Castro, Chavez, and Putin. In Venezuela's case, it is believed that large shipments of the country's gold reserves have been transferred to Switzerland in the name of Maduro and the small coterie he has paid off Communists, therefore, have fulfilled their promise to eliminate the wealth gap and income inequality by pushing everyone down to a uniform poverty level. Meanwhile, Putin, Maduro, Castro, and others have become among the richest in the world. As always, with the one-person rule, all the country's wealth is transferred to that man and his closest allies.

Although more than 50 countries recognize Guaido as President, Maduro has the support of the Cuban Praetorian guard and remains in the presidential palace. The United States and other members of the OAS have a great deal at stake in achieving a turnaround in Venezuela. Venezuela has been one of the world's least economically free nations since 1998 when Chavez came to power. Its economic freedom score is 24.8, making its economy the 176th freest in the 2022 Index of the Heritage Foundation. Venezuela is ranked 32nd among 32 countries in the Americas region, and its overall score is well below the regional and world averages.

Its modern democratic era lasted from the end of military rule in 1959 until the election of Hugo Chavez. His successor, Nicolas Maduro, completed the destruction of democracy and consolidated the authoritarian dictatorship in 2017. The deeply corrupt socialist regime's policies have led to one of historic economic depressions and a migration crisis. The regime has also bankrupted state-owned oil company PDVSA and is actively engaged in illicit trafficking. Property

By all measures, Venezuela is a failed state. The economy is in ruins, and the humanitarian crisis has resulted in Latin America's worst refugee and migration exodus. The political impasse has resulted in a proxy showdown between the United States and hostile foreign actors. U.S. policymakers cannot predetermine the outcome—but they can strongly influence events. They should maintain support for interim President Guaido and ask America's international allies and partners to help by increasing targeted sanctions against Maduro's illegitimate government. They can prepare for various outcomes in a post-Maduro Venezuela. Above all, U.S. policy must remain aligned with that of U.S. regional partners. The United States must remain committed to a peaceful and democratic transition in Venezuela.

In a post-Maduro Venezuela, the future government will find itself dealing with a complex security dilemma. It has to find a way of demobilizing and disarming over 100,000 paramilitary fighters loyal to Maduro. There are also Venezuelan guerillas, Colombia guerillas (FARC), and numerous domestic criminal organizations with entrenched interests throughout the country. Complicating the security conditions is the state's lack of control over many parts of Venezuela and the proliferation of criminal organizations. In terms of homicide rates, Venezuela is Latin America's most violent country, and the capital of Caracas is one of the most dangerous cities in the world.

The U.S. State Department must work with interim President Guaido's Administration to create a post-Maduro peace plan. Regardless of who assumes control, the United States should also develop plans with Venezuela's neighbors, Colombia, and Ecuador, to disarm and demobilize the paramilitaries and insurgencies. Fixing Venezuela's citizen security crisis must be a priority as well. There can be no free or fair elections under the current security circumstances.

The United States must strongly urge other countries to address Cuba and Russia's destabilizing role in Venezuela. Partner nations should not be investing in Cuban state-owned enterprises and should openly condemn the regime for undermining Venezuela's democratic ambitions. The United States should adopt targeted sanctions against the Russian state and state-supported enterprises for providing Maduro with security assistance. Russia's direct role in helping Maduro circumvent U.S. oil sanctions should be met with a similar combination of sanctions.

In Russian President Vladimir Putin, Maduro has an ally who can guide him through a crisis, like the way in which Russia has had success with Syria's Bashar al-Assad. For Russia's leader, propping up Maduro requires little investment and has the potential for high reward. Supporting Maduro does not require Russia to provide a massive troop deployment or significant financial investment like in Syria. While Venezuela is indebted to Russia, financial concerns are not the most important issue on the table. There could even be a scenario where Russia forgives Venezuela's debt in exchange for oil assets or other forms of collateral. U.S. policymakers should sanction Russian-backed, entities that are providing Maduro with security assistance and support for circumventing U.S. oil and gold sanctions.

For the Cuban regime, maintaining Maduro in power is in its national interest. Havana is economically bankrupt and unable to survive without a foreign benefactor and the Soviet Union had filled that role. Cuba's economic crisis following the fall of the Soviet Union brought a need for a new donor state. The current relationship with Venezuela emerged following the election of Chavez. The bilateral relationship is not simply an alliance—

Chavez himself described it as a merger of two revolutions. A sizeable percentage of Cuba's gross domestic product comes from Venezuelan subsidies and aid, peaking at 12 percent in 2012. According to numerous credible accounts, Cuba has thousands of officials embedded in the intelligence and security services of the Maduro government. For obvious reasons, Cuba's influence and presence have found their way into key Venezuelan government institutions. Cuba's survival depends on Maduro or a leader who shares Maduro's vision for the bilateral relationship. No other country, not even Russia, appears willing to replace Venezuela's subsidies.

Interim president Guaido has vowed to end the Cuban presence in Venezuela. The Trump Administration rightfully recognized that the road to liberty in Venezuela runs through Havana and ramped up sanctions against Cuba. A U.S. delegation from the Biden Administration reportedly visited Caracas, Venezuela, to meet with top government officials and iron out a deal to bring more Venezuelan crude oil to market. It was the highest-level visit by U.S. government officials to Venezuela in years. To send senior officials to Caracas to try to get more oil from a leader who is sanctioned and under indictment shows a real sense that increasing oil supply is of huge interest right now to the United States. It's especially noteworthy considering that the White House publicly criticized Venezuela recently for its disregard of human rights.

Venezuela's instability is spilling over into many countries in Latin America and the United States. Much of the crisis at U.S. borders is the result of millions of Venezuelan refugees. An estimated 5,000 Venezuelans flee the country daily to Argentina, Brazil, Chile, Ecuador, Peru, Mexico, and the United States. Many of these individuals and families lack the means to support themselves and rely heavily on their host countries. It is Latin America's worse refugee and migration crisis to date.

The exodus of Venezuelans can be traced back to a singular cause—the corrupt government of Nicolas Maduro. There are also no clear indications the end is near. Due to international actors meddling in Venezuela and the regime's tight-fisted grip on power, Maduro's weaknesses and unpopularity have not resulted in his removal from power. This could very well mean that Venezuela's instability will continue and result in a protracted crisis.

The Maduro regime would not be in power today were it not for the support it receives from its five key allies: Russia, China, Cuba, Iran, and Turkey. These states provide varying degrees of financial, diplomatic, and intelligence support to the Venezuelan regime. Some of these states have maintained close ties with Venezuela since the early years of the Hugo Chavez presidency. Others have emerged as new lifelines amid mounting international pressure. Russia, China, Cuba, and Iran, have distinct financial and geopolitical motivations for propping up the Maduro regime. Russia and Venezuela have a longstanding financial, political, and diplomatic partnership. Russia continues to help Venezuela circumvent oil sanctions and provide military supplies to the Maduro regime. China is owed by Venezuela at least $20 billion in loans, and Iran and Venezuela have had a partnership since the early years of the Chavez Administration. Cuba is existentially dependent on Venezuela but also continues to control the Maduro regime's intelligence apparatus and the Venezuelan military.

"The Venezuelan crisis long ago stopped being a local issue. It became a regional issue, and it is now an issue with diverse global implications. Understanding the influence and interests of other countries in Venezuela is a necessary condition to finding the way for a successful transition to democracy in the country and a route to lasting stability in the region," Francisco Santos, Colombian ambassador to the United States, warns.

15 | Ambassador to the European Community

AFTER THE 1984 ELECTION, Ronald Reagan asked George Shultz if he would stay on as secretary of State for the second term, and I believe that George said he would be pleased to stay. He saw an opportunity to swap out the left-over Haig team and put in his own. The word on the street soon had it that one by one, Shultz had been thanking various appointees for their loyal and valiant services, which were no longer required. My turn came: George called, "Can you come over and see me?" Our meeting was on a Sunday morning at his home. After the pleasantries—I'm sure that mine must have seemed a bit strained—he said, "Well, Bill, you know I've been asked to stay on, and I'm going to make some changes." Indeed. I put on my best good soldier smile and prepared to deliver the little speech I'd already rehearsed in my mind along the lines. "Grateful for the opportunity to have served the president, ready to assist in any way in the future, thanks, etc."

George continued, "I'd like to ask you if you'd be our new ambassador to the European Community in Brussels." I was startled and mumbled how much I enjoyed my position at the OAS, working on issues close to my heart: promoting privatization and working toward free market economies. I would have preferred to continue meeting those challenges in our own hemisphere, but George argued. There were more significant challenges, he implied, in an emerging coordinated Europe. New barriers to trade to overcome, changes in customs duties to be dealt with, and quotas on imports to be considered. Attitudes to overcome. "Let me give you an example," he said. "One of the things that I find difficult in relations with Europe is the French approach to trade. A very restrictive, narrow view focused only on what's in it for France. With your quiet and non-judgmental approach, you're the right man for the job and are needed."

My orientation was nowhere near as thorough as that for the Netherlands—I guess I was considered "qualified." But I was treated to a bit of history, which I share. The dream of a unified Europe began to take shape as a Pan-European Union in 1924, derailed in 1933 when Germany refused to play but was revived after the war. Winston Churchill called for a "United States of Europe" to begin, he suggested, with a partnership between France and Germany, one of many proposals that led to the European Coal and Steel Community (ECSC, comprising Germany, France, Italy, Belgium, Luxembourg, and the Netherlands), joined in 1958 by a newly created European Economic Community (EEC) and Euratom (for atomic energy cooperation). These three bodies merged under the umbrella of the European Community (EC), in 1965, informally known as the "common market" (and after 1993, were re-constituted as the "European Union").

As for the job, George was right. There were real challenges, not the least of which was trying to learn about, understand, and deal with what may have been the most complex political organization in the history of the world. When I arrived in Brussels in August 1985, the EC had employed some 12,000 staffers, conducted business in nine languages, and had major offices in Strasbourg, Brussels, and Luxembourg. It was organized into twenty departments, run by a policy-recommending Commission reporting to a policy-approving Council of Ministers, which listened to, but did not necessarily accept, advice from a fully separate organization, the European Parliament at Strasbourg, made up of an incredible collection of Reds, Greens, Socialists, Christian Democrats and members of the far-right National Front.

The EC had ten member states: those of the ECSC had been joined by Ireland, Denmark, Greece, and the United Kingdom (membership of which had been blocked for ten years in a French power-play). Spain and Portugal were added in 1986. There was some incentive—economics, pride, take your pick—to move the numbers. Most of my first few months on the job were taken up with the basic tasks of an ambassador: exchanging pleasantries with other members of the diplomatic corps, hosting visiting dignitaries, members of Congress, diplomats, and trade groups, and making courtesy visits to member countries. I visited eleven of the twelve in my eighteen-month tour, missing only Greece. I did squeeze in a few personal trips, including a visit to the Middendorf family farm in Germany, where I met with thirty distant relatives and slept in the 400-year-old farmhouse in the same bed as did many of my ancestors. I occupied some of my weekend time with music, for example, composing "European Overture," and was most pleased when the Symphonic Band of the Belgian Guides recorded it.

However, my real job was to participate in hard-nosed negotiations primarily over trade issues involving, on each side, hundreds of thousands of jobs. Willie de Klerc represented the EC. Our team included the new USTR, Clayton Yeutter, who had taken over from Bill Brock. I was on-scene as a facilitator and coordinator; Yeutter was the hammer who would willingly fly over on a moment's notice to help wrestle our opponents to the ground in long and exhausting sessions.

During my tour, the more essential issues included agricultural subsidies and tariffs; suspicions that the Europeans were trying to overwhelm the U.S. market with cheap steel; EC distress because the United States was reluctant to share advancing technology; disputes over alleged covert subsidies provided by the U.S. government to the Boeing Aircraft Company and open government subsidies given to Airbus (the prime European manufacturer of passenger airliners); and the EC refusal to accept American beef that had been fed growth hormones.

Let me start with the one that almost drove my team crazy: agriculture. The EC "Common Agricultural Policy" (CAP) was created to ensure a stable farm economy by providing subsidies and support (primarily but not exclusively, I was told, to some very wealthy farmers in France). The goal was to encourage production, partly due to the hard times that followed World War II. The reality: as reported in *Time*, September 8, 1986, "Too Much of a Good Thing," production was encouraged so far beyond the capacity of the marketplace, at home or abroad, that 1.4 million tons of butter and 750,000 tons of beef were sitting unsold in refrigerated warehouses (at the cost of $63,000 an hour) The stockpiled beef seems not to have been properly stored; what would you do with three-quarters of a million tons of spoiled meat? Turn it into fertilizer, I suppose. I don't remember what they did with it. And, what about the 300 million gallons of what *The New York Times* of December 27, 1986, "Food Surplus May Bankrupt European Bloc," called "undrinkable rotgut" wine? The whole program was costing $25 billion a year.

However misguided (and/or mismanaged), the CAP had a large impact on our trade. One of the first issues I tackled involved canned fruit, where European subsidies resulted in an unrealistically low price in the international marketplace. This was not a massive problem in the grand scheme of things—except for the American canned fruit suppliers who suffered from the unfair competition. Yeutter and I reached an agreement with the EC The deal fell through. We revisited, and they finally agreed to reduce the subsidies.

Of course, full disclosure, the United States had (and still has) a massive farm subsidy program of its own, and the goal in any of these international negotiations is to level, or at least moderate with some degree of fairness, the playing field. Subsidies and tariff protections are exercised to protect indigenous producers in whatever industry. There were other agricultural issues and a lot of tit-for-tat. For brevity (and your sanity), let me offer an oversimplified but accurate summary. One issue had been festering for sixteen years, EC tariff preferences that favored citrus fruit from Mediterranean growers—a clear violation of rules established by the General Agreement on Tariffs and Trade (GATT), a sort of a supreme court on international trade matters. GATT had ruled in our favor; the EC ignored the ruling. Therefore, three months after I assumed the post, the United States increased duties on heavily subsidized pasta from the EC (largely Italy); the EC retaliated by raising duties on lemons, almonds, and walnuts from the United States. These issues were resolved after about ten months; at the same time, we worked out an agreement on steel imports. We agreed to quotas that would not seriously harm European manufacturers who had long counted on the U.S. market while protecting our own steel companies. Then we learned that Italy would veto the fruit and nut pact, as inimical to Italian farmers. So steel was put on hold for a few months until we received assurances that fruit and nuts would be given a fair standing in the marketplace.

In the meantime, we calculated that the entry of Spain and Portugal would cost U.S. farmers some $400 million in lost sales of such products as corn gluten feed, a vast market, among our most extensive. That market would be compromised by favorable tariffs given to Spanish and Portuguese fruit and vegetable farmers whose products would eventually enter the EC duty-free. We threatened to impose 200 percent duties on wine, cheese, and brandy (directed like an arrow at France, the most adamant defender of CAP). The EC soon enough came up with a package to compensate us for the $400 million—by lowering tariffs on perhaps ten industrial products. (How would that help the farmers? Not very much, but such is the illogic of international trade).

The Europeans were upset because the United States had a close hold on emerging military technology; we would sell them fighter aircraft but not release the source codes for the fire control system. There was some logic to that because we had to keep the latest developments out of the hands of the Soviets. But what about navigation systems, computer programs, or telecommunications technology relevant to civilian and military applications? Such dual-use technology fell into a murky gray zone. The Europeans feared that they would fall behind. Of course, our policies gave them the incentive to go forth and develop their own technologies.

A consortium of aircraft manufacturers in England, France, and Germany—was supported by government subsidies, which brought charges of unfair competition from U.S. aerospace companies, notably Boeing. Airbus charged that Boeing received subsidies in the form of Department of Defense development funds, which often had direct application in civilian airliners. We were unable to come to either an understanding or an agreement.

On the recommendation of their veterinary committee, the EC blocked the sale of American beef from cattle that had been fed growth hormones. It didn't seem to matter that there were no residual growth hormones in the meat (the hormone-feeding stopped well before the slaughter) and that no one could show any harm to anyone who ate the beef.

A new British commissioner, Lord Caulfield, arrived just before I reported aboard, and I believe he was not too excited about his posting. I heard that he had somehow gotten himself cross-threaded with Prime Minister Thatcher, a lady who seems to have made a practice of rotating less-favored ministers out of her hair. To an Englishman, anything outside of Whitehall was exile. Thatcher might as well have sent Lord Caulfield to Abyssinia.

He and I spent many hours in pleasant socializing, and it was clear to me that he was a good man, careful and thorough, but at loose ends. He was looking for a project to prove that he was not the odd man out in Thatcher's circle to let her know she had made a mistake. During one of our conversations, we fell into a discussion about the general dysfunction of the EC. The goals of the organization, laid down in the 1957 Treaty of Rome, included the elimination of customs duties among members, creation of a common tariff and commercial policy toward outside nations, development of standard agricultural and transport policies, and removing barriers to the free movement of persons, services, and capital—but little progress had been made. Most attention was focused on wrangling over tariffs and quotas.

Lord Caulfield asked my opinion of a plan to unite the European Community, meet those goals, develop a common currency, and become a common economic force, a bulwark against Communism. I could only say that would have to be a winner! He created a magnificent white paper listing 315 action items to be studied and approved as the foundation for an actual single market. Over the next few years, as each member government ratified most, full credit went to Lord Caulfield. I don't think he was concerned about his standing with Thatcher afterward.

A grand irony: at the height of the Cold War, we encouraged Caulfield to pursue a unified Europe as a stalwart partner against the Soviets. Somewhere along the way, Henry Kissinger had warned me, don't count on a true "partnership" with an emerging Europe; their goals will not always be our goals. Well, Henry was right. The "improved" Europe sails on as a powerhouse economic competitor.

As with my posting to the Netherlands, I had to deal with threats from terrorists, anarchists, or just plain criminals; it's sometimes hard to tell the difference. The most significant: late one weekend night, when I was alone in my residence, a security guard notified me that "two men" had been seen lurking in the bushes on the nine-acre property. A team of policemen and dogs searched without result, and I was told, "Keep the doors locked." I'm not sure if that was good advice, but I complied. I would have preferred to have a very aggressive dog as protection. A few days later, I learned that two men had been sent from some Middle Eastern country with instructions to "kill an ambassador." They had traveled separately, each carrying half of a torn sheet of paper with the name of their intended victim—me. They would not know the identity of their target until they put the two pieces together. I believe I was targeted as a protest United States support of Israel. Still, the amateurish plan—like something out of the adventures of the Hardy Boys' teenage detective novels of my youth—would have been laughable if the intended result had not been so deadly.

But I moved on. I came home in 1987. Today, the EC/EU continued to grow at 500 million people in 27 nations (15 of which have adopted a common currency, the Euro.) Less than one-twelfth of the world's population generates an impressive 30 percent of the world's gross domestic product. But squabbling continues. Hormones in beef unresolved. Boeing–Airbus—in 2009, the World Trade Organization (WTO) ruled in Boeing's favor; Airbus protested. Issue unresolved.

A stable, secure, and economically viable Europe is in America's economic interest. Some of America's oldest and closest allies are in Europe. The United States is strongly committed to the rule of law, human rights, free markets, and democracy in this region. The economies of Europe and the United States account for almost half of the global economy. The United States and Europe are each other's principal trading partners and each other's top source of foreign direct investment.

Some members of the European Union had convinced themselves that war, the kind with bullets and missiles, was a thing of the distant past. Germany had essentially disarmed its military, reduced military spending, and refused to buy even armed drones because they were too "warlike." Other countries, similarly, let their militaries decline into obsolescence in favor of supporting a comprehensive welfare state. Putin's naked aggression in Ukraine in 2022 shocked these nations, producing an epiphany. Within weeks, Germany reversed course and declared it would exceed the NATO benchmark for defense spending. Moreover, it will now purchase cutting-edge F-35 jet fighters.

After counting Putin's tanks, planes, and missiles, many predicted Kyiv would fall in three days. They did not factor in their calculations the resolve of Ukrainians—many not even in uniform—to fight for the freedom of their family, village, and country. The media is full of stories about Ukrainian rock bands, politicians, and farmers who took rifles, Javelins, and Stingers to repel the Russians. Conversely, there are many stories of Russian soldiers told by their superiors that they would be welcomed in Ukraine, becoming disenchanted and demoralized when that was wrong. There are lessons here for Taiwan and other nations caught between major powers. Never underestimate the intangibles, the things you can't measure or count, in war. The fighting has severely crippled Putin's fighting force. But autocracies always value their military above all else. Once Putin gets the chance, he will rebuild his army and air force first; domestic priorities can wait. If autocrats like Putin and Xi hold power, the freedom-loving nations must maintain sufficient military forces to keep them in check.

Since Russia launched its most recent invasion of Ukraine, the United States and the North Atlantic Treaty Organization (NATO) have provided Ukraine with political, military, economic, and other aid and support. Kyiv's ability to defeat Moscow's unjust invasion is critical to defending Ukraine's territorial integrity and sovereignty, but also to returning stability to Eastern Europe, protecting the countries of NATO, and reestablishing deterrence against Russian nationalist ambitions fomented by Russian President Vladimir Putin.

On the diplomatic front, the United States initiated several calls and meetings with Russian officials before the second invasion, but none were fruitful. One significant meeting was the Biden-Putin Summit in June 2021, where President Joe Biden met with Russian President Vladimir Putin in Geneva to discuss many issues, including human rights, Ukraine, and cyberattacks.

President Biden asserted at the summit that the United States has an "unwavering commitment to the sovereignty and territorial integrity of Ukraine." This was an important statement given Russia's military buildup, which began in April 2021, the Russo-Ukrainian war that started in the Donbas region in 2014, and the ongoing illegal Russian occupation of Crimea. In the end, the diplomatic rhetoric was insufficient to prevent Russia's second invasion of Ukraine.

President Biden and Putin described the meeting as friendly and constructive, but they did not agree on anything of substance. Other significant meetings occurred in January 2022 among the United States, NATO, and Russia. At the bilateral Strategic Stability Dialogue (SSD) between the United States and Russia, the United States urged Russia to de-escalate the situation along the Russian-Ukrainian border. Still, Russia continued to claim that it had no intentions of attacking or further invading Ukraine and said the West should not fear "any kind of escalation."

A month before the January SSD meeting, Russia demanded security guarantees such as NATO retracting its membership offer to Ukraine and ceasing all U.S. and allied military activity in Eastern Europe and Central

Asia. However, the United States wisely did not capitulate. Instead, the United States made clear at the SSD that there would be significant consequences for Moscow "well beyond" what it faced in 2014.

In the NATO-Russia Council meeting in January, NATO allies insisted Russia "respect the territorial integrity of its neighbors." They reaffirmed that the alliance would not accept Russian demands to uninvite Ukraine into NATO. NATO even offered Russia a series of further meetings to discuss broader issues, but the Russian delegation demurred.

It is positive that the United States and NATO sought to utilize diplomacy in their approach toward Russia to prevent a second invasion of Ukraine. NATO Secretary-General Jens Stoltenberg, following the meeting, reported that "significant differences remained" between NATO and Russia. Besides these meetings, multiple calls were held between Biden and Putin. Still, the fact is that from Russia's perspective, the calls and meetings served as a means to buy time to decide its actions and build up its invasion forces.

Now, it is evident that Moscow crafted many contrived reasons for invading Ukraine, such as to "de-Nazify" the country or to "liberate" its population from nationalists. Diplomacy should always be attempted, but clearly, its use as a tool lacks proven success in dealing with Russia under Putin's control. In the end, the American and NATO diplomatic effort failed to prevent a Russian invasion of Ukraine in February 2022. The West, in some cases, has been challenged in garnering support against Russian aggression, including at the United Nations and among a number of major influential countries, such as India. In contrast, the United States, its allies, and partners have done well in the information space regarding Ukraine. In the weeks leading up to February 24, according to its intelligence agencies, the United States consistently informed Ukraine that a second Russian invasion looked imminent. On January 14, 2022, U.S. intelligence revealed that Russia could invade within the next month.

On February 18, President Biden, citing U.S. intelligence, reported that Moscow would target Kyiv within the coming week. In hindsight, these were highly accurate assessments, only a few days off. Now the United States and others reportedly continue to provide valuable intelligence to Ukraine. The United States also has done well in exposing possible Russian "false flag" operations, once again likely derived from intelligence, especially those revealing the potential use of chemical weapons, arguably deterring this weapon of mass destruction against the Ukrainian military or civilian population.

The weaponry and non-lethal equipment provided so far includes Javelin anti-tank missiles, Stinger anti-aircraft missiles, the Switchblade tactical unmanned aerial systems, body armor and helmets, commercial satellite imagery services, ammunition, and medical supplies, amongst many other items. These weapons were seemingly crucial in the first phase of the war, including blunting the Russian effort to take Kyiv. But these systems may not play as vital a role in the second phase of the war, which seems to focus on the South and East of Ukraine, where the topography is markedly different. Ukrainian commanders are pleading for weapons to counter Putin's assault in the East and South, which will likely feature more Russian heavy artillery and armor.

The United States and many of its NATO allies have imposed strong sanctions on Russia. Still, punitive economic sanctions can take time to have an effect, and, as such, many of these sanctions should have been imposed sometime last year when Russia was already increasing its troops on Ukraine's border. Ukrainian President Volodymyr Zelenskyy believed the same. On February 19, he was severely critical of allied leaders for waiting to impose sanctions until after a Russian invasion, accusing world leaders of "appeasement." He did not understand why the United States and NATO were waiting to impose sanctions, even though Western intelligence already showed that Russian forces would invade Ukraine.

Once Russia did invade, however, the West, in addition to Japan, South Korea, and Singapore, swiftly imposed harsh economic sanctions, devastatingly affecting the Russian economy. The United States sanctioned Sberbank, Alfa Bank, critical major Russian state-owned enterprises, Russian elites, and their family members, Vladimir Putin, and Sergei Lavrov, the foreign minister. The United States, in conjunction with Canada, the European Union, and the United Kingdom, also cut off Russian banks' access to the SWIFT international messaging system and imposed several other punitive sanctions. Many NATO allies sanctioned the same persons and entities. Russia's GDP is estimated to have up to a 15 percent downturn this year.

In addition, 750 companies, many of which are American or NATO-ally based, have curtailed their operations in Russia since February 24. Hundreds of other companies are retracting from Russia; some are temporarily halting their operations, some have reduced their current operations, some have merely held off on new Russian investments, and others have defied demands to exit the Russian market.

To have the most significant impact on the Russian economy, as punishment for Moscow's illegal invasion of Ukraine and disregard for Ukraine's territorial sovereignty and integrity, United States and NATO ally-based companies should not waver in halting their operations in Russia for the foreseeable future. Companies that have not retracted from Russia should do so immediately. Russia's military capabilities, nuclear superpower status, and concerns about the State of mind of the Russian leadership make this all the more difficult for the United States and NATO.

The Western response to Russian aggression so far has, unfortunately, been mixed and must improve significantly in the quantity, quality, and delivery of its diplomatic, economic, military, and intelligence support if Ukraine is to repel the Russian invaders, regain its territorial integrity and sovereignty, to return stability to the region, and to reestablish deterrence against Russia.

16 When Russia Nearly Became a Democracy

Soviet dictator Joseph Stalin was responsible for the deaths of 20 million citizens of the Soviet Union during his reign from 1924 to 1953. Most of them died in the purges of the 1930s. Thousands of survivors were sent to forced labor camps called Gulags. He promised a new society ruled not by the oligarchs of Wall Street but by the people—a society where everyone is equal. Instead, his bloody operations caused rampant terror throughout the Soviet Union.

When he came to power in 1924, one of Stalin's first acts was to take all guns and freedom of thought from his enemies. He explained, "Ideas are more powerful than guns. We would not let our enemies have guns. Why should we let them have ideas?" Walter Duranty, of *The New York Times* was the first Western reporter to interview Stalin (1930.) He described Stalin as "a quiet, unobtrusive man who saw much but said little." Duranty claimed that Russian peasants welcomed the Soviet seizure of their homes, their crops, and their farm animals. He wrote that the early 1930s famine that killed some 6 million people in Ukraine never happened. When asked about the millions of lives lost in the famine, Stalin said, "The death of one man is a tragedy. The death of millions is a statistic."

Vladimir Lenin, the founding head of the Soviet Union in 1917, used the term 'useful idiots" to describe the gullible intellectuals who supported the Russian Revolution. He reasoned that the same independent thinking they exhibited in supporting the revolution might make them dangerous counter-revolutionaries. The killing fields began. Stalin shared this same distrust for the useful idiots who supported his revolution. Many of them were imprisoned, executed, or exiled.

Despite the brutality of his regime, Stalin received favorable treatment from many of the intellectuals and statesmen of the time. No writer is more renowned for his ability to foresee the future than English novelist H.G. Wells. His books *The Time Machine* and *The War of the Worlds* predicted the airplane, space travel, the atomic bomb, satellite television, and the worldwide web. In 1934, Wells interviewed Stalin for the magazine *The New States-*

man. At the time, Stalin was in the middle of a wave of political purges while moving whole populations into Siberia. Yet Wells wrote that he "never met a more candid, fair and honest man. No one is afraid of him, and everybody trusts him." When the English playwright George Bernard Shaw visited Moscow in 1931, Stalin granted him a personal interview. Shaw wrote an article praising Soviet prisons where victims could stay "as long as they want." Joseph E. Davies, ambassador to Moscow, claimed in 1931 that Stalin's "eye is exceedingly wise and gentle." Rexford Guy, a member of FDR's brain trust, became an admirer of the Soviet Union after his 1927 visit. While admitting there was "ruthlessness and a disregard for liberties and rights," Guy insisted it was worthwhile.

Stalin was long gone when President Ronald Reagan initiated SDI—the Strategic Defense Initiative, which put the Soviet military in a state of fear and shock. In 1991, a Soviet admiral told me, "SDI defeated all our possible countermeasures." Reagan declared that "government is not the solution to our problem; government is the problem." He pledged that "your dreams, your hopes, your goals are going to be the dreams, the hopes, and goals of this administration, so help me, God." America would be prepared to defend its democratic way of life on the world stage, Reagan declared, just as it always had done. "As for the enemies of freedom . . . they will be reminded that peace is the highest aspiration of the American people. We will negotiate for it, sacrifice for it; we will not surrender for it, now or ever."

To back up these lofty goals, Reagan was a great advocate of "peace through strength" and ensured our military was vastly superior to that of the Soviet Union. He made a secret deal with the Saudis to reduce the price of oil dramatically, which ultimately contributed to the economic collapse of the Soviet Union. After his first term in office, with the American economy roaring back to life and the Soviet Union declining, Reagan won a second term, prevailing in 49 out of 50 states—one of the most significant electoral landslides in American political history. Behind these facts are lessons for the intellectually curious. Like no other political leader, Reagan united the considerable currents of modern conservatism: free-market economics, individual responsibility, limited government, a robust national defense, patriotism, populism, civic virtue, and faith. He made American exceptionalism his lodestar. Viewed objectively, his oratory—his natural eloquence, historical awareness, and moral clarity—rivals that of the greatest statesmen of the last century. Reagan neither bullied the American people nor treated them as hapless victims.

Reagan effectively ended the Cold War. He entered the Oval Office with a clear set of ideas he had developed over a lifetime of study. He forced the Soviet Union to abandon its goal of world Communism by challenging its legitimacy, regaining superiority in the arms race, and using human rights as a powerful psychological weapon. Reagan proved that the best way to move hearts and minds was to articulate a political philosophy clearly, compellingly, and with a touch of humor that could disarm even his harshest critics. His vision is needed more than ever. By the time Reagan left office in January 1989, the Reagan Doctrine had achieved its goal: Mikhail Gorbachev, the last leader of the Soviet system, publicly acknowledged the failures of Marxism-Leninism and the futility of Soviet imperialism. British Prime Minister Margaret Thatcher said, "Ronald Reagan had ended the Cold War without firing a shot."

I had been fighting the Bolsheviks through much of my adult life, and, whatever my modest contribution, I was delighted that toward the end of 1989 and thanks to the steadfast leadership of Ronald Reagan, we could claim victory! The Soviet Union began to unravel shortly after President Reagan said to the president of the Soviet Union, "Mr. Gorbachev, tear down this wall." Ed Feulner and I wanted to see with our own eyes the dismantling of that ultimate symbol of the issues that divided us from the Soviets. Upon arrival at the scene, we learned how we could help speed up the process: an entrepreneurial Berliner was renting a sledgehammer for $5 for a few whacks. With great personal satisfaction, Ed and I vigorously contributed to the cause.

At almost the exact moment, Poland formed the first non-Communist government that was still within the sphere of influence of the Soviet Bloc, and the hero/leader of the "Solidarity" movement, Lech Walesa, began exploring relations with other nations. He became, I believe, the first non-head of state invited to address a joint session of our Congress. I suggested he take Poland "cold turkey" into real-world free-market economics during a lunch we threw for him at the Heritage Foundation. His interpreter asked, "What is this 'cold turkey'?" We explained: free your markets from state control, abolish state-owned monopolies, privatize all government manufacturing and financial businesses, create an independent judiciary, validate the sanctity of contracts, make all commercial transactions transparent, slash tax rates, and provide for the full repatriation of dividends. All at once. If you do it piecemeal, I suggested, those who enjoyed special privileges under the Communists would find plenty of opportunities to preserve their advantages and defeat the purpose.

It must have seemed a bit overwhelming, but I added, "By doing all this, Poland would attract massive amounts of foreign direct investment and could become one of the fastest-growing countries in the world." He listened, and no doubt sought advice from some other economists. By the time he became president of Poland about a year later, something close to "cold turkey" was the name of the game. To what result? As foreign direct investment increased in Poland from $89 million in 1990 to $4.5 billion in 1996, Poland's gross domestic product grew from $59 billion to $134 billion.

Not too long after the fall of the Wall, our Heritage group made our first trip to Moscow. It was the first of one of the half-a-dozen trips I made to the former Soviet Union. I had pretty free rein, sponsored by a reformist, Deputy Premier Vladimir Shumeyko (whose confidence I gained when I offered staff space and support in my personal offices in D.C.). I journeyed through much of the country, looking for signs of economic life. I didn't find any. The Soviet Union, it seems, had been a hollow giant, with the economic sins of Communism aggravated by a budget that devoted a majority of GNP to building and maintaining military forces. When the country went bankrupt, industries collapsed, and millions were thrown out of work.

In the industrial heartland, I visited shipyards filled with rusting hulks and huge monster factories, now cold, dark, and dismal. Nuclear waste was everywhere. Those workers who still had jobs were sitting around with nothing to do; I was reminded of an old anti-Soviet joke: "We pretend to work, and they pretend to pay us." I did spot a lathe operator working at some task way down at the end of one cavernous building. I visited a truck factory in Novosibersk and saw the worst sort of Soviet production planning. The chassis was made in one place. The wheels, cabin, and engines came from factories, each one thousand miles away. And maybe one thousand miles away from each other. In the United States, with an efficient transportation infrastructure to move the parts from one plant to the next, this is called spreading the wealth, ensuring jobs in more than one state (and therefore greater support in Congress). In the Soviet Union, it was called paranoia. Stalin, always on guard against the revolution, scattered the production elements. Thus, in theory, it would be difficult for a revolutionary group to seize control of one or another vital industry. In practice, all industries functioned as wards of the state, too inefficient to ever turn a profit.

Our Heritage group was led by the great leader Ed Feulner and included Shelby Davis, Bob Krieble, Kim Holmes, and several others. We saw fertile ground upon which to plant free-market seeds, which we discussed with President Yeltsin and other government officials. We explained the formula for success and what had worked elsewhere. Ah yes, they said, and I believe our listeners understood. On one visit, our friends asked if we could help develop a proposed constitution for the new Russian Republic. This was a challenge eagerly grasped, and Heritage coordinated a draft, which among other radical Anglo-Saxon ideas, called for the sanctity of contracts and the protection of private property. When we presented the draft on our next visit to Moscow, one official questioned the inclusion of that right to "private property," a foreign concept throughout the seventy-plus-year life of the Soviet Union. He wondered if this was so important, why was it not included in the U.S. Constitution?

Fair question. It could be argued—and argue, we did—that the concept of private property was so well developed in English common law, which we inherited, that it did not need to be codified. We referred to our Bill of Rights, which put "property" in a defensible framework; the Fourth Amendment, "persons, houses, papers, and effects" were secure against unreasonable searches and seizures; and the Fifth Amendment, where "no person may be deprived of life, liberty, or property, without due process of law; nor shall private property be taken for public use, without just compensation."

In addition, we were asked to draw up a privatization program to encompass the hundreds of thousands of businesses, restaurants, factories, and construction companies that were now under the control of the government. I was one of the principal architects of this particular document. Yeltsin's team proudly presented me with a marked-up copy of the document that was later approved by the Duma. I was as honored as if I had been given a draft of the Magna Carta. I treasure this document, which is now an integral part of Russian law. Unfortunately, critical industries such as coal, iron, steel, and energy fell under the control of Communist leaders, oligarchs later beholden to Putin. We won the constitutional agreement with Yeltsin but not the Russian Parliament, the Duma.

Some months later, I was in the guest gallery with my Heritage comrades when the Duma considered the proposed constitution. Considered, that is, but barely, and it was defeated. The Russian Parliament was like much of Russia: the labels had changed, but not the players. At that point, there was still a large block of Communists in the Duma, and the private property clause might keep them from stealing everything in sight as they moved to privatize the oil companies and other major industries. "Private," in this case, meant in their pockets. Many of the Communists moved from being powerful but poor to being powerful and rich. Some of them are billionaires today.

Our basic efforts continued. I was guest of honor at a dinner Shumeyko gave at the same Moscow hotel, Oktiabrskaya, on our first visit, now renamed Hotel President to reflect the democratic shift in political attitudes and brought under the umbrella of a "free market" (to the extent, at least, that the vodka now was sold by the drink). The dinner was packed with powerful men, including the minister of Agriculture (whose name I have forgotten) and the head of the Central Bank, Viktor Gerashchenko.

Gerashchenko was skeptical of my proposition that high priority should be given to foreign direct investment to bring new technology, management skills, and capital to develop export markets. He admitted to the need for a great infusion of capital but was unpersuaded about the tactic. I argued that to attract foreign capital, Russia needed to make an explicit declaration affirming the rights of private property and the sanctity of contracts, all to be strengthened by an independent court system that enforced both.

Do these things, I emphasized, and after some 73 years of Communist misrule and with an enormous pent-up demand for everything, all else would quickly flow. Success. Employment. New markets. Gerashchenko, seated to my right, insisted that Russia had to move slowly, even on reform as basic as the privatization of farmland. This provoked a heated debate from the reform-minded Minister of Agriculture, seated on my left. As the man in the middle, I suggested that privatization should be done "cold turkey" across the board, the same argument we had used with Lech Walesa of Poland at our Heritage meeting. I argued that some 44,000 state-owned businesses—dubbed, by their economists, "parastatals"—should shift from making useless things like tanks and submarines to meeting consumer needs. Or shut down. Naturally, the central banker Gerashchenko took a cautious view, but I think he was beginning to soften in the end. Shumeyko was supportive throughout. He said that our earlier Heritage trips had been helpful by urging many of the free market reforms now taking place. However, he noted if they eventually succeed, he, of course, would take the credit. If they failed? He knew where to place the blame, as he pointed a friendly finger at me and smiled.

Following the Heritage Foundation mission and under the direction of Ed Feulner, we advised the Baltic countries Latvia, Lithuania, Estonia, Poland, Bulgaria, and the other newly liberated Eastern European countries. All those countries have had highly successful growth in the free-market principles recommended by our Heritage delegation. In my work with Latin America, I continued to press for free market reforms and, as with my efforts in the Netherlands, to look for joint business opportunities. I helped set up a Russian-American Business Council. We quickly signed up many leading American businesses to whom investment seemed like a good idea, and why not? Russia had by then declared itself open to foreign direct capital, and our corporations had checkbooks ready.

There were two problems: corruption and blackmail, including threats of harm to local facilities and employees unless "protection" was purchased from some willing vendor. It was like the 19th-century Wild West (or like some mob-controlled industries in 20th-century America). Promised contracts evaporated unless under-the-table payments were forthcoming. This was not a practical move for our companies. They were subject to the U.S. Foreign Corrupt Practices Act, which provides draconian remedies against individuals who offer bribes, however defined. And, even when contracts were solid and legal, other problems arose. For example, one of our drug company members sold $150 million worth of products to the Russian Ministry of Health for distribution to hospitals nationwide. A thoroughly above-board transaction—except the bill was never paid. Upon frequent inquiry, the response was always along the lines, "You're on the list…"

The Russian-American Business Council staggered for about five years until many of our members grew tired of dealing with the corrupt Russian bureaucracy. Russia seemed to prosper for a while, aided by massive loans, when the economy had nowhere to go but up. However, without a firm free-market foundation, any attempt at economic restructuring was doomed to fail. If Russia had early on followed the lead of Poland, Chile, or the Czech Republic, countries that exchanged state-controlled economies for the unseen hand of the marketplace, it would have attracted the one thing developing economies need most: substantial foreign direct investment. Instead, Russia got loans the oligarchs could (and did) transfer into Swiss bank accounts and paid off Putin.

The war against Ukraine has brought U.S.–Russian relations to their lowest point in modern history. Russia is demonstrating that it has no regard for human rights, sovereignty, territorial integrity, or nations' right to determine their future. Russian President Vladimir Putin clearly has imperialist ambitions. Ukraine did not provoke the war, and Putin would likely prefer to convert Ukraine into Russian territory again. This is not another Cold War. There is nothing "cold" about naked, violent aggression. This is a new kind of war, and the U.S. and its allies in the transatlantic community are going to learn how to fight. For starters, the transatlantic community needs to checkmate Putin's two most important weapons—his military and Russia's use of energy to blackmail, coerce, and profit.

Communism has imposed its tyranny in different countries at different times, and the reaction has always been the same: People resist, often at significant risk. We must remember Communism's crimes from East Berlin to Tiananmen Square, from Hong Kong to the invasion of Crimea and Ukraine. Harvard University's mammoth *Black Book of Communism* details the ideological roots of Communism's use of the firing squad, the Gulag, the KGB, forced famine, mass deportation, and suppression of fundamental human rights to stamp out any opposition to its tyranny. Lenin, Communism's founding father, relied on violence to further his ideological goal of a Communist world.

The Victims of Communism Museum opened in Washington, D.C., in June 2022 and is dedicated to an estimated 100 million human beings slaughtered, massacred, and killed by Marxist Communist regimes in the past 100 years. An additional 1.5 billion people still suffer under oppressive, tyrannical Communist regimes today. The museum has been more than 30 years in the making, starting with an idea from Anne Edwards, the wife of Lee Edwards, the prolific author, historian, biographer, and scholar at the Heritage Foundation, who was the driving force behind the museum's creation.

One exhibit shows a lone demonstrator staring down a column of tanks on June 5, 1989, at the entrance to Tiananmen Square in Beijing on the day after Chinese troops fired on pro-democracy students who had been protesting there since April 15. There are also photos of the freedom fighters who staged the first revolt against the Soviet Union in 1956 in Hungary, when NATO and the Allies stood by, ignoring the Hungarian freedom fighters' pleas for help as Russian tanks crushed the rebellion and ruthlessly arrested and killed everyone involved.

Some of the most moving artifacts in the museum are a series of paintings that finally have a home where they can be permanently displayed. In 1953, a Ukrainian painter, Nikolai Getman, was released from the Soviet Gulag, where he had spent eight years for being present at a meeting where someone had drawn a caricature of Joseph Stalin. The paintings were smuggled out of Russia in 1997 because Getman was afraid the post-Soviet Russian government would destroy them to hide a past it pretends never existed.

Getman's stark paintings cover everything from the transportation of prisoners to the camps in unheated trucks and ships to the horrible and almost unspeakable living conditions in the Gulag. We see the routine brutality with which prisoners were treated. The fragile existence they led is captured in Getman's paintings, which represent an enormous accomplishment, considering that all the scenes were painted from memory.

The paintings are haunting. They are the only visual counterpart to Aleksandr Solzhenitsyn's writings, which exposed this terrible mass imprisonment system that Robert Conquest rightly called "unexampled coldblooded inhumanity." The only difference between the Holocaust and the Gulag is that the Soviet Communists never used gas to kill their prisoners—just old-fashioned bullets, beatings, starvation, and working them to death.

One painting shows the despairing faces of men taken from their barracks in the middle of the night and executed by the NKVD (the forerunner of the KGB). This secret police organization ran the entire Gulag system. These kinds of executions constantly occurred and for no apparent reason. All the prisoners knew that if they were taken out of their barracks in the middle of the night, they never returned. And that's happening today in places such as China, where the Communist government has set up a gulag-type concentration camp system for the Uyghurs. A victims of Communism museum has long been needed. And every student in every college and university who thinks Marxism, Communism, and Socialism (which is just Communism under another name) is a wonderful idea should pay a visit to this museum to understand what that evil ideology has imposed on the world.

17 | Project Economic Justice: Private vs. Public Ownership of Industry

IN 1985, PRESIDENT REAGAN asked me to head a task force for an initiative called "Project Economic Justice." This major study was launched at the suggestion of Norman Kurland, president of the Center for Economic and Social Justice in Arlington, Virginia. It was funded by donations, not by taxpayers. "Task force" was an operative term: as chairman, I was nominally in charge, but most of the work was done by a team of experts: businessmen, labor leaders, economists, lawyers, and at least one religious scholar.

We wanted to confront, head-on, a critical issue that was keeping the Latin American nations from realizing their true potential (or any potential at all): government regulation of the economy and state ownership of many major industries—typically, heavily subsidized non-competitive failures that were a constant drain on resources. Corruption at the highest level was endemic. We encouraged free and open markets, private property expansion, and government ownership reduction. As Adam Smith wrote in *The Wealth of Nations*, 1776, "Basic institutions that protect the liberty of individuals to pursue their own economic interests result in greater prosperity for the larger society." It wasn't even a new idea, then: Ibn Khalduun, a 14th-century Arab jurist and historian, wrote in *Muqaddimah: An Introduction to History*: "When incentive to acquire and obtain property is gone, people no longer make efforts to acquire any." Or, as Norm Kurland put it, "To paraphrase Karl Marx, you could sum up the entire philosophy of communism in a single tenet: abolish private property."

Some nations knew that state ownership was a recipe for disaster. Still, when the more enlightened governments moved toward privatizing industry, they too often were blocked by the workers, who feared losing their jobs. We strongly recommended Employee Stock Ownership Plans, ESOP, as a vehicle to put ownership in the hands of the workers—whether in state-owned or private businesses. We found many examples of struggling companies worldwide that became successful when turned over to employee ownership, including some government-owned ones, such as Britain's largest trucking firm, the National Freight Corporation. You probably do business with an employee-owned company in the United States daily. When you give the workers a stake in the future, they are motivated to ensure that there will be a future and a profitable one to boot.

We presented our *High Road to Economic Justice* report to Reagan in August 1987. In commending the task force effort, the president reminded us all that "I've long believed one of the mainsprings of our own liberty has been the widespread ownership of property among our people and the expectation that anyone's child, even from the humblest of families, could grow up to own a business or corporation." Reagan also offered a kind personal comment: "Scientists say a perpetual motion machine is impossible. Considering that this task force completed its work without any appropriation from Congress, I think we should introduce Bill Middendorf to a few scientists."

At about this same time—an example of "government knows best"— Mexico had more than 1,000 state-owned businesses, including some of the largest industries in the nation, most of which were struggling to survive. As a corollary to my work at the OAS and on Project Economic Justice, I served as the first president of the Mexican/American Free Trade Association, an initiative that led to the North American Free Trade Act (NAFTA).

I also served on the Inter-American Foundation, providing small loans (dubbed "micro-loans" by economists), often less than one hundred dollars, to set up small home businesses or village cooperatives in Latin America. The payback rate has always run around 99 percent.

A personal note: Isabelle and I decided to step in and help one small "employee-owned" industry get a leg up. We contributed $5,000 to a group of cheese-making families with a factory high in the Bolivian Andes. Well, the women made the cheese, and the role of the men was to take it down to the market in La Paz (where it was rumored many of them drank up too much of the profits until the women started riding shotgun). Because of rampant inflation, by the time our contribution had worked through the bureaucracy and into the hands of the women, it had become the equivalent of $50,000. This was truly a boon because inflation had not much affected the cost of running the cheese factory, and the surplus was turned to road-building and bridge repair—undertaken by a local labor force whose wages also had not ballooned. Better roads, more trips to the market, greater sales.

I was invited to a ceremony to thank us for the gift. Imagine the scene: a village square in brilliant sunshine filled with several hundred people. A small table in the center of the crowd, upon which sat one bottle of Coca-Cola—a token reward for the honored guest. I think every child in the village was clustered around, longingly eyeing the Coke. I was almost too embarrassed to drink it, but an official had warned me that the women had made some effort to get that bottle (which was very expensive) and that not accepting it would be a huge insult. I drank slowly to show my appreciation and to great applause, after which the women launched into almost an hour of dancing—at an elevation of 10.000 feet, wearing heavy clothing, under a hot sun. I was induced to join them and, unaccustomed to the altitude and overwhelmed by the heat, I was barely able to hang on until the dance was over. Overall, it was one of the most rewarding experiences of my life.

This got me thinking: might there not be a method to compare all nations? Not just in the ease of starting a business, but in a range of activities? And would not this information be of great value to someone looking for a place to invest—or to avoid? I proposed to my colleagues at the Heritage Foundation what I called the "Index of Economic Freedom." We would assess every country on such vital factors as an absolute right to own property and fully realized freedom of movement for labor, capital, and goods, protected by an independent judiciary, give each category a score and each country a ranking. Heritage took the idea and turned it into a masterful program. For twenty-eight years, the Index of Economic Freedom has measured the impact of liberty and free markets around the globe. The 2023 Index confirms the formidable positive relationship between economic freedom and progress.

The 2023 Index, administered by the Heritage Foundation and *The Wall Street Journal*, scores 177 countries in ten specific areas:

1. Business Freedom
2. Trade Freedom
3. Monetary Freedom
4. Government Size
5. Fiscal Freedom
6. Property Rights
7. Investment Freedom
8. Financial Freedom
9. Freedom from Corruption
10. Labor Freedom

The top-ten rankings for 2023 are in order: Singapore, Switzerland, Ireland, New Zealand, Luxembourg, Taiwan, Estonia, Netherlands, Finland, and Denmark. At the other end of the scale, Russia is 113, China is 158, Iran is 170, Cuba is 175, Venezuela is 176, and North Korea is at rock bottom, 177.

Here are notable takeaways from the 2023 Index of Economic Freedom. On average, countries remain "moderately free," but barely. The global average score for economic freedom is now 60—a loss of 1.6 points from the previous year's 61.6. A loss of one more tenth of a point would drop the average score into the "mostly unfree" category. Data shows again that economic freedom correlates highly with overall well-being, including health, education, the environment, innovation, societal progress, and democratic governance.

A shake-up has occurred in the index's top-ten rankings. Although Singapore maintained its status as the world's freest economy, Australia, Canada, and the United Kingdom fell out of the top ten. Several small European nations performed well, with Switzerland becoming the world's second-freest economy and Estonia continuing to lead the Baltic region as the seventh-freest economy. Taiwan has become a "free" economy, achieving a rating of over 80 points for the first time. As the world's sixth-freest economy, Taiwan's openness, resilience, and competitiveness are impressive.

Quite regrettably, the United States has plunged deeper into the "mostly free" category, dropping to 25th place, its lowest ranking in the index's 28-year history. The primary causative factor eroding America's economic freedom is excessive government spending, which has resulted in mounting deficits and debt burdens.

Hong Kong sat atop the Heritage Foundation's annual Index of Economic Freedom for 25 years, but it is not even listed in the 2022 Index. In explaining the decision to remove Hong Kong (and Macau) from the index, the editors noted that while both special administrative regions "offer their citizens more economic freedom than is available to the average citizen of China, developments in recent years have demonstrated unambiguously that those policies are ultimately controlled from Beijing." Indeed, the loss of political freedom and autonomy suffered by Hong Kong over the past two years has made that city almost indistinguishable from other major Chinese commercial centers like Shanghai and Beijing.

Government spending around the world in response to the COVID-19 pandemic has hurt the fiscal health of nations. From the point of view of economic policy, the imperative now is for governments to steer clear of compounding the problem with misguided policy actions that distort markets, destroy incentives to work and innovate, and otherwise diminish prospects for rapid recovery and growth.

In the long run, the proven way to revitalize economic livelihoods most meaningfully is by restoring what we know has worked everywhere it has been tried for centuries: Leave individuals' economic freedom in their own hands. By contrast, socialism has failed everywhere it has been tried because it centers on government control and management over individuals as if the government knows what is best for them. Socialism is a failed system that denies economic freedom to people and, thus, opportunities to pursue and fulfill their dreams.

Why isn't the United States at the top of the rankings? We offer great freedom to conduct a business, for example, under a robust regulatory environment, and in the "Business Freedom" category, we score 91.9. However, the measures of fiscal freedom (burdensome tax rates) and government size (expenditures as a percent of GDP) are both below the world average and drag the United States down to number 25. With our well-protected property rights and a strong currency, we've been the beneficiary of one of the highest rates of foreign direct investment of any country in the world. It is a mixed blessing because the flow of so much foreign money into our coffers for many years allowed us to live beyond our means.

At the same time, we have been leveraging the future with massive amounts of additional debt, some held by foreign investors but most by our own citizens. Excess leverage leads to bubbles, and bubbles eventually burst. The harmful effects of our present excessive government spending have become the most pressing issue for Americans due to the worst inflation surge in decades. Washington's reckless choice to pump trillions of dollars into the economy is why we face more inflation than other top economies worldwide.

A more accurate way to evaluate whether the present administration has been good for the nation's financial health is to compare where things stood when a new administration took office with where they stand today. A recent report from the nonpartisan Congressional Budget Office helps underscore the severity of the nation's fiscal problems and the urgent need for a new approach. Compared to projections from February 2021, the latest analysis shows a combined $2.77 trillion in additional deficits over the 2021–2031 period.

My days as a formal diplomat ended when I completed my tour as ambassador to the European Union, but my participation in world or military affairs did not. For 12 years, I was co-treasurer (with Lord Jeffry Rippon) of the International Democratic Union (IDU) started by Margaret Thatcher and Ronald Reagan with members in Europe, Asia, Canada, and Latin America, including foreign ministers and heads of state. We promoted the idea of democracy across the world. In 1984, along with Fred Biebel, Frank Farenkopf, and Dick Allen, I founded the International Republican Institute (IRI). I became the long-term treasurer that worked with the similar National Democratic Institute (NDI) to develop democratic institutions in 50 countries. Forty years ago, I helped establish a Center for Advanced Research at the Naval War College and put up an annual personal award for the student contributing the most to the goals of the Center. I endowed a Naval History Research Chair at the Naval Historical Foundation. I have kept my hand in the world of business and public activities, especially as chairman of two banks. For more than thirty years, I have chaired the Defense Forum Foundation and the Committee for Monetary Research and Economics (CMRE).

As a trustee of the Heritage Foundation, I continue to be involved in worthwhile and exciting projects. One memorable day in 1993, Ed Feulner organized a Heritage Board meeting with Vaclav Havel in Prague when he was sworn in as president of the Czech Republic. Havel was a truly amazing fellow. He shunned American-style celebration and braggadocio to meet with us, and, later that evening as Howard Phillips and I were walking down a street of beautiful old Prague, past a row of austere cafes showing the wounds of the Communist past, bare light bulbs hanging down from the ceiling, in one of them was the president—discussing literature and poetry with friends.

Over the years, I have learned a few political lessons of my own. Let me touch on one of Barry Goldwater's guiding rules: if you want to run for office, arrange your finances before you announce your candidacy. I certainly agree. Too often, I've seen wanna-bes announce against patronage-laden incumbents with little more in their favor than an attractive family and oversized egos. Later they find that they must spend most of their campaign time in suburban living rooms pleading for funds. They are going up against entrenched incumbents—where the incumbent re-election rate is around 90 percent. Incumbents are well-supported by lobbyists (something like 23,000 are currently registered in D.C.) who know how to stick with winners who have risen to positions of power and authority (committee, sub-committee, sub-sub-committee chairmen) where they have a significant influence on the fortunes of the lobbyists. There is a pattern here and a strong argument for term limits. I thank God for the wanna-bes but let us hope they can learn to play the game before it is lost.

Like most games, politics (for that matter, almost any job) is a team effort, something too easily forgotten in the heat of the moment. If your team does well, you may win the election, solve a problem, or create a life-saving program, in which case you may be given some token of appreciation, perhaps a medal bestowed by a grateful government or an embossed certificate suitable for framing. You may justifiably be proud but don't get caught up in the fantasy that these came to you because you're such a wonderful person. They are more often symbolic representations of the work of your team. As noted earlier, I have thus been honored with almost a dozen honorary degrees and foreign decorations. Still, I know what most of these mean: that my team's efforts were considered essential or successful, or both. The lesson is to choose your team members wisely and reward them handsomely, especially with well-deserved praise. It may well be more important to them than money.

Russia's invasion of Ukraine shook and changed the landscape of international relations. Our chief adversary, the Soviet Union, is gone, but Bolshevik ghosts still animate much discourse. Moscow crafted many contrived reasons for invading Ukraine in February 2022, such as to "deNazify" the country or to "liberate" its population from nationalists. The United States and many of its NATO allies have imposed strong sanctions on Russia, but punitive economic sanctions can take time to have an effect.

Bringing back war to peaceful Europe, this conflict has broadened the fault line between the Free World countries that support Ukraine and the revisionist powers that side with Russia. On March 2, 2022, the U.N. General Assembly voted on a resolution demanding that Russia "immediately, completely and unconditionally withdraw all of its military forces from the territory of Ukraine within its internationally recognized borders." Thirty-five countries abstained, placing themselves in the Non-Aligned category, choosing an independent role in world affairs outside the strategic competition between the West and Russia, and China. Their goal is to avoid having to make a choice.

It didn't work in the past when Asian and African nations formally birthed the Non-Aligned Movement in 1955. The history of the Cold War was riddled with confrontations in Asia, Africa, and Latin America. The Free World is motivated by immediate security concerns: The North Atlantic countries do not want Russia to succeed in this aggression because it may trigger a broader war with NATO. The Asian Free World countries fear that a Russian success may encourage China in its expansionist designs, resulting in a war in Asia.

The Non-Aligned Movement doesn't address the challenges of living in a world divided between free nations that share commitments to human rights, freely elected governments, and free enterprise and those—like China and Russia—that see those equities as obstacles to expanding their power and influence. China and Russia have used their military might against their neighbors for years. China has had military clashes with most of its neighbors. Russia occupied territories in Ukraine in 2014, Georgia in 2008, and Moldova in 1992.

Russia and China are proponents of the Non-Aligned Movement. They still use the old Soviet-era anti-colonial, anti-imperialism rhetoric, often parroted by global leftists. Putin still has a lot of future aggression buttons that he can push. As for China, there is already handwringing over what

Beijing might do to Taiwan. China already has laid stakes in Africa and South America that are bound to lead to more head-butting with the Europeans and Americans. Nations that embrace the Non-Alignment Movement may do so for the wrong reasons—buying the favors of revisionist powers in exchange for favors, guarantees, or maybe just cash. China's Belt and Road initiative is a state-backed campaign for global dominance. China has poured nearly $700 billion into over 60 countries, some with shaky credit.

The Free World is vested in making a concerted effort to preempt the emergence of a new Non-Aligned Movement. Development based on free-market principles is critical. More free, secure, and prosperous nations will want to align with the Free World simply because Free World countries prosper and Revisionist countries do not. After over a century of Communist authoritarianism, Russia's gross national income (GNI) per capita was $10,690 in 2020. After 70 years of Communism, China's was $10,550. Several of China's formerly poor neighbors who chose free markets and democracy have made it. Taiwan's 2020 GNI per capita was $25,055, and South Korea's was $32,930. Several former Soviet Union republics that chose the freedom path to development, like Estonia and Lithuania, enjoy sharply higher GNI per capita: $23,270 and $19,620, respectively. The same holds true for former Soviet bloc countries like Poland ($15,260) and Czechoslovakia ($22,070). The Revisionist powers are not good role models for the Non-Aligned nations. The surest path to prosperity is followed by nations that did not align with the likes of Russia and China. Let's return to what actually works: free market-based reforms that attract private investment and mutually beneficial trade relations.

As most of the world has come together to condemn Russian aggression in Ukraine, China has refused to call it an invasion. China's foreign minister blamed NATO for pushing Russia-Ukraine tension to a breaking point. He described Vladimir Putin as China's most important strategic partner. China is also helping Russia deal with the sanctions imposed by the European Union and the United States. Russia and China's trade is currently around $150 billion annually. New agreements will grow that number to 250 billion by 2024 as China buys a significant amount of oil from Russia. China also signed new deals for Russian natural gas and weapon, including fighter planes, kilo-class submarines, and advanced service-to-air missiles. The Chinese also bought a hundred million tons of Russian coal for 38 new coal-fired power plants. Visa and MasterCard pulled out of Russia because of the Ukraine invasion. Within like 48 hours, Chinese banks with UnionPay and Alipay stepped in.

China has embarked on a naval-building spree—ballistic missile submarines, a new shore-launched anti-ship missile with a range of one thousand miles, and increasingly sophisticated cyber warfare capabilities—and seems focused on projecting military power and political influence well beyond their traditional areas of interest. Add bellicose North Korea and Iran, along with the possibility of nuclear proliferation spreading among freelance terrorists al-Qaeda and the Taliban, and the people of the world are far from safe.

But we don't have to focus on people who might want to kill us, just on people with vast oil and gas reserves who might be happy to control us. Russia and the states of the Persian Gulf sit on two-thirds of the world's proven oil reserves and about 70 percent of the natural gas. Even the most casual strategist—on their side, or ours—could devise a plan whereby, in concert, Russia and Iran could gain control of all that oil and gas. If Iran succeeds in developing a nuclear weapon and forms an atomic axis with Russia, how long could the oil-rich states of Saudi Arabia and the Emirates remain free? Would we go to war to save the Saudis and protect our access to the region's oil?

Where would a Russian-Iranian energy monopoly leave the United States and the rest of the world if not contested? A United States that restricts drilling and exploration for oil in our own territory because of a supposed impact on the environment contributes to the problem. We are so energy-dependent that if we lose access to even one-third portion of our imported oil from Russia, the Middle East, and Venezuela, we will see a chaotic rise in energy prices, and runaway inflation and won't worry much about the environment. Oh, some pundits might argue we will just increase our reliance on wind and solar energy. When and at what cost? In my judgment, it will be 20 or 30 years before the development of those alternatives will reach an economically rational level and have any impact on reducing our dependence on oil or natural gas—and I doubt that we will ever see battery-powered airplanes or ships. The issues I note are issues of the coming years, and unless we prepare to deal with them in a timely fashion, what "might" happen in 20 or 30 years will be moot.

Even more important is the wedge that Russian-Iranian energy domination would drive between us and our allies, who are vastly more dependent on imported oil and natural gas than we are. They all have greatly diminished military capabilities and would likely be forced into uncomfortable agreements and accommodations with Russia, Iran, and their allies.

As wise men have noted, eternal vigilance is the price of liberty. But vigilance means watching and being aware. You lose unless you are ready to act on what you learn or when you must. Our nation's security must come before all else. I fear subtle disarmament—one ship, one division, one squadron at a time—pushed by politicians who believe they need the money for something else. Politicians may forget or have never learned how long it takes to build a ship, develop a state-of-the-art aircraft or missile, or recruit, train, and equip a division of combat-ready soldiers in today's high-tech military world. We already seem to have over-mortgaged our grandchildren's future. Let's not continue to give it away.

18 | The Business of Banking

I FOUND A JOB after leaving my post as secretary of the Navy in 1977. George Olmsted called and asked me to meet him for lunch at the Metropolitan Club. I had known George for many years, since my days of monitoring the insurance and financial industries. A 1922 graduate of West Point, he left the Army after two years of obligated service and, with his father, started Olmsted & Olmsted, fire and casualty, in Omaha.

In World War II, he returned to active service, retired as a major general, and bought the International Bank in 1954—a diversified financial enterprise interested in insurance, manufacturing, leasing, financial services, and investments. However, despite the name, International Bank was not registered with the Federal Reserve Board as a bank, mainly because the company did not think of itself as a bank. However, it did have a 22.2 percent controlling interest in a company operated as a bank, Financial General Bankshares (called F.G.). The feds had ruled that the International Bank violated the law; the cure was to sell the controlling interest in F.G. George Olmsted, was looking for a buyer.

What he had to sell was a rare bird, indeed, a company that operated 15 banks (with some 141 branches) spread among Virginia, Maryland, the District of Columbia, and New York; total assets, $2 billion. The value of this prize had little to do with size. Under the anti-monopoly inter-state banking prohibitions enacted in 1927 (and in place until 1994), even the largest banks, such as Chase, Bank of America, and Riggs, were limited to (domestic) operations in their home states of New York, California, and the District of Columbia, respectively (international operations were not so constrained). At that time, I believe that only three or four banking companies had multi-state operations, F.G. among them, and they had been grandfathered in and allowed to continue. Given the states in which it was licensed and the rising prominence of the national capital area as a center for business as well as government, F.G.—a thoroughly respectable company, dating back to 1925 and now headed by retired Army general (and former chief of staff) Harold K. Johnson—was more than a collection of banks; it was an untapped goldmine.

We were joined at lunch by President Carter's close friend and incoming director of the Office of Management and Budget, Bert Lance, who was now chairman of a former F.G. bank in Georgia. I suppose Carter thought a banker would make a good leader of OMB. Maybe, but within a matter of months, banking regulators questioned some improvident loans he had made, there was a congressional hearing, and he was forced to resign from the OMB post. At the time of the lunch, Olmsted may have seen Lance as a candidate buyer for the whole company, and they may have had some discussions along that line. In any event, Lance, now entering government service, did not appear interested, but I—now leaving government service—certainly was.

It was not hard to assemble a small group of investors, some of whom I knew, some not, willing to put up about $15 million. Armand Hammer heard about the deal. With typical Hammer insensitivity, he called me at 3 am one morning and said, "Put me in for a share." I said, Do you know anything about this undertaking? He said, "If you like it, I want to be with you." Our offer to purchase the 1,204,231 shares of Financial General, then owned by International Bank, at $12.50 a share was accepted at the end of March. Within a month, we began transitioning from the old management to the new. I arranged to hold voting proxies from a number of major shareholders, giving our group effective control of 41.6 percent of the common stock and demonstrating to the Fed that International Bank was no longer in charge.

The annual meeting was set for June when an expanded board of directors was elected to include representation from the new investor group without Olmsted and Johnson. At the following board meeting, I was elected president, CEO, and chairman—and, to my surprise, one of the new shareholders handed me a 53-page memorandum outlining his plans for the business. Some of his suggestions merited consideration, but the most surprising element was that he presented me with a bill for drafting the memo. The next surprise: I hadn't been in the job for more than a week when another investor told me he expected to do business with the bank, selling us his company's services. It began to look like some investors thought they had bought into a private piggy bank. I said "no" to that foolishness, which did not sit well with that investor and a few of his cronies. Ten days after they elected me chairman, they secretly met to plot my downfall! It would be some time before I was entirely aware of the behind-the-scenes maneuvering—which became Byzantine before the year ended.

The company had a strange hands-off philosophy for a business run by military professionals whose careers revolved around such concepts as the concentration of forces and force multipliers. Olmsted believed that the most valuable asset was the image of each bank as a local, community-oriented institution, a position that might be damaged by too much centralization. Accordingly, they granted complete autonomy to each of the fifteen banks. In fact, when Olmsted announced the sale to the employees, he added, "We have insisted upon purchasers who would respect the long-standing Financial General policy under which its 15 banks operate as autonomous units of a mutually profitable partnership."

In a staff memo, Johnson reaffirmed that philosophy: "Financial General, as it exists today, represents the philosophy of General George Olmsted. Financial General has yet to determine the complete range of appropriate functions for a bank holding company that will continue to operate under a policy of autonomous operation for its individual banks. Making things easier for the holding company is not our objective."

Johnson's somewhat confusing memo reflected management uncertainty. In the meantime, and in happy ignorance of the plot just then getting underway, my staff and I were busy getting organized. We centralized the purchase of supplies, made plans for the merger of three large northern Virginia banks, and were soon to propose adopting a common name—First American—and a common advertising budget for all our banks. In deference to legacy managers who had long enjoyed the freedom to run their banks as they saw fit, most changes were phased in carefully and slowly.

We began promoting the national capital area as a business center—and what an easy thing that proved to be. The average household income in Washington was $21,000, 33 percent above the national average; 75 percent of area residents had a high school or higher education. In addition to government-related professions such as law and accounting, there were more scientists, engineers, managers, and technical workers per thousand population than in any other area of the country. Washington and surrounding communities hosted the headquarters of about 27 percent of all the trade and professional associations in the country. In 1978 alone, the area was to add 27,000 new jobs, only 5 percent of which were in the federal government.

In addition, not far to the north is my often-overlooked hometown, Baltimore. It was then the nation's eighth largest city; as a percentage of the population, Baltimore had more home-owning households than any other major U.S. city. The port of Baltimore ranked as the fourth largest in the United States in the total value of shipments.

I carried the message far and wide. I sent a letter to 131 New York City–based CEOs, suggesting the merits of headquarters relocation to the D.C. area. Most responses were along the lines, "We have no plans at this time" or "We just signed a ten-year lease," but there were several positive inquiries. For example, I made five trips to New York to successfully persuade Mobil to relocate its corporate headquarters to the Washington suburb of Fairfax County, Virginia.

In an August 13, 1977, profile, *The Washington Post* noted, "An interview with Middendorf is like attending a one-person pep rally for Washington. He believes, with an infectious earnestness, that the metropolitan area is in for a commercial boom and that his bank is bound to rise with the tide." It did, indeed: we would enjoy a rise in earnings over 17 successive quarters, possibly the best bank history on record (to that point). However, when the Post was extolling my virtues, the Securities and Exchange Commission heard rumors of a division between pro-and anti-Middendorf factions. The Commission sent a memo of inquiry and wondered whether a proxy fight was anticipated.

By then, the dissident group was not only trying to ease me out of control—they were trying to sell the bank without my knowledge and without the permission of the rest of the stockholders. I was to learn some of the details along the way; others, I did not know until some years later, when they were revealed in a series of congressional hearings transcribed in a 1991 *Report of the Federal Reserve Board* and in transcripts and press accounts of a series of criminal and civil proceedings. The collapse of the Bank of Credit and Commerce International (BCCI) became the greatest banking fraud in world history,

In October 1977, Bert Lance, having ended his brief term of government service, hooked up with Pakistani banker Aga Hassan Abedi, who also was looking for "an opportunity." Five years earlier, backed by a loan from the ruler of Abu Dhabi, Abedi had created BCCI with headquarters in London but with global ambition. He was off to a fast start, attracting deposits from wealthy Arabs who distrusted Western banks (widely believed to use Arab money to finance Israeli development.) Abedi wanted to establish a presence in the United States. The Bank of America considered BCCI an avenue to oil wealth and bought an early interest. This gave BCCI instant credibility— but was not much help in gaining a foothold in the financial center of America, New York City. Abedi made a clumsy attempt to buy two banks in New York—one of which, coincidentally, was owned by F.G.—by sending in sham purchasers, but the state regulators had rebuffed them. One of the applicants put forward for a multi-million-dollar bank was a young man with an annual income of only $34,000.

Nonetheless, when Bert Lance entered the picture, BCCI had become the fastest-growing bank in the world, with $2 billion in assets and 140 branches. It was, in fact, just about the same size as F.G. "I am building a bank headquartered in London," Abedi told Lance, "that has a deep and abiding interest in the problems of health, hunger, economic development."

Would Mr. Lance be interested in helping BCCI expand into the United States? Lance asked his attorney Clark Clifford (the former secretary of Defense under Lyndon B. Johnson), to run a check on Abedi. When Clifford reported that Abedi and his associates were men "of integrity and character," Lance signed on as BCCI's agent; for his trouble, BCCI arranged to buy Lance's interest in the bank in Georgia, advanced him some $3.6 million to pay off a loan, and hired him, at a reported salary $100,000.

And F.G. became the target—for the same reasons that I had become interested in the company; a multi-state franchise with headquarters at the seat of government and operations at the center of world finance. Lance sat down with the dissident group to develop a strategy, and they began contacting major shareholders, offering to buy stock on behalf of a "Washington law firm who was representing an undisclosed principal." Most of these shareholders would not sell to an anonymous buyer. Therefore, BCCI began buying shares on the open market.

To stay under the radar and not impact stock price, purchases were limited to ten thousand shares a day, and to avoid tripping the "5 percent" rule (which required a SEC filing if any individual holding in a company reached 5 percent of the outstanding stock), the shares were assigned to four theoretical purchasers. I say "theoretical" because, as I later learned, the funds came from BCCI as "loans" with no repayment obligation. BCCI held voting rights to the stock and indemnified the "purchasers" against any possible losses. Unknown to us, they soon controlled 1,076,590 shares, about 20 percent of F.G.

The increased activity in an ordinarily sleepy stock prompted the American Stock Exchange to inquire, and we issued a press release (January 7, 1978): "Financial General Bankshares, Inc., today stated that it knew of no reason for the recent market activity in its Common Stock."

We knew of no reason, but it was clear that something was up. We did learn that purchases were being engineered on behalf of an "undisclosed principal," but we assumed that to be one of the other stockholders. We knew, for example, that George Olmsted had sold his shares and that real estate magnate Frank Saul had not. We knew who had made the offers to those two men—one of the investors. I sent Jack Beddow, F.G. secretary and one of the finest men I have ever worked with, along with two of our attorneys, to visit that fellow to see if they could find out what was happening. The investor—who I thought was one of my team—refused to answer their questions and summarily ordered Beddow and the others to leave his office.

Frank Saul was one of F.G.'s largest stockholders and a very solid citizen. At my suggestion, he assumed my duties as chairman (leaving me as president and CEO), adding strength to our executive team. Then, *The*

Washington Post (December 18, 1977) reported that we may have been targeted by some sort of "Arab raid," apparently being led by Lance, who was in negotiations with some "Middle Eastern financial interests" to establish "a holding company to direct their capital into banks and other U.S. investments."

Now that the game was afoot, Saul and I arranged lunch with Lance to see where things stood. Lance was in fine form. He said something along the lines of, "Glad you came over, boys. I've got some good news and some bad news for you. Shall I give you the bad news first? The bad news is that you're out of there! We've bought 20 percent of the stock, and we're in control but the good news is, we're going to give you a big farewell dinner!" He made it abundantly clear that BCCI planned to buy more shares and intended to have control. He told Saul that there were three choices: We could sell them our stock, get together with them, or be taken over by them. It didn't seem to make much difference to Lance; he told us he fully expected to become either chairman or president of F.G.

I don't think I've ever heard of a theoretically responsible adult who was so blatantly unguarded in his comments. Lance had, in essence, admitted to material participation in a major securities fraud. Obviously, we lost no time in reporting the substance of this conversation to the SEC and the Federal Reserve. Then Bert Lance called Saul and tried to change his story—the purchaser is not BCCI, he now claimed, but a group of "individual investors," a fiction that all parties would maintain to the bitter end.

On February 17, 1978, we filed suit against "Bert Lance, Bank of Credit & Commerce International, Agha Hasan Abedi," and members of the dissident group who now were known to us ("Lance et al. ") for "unlawful conspiracy secretly to acquire control." It may or may not be a coincidence, but Bank of America began pulling out of the relationship with BCCI.

In March, two top BCCI officials admitted to *The Washington Post* (March 22, 1978) that the company indeed had a relationship with Lance but averred that he was merely "an informal adviser who pointed out investment opportunities in the U.S." and falsely affirmed that he was "not employed by the bank, was paid nothing by the bank and had received no loans from BCCI." The executives also told the Post that the Middle Eastern investors who had purchased F.G. stock at the advice of BCCI were "four individuals from different countries, absolutely unknown to each other."

Also in March, the SEC filed a complaint against those investors, charging violations of security ownership reporting requirements. Then the federal court granted a preliminary injunction in our suit against Lance et al., agreeing that BCCI had been deeply involved in the takeover attempt. We thought that we had won the day. But, no. Both the SEC and the Federal

Court said, in essence, that BCCI's illegal activities did not prevent it from continuing the takeover attempt, only from doing so in secret.

Now free to make a run on the bank, BCCI charged ahead but maintained that the takeover effort was by a group of individuals, unconnected investors who shared an advisor, BCCI. One of those investors stepped forward as the front man for the group: Sheikh Kamal Adham, former head of the Saudi equivalent of the CIA.

In June 1978—with the assistance of Clifford, who was now representing BCCI—Adham filed a suit against me and certain other directors ("Middendorf et al."), purportedly on behalf of other F.G. stockholders, alleging that we had breached our fiduciary duties and wasted corporate assets by pursuing our suit against Lance et al. There was a reasonably swift resolution to this nuisance. And Bert Lance, who had been kind enough to alert us to the secret plan, and who had expected to be appointed chairman or president of F.G., seems to have reached, in his employer's eyes, the level of his incompetence and had been eased out of the picture.

In June 1979—six months after losing Middendorf et al., BCCI announced a tender offer of $22.50 per share, which did not generate much excitement. By August, the offer was raised to $25. I was reelected president of F.G.; Armand Hammer was elected vice chairman. We were able to announce that "Financial General has enjoyed eight consecutive record quarters, each an increase over the comparable quarter of the previous year."

BCCI took a new approach: to acquire enough proxies from existing shareholders to win a vote. They asked for the names and addresses of all F.G. stockholders. We declined to provide it. BCCI petitioned a court for relief. The court granted the request. Adham told the SEC he was willing to spend as much as $1 million to bring the matter to a vote at the 1980 annual meeting; the tender offer was narrowly defeated. We had won another round, but there was no end in sight. In July, Hammer made an offer to Clifford: "Why don't we declare an armistice? This war goes on interminably, and I'll come along, and we'll sit down and talk this matter out." After a one-and-a-half-day meeting in Clifford's office, the ante was raised: a cash tender offer for all the outstanding common stock of the company at a price, net to the sellers, of $31.

It was clear that BCCI would never give up or walk away, and this was, after all, a reasonable price for the stockholders (most of whom had paid $12.50 or less per share), so the board voted to accept the offer. I added a clause that, in the event of any delay, the offering price would be adjusted to account for any increase in the book value at the time of the actual sale. In the event, this added about $5 to the final per-share price. All in all, not a bad deal: my original investors got a 300 percent return in a little more than three years, and this was when the market, in general, was not all that healthy, with stocks in disarray and mortgage interest rates around 20 percent.

With the deal set and government approvals almost in hand, BCCI thought it was home-free. Not quite. Virginia's chief bank regulator, Sidney A. Bailey, raised the most cogent question of the day: why would anyone launch such a protracted, expensive campaign to buy the company at a price well above its probable value? He answered his question: because of the company's unique position in the market, with operations in both the government and financial hubs of the nation. And, he wondered, what apparatus did our government have to ensure that foreign owners would abide by U.S. law or prevent them from stripping the bank of all assets?

This prompted a hearing of the Fed on April 23, 1981, during which Clifford introduced former spy master Adham as a "Saudi businessman" with the honorific "His Excellency." The regulators, in thrall, followed suit, addressing him as "Excellency" throughout. Clifford suggested it was the Fed's patriotic duty to assist the bank in attracting petrodollars, which were then leaving the country at a rate of $90 billion, back in the form of interest-earning deposits from the Middle East. BCCI, Clifford maintained, was not directly involved as a purchaser but was merely an "investment advisor" to Adham and the others—like the role of, say, Merrill Lynch, independently looking at investment opportunities for its clients.

On the last day of June 1981, I resigned as president/CEO of First American to accept a position as the United States Permanent Representative to the Organization of American States. During the 1980 election campaign, I had provided Republican candidate Ronald Reagan with briefing papers and other assistance; after his successful election, I helped with some transition matters and had now been offered an interesting and challenging assignment.

I was satisfied that I had met any commitments to my investor group—indeed, to all the shareholders—by helping move First American from relative obscurity to the first rank of banking. At the same time, I was worn out from four years of fighting against what I knew in my heart but could not prove was the rape of my company. Frank Saul took on the responsibilities of CEO and Beddow became chief administrative officer.

In August, the Fed approved the takeover, as did the Office of the Comptroller of the Currency, noting, "It has now been represented to us that BCCI will have no involvement with the management and other affairs, nor will BCCI be involved in the financing arrangements." BCCI installed its own management team. Frank Saul was replaced as chairman by Clark Clifford, and Clifford's law partner Robert Altman became president.

We had known the conditions for growth were exceptional, but under

BCCI, growth seemed to be explosive—but this was bookkeeping folderol. Within a few years, First American was in big trouble. Clifford made desperate efforts to sell the bank. All fell through. There was a bail-out of sorts: federal regulators arranged for $200 million in new financing to forestall the risk of a bank failure.

The whole cloth of BCCI deception was unraveling. There were rumors of growing instability in the bank's global operations and reports that the government of Abu Dhabi was poised to pump in large sums of rescue money. But on June 22, 1991, the U.K. branch of Price Waterhouse presented the Bank of England, the regulating authority in that country, with evidence of fictitious profits and concealed losses, fictitious transactions and charges, fictitious loans, misappropriation of deposits, shoddy lending, bad investments, off-book transactions, and falsified audits (juggled between two auditing firms that were not allowed to compare notes). Two weeks later, authorities moved in to close BCCI headquarters in London and branches in 72 countries worldwide.

BCCI turned out to be one massive Ponzi scheme. BCCI regularly had to pay interest and dividends on accounts and investments to appear safe and profitable. However, because they were siphoning off large sums of money for personal reasons, they couldn't pay dividends and interest in the usual fashion, so they had to attract ever-larger deposits from sources other than the typical customer. They did that, in large part, by bribing government officials around the world to deposit funds that had to be parked somewhere and by the laundering of vast sums of illegal monies, mainly from drug and illicit arms transactions. At one end of the scale, at least a million small depositors lost everything; at the other end, BCCI officials were suspected of embezzling $2 billion from one depositor alone. Early estimates pointed, overall, to at least a $20-billion fraud. I don't believe that has been refuted.

Clifford and Altman resigned from First American. BCCI dropped the "advisor" pretense, pled guilty to illegally purchasing First American and three other U.S. banks, and forfeited $550 million in U.S. assets. Abedi, living in Pakistan, was under criminal indictment in several countries, but Pakistan denied extradition. Sheikh Adham pled guilty to criminal charges in New York and paid a $105 million fine. I doubt that he was much bothered.

BCCI's day had ended, but litigation crept along. In 1998, Clifford and Altman agreed to pay $5 million to settle civil charges without admitting or denying wrongdoing. As *The Washington Post* explained (February 4, 1998), "The charges settled today involved the Fed's contention that Clifford and Altman lied when they told the regulators that BCCI would have no role in running First American."

A few years ago, when I was on the Hill giving testimony on another matter, one of the lawyers from the Treasury Department turned to me and said, "Weren't you the hero of that whole First American thing? Our records show that you tried to blow the whistle, and the regulators didn't pay attention. You even brought suit against them—now, there's egg on our face, big time."

19 | Advisor to Presidents and a Wanna-Be

Dwight D. Eisenhower

I MET DWIGHT EISENHOWER shortly after the end of World War II. My father and I sold him Black Angus cattle for his Gettysburg farm. I found him to be a humble, kind man as we did a lot of "over the fence" cattle negotiations. I am always surprised when I hear Eisenhower described as arrogant or a do-nothing president. He ended the Korean War, avoided a war in Vietnam, managed a potential confrontation with China, and soothed relations with the Soviet Union after Stalin's death. As part of his strategy to win the Cold War, Eisenhower expanded American military power, built a fearsome nuclear arsenal, and launched the space race. During Barry Goldwater's presidential campaign, I became closer to Eisenhower.

I became involved in politics during the presidential election of 1948: Republican Thomas E. Dewey against incumbent Democrat Harry S Truman. Dewey made his name throughout the 1930s by prosecuting dozens of big-name mobsters, including Lucky Luciano and Waxey Gordon. His record helped in his election to governor of New York in 1942. In 1944, he won the Republican nomination for the White House but lost the general election to President Franklin D. Roosevelt. In 1948, the Republicans again chose Dewey as their presidential nominee, with Governor Earl Warren of California as his running mate.

The keynote speaker at the Republican Convention, Illinois Governor Dwight H. Green, praised the Republicans as "the party of faith in the individual American." In my judgment, most Democrats believe that the government is a working tool that should be used to shape society. I think that individuals should shape society. Some Democrats seem to believe that earning a profit means abusing workers and that employing hundreds of people is a form of exploitation. Of course, demonizing businesspeople makes no sense: they provide the jobs in which most Americans earn a living. Demonizing "big" business just because it's big makes even less sense.

In the 1948 election, I served as a Republican precinct captain for the 8th Assembly District—the so-called "Blue Stocking" district on the upper East side of Manhattan—and worked sufficiently hard that I was honored to get an invitation to go to Albany and meet with the Republican state chairman. The Gallup Poll had Dewey at 50 percent, Truman trailing at 37 percent. The Republican politicians were already making lists of candidates for jobs in the Post Office. That was how the politicians rewarded local party leaders: there were post offices everywhere, and every post office needed a postmaster. Everyone knows that Truman won in an incredible upset, and a significant part of his reputation today rests upon that achievement.

My favorite political story was the result of Dewey's defeat. The day before the election, the confident Dewey asked his wife, Frances, how she would feel on election night sleeping with the president of the United States. After learning of Truman's victory, Dewey sat alone in his study, seeking solitude after his stunning loss. Suddenly Frances burst into the room with a question. "Now, Dear, am I going to Washington, or is Harry coming here?"

On November 10, 1962, I was invited to join a clandestine group of some 55 politically savvy men and women determined to make Senator Barry Goldwater the next president of the United States. I had just finished working on the losing congressional campaign of Connecticut advertising executive John M. Lupton, and F. Clifton White, a New York City PR man and political mastermind, sent me a kind note: "Congratulations on the tremendous run," Clif wrote. "I'm sure you feel as I do that it was a very important vote." He asked me to join him at a meeting at the Essex Inn motel in downtown Chicago, set for December 2. "This," he emphasized, "is the important one."

Clif's invitation was to seal my fate, the beginning of a transformation from Wall Street to a life of public service. I already knew about his group and their efforts. Jerry Milbank and John Lupton were both members, and Jerry and I had been paying the rent for the group's anonymous two-room New York City office. In tribute to our willingness and ability to produce needed funds on short notice, Clif called us "the Brinks Brothers." (In his own 1992 memoir of the campaign, *Suite 3005: The Story of the Draft Goldwater Movement*, Clif was kind enough to give me credit for many things, not just paying the rent, as "the man who stood at the dike and kept it from crumbling around our ears.")

The meeting at the Essex was the fourth—and indeed was the important one, as it was decision time, go or no-go. We were about to launch the first successful presidential draft in U.S. history. Twenty months later, we would head into the nominating convention with the winning votes already in hand.

We had picked Goldwater as our candidate, although he had not yet picked us. Why Goldwater? Because he was the conservative answer to the liberal policies of the Willkie-Dewey-Rockefeller crowd who dominated the Party, armed with plenty of money, a solid political base in the populous Northeast, and—in our judgment—no sense of shame. Goldwater offered straight-talk and blunt descriptions of what was wrong with America and challenged the EC—Economically Correct—thinking of the day: that the government was the solution to all ills. That only the government had enough money to tackle all problems. Only the government had the collective wisdom to make the right decisions. "The government," he liked to say, "does not have an unlimited claim on the earnings of individuals."

Goldwater found a ready audience, conservatives who felt locked out of the political process and who responded with an enthusiasm that sometimes slipped into adulation. He wrote a widely syndicated newspaper column, and a collection of his speeches—assembled and edited into the book *Conscience of a Conservative*—sold at a rate of 50,000 copies a month. When a *New York Times* reporter asked Goldwater if he hoped to make a run for the presidency, he replied, "I have no plans for it. I have no staff for it, no program for it, and no ambition for it." Our goal was to help him change his mind.

On April 8, Peter O'Donnell, Republican state chairman of Texas, launched the National Draft Goldwater Committee with a press conference at Washington's Mayflower Hotel "to mobilize the tremendous, spontaneous enthusiasm for Senator Goldwater that is sweeping the country and to encourage and channel the efforts of all volunteers who want to help Senator Goldwater." An article on March 26, 1963, in *The Chicago Tribune* was headlined: "Kennedys Fear One Man in 1964 Election—Goldwater." In truth, the Democrats hoped that no one noticed because their strategy, then and for the near term, was publicly to downplay any threat from Goldwater and build up Rockefeller as the man to beat in 1964—and they were doing a pretty good job of it. When delegates to the 1960 Republican convention were asked by *Congressional Quarterly* (April 3, 1963) who was most likely to get the 1964 nomination, Rockefeller or Goldwater, better than 2 to 1, said "Rockefeller." When asked whom they preferred, the score was about 4 to 3 in favor of Goldwater. A Gallup Poll taken at the end of April had Rockefeller the front-runner among Republican voters, at 43 percent; Goldwater, 26 percent. The other potential candidates: Michigan Governor George Romney, 13 percent; Pennsylvania Governor William Scranton, 7 percent. "Richard Nixon" was not included in the Poll, although considered a possibility.

By the middle of June, things were swinging our way. Dick Nixon told a reporter from *The New York Times* (June 13, 1963) that "Among professional politicians, Senator Goldwater has the lead, and they have more influence on nominations than anyone else." Three days later, the paper reported: "Goldwater Gaining in Northeast, Republican State Chairmen Say." *The Washington Star* noted that among a group of Eastern Republican party workers: "A surprising number—considering the scarcity of strong conservatives in the group—indicated a willingness, if not an eagerness, to see the nomination go to Senator Goldwater." The June 14 edition of *Time* noted, "If the Republican national convention were to be held today, Goldwater would almost certainly be its presidential nominee."

Wherever he went, Barry kept handing fat, juicy sound bites to the media. They were vintage Goldwater, as when he said that the government couldn't stop depressions, it only starts them, or that he had voted against federal aid to education because he didn't think educators could spend the money they sought. To a group of bankers at an Economics Club meeting, he said, "We are told that many people lack skills and cannot find jobs because they do not have an education. It's like saying people have big feet because they wear big shoes. The fact is that most people who have no skills have no education for the same reason—low intelligence or ambition."

Throughout the summer, he played a reluctant debutante. He didn't say "no," but he wouldn't commit. An AP poll of GOP state and county leaders, released November 2, asked, in essence, who would be the strongest candidate against Kennedy? More than 85 percent said "Goldwater." Rockefeller came in at just under 4 percent. The governor was not deterred; he formally announced his candidacy on November 6. To show that he knew how to play this game, he sent an announcement telegram and a bunch of red roses to every female delegate in previous conventions. When told of this, Barry was not much impressed; this was not his style. He told us—more than once—that he would not be packaged "by some Madison Avenue agency." He later would tell the brilliant campaign PR man Lee Edwards that if anyone tried to create "puff pieces" about hobbies and habits, Edwards would be out of a job. Nothing about Barry's years-long passion for ham radio. Nothing about his tinkering with autos (even though that had been a focus of the earlier *Popular Mechanics* profile). Nothing about his great skill as a photographer. By trying to force the campaign to stick with the issues, and only the issues, Goldwater, the politician, shut the public off from getting to know Goldwater, the man.

Despite what the press reported, Goldwater did have a keen sense of humor. In response to a question about living in Arizona, Goldwater was supposed to have said he liked it very much, although he had recently been turned down for membership in a local golf club because he was Jewish. "Since I'm only half Jewish, can I play nine holes?" Goldwater asked.

By mid-November, when we felt that we had lined up sufficient delegate strength, Jerry Milbank and I went to Washington and asked for his commitment. Barry was very gracious but not yet ready. He reminded me of the third leg of the campaign stool: "I'm not going to go," he said, "unless I see a big chunk of change in the kitty." To this point, fundraising during the "Draft Barry" period focused on raising working capital; our finance team had been reasonably successful, and we had brought in about $750,000. But much of it had been spent, and to Barry's point, we would need a lot more. Barry did try to be helpful. He said, "I have a buddy out in Washington who said he'd give me half a million dollars, and I have another friend who can raise a million bucks." So, I called Barry's half-million-dollar buddy out in Washington—no dice, he would contribute maybe $12,000. The million-dollar guy was astonished: "I don't know how Barry got that idea!" Discouraging, to say the least, but Jerry, Stets, and I kept plugging away, and eventually, we had a respectable treasury. The three of us went back to Barry with the numbers, and he said, all right, he'd declare, but probably not until January; otherwise, media coverage would disappear into the deep well of holiday indifference.

I had known the young Jack Kennedy slightly; I was an usher when he married Jackie Bouvier in Newport, Rhode Island, and once dated Jackie's sister, Lee Bouvier. It was a semi-blind date arranged by two of my old Owl Club friends, Bev Corbin and Steve Spencer. But paths diverged, and I didn't see Kennedy at all after he became president. On November 22, when the alarm bell on the stock ticker in my office began the urgent clanging that signaled "Bulletin, read immediately," the shock of the news was so great that I had to read it three times, thinking I was misreading some simple item. The president had been shot in Dallas.

At first, the assassination was blamed on the "radical right," especially the rabid right of Texas. The Draft Goldwater office in Washington was closed because of threats, and death threats forced Texas Senator John Tower's family to move into a hotel. Even the discovery of assassin Lee Harvey Oswald's connections to the Soviets and Cubans did not entirely quell the suspicions. The radical right was deemed capable of anything, according to the press. With his friend John Kennedy dead and replaced by a man he did not admire, Barry was ready to give up before even declaring his candidacy. He wasn't interested in competing with a man he knew to be "a dirty fighter . . . a wheeler-dealer . . . and treacherous to boot. He'd slap you on the back today and stab you in the back tomorrow." However, after a few days of serious reflection, he said OK. But in private, he told his wife that he didn't want to run, didn't want to be president, but wanted to give conservatives a cause and a voice. "Lose the election," he said, "but win the Party."

Barry made the formal announcement from his home in Phoenix on

January 3, 1964. We would have suggested he announce from one of the nation's media centers, Washington, and New York. No matter. January 3 was a Friday—a day of the week best suited to burying, not encouraging, media coverage. No matter. Barry wanted to show that he was his own man.

"I will seek the Republican presidential nomination. I have decided to do this because of the principle in which I believe and because I am convinced that millions of Americans share my beliefs. I have been spelling out my position now for ten years in the Senate and for years before that here in my own state. I will spell it out even further in the months to come. I was once asked what kind of Republican I was. I replied that I was not a "me-too" Republican. That still holds. I will not change my beliefs to win votes. I will offer a choice, not an echo. This will not be an engagement of personalities. It will be an engagement of principles."

"A choice, not an echo." This was a play on the then-typical Republican approach to American politics; the Eastern Establishment agreed with most Democrat positions and proposals but suggested that "they" would be better able to carry them out because they all had MBAs from Harvard. Goldwater proposed to lead us out of that wilderness. But there was a hint of what was to come: no members of the Draft Committee were invited to attend the event. We had expected that effective with Barry's announcement, he would also announce a campaign organization that would include our team. We had assumed, not unreasonably, that we would change the name of the Draft movement to something like "Goldwater for president" and soldier on. It was not to be.

Goldwater was uncomfortable with people he didn't know, and—perhaps partly because of the misinformation he had been given about Clif's motives—he was suspicious of Draft Goldwater. This all was made quite clear in the selections for top campaign staff, a close-knit palace guard that came to be known as the "Arizona Mafia." I find the term too pejorative; there is no question but that they ran protective interference for Goldwater and at times, made decisions for him that they were not qualified to make—but I found them all to be men of honor and goodwill.

Phoenix lawyer and long-time friend Denison Kitchel was campaign manager; Dean Burch, another Arizona lawyer who had once been Barry's Senate office administrative assistant, was number two, and Dick Kleindienst (a Harvard classmate of mine, although we didn't know each other at school), was director of field operations. The immediate staff was to include speechwriter Karl Hess, generally acknowledged to be one of the best in the business, and Bill Baroody, president of the proto-conservative Washington think tank, the American Enterprise Institute. Baroody had worked with Goldwater since the election of 1958 as an intellectual mentor— a role to which, staffers told me, he brought a large measure of arrogance, which would get in the way later in the campaign. Baroody did not seem to suffer fools, foolishness, or anyone who disagreed with his judgment or advice.

For example, *National Review* editors Bill Buckley and Brent Bozell met with Kitchel, Baroody, and another staffer at one point. They proposed, among other things, to provide academic credibility to the campaign by assembling a team of well-known educators and other credentialed experts. However, each suggestion they offered was turned aside by Baroody. He apparently viewed "Intellectual" as his territory; he wanted no help or interference from outsiders. As a result, Buckley, who practically created the conservative movement, was effectively shut out of the campaign.

Where the Draft Committee had built a solid infrastructure and established personal connections with Republican leaders nationwide, Kitchel and Kleindienst were largely unknown and without political influence—except with Barry. In what I can only characterize as an astonishing blunder, key members of the Draft Committee were shunted aside, some to be given subordinate roles, others ignored. While there were hurt feelings a-plenty and friction galore, the Draft rejectees continued to work on Barry's behalf throughout the primaries, the convention, and the campaign. As for me, I don't think Barry had any close friends who understood the duties and responsibilities of a campaign treasurer, so I was kept on in that capacity. I was the only member of the Draft group to be included in the immediate campaign staff.

Later, during a Chicago campaign finance committee meeting, Barry did at least acknowledge our collective role, our contribution to the effort. "I thank the group that met here in Chicago at that secret meeting that the whole world heard about. Sometimes I wished that Peter O'Donnell, White, Middendorf, Milbank, and their group would go home and run their cattle ranches, but now I'm grateful to them. Now, I want this job. And when I want something, I go after it."

Our fervor, he said, reminded him of a religious movement, and admitted that he had not yet been doing a very good job. "I'm a clumsy idiot," he said, "with five feet and six hands." He pledged: "This is a campaign I intend to win. I have never lost a campaign, and I'm too old to go back to work and too young to quit politics." He added, "My tail's too big to put between my legs." And he laughed. "Reporters throw up at the thought of me being nominated."

First up on the campaign trail: the New Hampshire primary. Barry was to spend 23 days clumping through the snow with a cast on a foot painfully sore from an operation, 18-hour days often wasted on the wrong audiences. How wrong? How about being scheduled to talk with a group of eight-year-olds at a primary school? The campaign was so disorganized that the term "campaign" is seriously out of place. Social historian Theodore White noted, "For mismanagement, blundering, and sheer naiveté, Goldwater's New Hampshire campaign was unique."

At the beginning of this campaign, Clif put together a briefing book—itinerary, officials' names, and people he would be meeting—but Kitchel and friends had not passed it on to Barry. Five days before the March 10 primary, Mary McGrory of the Washington Star would write, "Senator Goldwater has yet to give a statistic about New Hampshire. He does not even trouble to mention the town where he finds himself." Unprepared? Or, maybe, he didn't much care. Barry's core message should have had resonance where the state motto was "Live Free or Die," but he was impatient and irritable on the trail. His speeches were dull, and his delivery was flat. He made it crystal clear that he would rather be elsewhere. As he told one audience, "I'm not one of these baby-kissing, handshaking, blintz-eating candidates. I don't like to insult American intelligence by thinking that slapping people on the back will win you votes."

On his first day in New Hampshire, Barry's frank but blunt talk triggered the two most contentious issues of the entire campaign. At a press conference in Concord, he was asked whether he was in favor of continuing Social Security. His views on Social Security were no secret: he long had believed it to be an under-funded pseudo-insurance program, originally developed as a barely adequate safety net for older citizens, many of whom, in the depth of the depression, had no savings and little hope. Now, the depression was long past, and the wages of every worker were being taxed to fund the program, but not every worker would likely need the program. Therefore, he responded that he would offer "one change" to make participation in the program voluntary. "If a person can provide better for himself, let him do it. But if he prefers the government to do it, let him." There were many better ways to invest the payroll tax, he suggested, and "get a better Social Security program."

Headline writing is an art, not a science; the people who write headlines try to boil a story down to an attention-getting essence. The people who write headlines are not the people who write the stories. Thus, above a story that largely was accurate was the *Concord Monitor* headline of the day: "GOLDWATER SETS GOALS: END SOCIAL SECURITY." The Rockefeller team soon distributed copies of the article to every Social Security beneficiary in the state. The Rockefeller team knew that people who read headlines don't necessarily read the articles.

Later in the day, Goldwater set up what became the other key campaign issue. A *Washington Post* reporter asked him about President Eisenhower's recent suggestion that the six American divisions in NATO could be cut to one. Goldwater did not entirely agree but said that the number could be cut perhaps by one-third if NATO commanders in Europe had the power to use tactical nuclear weapons on their own in an emergency. At another meeting with the press a short time later, he was asked about nuclear weapons in Europe and gave the same answer: "I have said the commander should have the ability to use nuclear weapons. Former commanders have told me that NATO troops should be equipped with nuclear weapons, but the use should remain only with the commander."

He meant, of course, the commander of NATO, not unit commanders in the field. He was also referring to tactical nuclear weapons of limited reach—with a yield equal to perhaps 40 metric tons of TNT over a radius of about one mile (sub-microscopic compared with the 50 million-ton weapons of the day). No matter, his comment was interpreted to mean that any hot-headed major could start a nuclear holocaust. No matter that NATO was already equipped with tactical nukes. No matter also that the policy he suggested was the actual policy of both Presidents Eisenhower and Kennedy.

These two issues—or a willful and widespread misunderstanding—dogged him to the end of the campaign, when a touring Lyndon Johnson would encourage the crowds: "Vote Democratic on November 3. Vote to save your Social Security from going down the drain. Vote to keep a prudent hand which will not mash that nuclear button."

A February *Newsweek* poll of delegates agreed with our estimates: 425 firm, 124 leaning. We were bringing some political leaders aboard, but our greatest strength remained with the grassroots. We had pretty good control of fundraising and were reasonably on target toward Clif's original budget estimate of $3,200,000. However, the campaign leaders—Kitchel et al.—seemed to have no plan and were spending money in a scattershot fashion. Too much advertising money was spent in some places, not enough in others. They were spending too much money on charter aircraft. They were spending money on polls in areas where we didn't need the information, such as the District of Columbia.

This latter point sent my brother Harry (then president of the Conservative Party of NYC) off on a moderate tirade. "What on earth," he said, "is the reason for wasting money on polls?" Barry, he suggested—a creative politician with fresh new ideas—should create opinion, not try to conform to the popular notions of the day. "When moving into an uncharted sea, polls are useless." Harry had a point, but he was fixated on the Edsel debacle—the failed Ford product that had been designed by polls. He didn't understand the tactical value of political polling.

Barry wasn't concerned about the budget (or lack thereof) but had some issues, largely focused on the media's focus on his irrelevant off-the-cuff comments. "I have never in my life seen such nonsense," he told me but added, "I don't intend to butter up the press. I've made 125 speeches in Los Angeles, 125 in San Francisco, and 250 in New York. If I'm not well known now, I never will be." My brother didn't understand the tactical value of polls, but Barry was blind to the tactical value of working with the media.

Record-breaking, cheering crowds, the largest in the history of many towns, met his first trips into New Hampshire. However, along the way, Barry lost some voters to his own missteps; and aggressive attacks by Rockefeller cost him more. Goldwater and Rockefeller tried to outdo each other with public meetings and purchased media, succeeding only in pushing the "undecided" vote as high as 50 percent. A team pushing a write-in vote for Nixon's 1960 running mate Henry Cabot Lodge—who, as our ambassador to Vietnam, did no campaigning and wasn't even in the country—spent their time and money rounding up supporters and sending out sample ballots, on which they demonstrated how to vote for a write-in candidate. The man who had not set foot in the state captured "undecided" and won the race with 33,007 votes. Goldwater was second at 20,692, Rockefeller only about a thousand votes behind.

We watched the returns on TV in a room at the Madison Hotel, Washington, while a bunch of reporters waited downstairs. The networks announced the results no more than eighteen minutes after the polls had closed. Barry took the news quietly, went down to face the cameras, and offered one of the most honest comments ever spoken by a politician: "I goofed." Kitchel—the lawyer, dabbling in public affairs—issued a press release: "It is most gratifying that a candidate from the Far West, Senator Barry Goldwater, could do so well in the New England state of New Hampshire." No one was fooled.

We began to enjoy victories: South Carolina, Wisconsin, North Dakota, Kentucky, and Illinois—although press coverage of the Illinois primary was z bizarre. Goldwater had a big win against six candidates, but "It was the first contest I have ever been involved in," Clif said, "where the candidate got 62 percent of the vote and still came out a loser in the press." As columnist David Lawrence, *Washington Star* (April 16, 1964) offered: "Maybe two and two don't make four, after all, in national politics. Judging by some of the TV and radio broadcasts on Tuesday night and subsequent comments in the press, Senator Goldwater got the highest number of votes . . .but nonetheless suffered a 'setback.'"

Arizona, Louisiana, New Jersey, Iowa, Texas, Ohio, Indiana, District of

Columbia. Clif's unofficial reckoning soon put the total of committed delegates at more than 400. *Time* magazine, May 8, wondered at Goldwater's momentum: "It seemed impossible. Here was Arizona's Barry Goldwater, who only a few weeks ago appeared to be flat on his back in his quest for the GOP presidential nomination. Yet as of last week, Goldwater was the man to beat [at the Republican convention in] in San Francisco." *Time* ascribed his come-out-of-nowhere to "the national preoccupation with primaries, which usually make more headlines than delegates" and to an "obsession with the polls. But no pollster even nominated a presidential candidate." Slow and steady, *Time* noted, "Goldwater kept collecting delegates while the unavowed and disavowed collected press clippings."

On May 12, 1964, to show voters in the rest of the nation that, even in Rockefeller's hometown, Barry had pull, we held a "monster" rally in Madison Square Garden. *The Daily News*, the tabloid with the trademarked slogan "New York's Picture Newspaper," carried the banner headline "18,000 CHEER BARRY IN GARDEN" and filled the rest of the front page with an incredible shot of the band playing, the crowd applauding, balloons dropping, Barry and his wife at the podium—and, standing with them and looking quite happy, yours truly.

Clif's three years and a million miles had been well spent in lining up essential local support throughout the nation. Goldwater won all but two of the primaries he entered (he ran behind Rockefeller in Oregon) and piled up 2,150,000 votes—more votes than all other candidates put together. Along about here in the time-lime, one non-campaign event merits a brief discussion. The Senate passed the Civil Rights Act of 1964 by a vote of 73 to 27. Barry Goldwater was one of the 27 voting against it. It made no political sense for a soon-to-be presidential candidate to vote against a controversial but popular social issue on the eve of a national campaign. Barry did many things that made no political sense but that he believed were correct. On this measure, he was not alone: he was joined in dissent by a number of legislators of some stature: Albert Gore, Sr.. of Tennessee; Sam Irvin of North Carolina; J. William Fulbright of Arkansas; Norris Cotton of New Hampshire; Bourke Hickenlooper of Iowa; Edwin L. Mecham of New Mexico; Millard L. Simpson of Wyoming; and John Tower of Texas. Also opposed: George H.W. Bush, candidate for the Senate from Texas.

Goldwater voted against the 1964 Civil Rights Bill because he questioned the constitutionality of two sections relating to fair employment and public accommodation. The latter—the so-called "Mrs. Murphy" clause—held that you couldn't refuse to rent your home or a room in your boarding house to anyone. The goal was to ensure that African American or other ethnic minorities could not arbitrarily be excluded, but as written, the law forbade discrimination against drunks, felons, wife abusers, and people who smoke in bed.

"I am unalterably opposed to discrimination of any sort," Goldwater said from the floor of the Senate. "I believe that, though the problem is fundamentally one of the heart, some laws can help, but not laws that include features like these, provisions which fly in the face of the Constitution." Goldwater argued that states have all the rights not specifically reserved to the federal government by the Constitution and that employment and accommodation were local, not national issues.

He was swimming against the current and knew it but stood on principle. "If my vote is misconstrued," he said, "let it be, and let me suffer its consequences." In hindsight, his vote put a more significant hit on his legacy, an unfair tarnish on his reputation today, than on his election prospects. It matters not that he had voted for the Civil Rights Acts of 1957 and 1960, that he approved of the other nine Titles of the Act of 1964, or that he had offered four amendments to the Youth Employment Act of 1963 to forbid discrimination because of race, color, creed, or national origin. It matters not that Goldwater had integrated the employees of the family department store before World War II. It matters not that as the organizer of the Arizona Air National Guard after the war, he ensured and enforced integration. This was two years before President Truman ordered the desegregation of the armed forces. It matters not that he had been active in desegregating the lunch counters of Phoenix or that he had been a member of the NAACP and Urban League. That afternoon, we returned to the Cow Palace for Goldwater's acceptance speech. Dick Nixon made the introduction; unity was OK with him. It was time, he declared, not for the New Deal, the Fair Deal, or the "Fast Deal of Lyndon Johnson, but for the Honest Deal of Barry Goldwater."

Barry Goldwater took "freedom" as the theme of his acceptance speech. "This party," he declaimed, "with its every action, every word, every breath, and every heartbeat has but a single resolve and that is freedom—freedom made orderly for this Nation by our constitutional government; freedom under a government limited by the laws of nature and of nature's God; freedom—balanced so that... liberty, lacking order, will not become the license of the mob and the jungle."

He invited support. "Anyone who joins us in all sincerity we welcome," and clear thinking: "And let our Republicanism, so focused and so dedicated, not be made fuzzy by unthinking and stupid labels..." And then, as he came to the end of his speech and in one of the most-quoted phrases of any political convention, Goldwater took on the central theme of the opposition's pre-convention debate: that he and his supporters were "extremists" and the Rockefellers and Scrantons of the Party were the voices of moderation. "I would remind you," he said, "that extremism in defense of liberty is no vice. And let me remind you also that moderation in the pursuit of justice is no virtue!

At some point, a newsman in the press section exclaimed, "My God, he's going to run as Barry Goldwater!" Political science professor Henry Jaffee had written the offending words for Barry, but they became his own. In the firestorm that erupted among Democrats and liberal Republicans, he maintained that the sentiment was accurate, although widely misunderstood.

Most media reaction to the nomination was negative and, I suppose, predictable. Walter Lippmann claimed that Goldwater's election would lead to "a global, nuclear, anti-Communist crusade." Drew Pearson wrote, "The smell of fascism has been in the air at this convention." A writer in *The New York Times* noted that: Goldwater's nomination was "a disaster for the Republican Party and a blow to the prestige and the domestic and international interests of the United States." According to *The Chicago Daily News*: Goldwater "has the invaluable ability to give a latent, fear-born prejudice a patina of respectability and plausibility." *The New York Post* said that "... the Birchers and racists have never before enjoyed so big a night under such respectable auspices." *The Louisville Courier-Journal* predicted: "This will be a campaign to sicken decent and thoughtful people."

Time—in the post-convention issue of July 24, 1964—injected some balance: "Who are the Goldwaterites? They wear tennis shoes only on the tennis courts. They don't read Robert Welch or hate Negroes. They aren't nuclear-bomb throwers and don't write obscene letters to editors who disagree with them. They are reasonably well-educated and informed. They are, in fact, nuts about Barry Goldwater without being nutty in the process."

In their post-Convention issue of July 27, 1964, *Newsweek* editors also offered a portrait of the Draft Goldwater movement: "Jack Kennedy wanted the nomination, recruited his cadres, planned his own strategy, his eye always on victory. Goldwater had a nationwide organization handed to him while he remained aloof, longing to remain in the Senate. Kennedy captured his supporters; Goldwater's supporters captured him." The magazine defined these people who had "captured" the candidate: "Mostly obscure, humorlessly efficient, faintly Puritanical, they were propelled by motives as mixed revolutionaries. Some thirsted for authority; others delighted in the IBM technology of the new politics. Still, others yearned for a Free Enterprise Eden."

As for me—obscure, yes, I much preferred *Newsweek*'s description of "An eager young giant of a man (6 feet 4, 215 pounds) . . ." The magazine properly was fascinated with our fund-raising success, "300,000 individual contributions, most of them $1, $2, and $3." Still, it overlooked Jerry Milbank, Frank Kovac, and others to give me inaccurate (and un-warranted) credit as head of the fund-raising effort.

Overall, *Newsweek* let two young members of Congress speak about our effort: John Ashbrook wrote, "Most older politicians are afraid to make decisions. 'Well, son,' they always say, 'I've been that route before.' We haven't had that inbreeding"; Bob Dole said "We're not trying to turn back the clock; we're just trying to sound the alarm."

I stopped smoking at 3 am, on Thursday, July 16, 1964. This is easy for me to remember because I was locked in a bathroom with John Lupton, an advertising executive from Connecticut, at the Mark Hopkins Hotel in San Francisco. John and I were assigned to interview the potential candidates for vice president. We were sitting on the tub for several hours—we couldn't go out into the other room; the media was everywhere, trying to get an angle and interviews. The bathroom was the only place we could be alone. Well, "alone" is a relative term. There was me, another Goldwater staffer, and each potential candidate and his sponsors; two or three people standing in the bathtub, someone sitting on the edge, everyone talking loudly, and someone else would have to speak louder to be heard. Everyone smoking. In those days, we all smoked—it was glamorous and made us feel mature. And you didn't just smoke—you held your cigarette in a certain way, straight out of the movies. Sophisticated. Stupid. The smoke was so thick you could hardly see across the tiny room. By midnight, I was coughing so badly that I resolved that if I ever got out of that room alive, I would never smoke another cigarette. And I never have.

Barry had said, "Narrow down the list." I don't remember how many were on "the list" at the beginning, but in the end, there was only one: Bill Miller, chairman of the Republican National Committee. The runner-up was Walter Judd, endorsed to us by seven Minnesota members of Congress led into the bathroom by Clark MacGregor (it got really crowded). They put in a strong pitch for Judd, a true icon of the Party. However, we picked Miller like a Wall Street analyst picks a stock: run the numbers. In Miller's case, that included personality, religion, and home state. Miller was a genuinely nice guy, Catholic (to balance Barry's Protestant faith with semi-Jewish roots) and a New Yorker. Barry, the Westerner, branded as a "right-wing extremist," was out of the mainstream, and Miller was smack in the middle of it. We figured the New York vote would be locked with Miller on the ticket.

In hindsight, I think we should have gone with Judd. He stood for something more. As a medical missionary, Walter Judd had seen how the Japanese operated firsthand when they invaded China; following his return home in 1938, he gave more than a thousand speeches to warn the American people and Congress. "Stop trading with the Japanese," he said. "Stop giving them the sinews of war with which they may later fight us." He was right, but few people listened. "Give up silk stockings now," he said, "or your sons later." Powerful. After the war, as a ten-term Congressman, he was a fervent anti-Communist. In losing the race for vice president, Walter Judd would not have gone quietly down to defeat but would have remained a fiery voice on the national scene. Bill Miller disappeared.

Later in the morning, Peter O'Donnell, Republican National Committee member Ione Harrington, and I—a bit hung-over from too much celebration and a bit groggy from lack of sleep—served as the unnecessary official notification committee to let our candidate know that he had won and offered our recommendation for vice president. Barry accepted the notification with genial good grace, agreed with the recommendation, and called Bill Miller to give him his own good news.

Later in the morning, at a meeting with the 50 Republican state chairmen, Barry explained the choice of Miller—a man who had once called JFK the "foundering father of the New Frontier" and had advised that if Lyndon Johnson was offering a "Better Deal," someone had better first cut the cards. "Miller," Barry said, "drives Lyndon Johnson nuts."

Heading into the presidential campaign, Johnson had momentum; Barry took a vacation. Rather than capitalize on whatever public interest had been generated in his candidacy, the public campaign went into hiatus for almost six weeks. I suppose this was traditional—wait until Labor Day, it did not seem inappropriate at the time—but while we were getting organized, Lyndon B. Johnson was grabbing headlines, beginning with his acceptance speech at the Democratic National Convention, condemning the tactics of "fear and smear" and warning that "one rash act, one thoughtless decision, one unchecked action" could leave the world in ashes.

I still had a job in New York, of course, but also an understanding partner, and I was able to devote an increasing amount of time to the cause. The duties of RNC treasurer occupied some but not all of my time, and I was more than happy to be involved in various other campaign-related activities, from helping with advertising to going out on the road with Barry. Of course, everything was out of my own pocket, and I never took a cent for my 20 years of service to the Republican Party. At my own expense, I hired a photographer to document Barry's travels nationwide. He was responsible for some of the best photos of the campaign.

I directly coordinated the finances of the Republican National Committee, the Republican National Finance Operations Committee, the Republican Campaign Committee, Citizens for Goldwater-Miller, Citizens Campaign Committee for Goldwater-Miller, TV for Goldwater-Miller, National TV for Goldwater-Miller Committee, and Women Voters for Goldwater-Miller. Overall, 30 committees with similar titles may have been set up to avoid limits on individual contributions and spending by any group. Under the law of the day, no individual could contribute more than $5,000 to any one committee, nor could any committee collect more than $3 million.

We laid down the finance and accounting procedures and established controls over expenditures. Our new finance chairman was the former chairman of the board of General Electric, Ralph Cordiner. Ralph was a businessman, not a politician. In a departure from the usual campaign financing, he insisted that we run on a pure cash basis, not spending—or committing, which is about the same thing—any money we did not have in the bank. That made it difficult to plan for an uncertain future. Since radio and TV companies wanted funds in hand at least 48 hours before broadcast, our advertising agencies needed the money 72 hours ahead. That was for one-minute or 30-second "commercials," which often could be booked at the last minute. For a longer program, schedules were set at least a month in advance; we couldn't book a half-hour slot unless we already had the money, roughly $130,000, kept in a sort of escrow account. Welcome to "Ralph's Rules," which sharply reduced flexibility to confront fast-changing events.

The RNC had a lot of work to do, adding space, rearranging offices, installing new equipment, and taking the staff from about 100 people to more than 700. Staffers came in like a whirlwind, scrambling for office space like children playing musical chairs. One man introduced himself to another, adding, "I'm the finance director of Committee X. What's your job?" The other man was troubled because he thought he was slated for that job. In the event, neither man became finance director. When an incompetent national committee holdover was fired for what was deemed to be a good and sufficient reason, he triggered a telephone-daisy chain through George Humphrey to Kitchel to Dean Burch to me. All within thirty minutes. George—at home in Cleveland—was the 800-pound gorilla, and I immediately called him, to be treated to vituperation for another 30 minutes; we were "stupid and youthful." And those were the nice things he said. When he finally calmed down, I explained the issue; he listened and came on board.

Our fund-raising effort was exceptional; in truth, the techniques we pioneered during the primaries and the campaign set the standard for all who came after. Big money is usually easy to get, especially from lobbyists (usually, but in this election, they were betting on LBJ), but this gets very few people involved with the candidate. I pushed what I believe to be revolutionary fund-raising tactics: charging petition signers a dollar for the privilege, charging everyone a dollar for attending some rallies, and emphasizing our willingness, nay, eagerness, to accept small donations through the mail. Call it a buck for Barry. "But" someone complained, "it costs nearly that much for the mailing." Yes, but each mailing that brings in a contribution, no matter how small (our average was less than ten dollars), adds a member of the campaign, each not only likely to vote for Goldwater but to convince their friends and neighbors to do so as well.

Overall, we generated some 1.5 million contributions for the primaries and the campaign, an astonishing increase over the 50,000 supporters who contributed to the 1960 Nixon campaign, providing a tremendous base for the next election. Was this emphasis on small-dollar donors a breakthrough in political fund-raising? I can't say for certain—history is long, and details are often obscure—but Newsweek was kind enough to credit me for a "new money-raising technique." Frank Kovac assembled mailing lists of known conservatives and the 500,000 who had volunteered for Barry. After the election, Richard Viguerie, who already had cut his fund-raising teeth on telephone appeals, turned lists of Goldwater contributors into a national direct-mail network of conservative donors. And political fund-raising was never the same.

We hired the Opinion Research Corporation (ORC) for bi-weekly surveys; we learned—no surprises— that Goldwater "had strong convictions" and "spoke his own mind" and would likely hold down government spending. LBJ was seen as an unethical "deal maker" who would "promise anything to get votes" but, on the whole, had been doing a good job as president. The PR staff began to churn out brochures, advertising clip art, and campaign "Guidelines" for local organizations. Our main advertising agency Leo Burnett came up with the punning slogan, "In your heart, you know he's right," and PR man Lee Edwards managed one early coup: he leased a 106-foot-long billboard—just down the street from the Atlantic City convention center, then playing host to the Democrats—which he filled with the slogan and a photo of Barry.

In Barry's words, the basic campaign strategy was, "Let's go hunting where the ducks are, where we could expect to win some votes." Except for a few token visits, forget New England, New York, and Pennsylvania; concentrate on the Mid-West (especially Ohio, Illinois, 52 votes), the South (127 electoral votes), a smattering of traditionally Republican states (Oklahoma, Kentucky, Arizona, 22 votes; Nebraska, Kansas, Indiana, Wyoming, Colorado, the Dakotas, and the smaller mountain states, perhaps 50 or 60 votes)—and, of course, the big prize: California, 92 votes.

As he had in his senatorial campaigns—a good-luck talisman—Goldwater launched his presidential campaign schedule on the steps of the county courthouse in Prescott, Arizona (where his uncle Morris had been mayor for 26 years) and ended two months later in the Arizona hamlet of Fredonia, population three hundred. In between, he visited more than a hundred cities, covering 100,000 miles. During the first week, we saw gratifyingly large crowds: 53,000 in Los Angeles, 18,000 in Seattle, and 16,000 in Minneapolis, where Barry out-polled the former two-term mayor and now Democratic candidate for Vice President, Hubert Humphrey.

But as with New Hampshire, things quickly started going downhill. The crowds were there, but if "all politics are local," the locals were getting the wrong messages. On September 15, Barry never mentioned tobacco, cotton, or peanuts at a rally in the tobacco, cotton, cotton, and peanut center in Winston-Salem, North Carolina. He warned the citizens of the peaceful retirement community of St. Petersburg, Florida, about rising crime rates but did not discuss Social Security. In poverty-stricken West Virginia, he blasted Johnson's anti-poverty program. In Fargo, North Dakota, he reminded farmers that 17 percent of their income came from Federal subsidies and asked, "Do you want that to continue?" He did have a plan for a gradual phase-out of the program. He did not explain it. The Draft Goldwater veterans were appalled; the Kitchel-Baroody crowd didn't notice. We complained—not for the first time—about the lack of a cohesive message and our candidate's tendency to shoot from the lip. The criticism was not well received. And nothing changed.

Someone among the thousands of intelligent, active people involved with the campaign suggested that we take our messages directly to the people, with—perhaps—some control over the content, and we arranged to produce three 30-minute TV talkers. The idea was sound—witness Ross Perot's success with the format in 1992—but the execution was dismal. The first was an over-produced question-and-answer session, "Brunch with Barry." Barry sat in the middle of a group of seven women, which included Maine's Senator Margaret Chase Smith, several generic "mothers," a Vietnam widow, and an "Italian Nationalities Representative" (whatever that really means). They asked questions. He answered the questions.

The second was a filmed address in which Barry denied being impulsive, imprudent, and trigger-happy. The only bright spot was a highly successful fundraising appeal by actor Raymond Massey, tacked on to the end, which brought in $175,000. We had done this over the objections of both Kitchel and Baroody, who thought such public pleading for money was undignified. The third program was a 30-minute "Conversation with Ike," Goldwater, and Eisenhower at the Gettysburg farm. We wanted to show the two men in comfortable conversation discussing the issues, the future of the country, and whatever they wanted to talk about. Well, they didn't talk about much of anything—they might as well have been discussing the weather, all at four thousand dollars a minute (to the horror of the bean counter, me). The program started with an inane question from Ike: "Well, Barry, you've been campaigning now for two or three weeks. How do you like it? And how does it seem to be going for you?"

From that point on, the program was going nowhere. Dan Dornan—the photographer I had provided to the campaign—told me that there had been no focus, Eisenhower rambled along, it didn't seem as if there had been any advance discussion of goals or content, the on-scene campaign managers suggested no key questions; even Barry sensed that all was adrift and tried to get the managers to take charge, anything. He was told, "It's OK, don't worry about it." At the end of the program, Ike offered—I guess—an endorsement of Barry. To the charge that Goldwater was a "warmonger," Ike said, "Well, Barry, in this mind, this is actual tommyrot." We had intended to close off with another Raymond Massey appeal; Kitchel said no way. The dignity of the former president was more important than the money. I thought a fund appeal might bring in $1 million at the time, but that was before I saw the audience numbers. In a timeslot where "Petticoat Junction" pulled 27.4 percent of the viewers, and 25 percent watched "Peyton Place," "Conversation at Gettysburg" was seen by 8.6 percent.

Opinion Research (ORC) reported that the audience for those 30-minute programs was minuscule—conservative junkies looking for a fix and Johnson campaign workers looking for fodder. Almost everyone who tuned in out of curiosity quickly switched to something else. I would note, however, that despite the poor execution of those voters who stayed the course, 67 percent of Republicans and 39 percent of Democrats came away with a more favorable impression of the candidate. ORC also noted a positive response to one of Barry's key messages: America was falling into a moral cesspool. Replaying one theme of his convention acceptance speech, and in one of his more successful approaches, our candidate charged that a lack of national leadership had "turned our streets into jungles, brought out public and private morals into the lowest state of our history" with climbing divorce rates, juvenile delinquency, street violence. "When morals collapse," he said, "they don't collapse upward."

Clif saw an opportunity to confront the issue head-on with a 30-minute TV documentary. "Agree completely with you on morality issue," Barry said in a memo to Clif. "Believe it is the most effective we have come up with. Also, agree with your program. Please get it launched immediately." The program was called "Choice." It was filled with images of immorality (women in topless bathing suits), depravity (drunken college students on a spree), anti-social behavior (rioting and looting in the streets), and failed leadership (a tall man in a cowboy hat driving a Lincoln convertible remarkably like LBJ's car, throwing out beer cans as he careened down the road). The stated goal of "Choice" was "To portray and remind the people of something they already know exists, and that is the moral crisis in America, the rising crime rate, rising juvenile delinquency, narcotics, pornography, filthy magazines . . . [The American people] will see all this on television, and there is only one way they can go, and that is with Goldwater."

I saw a screening of the show on October 14, and I thought it was outstanding. I had been working most of the day on the budget; income was projected at $11.6 million, outgo $12.2 million. Not too encouraging; nonetheless, I scrambled around to find the $40,000 needed to purchase the airtime. We scheduled the broadcast for October 22. The program never ran. The Democratic National Committee obtained a print and showed it to a group of journalists, thereby triggering an avalanche of adverse comments. When Goldwater screened it (for the first time), he said, "It can't be used." Period. "It's nothing but a racist film." Although "Choice" gave equal time to black and white miscreants, I had to agree that Barry was right on reflection.

Since I wrote the checks that covered their expenses, I was in almost daily contact with surrogates in the field—notably Dick Nixon and Ronald Reagan—and helped arrange their schedules. I discovered that they needed something to talk about. Barry's speechwriters were wrapped up with his needs, so I also found myself in the part-time speech-writing business, penning remarks for both Nixon and Reagan.

Nixon gave his all for Goldwater, 237 speeches in 36 states. Once, without mercy, I asked him to go to Hawaii, then to San Francisco, to Los Angeles, to Kansas, and back to Hawaii in three days. He never complained, which didn't hurt his standing with the Party. Reagan, who didn't like to fly, was co-chair of the California Goldwater campaign and pretty much stayed in the state, but he gave about 100 speeches and did terrific TV work, as well. In fact, by all accounts, the best speech of the campaign, perhaps of any campaign, was Reagan's October 27 TV broadcast, dubbed "A Time for Choosing." But it almost didn't happen because of objections by Kitchel and Baroody. They told Barry the speech was unacceptable and proposed putting "Conversation at Gettysburg" into the booked time slot. I told Barry that was foolish, but he called Reagan to ask him to cancel; Reagan said, well, it's not up to me. Some other fellows are paying for the time out of their own pockets, and, besides, what's wrong with the speech? Barry said I don't know. I'll take a look. When finished, he looked at Kitchel and Baroody and said, "What the hell's wrong with that?"

But Kitchel and Baroody would not give up—goaded, I believe, by our ad agency, which stood to gain a $23,000 commission if they took over the booking—and within three hours of airtime, they were still trying to plug in "Gettysburg." However, the spot was being funded by a group led by friends of mine, Henry Savitore, and John Wayne. The Californians said Reagan gets the time or no one. The speech was an updated version of one that Reagan had made many times for his then-employer, General Electric. "A Time for Choosing" articulated Goldwater's positions better than Goldwater and launched Reagan's political career. The first "Reagan for President" club was established soon after, and he was elected governor of California in 1966 with a plurality of one million votes.

Our TV plan for the last couple of weeks before election Tuesday included one 15-minute show, five 30-minute visits with the candidate or his surrogates, and twenty-six 5-minute spots inserted in some of the most popular television shows, ranging from *Today* to *As the World Turns*. The final push would have been much more significant, but for one thing. On this, there is confusion in the published record. Let me clarify.

It is true that under Ralph's Rules, we had to run the campaign on a cash basis, spending no money that was not already in the bank. However, as often reported, it is not true that Ralph's Rules prevented us from buying extra TV and radio time in the hyper-critical final week. Then, our mailings were paying off, and we had the money. One typical day in the middle of October, the Post Office delivered some 14,000 letters. A majority included checks, although many were empty. The senders were not forgetful: they wanted to make us pay the return postage. Why so many adversaries? Unlike the earlier mailings that targeted probable supporters, these went to lists purchased from commercial suppliers. But overall, during the campaign's last week, almost $3 million came in from mail and TV solicitations.

As we entered the last week, Barry asked, "How are we doing?" I—ever the optimist— said, "Great!" and showed him the latest, revised broadcast schedule. I told him we had the money. He put his hand on my arm and said, "Don't spend it." He said to cancel the additional radio and TV and leave money in the bank to keep the Party alive after the election. Of course, he was right, and thus, perhaps $1 million was not wasted in the past but passed along for the future.

We campaigned for Goldwater. The Democrats campaigned against Goldwater. In the Democrat's TV and radio commercials, produced under the direct supervision of the White House, Barry was a bomb thrower who would ignite World War III and tear up Social Security along the way. The commercials were brilliant and devastating. The best-known hit was the infamous "Daisy" TV ad, which may have been broadcast—as a paid spot—only one time, on September 7. The scene: a pretty young girl playing "loves me, loves me not" with a daisy, picking off the petals as she counts, "One, two, three . . . " As she reaches "nine," a somber male voice cuts in and counts down, "ten . . . nine . . . eight . . ." until the image explodes in the mushroom cloud of an atomic blast. We hear the voice of LBJ: "These are the stakes, to make a world in which all of God's children can live or go into the dark. We must either love each other, or we must die." The voice-over announcer closes the spot: "Vote for President Johnson on November 3. The stakes are too high for you to stay at home."

Goldwater was only four days into his campaign when the "Daisy" bomb was dropped—and from then until the end, he was on the defensive. By the middle of September, 53 percent of women and 45 percent of men believed that Goldwater would take the country to war (Harris Poll). I heard that LBJ's assistant, Bill Moyers bragged that they hung the nuclear noose around Goldwater and finished him off. He was right, but what right did he have to be so proud? And, of course, there was the advertising of a different sort: the ubiquitous placards and signboards—"In your guts, you know he's nuts"—that showed up everywhere Barry went.

Johnson played the father of his country, campaigning with unabashed zest. Eighteen-hour days, twenty speeches a week. He offered peaceful reassurance on the festering troubles in Vietnam. "We are not going to send American boys nine or ten thousand miles from home to do what Asian boys ought to be doing for themselves." And offered a grave warning. "By a thumb on a button," he told a crowd in New Orleans, "you can wipe out 300 million lives in a matter of moments."

It may seem hard to believe, but most of the traveling press—especially those who had been with Barry throughout the campaign—liked the man, and some tried to protect him from himself. When he gave one of his off-the-top-of-his-head answers to a tough question, they might ask, is that what you really want to say? Of the 53 reporters on board for the last big swing, I think only three were really belligerent. Barry's big problem now was not with reporters but with editors. Of all the major newspapers in the country, only three—three! —came out in support of his candidacy: *The Los Angeles Times*, *The Chicago Tribune*, and *The Cincinnati Enquirer*, which offered this perspective:

> Barry Goldwater has become the most slandered man in American political history. He is portrayed as a poisoner of children, a creature of the night riders, and a pawn of the militarists and the warmongers. To see the viciousness of the vilification heaped upon him

is to understand the desperation with which his enemies are trying to cling to the perverted political order they have been imposing upon America. Their purpose is to do considerably more than defeating him at the polls: they seek literally to crush him lest any other muster the courage to ask them to account for their sordid works.

We began the final campaign swing on October 26 with another capacity audience at Madison Square Garden, ending at sunset in Fredonia, Arizona, on November 2. In between, we made eighteen stops in seven days—in Tennessee, Ohio, Iowa, Wisconsin, Illinois, Pennsylvania, Wyoming, Nevada, Arizona, California, Arizona again, Texas, and South Carolina, back to California, and then to Arizona. Air Force Reserve Major General Goldwater delighted in frequently taking the controls of the campaign airplane, but his skills were, well, a bit rusty—if triple-bounce-landings signify anything. Some reporters in the back of the plane became sick because of the bumpy landings. Goldwater smiled when he became aware of their discomfort.

At the wrap-up in Fredonia, Barry thanked many people but said nothing memorable. As we headed to Phoenix for the returns, he gave me a weary smile and asked, "Well, Bill, how are we going to do tomorrow?" The latest Gallup and Harris polls both had it at 64 percent for LBJ and 36 percent for Goldwater, but I, the team cheerleader, said, "Barry, it's in the bag. The silent majority will turn out in force." You may think my optimism was incredible, but lulled by the roar of the crowd everywhere we went, I believed it to be true. Any experienced politician will warn you, don't see or hear what you want to see or hear. Never consider the roar of the crowd as an accurate poll. It's only temporary. They'll be another hero tomorrow when the road of the crowd for you has become a giant echo. I was right that it was "in the bag," but unfortunately, it was in the bag for Lyndon Johnson. Goldwater lost in one of the largest landslides in U.S. History.

Just after Goldwater's nomination, James A. Farley, postmaster general in the Roosevelt Administration, predicted that Goldwater would only carry six states. On November 3, Barry Goldwater carried just six states. Popular vote: Johnson, 42 million. Goldwater, 27 million. As the polls predicted, it was 64 percent to 36 percent. NBC called the election for LBJ four hours before the polls closed in California. Barry was visibly stunned and went to bed.

The New York Times comment of James Reston, November 4, 1964, was typical: "Barry Goldwater not only lost the presidential election yesterday but the conservative cause as well. He has wrecked his Party for a long time to come and is not even likely to control the wreckage." Reston, Teddy

White, Bob Novak, and I don't know how many others had us down for the count. The Party is in tatters—leadership in the sewer.

At that point, I was part of that Party leadership—and we saw things a bit differently. Yes, there were problems within the Party. The Rockefeller-Scranton-Romney crowd was not happy with the conservative tilt. They wanted back in the driver's seat: they did not understand the sea-change; that the center had shifted away from Philadelphia, New York, and Boston; that for the first time since 1932, power in the South was shifting back to Republicans; that more people had contributed to our campaign than had ever given financial support to the presidential campaign of any party. Three times as many as contributed to the Democrats.

Not to put too fine a point on it, but the Republicans, "destroyed" by the Goldwater campaign, came back strong in the 1966 elections, adding four senators and 47 representatives, returned Goldwater to the Senate in 1968, and won five of the next six presidential elections. In the 1966 mid-term elections, the Republicans picked up 700 seats in state legislatures, more than erasing the 529 seat loss of 1964. Where we lost 37 House seats in 1964, we had a net gain of 47 in 1966, plus 3 Senate seats and 8 governorships.

Barry Goldwater was returned to the Senate in 1968. He served for three more terms, retiring in 1987. In the meantime, the conservative movement, anchored by the Draft Goldwater veterans and a host of new volunteers, continued to grow, gaining sufficient influence to bring a true conservative, Ronald Reagan, to the presidency in the election of 1980.

Richard M. Nixon

The real winner of the 1966 election, virtually ignored, had been Dick Nixon. From the beginning of 1965 until Election Day, he helped raise 6.5 million dollars, visited 35 states, and spoke on behalf of some one hundred candidates. He was building grassroots support by planting seeds. On November 26, 1966, a *New York Times* statistician concluded that "a GOP House candidate for whom Nixon did not campaign stood only a 45 percent chance of winning while a man he embraced stood a 67 percent chance."

Nixon's campaign trial competition included LBJ, Herbert Humphrey, and Senator Robert Kennedy. A contrast? Twenty or more reporters usually followed Robert Kennedy; Nixon's entourage, if thus it might be called, was usually two. Maybe four. But, as *The Chicago Tribune* later would muse, "Bobby made a big hit with the teenagers. Richard Nixon put himself across with adults."

Nixon was an awkward, insecure guy who came up the hard way. He was born poor and never made much money when working for the government, but the royalties from his book, *Six Crises*, weren't bad, and he became relatively well-off when he joined the law firm of Mudge, Stern, Baldwin, and Todd in Manhattan. His involvement in politics always seemed something of a paradox. He was a loner by inclination and had thrust himself into the public arena with mixed emotions.

Over lunch on November 10, 1965, Dean Burch, Jerry Milbank, and I agreed that Nixon was probably the front-runner for the 1968 nomination. His efforts for Barry and others had earned a lot of goodwill throughout the Party and merited consideration. However, other credible players might emerge after the 1966 midterm elections, heavy with gubernatorial contests. Our consensus, as recorded in my meeting notes, was that: "Nixon is all we have at present and makes good speeches to boot. He suffers only from a lack of television personality and the fact that he has been licked a couple of times in other elections." According to a poll taken a few months later, Nixon was the front-runner with 27 percent of Republican voters. George Romney was 14 percent, and Goldwater ran a close third at 13 percent.

In February 1966, Peter O'Donnell, Jerry Milbank, and I agreed that siding with Nixon was a reasonable choice. Toward the end of April, five Goldwater veterans spent a weekend at Peter's Dallas office: Peter, John Grenier, Fred LaRue, Fred Agnich, and me. We aimed to launch "Project X" to determine whether Dick Nixon was the best hope to win back the presidency and, if not, to decide who was. We felt it was time to offer our support to a presidential candidate for 1968.

LaRue, who had just attended a strategy session in Chicago with Nixon and some of his advisers, offered a persuasive bit of intelligence: Nixon was spooked by the thought of having too many Goldwater supporters. Nevertheless, we knew we had a few things to offer. First and foremost, we could deliver delegates. We had a line on perhaps 500 of them by our best estimate. We could also raise cash. Though our experiences had burned us on the campaign trail, we felt we could deliver reasonably good advice. But we had to consider two key questions; Would we be comfortable working with Nixon, and would he accept our assistance?

Nixon answered the second question himself without being asked. In June, he invited Jerry Milbank and me to join him for lunch and some friendly probing. Dick was in a most expansive mood, drifting into something resembling humor. The current issue of *Time* magazine had an extraordinarily favorable write-up about Bill Buckner. "Maybe all along he's just been a Trojan horse for the liberal left, assigned to infiltrate and sabotage by becoming a spokesman for the right," Nixon joked. But when he got down to business, he was straightforward. "Look, I gave my all for you guys, gave it everything I had, and I want you to give some thought to turning those delegates loose to support me in "68."

It was our turn to probe. How did he feel about our team? What did he think about, and what were his connections with the RNC? What were his plans for the immediate future? It was like an employment interview, and I took notes like a good interviewer. "Overall impression ... a man of great energy, but not particularly prepossessing, a man of great devotion to the Party, but perhaps motivated a touch by self-interest, a man so much on the run perhaps to obscure a shallowness that would show up if he slowed down and could be analyzed?"

A "Nixon for President Committee" opened a Washington office headed by San Diego obstetrician Dr. Gaylord B. Parkinson. As GOP State Chairman for California, Parky wrote the so-called 11th Commandment ("Thou Shalt Not Speak Ill of Other Republicans"), which later became a keystone of Reagan's political philosophy. Nixon himself went on a six-month "political moratorium," which included an extended overseas fact-finding tour: Bucharest, Prague, London, Paris, Berlin, Rome (where he met with the Pope), and Moscow (where Soviet officials declined an invitation to meet). The main topic of interest everywhere was Vietnam, followed by East-West tensions and Chinese hostility.

When he opened his New Hampshire campaign on February 2, 1968, the up-tight Nixon of 1960 had bloomed into a relaxed, jovial master of the press conference. A newsman asked why did he want to be president? He parried; why would anyone want to be a reporter? "I think," he said, "covering a presidential campaign is worse than running one." Nixon's strategy from the beginning was to take on LBJ and not run against any of the Republican candidates. Well, he won New Hampshire with more votes than all other candidates, Democrat, Republican, and write-ins, put together. More votes than any candidate in any New Hampshire primary, ever.

Rockefeller was more or less a non-candidate until, right in the middle of the New Hampshire campaigning, North Vietnam's Tet offensive demonstrated that it still had considerable force despite years of American efforts—and pronouncements—to the contrary. Tet was a military defeat for the North; they achieved no objectives and did not, myth to the contrary, "capture" the U.S. embassy. But Tet was a major morale-buster for America and would drive Lyndon Johnson out of office. On March 31, 1968, an over-burdened LBJ announced: "I shall not seek, and I will not accept, the nomination of my party for another term as your president." And Rockefeller was back in the game.

He tried but seemed to have lost his rudder. Rockefeller fell flat on his face at a meeting of editors and reporters, according to a friend who was there.

He read a speech that seemed to have been put together by a committee. He did enter some primaries but was pretty much ignored. Rockefeller twisted some arms to convert Nixon delegates; perhaps he could keep Nixon below the magic number, 667, force a second ballot, and then go head-to-head with whoever was still standing.

Then, just as the convention ramped up, another late-comer entered the race: Ronald Reagan created a first-ballot deadlock. And Clif White was back in the saddle, counting delegates. He asked me to meet with Reagan; the reason was apparent, and Reagan made a firm but friendly pitch. Would I shift my vote and bring along as many of my friends as possible? I had to say "No," that it was too late in the game, and while I truly believed Reagan to be the ideological successor to Goldwater, I was honor-bound to stick with my commitment to Nixon.

At a gala on the eve of the Convention, John Wayne was working the tables, warning, "Look fellows, if you don't vote for Nixon, I'll break all your heads open." I guess most of them were listening, because Nixon won with 692, Rockefeller got 287, and Reagan, 182. I could not help but recall the "consultant" quoted in David Broder's column, "Nixon is trying to take the remnants of the Goldwater team and give it some responsibility, but it won't work." But that is exactly what he did, and the grassroots "remnants of the Goldwater team" were behind Nixon. Along the way, in every Poll taken by Republican local officials and potential delegates, Nixon came out ahead. He had earned that support.

Here's a minor, little-known footnote to political history: Jerry Milbank and I had decided, early on, to push George Bush for vice president. We thought he could run well with any of the three leading candidates, no matter which was nominated. Granted, he was a first-term congressman and not well known, but I felt his relaxed personality was natural for television. He would quickly make his mark as the ideal candidate: young, with a fresh face, a mix of East Coast and Texas to balance Nixon's California background, and a politically well-connected father who could facilitate fundraising.

I tested this idea on friends from New England and a few journalists from Texas. They were encouraging. I called Bush, and told him I was nosing around, testing the waters, and asked if he would like to be vice president? He said, "Who wouldn't?" Jerry and I worked the floor at the convention, lining up what were probably sufficient votes to put him over. We obtained letters of support from delegations from seven states. And, as noted in August 5, 1968, *San Antonio Light*: "Houston Congressman George (Poppy) Bush's vice presidential stock went up this weekend, with the national Republican treasurer pushing his candidacy for the GOP No. 2 spot."

Well, I was not pushing for Bush in my official RNC capacity but as a friend and member of the Connecticut delegation. I had a "Bush for V.P." banner in his hotel's lobby. I spoke up at a press conference, encouraging support. Poppy was surprised by the number of reporters who met his plane when he arrived in Miami a few hours later.

As soon as Nixon had the nomination, Milbank and I made an appointment to make the pitch. "Mr. President, we'd like to put forward the name of George Bush for vice president." We assured Nixon that we had lined up the votes. "Oh, gosh, fellows," he said. "Gee, that's too bad. We're not going that way. I've already decided to put Agnew on the ticket." Spiro T. Agnew, governor of Maryland, was little known to the rest of the country, but that didn't matter. "Agnew," Nixon explained, "will unite the Party with Rockefeller, and he made a terrific nominating speech on my behalf." I think we both blurted out, "Who?" We tried to talk about it, but Nixon was adamant. "This is my man! My Man! Sorry fellows, you've really done great work, but Agnew's my man!"

The night of the election, Nixon's secretary, Rosemary Woods, called and invited a few of us—Strom Thurmond, Fred LaRue, Jerry Milbank, and a couple of others—to come to campaign headquarters at the Waldorf-Astoria and help count the votes. We were stationed outside Nixon's suite in the hall by the elevators, with some chairs and a TV set. Now and then, Rosemary would come out of the suite and assure us that Nixon wanted to thank us for our outstanding support; we were "his team." The election was in doubt until well into the morning. I don't think the TV pundits were calling it for Nixon until breakfast time, and Humphrey didn't concede until 11:30 am. The final numbers were interesting: Nixon, 31,770,237; Humphrey, 31,270,533; Alabama governor George Wallace, 9,906,141. Nixon had 2 million fewer votes than in 1960, even though the total number of votes was higher than in 1960 by some 4 million.

At about 12:30 am, Herbert Brownell and some other Rockefeller types stepped out of the elevators and went past us to Nixon's suite; the door opened, they went in, and the door shut. Perhaps an hour later, the door opened, and they came out, got back in the elevator, and went down. I don't remember if they said anything to us, going or coming. As I later learned, Nixon had invited them over to discuss cabinet positions. At about 2:00, Rose Mary came out and apologized. She said the boss had gone to bed; he'd have to see us in the morning. I later found out that Nixon actually didn't go to bed until about 8 am; and that, as soon as we had left, he called in his campaign manager H. R. Haldeman and they began working the phones; then he brought in the rest of the immediate campaign staff for an impromptu celebration that went on for several hours. Gratitude, I came to realize, is the most fleeting of human emotions. I decided if Nixon ever really wanted to thank us, he knew how to find us.

Some years later, I was giving a talk at the Breakers Hotel in Palm Beach. It was a conference of high-level corporate CEOs, and Brownell was there. It was the first time I'd seen him since that election night, and I asked him what had happened. "Don't blame me," he said. "I got a call from Nixon, and he asked me to get together with some other members of the Rockefeller team, draw up our suggestions for the Cabinet, and bring them over immediately. We presented our list; he accepted some, not others."

I find it sad that few of the Rockefeller types would give Nixon the time of day until he was elected—and then he was courting them. Some might think this was a brilliant move and argue that Nixon was giving the opposition a hand in friendship. It was more of an example of Nixon's insecurity, a need to be liked. He tended to ignore those loyal to him, but those who fought or stood up to him would find him seeking their friendship.

Gerald R. Ford

America was shattered in 1974. The Nixon presidency was in its last days. The vice president had already resigned. Soviet Communism, with its Castro proxies, was rampaging through Africa. OPEC held Europe by the throat. Saigon was teetering, and our armed forces were falling apart. The scourge of inflation was wrecking the economy, and many proclaimed the end of the American experiment. In stepped Gerry Ford, who helped restore the Oval Office's integrity during a crisis.

Ford quickly began assembling the plans for transition with an eye to both the Cold War and the unrest at home. He selected Donald Rumsfeld as his chief of staff, and the two began to right the ship of state after Watergate. Rumsfeld later served as the youngest and oldest secretary of Defense in the nation's history. In foreign policy, Ford convinced the two most famous members of the Cabinet—Secretary of State Henry Kissinger and Secretary of Defense James Schlesinger—to stay to signal to the Soviet Union that the new president would not be trifled with. To buttress the Nixon staff who survived, he assembled a group of seasoned professionals, including former members of Congress and businesspeople.

The instructions were clear—restore the integrity of the Oval Office. That charitable grace led to the pardon of the former president to spare him, his family, and the nation the destructive spectacle of seeing a former leader on trial. It may have cost Ford the White House in 1976 but it saved the constitutional balance. Ford and Rumsfeld threw out the "Berlin Wall" system of Bob Haldeman and John Ehrlichman that cordoned Nixon off from those with his best interests. The "Spokes of the Wheel Theory" that Ford liked created an open door with the president at the center of numerous advisers. Donald Rumsfeld reminded him that the hub of the wheel could get overheated and that the key to success was that everyone meeting the president had to first work from his "outbox," not their "inbox." Rumsfeld brought order to the system and capitalized on the president's easygoing personality.

Ford had to make tough decisions—the most influential being to have Henry Kissinger focus on the State Department while handing his national security advisor duties to a Ford man, Brent Scowcroft. Ford sent Marines into Cambodia to rescue the crew of the Mayaguez, and he was there asking Congress not to forsake the South Vietnamese in 1975. Through it all, America slowly righted itself. Ford made the White House function during a crisis, the likes of which had not been seen since the Civil War. His selfless patriotism and mastery of people helped the quiet man from Michigan save the presidency.

Although Nixon had appointed me secretary of the Navy, I served most of that term under Ford, an old friend, much more relaxed than Nixon ever had been. At one point, he said, "Bill, you've got a great job with more than a million men and women united in a common cause, the crew standing at attention and saluting you as the carrier steams past with the band up on the bow playing one of your marches, and there you are in all of your glory. I'm over here wrestling with our country's future with a staff of 350 people while some of my senior staffers are wrapped in a battle of ego, and I've got to try to keep everyone happy." He seemed to long for the days when, in Congress, he could bring people together; now, he had to play referee.

Ford brought in Nelson Rockefeller as an appointed vice president, and while I was initially disturbed by that selection, I can only say that Nelson became a staunch ally. Yes, you never know. Nelson Rockefeller had always been "the enemy." He may have been a Republican, but he seemed to stand for everything I didn't believe in. He had always been this devious plotter, sitting in his castle on the river, finding ways to spend his vast fortune in support of liberal causes. In my circle of friends, he was known as "Old BOMFOG," for his frequent use in speeches of what seems to have been his favorite phrase, the "brotherhood of man, fatherhood of God." Yet, when I bumped into him at the Pentagon, he was a most engaging fellow, very outgoing, who seemed interested in my efforts to boost the Navy. He said, "Bill, I'm underemployed here as vice president. I've always been fond of the Navy, and I want to help." And I said, "Welcome aboard!"

Rockefeller became a strong supporter of our efforts; he made phone calls on our behalf and went along with me on several congressional visits. He also accepted my invitation to be the graduation speaker at the Naval Academy and principal speaker at the commissioning of the nuclear aircraft carrier, USS *Dwight D. Eisenhower*. For reasons not clear at the time, the Party dumped Nelson and put in Bob Dole as the vice-presidential candidate for the 1976 election.

In 1975, Ford came to me with an urgent message—prepare a helicopter plan to rescue Americans and Vietnamese sympathizers from Saigon during the last days of the war. Admiral James Holloway was in control throughout the operation. He took charge, trying to gauge results and assess remaining needs. "How many are left at the embassy? How many more lifts?" It was clear to me why this man had been chosen to be CNO; with calm authority, he called for a final nineteen sorties, and that was that.

Most Americans believed that Gerald Ford was an innately decent and good man and would and did bring honor to the White House. Although this sentiment proved too little to get Ford to victory in 1976, it is an assessment that most Americans and scholars still find valid in the years after his presidency.

Ronald W. Reagan

As the 1980 presidential campaign approached, I was no longer an official of the RNC or an official delegate to the nominating convention held in Detroit. I provided policy assistance to Governor Reagan as chairman of both the International Economic Advisory Committee and the Naval Advisory Committee. Just after Reagan won the nomination but before a running mate had been picked, we learned that a group of Republican insiders viewed the candidate as a political upstart, good at reading his lines but without a brain in his head. They seemed to have missed Reagan's two-term service as an elected governor of California who wrote his own speeches. They felt that Reagan would need on-the-job assistance from an established person, such as the previous president, Gerald Ford.

Reagan did not reject the idea out of hand, agreeing there might be some merit in giving the vice president some responsibilities in the international arena as sort of an overseer of the State Department. We held a meeting aboard the yacht of Republican fundraiser John McGoff, with Henry Kissinger, Alan Greenspan, Dick Allen, Bill Casey, and me to discuss the possibilities of such a plan. Before any decisions were made, Ford told CBS newsman Walter Cronkite that as vice president, he would share responsibilities across the spectrum, implying that he would be an equal partner with the president. Reagan saw the Cronkite broadcast and exploded. Within hours, the vice presidency was offered to George Bush.

On January 20, 1981, Ronald Reagan was sworn in as president of the United States. After the election, I served as finance chairman for the Inaugural, where I was asked to raise $15 million in ten days as a loan to cover the up-front costs. It was all paid back in about three weeks, with proceeds from ball tickets and trinkets. I even wrote a new march for the occasion, "Thumbs Up America." This one came with lyrics by Sammy Kahn, head of the Songwriters Hall of Fame.

Reagan faced turmoil at home and abroad: His predecessor had presided over the worst recession since the Great Depression, staggering rates of inflation and unemployment, the Soviet invasion of Afghanistan, the Iran hostage crisis, and a mood of defeatism and exhaustion in the aftermath of the Vietnam War and Watergate. Reagan laid out a bracing vision of American renewal in his inaugural address despite all this. In plain and stirring language, he appealed to the "moral courage of free men and women," asking Americans to rededicate themselves to noble purposes.

As Ronald Reagan assumed the presidency, he was greatly troubled by what he saw worldwide. For more than three decades, the U.S. and its allies had striven to contain Communism through diplomatic, economic, and military initiatives that had cost hundreds of billions of dollars and tens of thousands of lives. Yet Communism still gripped the Soviet Union, Eastern and Central Europe, China, Cuba, Vietnam, and North Korea and spread to sub-Saharan Africa, Afghanistan, and Nicaragua.

"Detente," Ronald Reagan once quipped, "isn't that what a farmer has with his turkey—until Thanksgiving Day?" When Reagan took over the White House, he planned to make his foreign policy everything Jimmy Carter's was not. Carter had tried accommodating America's enemies. He cut back on defense. He made humility the hallmark of American diplomacy.

Our foes responded aggressively: Iranian revolutionaries danced in the rubble of the U.S. embassy; the Soviets sponsored armed insurgencies and invaded Afghanistan. Later in his presidency, Carter tried to look tough. He proposed a modest increase in defense spending, pulled the United States out of the Moscow Olympics, and slapped an embargo on wheat exports to the Soviet Union. These actions hurt athletes and American farmers but didn't faze our enemies. It was too little, too late.

As Reagan entered his presidency, the U.S. economy and the American spirit were low. Still, he committed to a policy of "peace through strength." And, even before he put his plan into action, our enemies began to worry.

Yuri Andropov, the chief of the KGB—the Soviet's spy network—feared that Reagan planned to attack. "Andropov," wrote Steven Hayward, in his *Age of Reagan*, "ordered the KGB to organize a special surveillance program in the United States—code-named Operation RYAN—to look for signs of preparations for an attack."

Reagan's assertive approach to foreign policy did not spark a war. It produced peace. The Kremlin discovered Reagan was not the cowboy they feared. But they respected the more muscular United States. Russia agreed to the most effective arms control treaty in history.

Reagan's opponents never understood the importance of peace through strength. When Reagan went to negotiate an economic strategy with House Speaker Tip O'Neill, he was told Congress would cut $35 billion in domestic spending only if Reagan pared the same amount from the Pentagon budget. Reagan refused. Defense was not the problem, he told O'Neill. Defense was less than 30 percent of spending, down from nearly half the budget when John F. Kennedy had been president. (Today, Pentagon spending is less than one-fifth of the budget.) He concluded that keeping America safe, free, and prosperous doesn't start with making the nation unsafe.

Whatever its early success, the policy of containment no longer worked. Reagan determined the time had come for a new strategy: "We win, and they lose." In his first presidential press conference, Reagan denounced the Soviet leadership as still dedicated to "world revolution and a one-world Socialist-Communist state." He wrote in his official autobiography, "I decided we had to send as powerful a message as we could to the Russians that we weren't going to stand by anymore while they armed and financed terrorists and subverted democratic governments."

Based on intelligence reports and his life-long study, Reagan concluded that Soviet Communism was cracking and ready to crumble. In May 1982, he went public with his assessment of the Soviets' systemic weakness. He said the Soviet empire was "faltering because rigid centralized control destroyed incentives for innovation, efficiency, and individual achievement." In his first address to British Parliament, Reagan said a "great revolutionary crisis gripped the Soviet Union" and that a "global campaign for freedom" would ultimately prevail. He predicted that "the march of freedom and democracy will leave Marxism-Leninism on the ash-heap of history as it has left other tyrannies which stifle the freedom and muzzle the self-expression of the people."

He directed his top national security team to develop a plan to end the Cold War by winning it. The result was a series of top-secret national security decision directives that:

- Committed the U.S. to "neutralizing" Soviet control over Eastern Europe and authorized covert action and other means to support anti-Soviet groups in the region.
- Adopted a policy of attacking a "strategic triad" of critical resources—financial credits, high technology, and natural gas—essential to Soviet economic survival. Author-economist Roger Robinson said the directive was tantamount to "a secret declaration of economic war on the Soviet Union."
- Determined that, rather than coexist with the Soviet system, the U.S. would seek to change it fundamentally. America intended to "roll back" Soviet influence at every opportunity.

Following these directives, the administration pursued a multifaceted foreign policy offensive that included covert support of the Solidarity movement in Poland, removal of a Cuba/Soviet threat in Grenada, a global campaign to reduce Soviet access to Western high technology and a drive to hurt the Soviet economy by driving down the price of oil and limiting natural gas exports to the West. A key element of Reagan's victory strategy was the support of anti-Communist forces in Afghanistan, Nicaragua, Angola, and Cambodia. The "Reagan Doctrine" was the most cost-effective of all the cold war doctrines, costing the United States less than a billion dollars a year while forcing the cash-strapped Soviets to spend some $8 billion annually to deflect its impact. It was also one of the most politically successful doctrines in Cold War history, resulting in a Soviet pullout from Afghanistan, the election of democratic governments in Grenada and Nicaragua, the removal of 40,000 Cuban troops from Angola, and the holding of United Nations-monitored elections there.

Reagan also initiated SDI—the Strategic Defense Initiative that put the Soviet military in fear and shock. In 1991, a Soviet admiral told me, "SDI defeated all our possible countermeasures." Reagan never missed an opportunity to educate the world about America's democratic achievements. He lauded the American democratic ethos that knows no ethnic or racial divisions in times of crisis. "All of us together, in and out of government, must bear the burden," he said. "The solutions we seek must be equitable, with no one group singled out to pay a higher price." The key was to recover a vibrant, dynamic free-market economy. This objective—not massive government spending and tax increases—was the surest path to providing "equal opportunities for all Americans with no barriers born of bigotry or discrimination."

Reagan declared that "government is not the solution to our problem; government is the problem." In the next, he pledged that "your dreams, your hopes, your goals are going to be the dreams, the hopes, and goals of this administration, so help me, God." America would be prepared to defend its democratic way of life on the world stage, Reagan declared, just as it always had done. "As for the enemies of freedom . . . they will be reminded that peace is the highest aspiration of the American people. We will negotiate for it, sacrifice for it; we will not surrender for it, now or ever."

After his first term in office, with the American economy roaring back to life and the Soviet Union declining, he won a second term, prevailing in 49 out of 50 states—one of the most significant electoral landslides in American political history. Behind these facts are lessons for the intellectually curious. Like no other political leader, Reagan united the significant currents of modern conservatism: free-market economics, individual responsibility, limited government, a strong national defense, patriotism, populism, civic virtue, and faith. He made American exceptionalism his lodestar. Viewed objectively, his oratory—his natural eloquence, historical awareness, and moral clarity—rivals that of the greatest statesmen of the last century. Reagan neither bullied the American people nor treated them as hapless victims. He proved that the best way to move hearts and minds was to articulate a political philosophy compellingly and with a touch of humor that could disarm even his toughest critics.

The American president who effectively wrote the end to the Cold War was Ronald Reagan. He entered the Oval Office with a clear set of ideas he had developed over a lifetime of study. He forced the Soviet Union to abandon its goal of world Communism by challenging its legitimacy, regaining superiority in the arms race, and using human rights as a powerful psychological weapon. His vision is needed more than ever. Indeed, the outcome of this struggle depends upon its revival: on ordinary Americans, united by their love of country, fighting to preserve the world's most daring experiment in human freedom. By the time Reagan left office in January 1989, the Reagan Doctrine had achieved its goal: Mikhail Gorbachev, the last leader of the Soviet system, publicly acknowledged the failures of Marxism-Leninism and the futility of Russian imperialism. British Prime Minister Margaret Thatcher said, "Ronald Reagan had ended the Cold War without firing a shot."

20 | Music, Poetry, and Art

As ambassador to the Netherlands, the Organization of American States, the European Community, and as secretary of the Navy, I was involved in trade negotiations and ship and weapon systems procurement. Composing music, reading poetry, and creating art was such a great change from the hard grind of diplomacy and economic and military activities on occasional weekends when my busy schedule allowed it. It brought joy and a sense of balance to my life. Planning for our nation's defense never diminished my love for music, poetry, and art.

The most significant non-official and non-family event of my tour as ambassador to the Netherlands was my re-entry into the music world. Not in performance (I had studied music and piano in preparatory school but was indeed not well grounded) but in composition. In the spring of 1971, I was most fortunate to meet an absolute musical genius, Somtow Sucharitkul, son of the Thai ambassador to the Netherlands. When he discovered that I had always been interested in composing but had no idea how to go about it, he volunteered as a teacher and, more critically, collaborator. This was a wonderful interlude for me in the evenings after my 8–9 hours days.

We started with a few hymns for my Church in the Hague, then a short piano concerto and some other minor pieces. I worked out the melodies, and Somtow helped me develop the orchestration. With Somtow's invaluable assistance, I composed a symphony to commemorate Queen Juliana's 25th year on the throne. I was most flattered when Philips recorded a performance of my "Holland Symphony" for release during the Jubilee Year celebrations and honored by its broadcast, along with an extended interview of yours truly, on Dutch national television. I presented the score to Her Majesty during a farewell lunch she held in my honor. Every month, with a particular focus on music, Somtow contacted the different musicians and organized the events. On several occasions, I invited Dutch composers to create something new to be played during a soirée. Perhaps 15 took up the challenge, and each of their compositions was performed that evening for our critical review. One of the composers was Princess Margriet's husband, Peter van Vollenhoven.

One dinner, in honor of the pianist Arturo Rubinstein, was not so successful. Oh, the dinner was delicious, and the company gregarious, but the music portion ended on a different note. There was a marvelous Bösendorfer grand piano in the residence, my own piano, and I asked Mr. Rubenstein if he would care to play something for the guests, anything at all. He said, "Oh, I have to tell you, I am under contract with Steinway, and I am not permitted to touch another instrument." Not even in a private party at an American embassy?

Over the years since, and always with the technical collaboration of Somtow and others, I've put together a fair number of compositions, ranging from nocturnes to operas, marches, eight symphonies, and an opera. Many, if not most, have been in commemoration of something: a visit to a foreign country or the launching of a new Navy ship. I've put a particular focus on marches for Navy ships, and a few years ago, I was most gratified to receive the "Edwin Franko Goldman Award" from the American Bandmasters Association. I have been honored when my compositions have been played by such stellar orchestras as the National Symphony and the St. Louis Symphony, and I served as guest conductor at a number of orchestral and band performances, at home and abroad, usually playing one of my own works.

I make no claim whatever to any skill as a conductor; my style, if you will, has been described as enthusiastic but stiff—what Isabelle called the "Al Gore school of conducting." While I gained some confidence in making music over the years, I was not at all grounded in the conducting thereof. As I was preparing to conduct the Boston Pops in one of my compositions, Maestro Arthur Fiedler told me everything I needed to know: "The secret of conducting? When the band stops playing, stop waving." Fiedler was not a great fan of those fancied conductors with flying arms, legs, and tails feverishly waving while being ignored by the orchestra.

In the fall of 1976, my Violin Concerto in D minor premiered under the baton of Richard Hayman, principal Pops conductor of both the Detroit and St. Louis Symphony Orchestras and chief arranger for Arthur Fiedler and the Boston Pops Orchestra for 22 years. Maestro Hayman commented:

> Here, indeed, is a concerto by an American composer that will hold a powerful appeal for both the performer and audience alike. This is due to the fact that it is a moving poetic work of intense romantic expression that demands of the soloist not only great virtuosity but also a warmth of expression and elegance of style that causes an immediate effect on the listener's emotions. There is breadth of soul in its themes and well-contrasted rhythmic ideas in the individual movements.

One of the great compliments about my music came from Yehudi Menuhin, one of the world's foremost violinists. He wrote to me: "I listened to the Violin Concerto, and its spontaneous warmth and melodiousness are among its most pleasing qualities. Surely, you must be the first Secretary of the Navy to have composed a violin concerto! How fortunate we are that so sensitive and responsible a position in government is vested in a person of such great musical sensibility as yourself." Of course, I was very grateful for the quotes from Maestro Hayman and Yehudi Meduhin, but a review from my eight-year-old granddaughter gave me another perspective. In a quote from Mark Twain, she cheerfully said, "Granddaddy, your music is not as bad as it sounds." My opera, *The Lion and the Rose*, was based on the adventurous King Richard the Lionhearted, who tried twice unsuccessfully to regain the holy city of Jerusalem from Saladin at the end of the 12th century. The entire opera is approximately two and one-quarter hours. The Cambridge Symphony Orchestra in England, under conductor Somtow Sucharitkul, recorded two excerpts of the opera in 1977.

As ambassador to the Organization of American States, I realized that to really understand the Latin culture and its traditional values, you must learn the way music plays a major role in their lives. I wrote symphonic pieces for 14 separate Latin American countries. They included *To Trinidad with Love*, a composition performed in Trinidad by their leading steel bands. One of my favorite types of music is that of the steel band, which originated in Trinidad and Tobago and caught on with much enthusiasm in our own country. I was asked to be a judge in Trinidad's National Steel Band Contest in August 1982. It was like a world series in baseball, and very difficult to pick out a winner. Some bands had as many as 120 members and played classical music, such as Beethoven's *Fifth Symphony*.

I wrote a symphonic piece for Venezuela called *Fantasia de Marfacaibo*, performed by the Maracaibo Symphony Orchestra at the OAS Music Festival in Washington in 1983. I also wrote *Mexican Rhapsody* and *Brazilian Triptych* for a chamber orchestra that was played at the OAS Music Festival in 1983. *Brazilian Triptych* made its world premiere by the New World Chamber Players at the National Academy of Sciences in Washington, D.C. on May 18, 1983.

"Nobody's pretending the ambassador is the new Stravinsky, least of all Middendorf himself," Lon Tuck, music critic for *The Washington Post*, wrote in his review. "But Middendorf does have a way with tunes. They are individual, with an exotic touch to some. They are also eclectic."

When Belize gained its independence, I wrote the *Belize Independence March* for the occasion. When the British flag came down and the Belize flag went up, and they played my march, I can't tell you how thrilling it was.

Years earlier, in the mid-1950s, I developed a fascination for the poetry of Robert Frost and was determined to meet him in person. Boston book dealer George Goodspeed called a friend who lived at the foot of the hill where Frost lived part of the year with no telephone or even electricity. The neighbor asked the poet for an appointment on my behalf. It was granted, and Isabelle and I went up to the little log cabin in Ripton, Vermont, where Frost lived in spring and summer. Frost looked like a stonewall builder with big paw hands, but he was a sophisticated man with passionate loves, hates, and a load of insecurities. He made us feel welcome, sitting on the hillside. He took a book and wrote the poem "Stopping by the Woods" on the flyleaf and endorsed it to Isabelle and me. Frost and I became good friends, and I sponsored his visits to the Frost Library at the University of Virginia and the Grolier Club in New York, where he recited his poems.

Over the years, I collected a number of Frost originals. In 1961, president-elect John F. Kennedy invited Frost to write something for the inauguration. Frost declined but agreed to recite one of his poems, "The Gift Outright" at the ceremony. A few days before the ceremony, Frost changed his mind and began to write a new poem, finishing some 42 lines. At the inauguration, Frost was so blinded by the sun that he couldn't read the new poem, but he easily quoted "The Gift Outright" from memory. I have one of his handwritten copies of "Dedication," which Frost later renamed "For John F. Kennedy His Inauguration." Frost remained a close friend until his death in 1963.

I began to collect art, focusing on several well-known contemporary American artists such as Edward Hopper and Andrew Wyeth. I met both of these artists through Lloyd Goodrich, director of the Whitney Museum. I was intrigued by an ad placed by a lady who offered a Frederic Church painting her family had acquired directly from the artist in the 1860s. Frederic Church was a giant of art in the 19th century. I contacted the lady, and she led me to the painting hanging in a solarium with a very leaky roof, with the only light coming from a nearby streetlamp. The painting was torn, partly out of the frame, flopped down on a bunch of plants, and drenched by rain blowing through some broken windows. It was not an auspicious introduction, but upon prodding, the lady produced a flashlight, and after a quick look at the grimy, four-by-seven-foot canvas, I knew this was a wonderful painting. In truth, *Rainy Season in the Tropics* is now rated as one of Church's best. Many years later, pinched for cash from living on a government salary and putting five kids through college, I sold it to John D. Rockefeller IIII, and it is now at the DeYoung Museum in San Francisco.

When I was ambassador to the Netherlands, in addition to my hundreds of routine embassy duties, occasionally, a Dutch industry would make a special request. For instance, KLM, their leading airline, would request landing rights in Chicago. At this point, reciprocal negotiations would take place. On one occasion, a certain Dutch-born Swiss citizen whose family steel company had dealt with both sides during World War II approached me. They had a large operation in Rotterdam, but his visits, I think, were not to check on his business but to curry favor with the Americans. For a big-time industrialist, he was an odd dresser, with lederhosen and an open shirt carefully arranged to highlight the hair on his chest. Rather like a male bird sporting his plumage. I think he had five wives, favoring models and beauty queens, most 5 or 10 years younger than the wife he was leaving. He always gave each a valuable painting as a going away present.

During one visit, looking around my residence, which I had decorated with some classic-era Dutch paintings from my own collection, he said, "You don't have any Impressionists. You really should have at least one. I gave a nice Monet to my last wife. She lives in Switzerland, and she might loan it to you. Give her a call." I did call. She said, "You want to borrow the Monet? Come pick it up, fine." I drove over to Switzerland.

The ex-wife was very gracious if a bit vague: "Let me see . . . if we can find the painting. It was of what? Oh, wait, yes, the one that my ex-husband gave me. His reward." Her sour expression told me what she thought of her ex-husband. We found the painting behind a couch—*Three women in a blue boat*. With a wave of her hand, she said, "Please, take it." I'm not sure if she had any idea who I was or where it was going.

I hung it in the embassy, but it was too much of a contrast compared with the Old Masters on display and was not on my list of favorites, either. I considered it to be superficial, lacking technical skill and emotion—but I guess that's why they called Monet and friends "Impressionists." I tolerated it for six months and then took it back. The owner was as disinterested in its return as she had been with its leaving.

Armand Hammer, usually identified as "the millionaire Chairman of Occidental Petroleum," was an acquaintance of some years standing, growing out of his own passion for art (he and his brother owned New York's Hammer Galleries). Armand visited me at the embassy and, I guess, assumed that I owned the Monet because soon after my tour had ended, he called to offer me $10 million for the painting. I gave him the owner's name and have no idea whether or not he followed through.

I was offered the chance to buy an Old Master painting from a church in Spain, where it had been hanging over the altar for almost four hundred years. The church needed money to fix a roof badly in need of repair, so it put the painting up for sale. I asked Renaissance art expert Daan Cevat to join me to take a look. The chancel was dark (they used candles to light the services) and filled with the gentle sound of the nuns, hidden behind a screen, watching our every move and praying for the new roof. We had a flashlight. When Daan saw just the bottom of the painting, he whispered, "We must leave."

When we were out of the building, Daan explained: "That's a copy. The original is in a museum in America." But how could this be? I was told the painting had been owned by the church since it was painted in 1577. As it turned out, the painting had been sent to a restorer in the 1870s and, yes, came back as a copy while the original was quietly passed through a series of owners, finally to come to rest some 40 years later in an American museum.

I experienced another "art" adventure of a more pleasant sort—early in my tour, before Isabelle and the kids came over. I had some spare time on weekends, and I took the opportunity to study stained-glass window-making with one of the world's leading experts, Joep Nicolas, and I helped him create an enormous window for the William of Orange Church in Delft. Joep allowed me to paint some areas near the top, reserving the important main figures for himself. A plaque at the bottom of the window credits both of us for the work. A few feet in front of the window is the floor burial of the great Dutch artist Johannes Vermeer. Satisfied that I had some skill, Joep allowed me to make more than a dozen much smaller windows, including a baptismal window for the American Anglican Church in the Hague.

I also learned to make "Delft" plates, commemorating something or other and illustrated in a characteristic blue paint. I presented them to various friends and associates, including Joseph Luns, foreign minister, making his final speech in 19 years to 30 members of Parliament, all of whom are portrayed. One member was sleeping. My friend Luns told me he would donate the plate to the Rijksmuseum upon his death. I presented President Nixon with a Delft plate on behalf of the Dutch people.

I am also a collector of Dutch and Flemish Masters paintings, some of which are regularly lent out to museums. Over the years, I've given many paintings and whole collections to museums. As long as 60 years ago, I became a major donor to the Metropolitan Museum, including a major collection of American miniatures, among them ones by Copley and Peales. Recently, I donated a painting by Hans Memling to the Bruges Museum in Belgium. I've been visiting Bruges for more than 60 years. It's one of those rare world treasures preserved mainly as it was in medieval times. Its beauty and my passion for the paintings that echo through the centuries has drawn me back there over the years.

Born in Germany around 1430, Hans Memling worked in the Brussels workshop of Rogier van der Weyden by 1465. He later settled in Bruges, where he became one of the most influential northern European artists of his time. His religious paintings often incorporated portraits of his wealthy patrons: bankers, merchants, politicians, clergymen, and aristocrats. The Memling painting is most widely believed to portray Francisco de Rojas, the Spanish ambassador to the Burgundian Court. Till-Holger Borchert, the director of the Bruges Museums, is one of the great art historians in the world, and I admire him tremendously. All these factors played a part in my decision that the painting would return to Bruges, where it belongs.

"This is the first time we've received such an important donation," Borchert said in acknowledging the gift. "It is one of the very few examples that we will have to remind us of the Spanish presence in Bruges during the Middle Ages. The city was an important trading hub at that time. While we have a lot of archives documenting the presence of Spanish merchants, we don't have many images showing them. So having a depiction of a prominent Spanish family makes it very interesting, especially as it is by Memling, another prominent citizen of Bruges and an extremely important artist."

Borchert added that the source of the gift brought an even deeper meaning. "I've known Bill Middendorf since 2002, and he has become a friend. I feel extremely honored that he thought of us. Bill is a remarkable person—part of a generation of great collectors that has shaped the taste of the American public. So not only will we have a great Memling. We will also have a painting that keeps the memory of a great collector alive."

My love of drawing began at an early age with my mother's encouragement. I attended the Middlesex School in Concord, Massachusetts, where I studied art under the visiting art teacher Frank Benson, from the Museum of Fine Arts in Boston. He was very kind when I was a young kid, getting me excited about watercolors. As a student at Harvard, I signed up for a fine arts course at the Fogg Museum because I had heard it was an easy a gut course in which one might catch up on sleep during slide shows after a strenuous crew practice in the morning. Instead, I became hooked, riveted by the wonderful slides displayed, including Rembrandt and those colorful impressionists. It changed my life and led to my participation as a board member of several art museums, including the Baltimore Museum of Art and the Corcoran in Washington, D.C. I was the founding chairman of the Friends of the American Wing at New York's Metropolitan Museum. My name is carved in the marble staircase as a major benefactor of the museum.

One of my most rewarding experiences as an artist was the result of an invitation from a minister who asked me to teach a course in drawing for the inmates of the Bristol County House of Corrections in North Dartmouth, Massachusetts. Every Tuesday night for five years, I met with male and female inmates in separate groups, teaching drawing and painting with watercolors in their prison cells. I had two rules my mostly young prisoners recited before each class:

1. Never say you can't draw. Of course, you can draw. Anybody can.
2. Never use an eraser. I want you to see your mistakes. Leave the bad line on the paper and draw the good line next to it. Then you can see the difference. That's how you learn to do it the right way and don't use the eraser as a crutch.

At the end of each class, I would pass out cardboard mats so my prisoners could frame their artwork. It gave them a chance to see their work as a framed, finished piece and helped establish a work ethic, a goal. Some appeared to show for the first time a feeling of personal accomplishment. I saw a lot of pride develop on their faces as their drawing skills developed. In a letter to me Thomas Hodgson, Bristol County sheriff, said, "Thank you for all you have done volunteering to teach our inmates the transformative value of learning to create artwork and the wisdom of finding beauty and peace in the friendship you share with them. Your character and love of humanity shine in your willingness to share your time and talents with us." Sherriff Hodgson also told me that the rate of recidivism—the tendency of convicted felons to return to prison—was at a very low percentage for my students.

"Bill, I have never known you to call a press conference to put the spotlight on yourself," President Reagan said to me when I was serving as secretary of the Navy. The president was right. I never called a press conference as a vehicle for placing myself in a favorable position or using it to advance my career. Yes, I attended press conferences and never ducked any questions, particularly in regard to our Ohio class ballistic missile submarine fleet and their Trident missiles that remain the backbone of our strategic nuclear deterrent.

Former British Prime Minister Margaret Thatcher once told Ronald Reagan that I was one of the best U.S. ambassadors she had ever met. The president replied, "Oh, Maggie, I love Bill. But I've got 152 ambassadors. Why do you think Bill was the best?" he asked.

"Whenever I gave a speech, I noticed the Ambassador, from the front row, carefully taking notes," she replied.

"He wasn't taking notes," Reagan said. "He was sketching you, something he's been doing for public figures for years. I'm surprised he didn't ask you to sign them. I've been signing the drawings he made of me for years." President Reagan was right, as I confessed to Margaret Thatcher when she attended a meeting at the Heritage Foundation in Washington some years later. I showed her four or five of the drawings I had made of her, and she graciously signed each one, "To Bill, my great friend." During this visit to our foundation, she donated $10,000,000 to us on a matching basis, which was swiftly matched, and we made the "Iron Lady" our honorary chairman.

My sketchbook has always been at my side, recording dignitaries and friends from all over the world. I'd be at a conference, and I'd sketch them. Speeches are forgotten soon after they are delivered. My drawings would bring back memories of what the speaker said and why. As a visual person, I found that sketching friends brought back memories of the key points of what they said, much more than dry recitations of their speeches which end up in a dead file drawer.

No matter where I go, I sketch practically everyone I encounter. I have about 620 sketchbooks filled with drawings of people (some famous, some anonymous), pets, and landscapes. I made several thousand sketches of leaders and associates, 150 drawings of art historian friends, and many thousands of drawings of my children, grandchildren, and great-grandchildren, recording every stage of their younger lives. My assistant tells me I have over 10,000 drawings in my collection. Regrettably, my eyesight has failed me, and I must rely on my visual memory only.

In recent years, my daughter Franny, a wonderful artist and art teacher, exhibited her and my paintings in solo exhibitions in New York. Since 1989, my son, Roxy Paine, has been filling galleries, museums, and sites worldwide with his dark, whimsical installations and sculptures, melding the industrial and the organic to explore manmade and natural systems as well as their ramifications. One of his great sculptures is in the National Gallery in Washington, D.C.

By getting close to the culture of each of my tours of duty, I felt diplomatic doors would open more readily, and they did. The State Department must have agreed because they presented me with the prestigious Superior Honor Award on two occasions.

Some of my drawings of prominent world leaders I sketched while serving as ambassador to the Netherlands, secretary of the Navy, ambassador to the Organization of American States, ambassador to the European Community, and retired resident of Little Compton, Rhode Island. They are shown after page 183.

21 | My Life Story

My lifetime journey got off to a rocky start when I flunked kindergarten at Towson (Maryland) Normal School. They told my father I was not ready to go to first grade and would have to repeat. Five years later, my mother left us to go and live in England. I must have tried to make some connection between these two events—there was none, of course—but both were traumatic. Being kept back in school turned out to be a good thing: for the rest of my grade school years, I was always, on average, about six months older than my classmates. This gave me an advantage in sports and made it easier for me to appear intelligent.

My mother, Sarah Boone Kennedy, and my father, Harry S. Middendorf, were married in the early 1920s and had four children: my brother Harry, Jr., my brother William Kennedy Boone "Took," my sister Sally, and me (1924), named John William, for both my grandfather and my father's twin brother, called Billy.

Mother was unhappy as a homemaker in what she saw as the dull world of Baltimore investment banking, my father's profession. Dad was all business; Mother wanted to be more out in the World. When I was 10, my mother was among a group of 40 women from Baltimore who were presented to the Court of St. James in England. This was the "in" thing for the in-crowd, and a gaggle of Baltimore society women made the trip. My mother's distant cousin, Wallis Warfield Simpson, married to a shipping executive then and living in London, gave them a warm insider welcome.

Mother was enchanted with England; she was captivated by the pomp and circumstance, but more to the point, she fell in love with a much older, well-connected nobleman, Lord Mount Temple, who served as minister of Transport in Stanley Baldwin's cabinet. Mother's vacation romance proved stronger than her family ties, and she divorced my father. Lord Temple was the father-in-law of Lord Mountbatten, a World War II hero who later became my good friend. Over one hundred letters from Mother to Lord Mount Temple are preserved in his archive at South Hampton University.

In the meantime, Mrs. Simpson had become involved with the Prince of Wales and divorced Mr. Simpson. The Prince of Wales soon became King Edward VIII and wished to make the former Mrs. Simpson his queen.

Church and state were reluctantly willing to have a ruler married to a non-noble American divorcée. Still, they would not allow her the title of queen nor for any issue of the marriage to be in the line of succession to the throne. Therefore, he resigned. Everyone knows that story: giving up the crown for "the woman I love."

While my mother was away all those years, my father had the entire burden of bringing up his four children. He was a remarkable father, paying attention to every detail of his children, including writing them every day when they were in school.

When she first left, I asked, "Where's Mother?" Two years later, it changed to "When is Mother coming back?" After that, there was silence on the subject. Then, in the late 1930s, the war clouds formed in Europe, and my mother did return and asked for a reconciliation with my father. My father—angry and hurt and with very little respect for my dissolute Royals—said no. It ended when Father's pistol discharged mysteriously and left a hole in a bedroom window. Who fired the shot and why remains a mystery. But Mother was gone again, this time for good.

Although the marriage ended, Mother did reconnect with her children. During World War II, she became a welder at Sparrow's Point Shipyard in Baltimore, joining thousands of other women answering the call of "Rosie the Riveter." She worked her way into a supervisory position before the end of the war. Mother never remarried, and she died on October 21, 1971, at the age of 69.

Here's another family story that significantly impacted a growing boy, but with a better outcome. Around the turn of the 20th century, my grandfather, John William Middendorf, one of the leading investment bankers of the South, had acquired the Seaboard Air Line Railroad in partnership with John S. Williams, raising necessary capital with corporate bonds. However, they were hit by a market crash in 1903, and my grandfather was wiped out. He not only lost all his money but was left with a personal debt of $5 million. The world of high finance was a small world, a club. Grandfather received sympathetic letters and cables from all over the world, especially from railroad executives such as William G. McAdoo, then building tunnels under the Hudson River and who later served as World War I secretary of the Treasury. "What can I say," he wrote, "that will adequately express how deeply I feel for you and Williams in your troubles? Words seem so empty under such circumstances." In this club, your reputation was everything; it was unheard of for a member to declare bankruptcy. Gentlemen incurred obligations, and gentlemen met them. Grandfather worked to pay off his debt, every penny. In 1928, after the debt was discharged, he died.

My father and Uncle Billy had joined grandfather at Middendorf & Williams in 1920, helping to work down the debt, and carried on the business after his death. They helped form the Middendorf, Hartman & Co. firm in Baltimore in 1921. The following year, they included Brinkman & Co., investment bankers. In 1930, they bought three companies that were in bankruptcy: Madura Portland Cement, North American Cement, and Oklahoma Natural Gas. All three companies emerged from bankruptcy, returning 15 to 20 times the initial investment.

All my father ever wanted to talk about was economics—not the good things that could happen, but the bad things that did happen. In those days, the economy went through many more cycles than today—boom, bust, and between. He had seen it all firsthand. Economics might seem like a pretty heavy dinner topic for a teenager, but I found it fascinating, and, living in the middle of the Great Depression, real-world lessons were everywhere at hand. President Hoover raised interest rates and taxes when he should have done the opposite. Franklin D. Roosevelt distorted the economy to meet social goals. Father had started as an FDR supporter—he made us listen to the weekly radio broadcasts—but turned away from "that man" as the excesses of the New Deal became clear. And we saw the unintended consequences of the protective tariff of the Smoot-Hawley Act. Rather than shield American industries from international competition, it raised consumer prices and provoked a tit-for-tat game of trade barriers.

Father also had a brief flirtation with politics. In the 1930s, he had attracted some notice as head of the Maryland Taxpayer's Association. Senator Harry Byrd, Sr., dropped by the house to unsuccessfully persuade him to run for governor. I listened in awe to that great Virginian, known even to me for standing almost alone against his fellow Democrats and the New Deal.

Thus, much of my childhood involved talk about my grandfather's problems, the 1929 crash, and living through the long Depression that followed. Money was tight; once-proud businessmen were standing on the corner of Calvert and Redwood streets, peddling apples, a nickel apiece, and "Brother, can you spare a dime?" was not just the title of a song. Some summers, my two brothers and I worked at a nearby farm, pitching hay to bring in a few extra dollars. In 1938, I worked for my father's firm—twenty-five cents a day—as a "runner," picking up or delivering certificates for stocks and bonds bought and sold. I have to say, I took the term "runner" seriously. I got a lot of healthy exercise.

One memory has stuck with me all these years: the annual Memorial Day encampment of Civil War veterans out along the Joppa Road in Towson.

These hundred or so men, well into their 90s, would proudly march in the parade, cheered on by the crowd lining the street. Symbolic on so many levels—reconciliation, remembrance, reflection.

The economy improved for a time, but a recession in 1937 was exacerbated by labor issues and ever-higher taxes (the top marginal tax rates eventually hit 91 percent). But by late 1938, the growing threat of war in Europe turned everything around. Industry began churning out vast quantities of war material, and export business was booming. Then, in September 1939, the threat became a reality when Germany invaded Poland, brought to the screen of my local movie theater with newsreel footage of Stuka dive bombers raining death.

The New York Times, as I recall, looked for a short, sharp contest. I remember this because I had been following developments with avid interest and decided to get a scrapbook and save newspaper clippings on the war. The clerk at Reed's Drugstore in Towson asked whether I wanted the 32-page scrapbook for 25 cents or the 96-page version for 75 cents. I bought the shorter version, based on *The New York Times*' prediction that the war would be over in a month.

I was in prep school soon after the European War began and at Harvard by March 1943. Harvard, in wartime, was a great place to be. For one thing, the university was glad to have us; students were in short supply. Class enrollments were wide open, and we could study with some of the finest professors in the world. It was relatively easy to be accepted on any of the sports teams—mine was rowing. Then, there was the general excitement of a nation at war: rationing, air raid drills, the nightly blackout with heavy drapes on the windows, no streetlights, and car headlights taped over so that only a tiny slit remained at the bottom.

In some respects, Harvard was too great because it offered too much freedom. I was relieved to be out of the strict regimen at my prep school, Middlesex, which had temporarily put me ahead of some of my Harvard freshman classmates. For a time, I stopped going to classes. Then, to make matters worse, I was invited into the Owl Club, one of those exclusive eating and drinking clubs. This carried on a family tradition, as both my father and uncle—the twins—had been members. I discovered that socializing was more fun than studying and fell victim to a triple whammy: too much freedom, drinking, and ego. I darn near got thrown out of school.

However, it wasn't long before the reality of the war began to hit home, and it was time for Middendorf to stand up and be counted. If I were to serve in the military, I knew it should be as a naval officer. This wasn't Harvard snobbishness. It was because I'd learned too much about the Army from the veterans closest to me; my father and uncle had served as Army officers in World War I, and my cousin Alex Smith was a colonel in the Army Reserve as I was growing up. His stories of impoverished training—recruits drilling with wooden rifles right up to the very eve of the war—reinforced my negative impression of Army life. Therefore, when the Navy established a V-12 Officer Training Program at Harvard, I was among the first to sign up.

I soon learned that V-12 was limited—it prepared men for Officer Candidate School (OCS) but offered no degree. I learned that I was eligible for another program, an accelerated wartime version of the Naval Reserve Officer Training Corps (NROTC). This was a degree-granting program, offered at a number of universities. Because naval science courses were part of the curriculum, the NROTC was considered to be academically equivalent to the program at the Naval Academy at Annapolis. Graduates were commissioned in the Naval Reserve rather than the "regular" Navy. Soon after the war, the program was modified, and U.S. Navy commissions were given to some NROTC graduates.

I signed on to the NROTC, assuming I would continue with the already-established unit at Harvard, but as it developed, there were not many openings in the unit at Harvard. A few of my classmates got that assignment, but most were transferred to units at Yale and Brown, and other New England universities. As for me, I was sent to Holy Cross.

It bothered me to transfer to another university because a Harvard degree meant more to me than one from anywhere. I was sure that I would never be allowed back into Harvard, but my brother Harry—showing a fine legal mind so early in life—offered a winning suggestion: see the Dean and get a letter of "withdrawal with permission to return."

A veteran of World War II, Harry practiced law in Manhattan until his death on March 9, 2000. He had been president of the Sons of the Revolution, the New York Genealogical Society, and the Youth Foundation. Harry was active in conservative politics, serving as vice chairman of the Conservative Party in New York from 1970–1974. He worked with me on the presidential campaigns of Barry Goldwater in 1964 and Richard Nixon in 1968.

When the war ended, a huge group of returning veterans came home to Harvard, and every applicant for admission who already had a degree (as from the NROTC at another school) was turned down—including me, initially, until I produced the letter. The dean knew me—rowing had been his sport—and gave me a sympathetic hearing and a letter that addressed my request to be re-admitted after the war, even if I had a degree from another school. I may have been the only exception.

I did not choose Holy Cross, and I doubt that Holy Cross would have chosen me in normal times. My group of NROTC midshipmen may have been among the first Protestants to attend this solidly Catholic university, where we studied philosophy and theology from a Catholic viewpoint, along with naval science and other core courses. However, the teaching fathers, Jesuits, offered sympathy and enough extra attention that I survived. The naval science courses were of great interest—navigation, naval history, engineering, gunnery, ship stability, rules, and regulations—and I quickly realized that having to cram the essence of a normal four-year program into a year and a half would require efforts more focused than any I had exercised at Harvard. I gave up partying for the duration. By the time I finished Holy Cross, the war was ending, but not my commitment to the Navy. Graduation brought an accelerated B.S. centered on the Thermodynamics of Steam (a miserable subject for a future career, but a degree nonetheless), a commission as ensign, U.S. Naval Reserve, and orders to report to the headquarters of the Pacific Fleet, at Pearl Harbor, for "further assignment."

I journeyed by train to California and then aboard the troop transport USS *Doyen* to Hawaii. En route, I had a most unpleasant shock: I was subject to almost constant seasickness. Arrival at Pearl Harbor brought a more pleasant surprise. I had exchanged a chilly New England for a lush tropical paradise. Well, "paradise" may be too strong; Honolulu had just endured a bloody riot by servicemen ostensibly protesting the slow pace of repatriation. Everyone wanted to go home, and here was Ensign Middendorf, swimming against that tide, off on his great adventure.

Here also was my first authentic look at the wartime Navy, which was awesome. The piers were crowded with ships, some moored four or five deep; some parked bow-to-stern in the shipyard drydocks, where the sounds of pneumatic chisels cutting away damaged steel mingled with the smell of burning metal as new plates were welded in place. The remains of the battleship USS *Arizona*, a victim of the December 7 attack, had been cut down to the main deck but were still very visible. When the water in the harbor was calm, you could see a sheen of fuel oil floating on the surface, steadily seeping from a sunken hull in which one thousand sailors were entombed. It was a clear reminder of where the Pacific War had begun and where, for many, it was now winding down.

Except, of course, for Middendorf. Where should I be sent for duty? I was offered an assignment on PT boats, but I was pretty sure that chronic seasickness and 80-foot wooden boats would not be a good match. "Send me anywhere else," I asked. In the geography of the Pacific Theater, that was determined to be somewhere on the coast of China. I was duly issued orders to the LLCS (L) 53 (then anchored in the Whangpoo River, Shanghai) as a replacement for another officer whose turn had come. LCS stood for "Landing Craft, Support" and the other (L), for "Large"—although in usual practice, the second (L) was dropped. LCS 53 was a floating rocket launcher armed with 150 rockets, mounted in a fixed position on the bow. The rockets were aimed by pointing the ship at the target. LCS 53 was twice as long as a PT boat and therefore considered a "ship," more or less. It was powered by eight GM 671 diesels, arrayed four to a shaft—well, so much for that degree in steam engineering. Wartime complement: five officers, sixty-eight enlisted men. Post-wartime, I later learned, was as few as possible.

The rest of my westward journey was by air: Honolulu to Johnston Island (the wettest place I have ever been, I think "torrential downpour" is a synonym for Johnston Island), thence to Okinawa (where mopping up operations were still underway against scattered Japanese holdouts), then China, handled from one leg to the next by teams of sailors with a practiced but disinterested efficiency. The final leg was by a small boat from the Fleet Landing in Shanghai, weaving through a river crowded with tramp steamers, huge Chinese junks, and business-like destroyers—to catch the first sight of my new home. If you've ever seen the 1961 movie (starring my Harvard classmate Jack Lemmon) *The Wackiest Ship in the Army*, you have a sense of this experience: Lemmon thinks that his new duty station is a spit-and-polish Navy ship just ahead when, slowly, that ship pulls away to reveal a grimy, decrepit hulk. For me, it was—voilà! —LCS 53 .

I managed to lug my seabag up the companionway to an apparently deserted ship and, true to my midshipman training, did the proper thing: I stood at attention, faced aft, and saluted what I assumed would be the flag hanging at the stern. Of course, I couldn't see the flag (part of the ship was in the way), but I took no chance of being caught in a violation of naval courtesy. I was about to say, "Ensign Middendorf reporting for duty, sir," when an officer popped out of a doorway, guessed at my identity, and shouted with glee, "That shithead Middendorf is here! I can go home!" So much for the formalities of the hallowed quarterdeck.

The wartime skipper went home soon after I reported aboard, and his duties were assumed by the communications officer, one rank higher than I, a lieutenant (junior grade). LCS 53 had been through two of the heaviest actions of 1945, Iwo Jima and Okinawa, and in my judgment, both the ship and the new skipper were considerably the worse for wear. This class of ship was basically built for one event: the invasion of Japan. Six Japanese flags were painted on the superstructure, the tally for the destruction of Kamikaze aircraft for which the crew could claim some credit. There was no way to know who may or may not have brought down an attacker because everyone for miles around was under fire. The Kamikaze phenomenon was bizarre; you had these young men in their late teens and early twenties who had been taught enough to get the plane off the ground, follow a leader to the target area, and then try to fly the plane into one of our ships. During the Okinawa campaign, they sank 5 ships and damaged another 87. I think LCS 53 had been hit by some pieces of a Kamikaze aircraft that had been shot down just in time.

For six months, we listened to gunfire being exchanged by the Nationalists and the Communists in the distant hills above Shanghai. We also witnessed the frustration of General George Marshall, who was attempting to broker a peace deal. We watched in disbelief when Marshall withheld arms shipments to the Nationalists, effectively delivering China to the Communists. Our squadron commander called us all in for a briefing in April 1946. We had orders. Eastward, home! The thirteen ships in our squadron would be sailing together, and there was an immediate rush of activity among the officers and crews, largely confined to running ashore and celebrating. But I had been assigned as an engineering officer and did, after all, have a degree of sorts in engineering and was smart enough to be terrified. We were about to set out across 7,000 miles of trackless ocean with a tired powerplant, pumps, and motors and no spare parts. I took our chief engineman and a couple of sailors on a scouting party, and we located a supply of spare parts in a building a bit upriver. I requisitioned every spare injector, gasket, belt, and anything else we could find that looked as if it might be helpful. We spent almost a week getting the stuff, bringing it aboard, and finding places to stow it.

Our diligence paid off. Not so much for LCS 53, although we had a few problems underway. Other ships in the squadron kept breaking down, and we had the parts they needed. We passed them over on a light line: you throw one end of a long line (attached to a small weight) to the other ship, tie the spare part in the middle of the line, and hold on to your end while they pull the part across. We all made it as far as Pearl Harbor, but as I recall, a couple of ships with more severe problems were to drop out at that point.

Finally, loaded and ready, we headed down the Whangpoo for the deep blue sea. Now, please understand: I had no training in the operation of any ship, let alone this one. My NROTC experience was limited to classroom work; we didn't have the summer training cruises of today's program. LCS 53 had gotten underway a few times while in the Whangpoo, primarily to turn the ship around, blow out the lines and make sure we weren't about to be stranded on an island of our coffee grounds. Still, then I was learning about engine room operations, not ship driving.

The skipper posted the watch bill once we were about to get underway. If your name was on the list, you were a qualified officer of the deck. If that seems pretty cavalier, it is, but the rest of the crew had been aboard for a long time, and they knew how to run the ship even if Ensign Middendorf didn't have a clue. So I took my turns at the watch (four hours on, eight hours off) and watched the quartermaster, the boatswain's mate, and the helmsman and took my cues from them. After a few days of steady steaming and except for occasional bouts of seasickness, I felt like an old hand.

In addition to my duties as an engineering officer and watch officer, I was assigned—in an even greater leap of faith by the commanding officer—as navigator. It was my off-watch job to figure out where we were and tell the skipper how we would get to our next port of call. If I thought I could count on the other ships in our squadron, I was quickly put straight: we were the lead ship, and they would all rely on me. I was blessed by having a chief quartermaster who knew what he was doing. Celestial navigation—in those days of yore before the invention of GPS—was the only way to determine your position at sea when out of range of radar or Long-Range Navigation (LORAN) aids. Both at dusk and just before dawn, when the sky is dark enough to see some stars but there is still enough light to see the horizon, you use a tool called a sextant to measure the angles between some selected stars and the horizon and note the precise time of that measurement. You match the information against some tables published by the Navy's Hydrographic Office (covering the part of the world in which you are operating), and that's about all you need to "fix" your approximate position. The skill comes in making the measurements in the first place, the more accurate the measurement, the more accurate the fix. A seasick navigator on a rolling ship requires a special skill, and an even greater skill comes in figuring out where you are after a week of solid overcast.

Our first stop, eight days out of Shanghai, was Saipan, ostensibly for some rest and recreation (R&R), but it was a quarantine to screen for venereal disease and smallpox. A team of medics came aboard; a few crewmen apparently failed one or the other test and were taken ashore. As for the R&R, it was real enough, although a bit limited. After the medical formalities, we shifted our berth to Apra Harbor, Guam, where we were allowed to take our turn at a barbed-wire enclosure on the beach, a party spot furnished with tables already set up with booze—an unlimited stock of government-supplied Johnny Walker Red or Black Label—and piles of Lucky Strike cigarettes. We began to party under a blazing hot sun; within an hour, we had become a crowd of glorious, roaring drunks regaling each other with a great song ("There's none so fair as can compare with an L C S at sea").

Off on the next leg of our journey, I produced one superb fix after another, growing increasingly confident of my skill as a navigator—until I lost Wake Island. My plot said we were within a couple of dozen miles, and the mountains should be looming over the horizon at any moment. We slowed down, circled for a while, and someone finally spotted the island when we were almost aground. I learned the hard way: no mountains. Wake Island is flat as a pancake; the highest point was the top of some palm trees. Lesson learned: you can discover a lot by looking at the chart.

I noticed a lot of activity in the signal flags of the other ships immediately after I lost Wake Island. Curious, I asked one of the sailors to translate the messages. He looked, shook his head, and said, "You don't want to know." After a few threats, he finally translated. "The ass who lost Wake is supposed to be a Harvard graduate." Once again underway, with Pearl Harbor, the next port of call, some of my Holy Cross book learning was to be put to a real-world test. The weather began to turn sour and then got really rotten. You know when you've reached "rotten" when standing on the bridge—the conning station, some 30 feet above the waterline—you are looking up, way up, to the top of the waves.

I was officer of the deck, effectively in charge of driving the ship for my four-hour watch, when we began some very heavy rolling. Now, I had learned that a ship could roll from one side to another in safety, even heavy rolls if the recovery is quick and the period of the roll from one side to another remains about the same. However—as I found out—you are in big trouble if a ship rolls over to one side and hangs there for a moment, or two or three moments, before slowly coming up. The "metacentric height influences the timing of the rolls," the relationship between the center of gravity —that point which is the mathematical average of the mass of a ship—and the center of buoyancy, which is the geometric center of the mass of water displaced by the hull. In basic terms, the lower the center of gravity, the better. However, the center of gravity does not remain fixed on a ship underway. It is constantly raised as fuel and water are consumed.

The design of LCS 53 put six feet of the hull, with the heaviest machinery and fuel and water tanks below the surface, and about 61 feet, with the superstructure, mast, and so forth, above the waterline. The nominal stability was marginal, and the ship could handle moderately heavy rolls—if it was in normal trim, with tanks essentially full. However, we had been at sea for some time, and our tanks were far from full as the weather deteriorated into a full-blown typhoon. The term "moderate" could not be applied to anything we began to experience. A wave would hit; the ship would tip over to a frightening angle and shudder for a terrifying moment before slowly coming back, temporarily, to the vertical. Every roll brought sounds of things crashing to the deck, things that should have been secured for heavy weather and maybe had been, but not against a rolling so great that gravity was almost working sideways.

The skipper had locked himself in his cabin. I may have been driving the ship, but as commanding officer, he was responsible for the safety of the ship and crew. No matter—he refused to come to the bridge, leaving one very seasick, young, inexperienced officer of the deck to do the best he could. I had been struggling to keep the bow pointed into the violent seas, trying to minimize the roll, but a shallow, flat-bottomed hull does not provide much directional stability. I took what the Navy calls "bold corrective action" and ordered empty fuel and water tanks to be flooded with seawater. I called the skipper on his cabin telephone and told him what I was doing; he ordered me not to do it. "You'll contaminate the tanks," he yelled. "We'll never get them clean!" I did it anyway. Soon enough, the rolling was not so dramatic, and the recovery was more dynamic.

Did I save the ship from foundering in the storm? I don't know for a certainty, but I do know that the other ships in Company with us took the same action and that removing all traces of salt water was not all that much of a problem once we were safely berthed at Pearl. Does this story sound vaguely familiar? Yes, it's very close to the fictional account at the center of the movie *The Caine Mutiny*, where in the middle of a huge storm, Van Johnson dramatically relieved his commanding officer, a frozen-with-fear Humphrey Bogart ("Captain Queeg") and assumed command. Captain Queeg would not change course the better to ride out the storm because the fleet commander had ordered their course, and Captain Queeg would not disobey an order. The Van Johnson character later was court-martialed for mutiny but found not guilty.

Author Herman Wouk, a World War II naval officer, based his drama on several real-life incidents. Mine was not one of them, but massive storms in the Pacific claimed a number of ships. In December 1944, three destroyers capsized and sank in a single storm; 790 men were lost, with another 25 ships severely damaged, in part because they continued to try to steam on an ordered but increasingly dangerous heading. They held on and held on and held on until they had sustained too much damage to recover. The loss of the destroyers was most certainly because they were low on fuel and were scheduled for ship-to-ship refueling the following day,

Admiral Chester Nimitz, commander-in-chief, Pacific Fleet, sent a strongly worded message to all commanding officers reminding them that when sailing into heavy weather, the skill and judgment of professional seamen must always take precedence over often arbitrary "orders" from higher authority. "No rational captain will permit his ship to be lost fruitlessly through blind obedience to plan or order," he wrote, "since by no chance could that be the intention of his superior." Regarding my own disobedience of orders, I find both moral and legal support in the final words of the Nimitz message: "The time for taking all measures for a ship's safety is while still able to do so. Nothing is more dangerous than for a seaman to be grudging in taking precautions lest they turn out to have been unnecessary. Safety at sea for a thousand years has depended on exactly the opposite philosophy."

At Pearl Harbor, our crew was reduced: 6 officers down to 4, 58 enlisted now at 49. One of the departing officers was the skipper, and another, more or less old hand, took over. We sailed to San Francisco, where more of the crew were released. Our next stop was the Kaiser Shipyard on the Columbia River in Portland, Oregon, for de-commissioning, where, in the biggest leap of faith ever, I was appointed acting squadron commander. Our mission was to put the ships into long-term storage in the Reserve Fleet to be ready in the event of some future need. As we were approaching the shipyard, an omen: we passed a little riverside tavern identified by a large sign, "Jack's Lighthouse." We passed close enough for some of the crew to converse with some idle women, and I knew we were in trouble when I heard them inviting the sailors to come back for a visit. It was straight out of Greek mythology, gorgeous Sirens luring seamen to death on a rocky shore. One 17-year-old country lad, not more than six months off a Nebraska farm, was married within three days.

I had trouble of my own, which could have ended any hope I might have had for a naval future. Over time, the pounding of waves against a steel hull turns a ship into a big magnet—making it a sweet target for magnetic-influence anti-ship mines. Occasionally, a ship needs to sit in the middle of an electric field in the middle of a special "deperming" dock, a U-shaped affair floating in the river but tethered to the shore. We had to be de-magnetized before heading for our assigned berth. I may have been legally in control of LCS 53, but I realized how little technical control I had when I tried to turn through the swiftly running current. My ship-driving experience, other than the big storm, had been pretty much straight and steady up to that point. My training barely touched on "parking," certainly not under these conditions.

I headed upstream, started a gradual turn, and the huge current hit the bow, Wham! I ordered all engines back full, with full rudder, and we backed off and got stabilized, backing up against the current. Well, the ship may have been stabilized, but I was shaking like a leaf. On my next approach, I saw that I was too close to the shore, so I ordered all back two-thirds and another big rudder order. By this time, the helmsman was more flustered than I, and he swung the wheel in the wrong direction. So, instead of my intended graceful slide to a stop, we headed straight for the dock—straight, actually, for a brand-new three-thousand-dollar generator sitting at the edge. We knocked it into the river while at the same time pushing the floating dock halfway up on the shore.

This mightily upset a lieutenant who was standing on the dock. Whether he was upset about the destruction of government property or jeopardy to himself, I'm not sure. "Asshole!" he yelled, along with a string of vivid obscenities more appropriate to a boatswain's mate. We finally got in position and were de-permed and shifted to our berth. However, I bought the lieutenant a liquid dinner that night to assure him that I was a decent sort of guy, albeit inexperienced, and merited his understanding, not the court martial charges I'm sure he had considered filing. The generator, of course, was fished out of the drink, dried out, and because it had been immersed in fresh water, not salt, was none the worse for wear.

Preparing a ship for mothballing was routine: inspect every piece of equipment and clean it up; or, if not worth keeping, such as a worn-out battery or a broken pump, get rid of it. Getting rid of it the proper way meant weeks and weeks of paperwork. Even a burned-out light bulb had to be accounted for. The innovative American sailors preferred a more straightforward method of disposal: a late-night evolution they called the "Splash Detail." Of course, had I known about it, I would not have approved.

I seem to have given one class of material special treatment: a bunch of autographed movie-star photos, Betty Grable and friends in bathing suits had been taped on the bulletin board in the communications shack. These must have seemed like pretty exciting stuff to this naive young naval officer because when I began sorting through a lifetime's collection of files in preparation for writing this memoir, I found four of them tucked away in a scrapbook.

We devoted a month to cleaning everything that could be cleaned, draining everything that could be drained, and putting on a fresh coat of paint on everything that could be painted. We must have done a pretty good job because some 20 years later, several were pulled out of the Reserve Fleet and transferred to the Vietnamese Navy (LCS 53 was not among them; it had been sold for scrap in 1949). Another LCS of our vintage was until recently in active service in Thailand, the only survivor of some 130 built for the war. A few years ago, I teamed up with a group of former LCS sailors, along with Secretary of the Navy John Lehman, whose father served aboard an LCS, to pull that ship out of Thailand and bring it home as a floating museum and memorial. Here's a truly international pedigree: this American ship was with the Japanese Maritime Self Defense force, then the Thai Navy, and came back to the United States as deck cargo on a heavy-lift freighter that flew the Panamanian flag, was manned by a Chinese crew, and owned by a company in the Netherlands.

Mothballing finished, I was sent back to Boston, where I was mustered out of the Navy in August 1946, three and a half years from the time I signed up for the V-12. With about a month to go before returning to Harvard, I took a job at the Graves Shipyard in Marblehead—well, it was more a boatyard than a shipyard, and I was assigned to scraping barnacles and painting. It was mindless work but good exercise. To get the job, I had to join a union. This gave me my first taste of union work rules and attitudes. The other workers came to me and said, "Slow down." I was upsetting the standards. I thought, if you had a job, you were supposed to do some work. I quit. By the end of September, I was back at school.

The "letter of withdrawal" put me back in Harvard, and the G.I. Bill helped pay the way. The campus was full of veterans, but the unwritten rule was that we did not discuss our wartime experiences, great or small. We demonstrated that we were veterans by wearing our old khakis; the more beaten up, the better. It's funny, but I didn't find out what some of my classmates had done in the war until 25 years later at a class reunion, from a brochure of capsule biographies.

I knew that my earlier time at Harvard and the accelerated B.S. degree from Holy Cross would allow me to finish a Harvard degree in a year. But, with only a year of freedom before I had to find a job, I reverted to some of my earlier bad habits and often found socializing more interesting than studying. By great good luck—because only a few students had signed up—I was able to enroll in a graduate-level course taught by Austrian libertarian economist Joseph Schumpeter, which also changed my life. Libertarian? He put forth the "entrepreneur" as the hero of economic growth, introducing new products, new production methods, and new competitive strategies, all of which give rise to new clusters of business investment that propel economic expansion. The individual entrepreneur accomplished this, not the government. It was the opposite of the Keynesian school of economics then so prominent at Harvard.

Schumpeter introduced the concept of "creative destruction." As entrepreneurs bring new products and services to market, they will likely displace whole families of products (the electric refrigerator displacing the icebox). There may be—often has been—entrenched resistance to change. I own a 1901 Crestmobile single-cylinder gas-engine automobile that came complete with an installed buggy whip-holder. This accessory was required by a law engineered by the buggy-whip industry of Massachusetts because should the engine fail, a horse would surely be needed to move the machine.

Schumpeter also was a champion of business cycles—highs and lows, he suggested, can be predicted with some accuracy because they recur at relatively consistent intervals. There was the Kondratiev cycle, signaling a sharp recession about every 54 years. There were shorter cycles with equally exotic names—the Kitchin inventory cycle (3 to 5 years) and the Juglar fixed investment cycle (7 to 11 years). As a young student, I was impressed with the concept and pleased to find such a handy set of measuring sticks. I would later learn that things in the real world don't work with such comforting predictability.

I was later told by another of my own economic heroes—Ludwig Von Mises, whose course I was able to audit in graduate school—that Schumpeter, while finance minister of Austria, had screwed up that nation's economy. Perhaps, but no matter: those who teach may not always be as effective at doing. Schumpeter himself told me that he had only two ambitions: to be the world's most outstanding horseman and the world's greatest lover.

On the downside, I failed an economics course on the Federal Reserve. I will agree that holding a low regard for the Federal Reserve—an attitude I made clear to my professor on the first day of class—is not a valid reason for screwing up my record, but it made perfect sense at the time. I went into the course telling all who would listen that Woodrow Wilson was one of the world's great sinners for creating the Federal Reserve, as well as the individual income tax (it was to be "only" 1 or 2 percent but hit that 91 percent high within a generation or so; so much for government promises). I had to repeat the course in summer school and did not receive my degree until two months after the rest of my class. However, I was allowed to attend the June graduation ceremonies. The commencement speaker was General of the Army/Secretary of State George C. Marshall. His topic: a new plan to bail Europe out of post-war bankruptcy. A plan that Arnold Toynbee would call "The signal achievement of our age" and Winston Churchill described as the most unselfish act in history.

Well, it was a brilliant, sunshine-filled day, and Marshall was perhaps the most boring speaker we had ever heard. Whatever the significance of his remarks, they escaped most of the graduates. Europe was 3,000 miles and many generations away from most of us; the graduation parties couldn't begin until he stopped rambling on. Twenty-five years later, when serving as ambassador to the Netherlands, I was often reminded of that day and that speech when grateful Dutch citizens would offer a toast, "To the United States and the great Marshall plan that pulled us out of devastation."

Most of my classmates went into one industry or another. America had emerged from the war with industry intact and robust, many senior executives would soon be retiring, and there were limitless opportunities. I was one of very few who chose the long-depressed world of finance, but it was a world that I understood. I benefitted from those nightly discussions with my father and some personal albeit low-level experience from that summer job with my father's firm. In any event, I knew early on that I wanted to be an investment banker. I do, however, admit to a short—very short—flirtation with show business. At Harvard, I had a choice role in a "Hasty Pudding" theatrical extravaganza with Jack Lemmon, George Plimpton, Dave Finger, and Fred Gwynne–showmen all. I blew my lines.

I moved to New York and briefly stayed at the home of a former congressman from New York, Kenneth F. Simpson, father of one of my close friends, William Kelly Simpson. During that time, the former prime minister of Russia, Aleksandr Kerensky, was staying there as well. He was a leading figure in the Russian Revolution. I was impressed by the humility of this former Socialist-Communist, but I also felt the despair of a person who had been misled by a former family friend. Kerensky's parents and the Lenin families were close friends and Kerensky's father had been a teacher of Lenin.

Kerensky told me that he had been influenced at the University of St. Petersburg by the Narodnik Populist Movement to become a Socialist-Marxist revolutionary with all the popular slogans of income inequality and wealth redistribution. These slogans are still being used worldwide to promote what always turns out to be a one-man rule and the inevitable killing fields. Starting in 1912 with several tours of duty in the Duma and as minister of War and the Navy, Kerensky became prime minister in October 1917 with his full socialist agenda. Almost immediately, the violent Bolshevik Revolution occurred. Lenin took over, and one-man rule ensued. Stalin succeeded Lenin and eliminated 30 million "Enemies of the People." Many of the naïve socialists, which Stalin called "useful idiots" were among the first to be executed. Kerensky went into hiding and escaped to Europe in 1918. He immigrated to New York in 1940. Years later, I became a trustee of the Hoover Institution of Palo Alto, California, where Kerensky was a visiting scholar writing his memoirs, and we continued our friendship.

I also met Nicholas Debasisley, another participant in the Russian scenario, who had drawn up the abdication papers for the Czar in 1917. He had escaped Russia in 1917 to avoid execution and later settled in Baltimore in the early 1930s with a small amount of money and a LaSalle car. With the guidance of my father and uncle, both prominent Baltimore investment bankers, Debasisley ended up with a multi-million dollar fund many years later. Through my efforts, Debasisley left his estate to the Hoover Institution for the study of the Russian Revolution. Unfortunately, these funds were diverted from Hoover when his widow journeyed to Switzerland and was coerced into signing the funds over to two Swiss lawyers who apparently took advantage of her. Despite lawsuits by Hoover and overtures by the U.S. ambassador, this could not be overturned.

My embarrassing senior year encounter with the Federal Reserve notwithstanding, I had several job offers in Boston and New York City. I picked the Bank of Manhattan Company, starting as a trainee. Although we were making only $2,000 a year, my fellow trainees and I were impressed that working for a bank was such an enormous privilege that candidates paid the bank for a job before World War I.

The trainee's first three months were spent in the security vaults at 40 Wall Street. Here, the wealthy old-family New Yorkers kept their stocks, bonds, and jewelry. They were satisfied with the protection offered for their stocks and bonds but expected some extra services on the jewelry. Especially pearls. We were told that one of the wealthiest women in the World, Hetty Green, had swapped the 5th Avenue plot on which Tiffany's now stands for a string of pearls. Therefore, pearls had exceptional value. However, we were warned natural pearls would deteriorate over time unless occasionally worn against the skin. It didn't seem to matter whose skin; we trainees took turns wearing those damn pearls for a few hours at a time.

My next assignment was handling bonds, the prime investment tool in those post-Depression days. Bonds had coupons, which were redeemed for cash on a stipulated schedule. However, the coupons must first be cut away from the bond—no doubt you've heard the phrase "clipping coupons," a favored activity of the idle rich at our bank. They were then fastened together with a straight pin. I cannot begin to explain the reason for this awkward practice, but I can affirm that unless properly inserted, with the point tucked back into the stack of coupons, the pin would pose a hazard to unwary clerks. My skill with this maneuver earned my first positive performance rating: "Middendorf, you're the best pin-pusher-under we've ever had." I was clearly on the cusp of a promising career.

After about a year cycling through a couple of branches, and a long stint in the credit department, I figured that basic training was over and it was time to take my knowledge and skills to a higher level. I applied to and was accepted by Harvard Business School. My father's reaction was, who's going to pay for it? I said, I was sort of hoping you would, since I did Holy Cross on the Navy and Harvard on the G.I. Bill, and he said, you sure got that wrong: "Get back to work!"

I stayed at the bank for about four years, working on commercial loans—essentially, loans to credit-worthy businesses that didn't need the money but were looking for opportunities to expand or were temporarily swapping assets. On one transaction, for example, we accepted collateral in gold—from Brazil, as I recall—for the full amount of the loan. Another transaction stands out in my memory for two reasons. First, the nature of the loan itself to the Socony Vacuum Company—$50 million for ten years at 2⅝ percent, interest-only (at about twice the then-going rate) with a balloon payment for the total when the loan came due. Second, our boss, Fletcher Gill, was so pleased with this deal that he jumped up on a desk, champagne in hand, to offer congratulations to all. Very soon after that, he announced his retirement.

My time as a Bank of Manhattan loan officer came to a logical end in 1951 when, following a friendly squash game with one of our vice presidents, I made so bold as to make a personal inquiry. "When," I asked casually, "might I expect to make V.P.?" His answer, "Oh, easily in fifteen or twenty years," sent me on a search for a job with better prospects. I was hired at Wood, Struthers Company, a member New York Stock Exchange, as a research assistant with a starting salary of $15,000 a year.

This was the perfect time to become involved with the stock and bond markets. For one thing, the Federal Tax Code greatly encouraged certain types of investment—that top tax bracket of 91 percent provided a powerful incentive for investment in tax-free municipal bonds. A 10-year bond yielding 0.78 percent was equal to about 8.0 percent of taxable return. For another, the rules governing investments by New York–based trusts and pension funds had just changed to allow them to own stocks, greatly expanding the marketplace. The volume of sales on the New York Stock Exchange began to rise dramatically. In 1949, a big day on Wall Street would have seen 1 million shares traded. By the 1960s, that number had grown to 25 million (and today, a slow day may involve more than a billion shares).

This also was a good time to start a family. Isabelle Paine and I were married in 1953, eventually having five wonderful children. We lived at Peter Cooper Village in Manhattan for the first year, then moved up to 1170 Fifth Avenue, where we purchased a cooperative apartment for $40,000: seven rooms, high ceilings, and a pretty nice place overlooking Central Park. The price was so low because co-op owners needed to bail out of debts piled up during the Depression, when other owners moved out to avoid paying their share of maintenance, leaving those who remained stuck with all the bills.

My first challenge as a Wood, Struthers research assistant was to assess the viability of some railroad bond issues by studying the turnaround time in the Chicago rail yards. Busy work? No, it was an excellent measure of efficiency. Boxcars did not earn money while sitting idle. I soon became an insurance and bank stock analyst, teamed with another analyst, Austen Colgate (of the "Colgate" toothpaste and the university.) Austen and I quickly became close friends and remained so until his passing.

Wood, Struthers was a wonderful place, serious and professional but not at all stuffy. The management was willing to encourage youngsters with bright ideas. Austen loved to run the numbers in the back office, while I liked to get out front with our customers. I visited insurance companies and banks—acting almost like an old-time Dunn and Bradstreet "reporter"—to assess their operations and prospects. After I had shared my observations with Austen, we would make our recommendations. It was not as easy as it sounds. Compiling and analyzing the data was tedious—no computers, of course—and we enjoyed a lot of late-night work studying the Pink Sheets covering obscure OTC insurance stocks. But we got a lot of business.

Our clients included the Union Pacific and G.E. Pension Funds, J.P. Morgan, City Bank, and ITT, for which we would recommend investments. Most Wall Street firms in those days were simply brokers, buying and selling. Few did any in-depth research because it cost money to run an extensive research department, and firms that specialized in trusts and estates were relatively rare. I turned some of what I learned into my 1954 book, *Investment Policies of Fire and Casualty Insurance Companies*.

We also took advantage of opportunities for Wood, Struthers's own account. We developed a special interest in insurance stocks—searching for undervalued, obscure, and thinly traded companies, usually locally owned. Because of the Depression, their stock value may have slipped, but they often had equity backed by treasury bonds worth more than the value of the whole Company. I began advertising in selected newspapers nationwide, soliciting information about well-established old-line insurance companies that might be for sale.

One night I got a call from a trust officer who had control of the Lincoln Liberty Life Insurance Company stock in Lincoln, Nebraska. He said that the trust had a dispute with the president of the Company, who wanted to buy all the stock at an unreasonably low price, and while they were willing to sell, they wanted fair value. Was I interested? Yes. "Well," he said, "if you can get out here tomorrow, I'll sell it to you."

I caught the next plane out and traveled all night. Less than an hour after my arrival, we had a deal: I could buy controlling interest in the Company, 75 percent, for 1.5 million dollars. I called Jerry Gantz, one of the partners at Wood, Struthers. Jerry was a solid performer who had helped hold the Company together through the Depression. "What's the problem?" he said. "I need a million and a half dollars," I said, "wired out here right away," I explained the deal.

He said, "I've never heard of that Company. . . are you sure you want to do this? "Well," I said, "I already did." The acquisition was one of the most profitable I have ever put together.

A month or so before I closed the deal, Dale Clark of the Union Pacific Pension Fund had called and asked if he could send over a brilliant young man from Omaha, someone I should meet and who might be a candidate for a job. It was Warren Buffett, who was so relaxed and so confident that he admitted that his goal was to come into Wall Street for a year, make a million dollars, and then go back to Omaha. Warren was very impressive, with a solid family background (his father was an investment banker and two-term congressman), and I had no doubt that he could do exactly what he wanted. However, it was obvious that, although Warren would have been a fabulous addition to the staff at Wood, Struthers, and Company, it was too small for him. But I made so bold as to pass on some advice.

I was by this time working on my MBA at New York University—Harvard was left to the past. I needed a school I could attend in the evenings while earning a living. It was a miserable life, with little time for anything else. Still, I was highly motivated, spurred on, in part, by the competition from NYU classmates who were determined to get somewhere in life. I atoned for my earlier academic failings and pulled straight "A"s. One of our textbooks was *Security Analysis: Principle and Technique* (better known for its co-authors, Graham and Dodd. It was literally a handbook for buying companies under book value, and it is still in print today. When I recommended the book to Warren, he said that he had already not only read the book but had enrolled in the MBA program at Columbia, where Graham was a professor.

The story is told that Warren earned the only A+ grade ever given by Ben Graham. Warren then took his natural skills to a job with his father's company in Omaha and next went with Graham's firm, Graham-Newman, in New York. Somewhere along the line, he did make his million and a lot more and moved back to Omaha. While they were living in New York, Warren and Susan Buffett invited Isabelle and me for dinner a few times. I brought Warren into the Lincoln Liberty Life deal. He and I each invested $25,000 and tripled our money in six months. To return the favor, Warren later asked to go in with him on buying the entire press run of a forthcoming United Nations stamp issue. For a $50,000 investment, we would have controlled the market. I got cold feet and passed.

I became involved in politics with the presidential election of 1948: Republican Thomas E. Dewey against incumbent Democrat Harry S Truman. The keynote speaker at the Republican Convention, Illinois Governor Dwight H. Green, praised the Republicans as "the party of faith in the individual American." In my judgment, most Democrats believe that the government is a working tool that should be used to shape society. I believe that individuals shape society. Some Democrats seemed to think that earning a profit meant abusing workers and that employing hundreds of people was a form of exploitation. The demonizing of businessmen, of course, makes no sense: they provide the jobs in which most Americans earn a living. The demonizing of "big" business just because it's big makes even less sense.

Friedrich Hayek wrote a seminal work, *The Road to Serfdom*, subtitled *A Classic Warning against the Dangers to Freedom Inherent in Social Planning*. Hayek wrote of encroachments on liberty and human dignity.

In the 1948 election, I served as a Republican precinct captain for the 9th Assembly District —the so-called "Blue Stocking" district on the upper East side of Manhattan—and worked sufficiently hard that I was honored to get an invitation to go to Albany and meet with the Republican state chairman. The Gallup Poll had Dewey at 50 percent, Truman trailing at 37 percent. The Republican politicians were already making lists of candidates for jobs in the Post Office. That was how the politicians rewarded local party leaders: post offices were everywhere, and every post office needed a postmaster. Everyone knows that Truman won in a great upset, and much of his reputation today rests upon that achievement.

By the mid-1950s, I was a partner at Wood & Struthers. At the end of the decade, my starting salary had grown twenty-fold. Nonetheless, Austen Colgate and I left Wood & Struthers in 1961 to set up our own firm, Middendorf, Colgate, and Company. We bought a seat on the NYSE for $155,000, and its value quickly dropped to $90,000. We blamed it on bad timing, not a bad omen. We saw an opportunity to carve out a needed but largely overlooked niche, became specialists in insurance stocks, and prospered. I brought my father and uncle into the firm in their early seventies to show them how much I appreciated their support. We soon had offices in Boston, Baltimore, San Francisco, and New York.

After Isabelle and I had our first child and with another on the way, we decided it was time for a more suburban environment and picked Greenwich, Connecticut, where we already had some friends. We rented for about a year and then bought a house on four acres, a really nice place. My neighbor was U.S. Senator Prescott Bush, Sr., father of George H.W., and grandfather of George W. Bush. It was quite a family. At that time, George H.W. was getting started in his Texas oil business.

They were good neighbors. Some evenings when the Bush clan got together, I would hear the Yale Whiffenpoof Song drifting across the lawn to my house. They had wonderful voices, and it was a joy for me to sit and listen, especially after a tough day at the office and a 90-minute commute. I had taken my own interest in politics along with the move to Connecticut, where I was encouraged by a friend, Orson St. John, to become a member of the Greenwich Representative Town Meeting. There I discovered what I call the "stoplight" mentality of local politics. Most people cannot get their arms around a large civic project, and they leave the details to the experts. But if it's small—like where to put a new stoplight—they will debate it forever.

In 1969, Greenwich was a lovely place to bring up a family and a refuge for many financial executives, and they were astonished when I told them I was leaving a seven-figure-a-year Wall Street partnership for a $40,000 job as ambassador to the Netherlands. Well, I had learned how to make money. I wanted to learn how to make a difference. I had been bitten by the bug of public service, which so overwhelmed my immune system that over the next 18 years, I never looked back. For me, it certainly was, to quote my friend Robert Frost, a journey on "the road less traveled."

I know now but was not sensitive to the fact then that it was unfair to negotiate such a major change without fully discussing all the implications with my family. Isabelle and the children were taken off-guard and were not happy when I announced we were all moving to Europe. Isabelle wanted to be a stay-at-home mother, not a diplomatic hostess. Public service brings penalties, especially to families. An unexpected crisis somewhere in the World may seem to take precedence over your son's soccer game. But your son will not understand or be quick to forgive.

There was an event practicality every night: dinners at the residence, receptions, and formal and informal parties. I got all the glory, rubbing shoulders with the high and mighty. It fell to Isabelle to be the constant hostess, to make sure everything was in order, and to deal with the frustration of not having enough time to spend with our children.

Isabelle was much more comfortable in dealing with practical matters, such as fostering 28 babies while we were living in Washington, D.C. when I was secretary of the Navy. A registered nurse, she worked with the Barker Adoption Agency, established during World War II, to support Navy wives. This agency plays a vital role in the significant minority community surrounding Washington providing desperately needed services for foster care and final adoption for babies. There were occasions when I may have put the country at risk, attending early morning meetings with Navy admirals and Marine generals after spending early morning hours burping babies and changing diapers.

For many years I served as chairman of the Harlem Facility of the Boys Club of New York located in the Harlem Building at 321 E 111th Street. We administered an after-school program for over 1,000 boys from ages 7–21. The after program included an array of sports in physical activities, as well as the arts, dance, and designer programs, literacy, math, and science challenge programs. I also served on one of Nelson Rockefeller's New York State commissions for the mentally ill. I was appalled at the terrible conditions at the Creedmoor Psychiatric Center in Queens, where thousands of mental patients were often neglected. I wrote many stern recommendations about the awful conditions there. I taught an art class for the prisoners at the Bristol County House of Corrections for five years, and Sheriff Hodgson told me afterward that this program significantly reduced recidivism in Massachusetts's prison system.

I have always had an active interest in sports. At age 15, I attended a private camp in Pleasantville, New York. It was 1939, and the Baseball Hall of Fame was inducting its first class at Cooperstown. Games were played all that week, with professionals including Hank Greenberg, Lloyd Waner, Charlie Gehrenger, Billy Herman, Arky Vaughan, Joe Medwick, Lefty Grove, Stan Hack, Mel Ott, and Johnny Vander Meer playing exhibition games against college and local camp teams. As a member of the Hi Dee camp team, I was playing a deep left field when Mel Ott, the Hall of Fame right fielder for the New York Giants, hit a ball over my head.

The highlight of the week was an exhibition game featuring the greatest ballplayers of that era. In the fifth inning, the 44-year-old Babe Ruth strode to the plate as a pinch hitter. Everyone was pulling for him to put one into the stands, but he popped out to the first baseman. Later Ruth said, "I'm too old. I can't hit the floor with my hat."

About five years later, I had another experience with Mel Ott. I had a reputation for being able to throw a baseball through a wall. My problem was in control, not speed, as I never knew which wall I would hit. Despite my control problem, I received the following letter from John S. Schwarz of the New York Giants baseball team in February 1944:

Dear John:

This is to notify you that you are invited to report to our training camp on March 12, 1944, for a spring training trial at our expense. We have notified Mr. David Beck of the Southern Railway to have your local representative supply you with a railway ticket to Lakewood. Please bring your uniform, shoes, and glove with you.

P.S. You are to report to Manager Mel Ott at the Hotel New Yorker Sunday, March 12, 1944, in New York City.

My baseball career ended about a week later when I joined the U.S. Navy. I had better success in another sport when I started rowing as a teenager and remained active into my nineties. My rowing career was inspired by my father and uncle, both legendary Harvard oarsmen and members of the team that won the Grand Challenge Cup on July 4, 1914, at the Royal Henley Regatta. The final in the Grand Challenge Cup was rowed between a Harvard crew and the Union Boat Club of Boston, the first time in the history of the regatta that an English crew was not in the finals. The Harvard crew was coached by Robert F. Herrick '95, a great benefactor of Harvard rowing. According to the records, the crews between 1899 and 1914 had rowed their annual races in four-man crews. The change was made to eights in 1914 for Harvard's trip to Henley.

The Harvard crew included Leverett Saltonstall; Henry Meyer; Laurence Curtis; David Morgan; Charles Lund; my father, Harry Middendorf; and my uncle, Bill Middendorf. Saltonstall served two terms as governor of Massachusetts and more than 20 years in the U.S. Senate. Meyer and Curtis became successful lawyers. David Morgan was a prominent New York financier, and Charles Lund was a renowned Boston physician. My father and uncle became successful financiers. Within weeks of the 1914 event, most English and German crews were involved in World War I. A few years later, my father and uncle joined them.

I can still remember my father and uncle's excitement when it was announced that the 1914 crew would row again in 1939 at Henley to commemorate the 25th anniversary of the original victory. Fifty years later, my father's winning Harvard crew of 1914 was reassembled and rowed the Henley course again in 1964.

I served as a judge for the 1960 Olympics in Rome. In the 1963 World Championships of Men's Field Hockey in Lyon, France, I played on the U.S. National Team. In 1964, I served on the U.S. Olympic Selection Committee for field hockey and was selected for the team as player manager. We were not invited to the Olympic games in Tokyo because we didn't qualify as one of the top 16 teams.

I have been active in many rowing contests, winning both a U.S. National Masters and a World Masters Rowing Championship. I was awarded The Hero Sportsman of the Year Gold Medal Award for stopping during a race to help a fellow oarsman who had suffered a possible heart attack and was at risk of drowning. This is only the second that this award has been given in over fifty years. I stroked the victorious Thames Rowing Club Crew in the famous Vogalonga 20-mile regatta race around the Islands of Venice, in which 4,000 boats participated. I participated in 20 "Head of the Charles" races in Cambridge, Massachusetts, and won a national championship in Masters Sculling in 1979. New Zealand's Jay Limerick and I were presented the World Masters Rowing Championship Globe (Pairs) in Toronto in 1985.

In 2020, at the age of 96, I competed in seven virtual Regattas, winning all but one of these in the over-85 category. These virtual international Rowing Regattas against worldwide competition average 3000–5000 meters each. In the famous Head of the Charles Regatta, I placed second to a rowing colleague of the Rocky Mountain Rowing Club.

When I was secretary of the Navy, CNO Admiral James Holloway complained about the high percentage of senior officers and chief petty officers who were overweight and out of shape and wanted to do something to encourage physical fitness. I started the "Twenty Minute Club," where I would visit a base and invite everyone to run a three-mile course in 20 minutes. I would hold the stopwatch. I do admit to a bit of fudging, which I might blame on "a faulty stopwatch." If some struggling soul made it across in, say, 24 or 25 minutes, I called out the time as "twenty." All told, many thousands received "Twenty Minute Club" certificates.

Around the same time, a group of Marine Corps Reservists asked me to endorse an effort to enhance morale and physical fitness and perhaps encourage some young men and women to enlist. They wanted to stage a classic 26.5-mile Marathon to start and end at the Marine's Iwo Jima Memorial in Arlington, Virginia. I not only endorsed the idea but put up a scale model of the Memorial as a trophy for the winner. The first Marine Corps Marathon was run in 1976, with just more than one thousand finishers. These days, perhaps 30,000 may enter the race. In truth, the race has reached maximum capacity (as determined by the police and other safety forces), and online registration is usually filled out within a few days of opening. It is now the fifth largest marathon in the United States. A small computer calculates each runner's time on the shoe, recording when they cross the starting and finish lines. Thus, a runner would not be penalized by starting at the back of the pack. The race has been dubbed the "People's Marathon" because anyone can enter; there are no big cash prizes to attract elite runners, just the "Middendorf Award," for the winner. It is not unusual for a first timer to win. I have entered (and finished) eight times. My best time was 4:22, just about twice that of the winner. I do not feel that I was a top athlete, but I had a secret. When in every race, you reach a point when it is impossible to do better, you call on all reserves built up over months of training, turn a corner, and new energy arises. I call it "The Middendorf Corner," which makes all the difference. Isabelle and I had five children, Frances, Amy, John, Roxy, and Martha, who left us too soon, dying suddenly on February 1, 1979, at the age of 20. Despite our frequent moves, all four children are highly successful.

Frances is an outstanding artist with numerous shows in Paris, Rome, and New York. She received her BFA from the Rhode Island School of Design and her MFA from the School of Visual Arts in Manhattan. She teaches at the Rhode Island School of Design Museum and serves on their fine arts committee. An accomplished rower, Frances is a member of the Narragansett Boat Club and competed successfully at the Head of the Charles Regatta 2022.

Amy Givler is a family physician in Monroe, Louisiana. She and her husband, Don, also a physician, have a heart for missions. They served as volunteers at a hospital in Kenya. Amy graduated from Wellesley College and

Georgetown University School of Medicine and completed her family medicine residency at the same indigent-care hospital where she now works part-time. She also works at an urgent-care clinic and is the medical director for a Shots for Tots clinic. Amy loves to write and has written many articles and one book, *Hope in the Face of Cancer: A Survival Guide for the Journey You Did Not Choose*. She and Don hope to do more volunteer work now that their three children have launched from the nest.

John is an outstanding rock climber and designer of climbing equipment. He climbed the largest rock wall in the World, the Great Tango Tower, and pioneered numerous big wall routes in Zion National Park in Utah. A teacher, John, lives in Australia with his wife Jeni and their son Rowen.

Roxy Paine is a sculptor and painter best known for his large-scale, tree-like structures. He attended the College of Santa Fe in New Mexico and the Pratt Institute in New York. In addition to his outdoor tree sculptures—which he calls Dendroids—he creates sculptures and paintings using computer-operated devices and robotics. Roxy's art has been displayed in various museums, including the Hirschhorn Museum and Sculpture Garden in Washington, D.C.; the Museum of Modern Art in New York; the San Francisco Museum of Modern Art; the Whitney Museum of American Art in New York; and the National Gallery in Washington, D.C. He lives with his wife Sofia and daughter Laila in Wyoming.

Life is all about seeking equilibrium, the rarest of human conditions. We are always a little off balance—moving forward without going over the cliff, finding success without losing our way, smelling the roses without getting stung by the bees. I've learned that the dreams I've spent so much energy chasing are worth less than what I had initially but tossed aside. I can stop running after shadows and be happy with what I've got at long last, to discover happiness in things that so many others take for granted, like a loving (and loved) family, a few good friends, a wonderful piece of music, a great painting, and a simple sunset.

Sadly, these insights only arrive when the old joints and eyesight give out. On September 22, 20223 I turned 99, certainly a long life. Yet I want more, especially with the news that a new Navy ship will be named in my honor. I'm planning on being there when my daughters Frances and Amy smash a bottle of champagne on the *J. William Middendorf* destroyer in 2025.

I've lived a life filled with interesting people, events, and jobs. Along the way, I've met dictators, murderers, liars, cheats, humanitarians, and diplomats. Perhaps we can call this book an autographical tribute to the interesting people and events that shaped my life.

J. William Middendorf II
Little Compton, Rhode Island

Notes

1: Five Characteristics Present in Communist Takeovers and an Islamic Revolution

Mao Zedong speech at the beginning of the Communist era, Aug. 27, 1927.
"After the Guns Were Removed, the Killing Fields Began," J. William Middendorf, *The Daily Signal*, June 16, 2022.
Red Star Over China, Edgar Snow, Grove Publishing, 1939.
Mission to Moscow, Joseph E. Davies, Simon & Schuster, Jan. 1, 1943.
The China Mission: George Marshall's Unfinished War, 1945–5947.
George Atcheson Papers, 1917–2004, Bancroft Library University of California at Berkeley.
"The Man Who Lost China, John Service, A Purged China Hand Dies at 89," *New York Times*, Feb.4, 1999.
The Long March: The True History of Communist China's Founding Myth, Sun Shuyum, Anchor Books, 2008.
Mao: The Unknown Story, Jung Chang and Jon Hallidan, Anchor Books, 2005.
The China Civil War, 1945–1949, Michael Lynch, Osprey Publishing, 2010.
"General Albert C. Windemeyer's Mission to China, 1945–1947—An Attempt to Achieve the Impossible," Defense Technical Information Center, August 1990.
Diaries of General Joseph W. Stillwell, 1904–1946, Hoover Institution Library.
"Cuban Rebel Is Visited in Hideout; Castro Is Still Alive and Still Fighting in Mountains," Herbert C. Matthews, *New York Times*, Feb. 24, 1957.
The Papers of Earl E. T. Smith, the Last Ambassador to Pre-Castro Cuba, Hoover Institute, Nov, 24, 2010.
Fidel Castro Interview on *Ed Sullivan Show*, Aug. 2, 1959.
Face the Nation Interview With Fidel Castro, Aug. 9, 1959.
The Man Who Invented Fidel Castro—Herbert Matthews and the New York Times, Anthony De Palma, Public Affairs, April 2006.
The Cuban Missile Crisis, October 1962, Office of the Historian, Department of State, Washington, D.C., 1998.
"The Nixon-Castro Meeting," Jeffrey Safford, Oxford University Press, Fall, 1980.
"Iran's Shah Leads a White Revolution," Jay Walz, *New York Times*, Oct. 27, 1963.
"Iran: Heart of the Matter," R. W. Apple, *New York Times*, March 11, 1979.
"Trusting Khomeini," Richard Falk, *New York Times*, Feb. 16, 1979.
"An Interview With Khomeini," Oriana Fallaci, *New York Times*, Oct, 7, 1979
The Making of Iran's Islamic Revolution From Monarchy to Islamic Republic, Mohson M. Miloni, Westview Press, 1994.
The Last Shah: America, Iran and the Fall of the Pahlavi Dynasty, Ray Takeyh and Eric Martin (Blackstone Audio) 2003.
The Fall of Heaven: An American Coup and the Roots of Middle East Terror, Stephen Kinzer, Tantor Media, 2003.
Sen. Joe Biden Argues for Better U.S.-Iran Relations, AIC Conference, June 16, 2002.
Boland Amendment Iran-Contra Affair, Dec. 8, 1982.

"America Dealt With A Nicaraguan Dictator—It Didn't Go As Planned," Nahal Toosi, *Politico*, 3/18/2023.
Daniel Ortega's Net Worth $50,000,000, celebritynetworth.com, 2023.
"Castro, Chavez and the True Origins of Autocracy," worldcrunch.com, 2008.
"Mr. Chavez is a Godsend," Larry Rohtor, *New York Times*, July 28, 2000.
Inside the National Security Council, Constatine C. Menges, Simon & Schuster, 1998.
Chavez's Speech to the General Assembly of The United Nations, Sept. 20, 2006.
From Benito Mussolini to Hugo Chavez, Intellectuals and a Century of Political Worship, Paul Hollander, Cambridge University Press, 2016.
"A Close Bond: Fidel Castro and Hugo Chavez, *Wall Street Journal*, March 1, 2013.
"Castro, Chavez and the True Origins of Autocracy," worldcrunch.com, Sept. 28, 2017.

2: Ready, Aim, Misfire: Who Gave China to the Communists

Mao Zedong speech at the beginning of the Communist era, Aug. 27, 1927.
Red Star Over China, Edgar Snow, Grove Publishing, 1939.
"After the Guns Were Removed, the Killing Fields Began," J. William Middendorf, *The Daily Signal*, June 16, 2022.
Mission to Moscow, Joseph E. Davies, Simon & Schuster, Jan. 1, 1943.
The China Mission: George Marshall's Unfinished War, 1940–1947, Daniel Kurtz-Phelan, W.W. Norton & Company, 2018.
George Atcheson Papers, 1915–2004, Bancroft Library University of California at Berkeley.
"The Man Who Lost China, John Service, A Purged China Hand Dies at 89," *New York Times*, Feb. 4, 1999.
The Long March: The True History of Communist China's Founding Myth, Sun Shuyum, Anchor Books, 2008.
Mao: The Unknown Story, Jung Chang and Jon Hallidan, Anchor Books, 2005.
The China Civil War, 1947–1949, Michael Lynch, Osprey Publishing, 2010.
"General Albert C. Windemeyer's Mission to China, 1945–1947—An Attempt to Achieve the Impossible," Defense Technical Information Center, August 1990.
Diaries of General Joseph W. Stillwell, 1904–1946, Hoover Institution Library.
Stillwell and The American Experience in China: 1910–1945, Barbara Tuchman, Random House, 2017.
The Man Who Loved China, Simon Winchester, Harper, 2009.
The Private Life of Chairman Mao, Li Zhnissi, Random House, 1996.
Out of Mao's Shadow, Philip Pan, Simon & Schuster, 2008.
Red China Blues: My Long March from Mao to Now, Jan Wong, Anchor Books, 1997.
The Last Days of Old Beijing: Life in the Vanishing Backstreets of a City Transformed, Michael Meyer, Walker & Company, 2008.
China Wakes: The Struggle for the Soul of a Rising Power, Sheryl Wu Dunn and Nicholas D. Kristof, Crown Publishing, 1994.
The China Mission: George Marshall's Unfinished War, Daniel Kurtz-Phelan, Norton & Company, 2018.

3: Ready, Aim, Misfire: Redux—Who Gave Cuba to the Communists

"Cuban Rebel Is Visited in Hideout; Castro Is Still Alive and Still Fighting in Mountains," Herbert C. Matthews, *New York Times*, Feb. 24, 1957.
The Papers of Earl E. T. Smith, the Last Ambassador to Pre-Castro Cuba, Hoover Institute, Nov, 24, 2010.
Fidel Castro interview on *Ed Sullivan Show*, Aug. 2, 1959.
Face the Nation, Interview with Fidel Castro, Aug. 9, 1959.

"The Man Who Invented Fidel Castro—Herbert Matthews and the New York Times," Anthony De Palma, *PublicAffairs*, April 2006.
"The Cuban Missile Crisis," October 1962, Office of the Historian, Department of State, Washington, D.C., 1998.
"The Nixon-Castro Meeting," Jeffrey Safford, Oxford University Press, Fall, 1980.
"After the Guns Were Removed, the Killing Fields Began," J. William Middendorf, *The Daily Signal*, June 16, 2022.
"Belize Independence March, J. William Middendorf played at Independence Day, Sept. 21, 1981," R. Hart Phillips, *New York Times*.
Fidel Castro: My Life, translated by Andrew Hurley, Penguin Books, 2007.
The Double Life of Fidel Castro, Juan Sanchez, St. Martin's Press, 2016.
William F. Buckley Jr., "The March of Freedom," Heritage Foundation, March 25, 2004.

4: Ambassador to The Netherlands

"President Nixon appoints J. William Middendorf as U.S. Ambassador to the Netherlands, *Time*, July 7, 1969.
"World Trade: A U.S. Ambassador New Business Role," *Business Week,* Dec. 16, 1972.
The Hiding Room, Corrie Ten Boom, Bantam Books, Oct. 1, 1974.
J. William Middendorf receives the Grand Marte Order of Orange Nassau, 1985.
"Top 10 Remarkable Facts About Joop den Ure," *Wikimedia*, Sep. 19, 2002.
Jonah Lans appointed Secretary General of NATO, Oct., 1971.

5: Secretary of the Navy

"The Military Goes Mad," *Time Magazine*, Dec. 21, 1970.
Hyman G. Rickover, "The Father of the Nuclear Navy," Atomic Heritage Foundation, Oak Ridge, TN, 1985.
Admiral Hyman Rickover and the Birth of the Nuclear Navy, The Mariner's Museum, Sep. 29, 2022.
The Great Nightfall, J. William Middendorf II, Heritage Harbor Foundation, 2020.
Admiral James L. Holloway III, A Lifetime of Service, Albert Murray, Naval History and Heritage Command, Nov. 20, 2019.
"Women of the Academy," U.S. Naval Academy Class of 1980, May 28, 1980.
"A Lavish Lifestyle Strains Credibility, T.K. Veliotis," *Chicago Tribune,* Dec. 2, 1985.
Aegis Ballistic Missile Defense, Center for Strategic and International Studies (CSIS) Feb. 1975
Ohio Class SSBN: Submarine Industrial Base Council, March 1976.
Trident Missile Threat, CSIS, May 1975.
Navy Aegis Ballistic Missile Defense (BMD) Program, Federation of American Scientists, April 1975.
"Why Ohio-Class Submarines Are So Badass," *Popular Mechanics*, May 1, 2023.
United States Submarine Capability, NTI, March 1979.

6: Queen Elizabeth II Joins the Navy

"Ship Named for Comte de Grasse, Spruance-class destroyer" Navy Historian, 1987.
"Queen Elizabeth II Visits Boston," Brittany Bowler, *Boston Globe*, July 6, 1976.
"Parade of Ships, New York Harbor," *New York Times*, July 5, 1976.
"Operation Sail," *International Naval Review*, July 4, 1976.
"Parade of Ships, USA Bicentennial," Pinterest, July 5, 1976.
"Lone Sailor Statue, 1987, Stanley Bleifeld, U.S, Navy Memorial, Washington. D.C.

7: Iran: With Friends Like These

"Iran's Shah Leads a White Revolution," Jay Walz, *New York Times,* Oct. 27, 1963.
"Iran: Heart of the Matter," R. W. Apple, *New York Times*, March 11, 1979.
"Black Friday: The Massacre that Ignited a Revolution in Iran," Britannia 1971–1979.
"Trusting Khomeini," Richard Falk, *New York Times*, Feb. 16, 1979.
"An Interview With Khomeini," Oriana Fallaci, *New York Times*, Oct. 7, 1979
The Making of Iran's Islamic Revolution From Monarchy to Islamic Republic, Mohson M. Miloni, Westview Press, 1994.
The Last Shah: America, Iran and the Fall of the Pahlavi Dynasty, Ray Takeyh and Eric Martin (Blackstone Audio) 2003.
"Richard Nixon's Road to Tehran: The Making of the U.S.–Iran Arms Agreement of May 1972," Stephen McGlinchey, *Diplomatic History*, Vol 37, No. 4.
The Fall of Heaven: An American Coup and the Roots of Middle East Terror, Stephen Kinzer, Tantor Media, 2003.
Sen. Joe Biden Argues for Better U.S.-Iran Relations, AIC Conference, June 16, 2002.
"The Past and the Present of Women's Rights in Iran," *The Borgen Report*, Oct. 24, 2121.

8: The Vietnam Extraction: Operation Frequent Wind

Daniel Harkman, Department of Defense, *Midway Times*, April 28–10, 1975.
"I have One More Hour of Fuel Left," Operation Frequent Wind, *Midway Times*, April 29, 1975.
"Midway Skipper Who Pushed Chopper Off Deck in Fall of Saigon," *Midway Times*, May 8, 1975.
Ambassador Graham and the Saigon Embassy, 1969–1975, Archives Unbound, 1963–1975.
"Hoa Lo Prison nicknamed the Hotel Hilton by American POWs in reference to Hilton Hotel Chain," *Midway Times*, 1977.
President Gerald Ford, Paris Peace Agreement, Jan. 23, 1973.
History of the Communist Party of Vietnam, Sophie Quinn, Cambridge University Press, 2017.

9: How 9/11 Could Have Been Prevented

"Middendorf Transition Team Recommends Sweeping Changes in the Organization and Operations of the Nation's Intelligence Program," *New York Times,* Dec. 8, 1980.
"Tension Between the Reagan Advisors and the CIA, *The Washington Times,* Dec. 18, 1980.
"Meetings Between Middendorf Transition Team and the CIA called hostile and acrimonious," The Washington Post, Dec. 29, 1980.
9/11 and Terrorist Travel, Staff Report of the National Commission on Terrorist Attacks Upon the U.S., Aug. 21, 2004.
America's Rise and Fall Among Nations, Angelo Codeville, Encounter Books, 2014.
"Preserving Our Freedom While Defending Against Terrorism," Department of Justice Oversight, Washington, D.C., Nov. 28, 2001.
"Military Implication of the U.S. Convention on the Law of the Sea," J. William Middendorf II, Heritage Foundation, Nov. 28, 2001.
"9/11 Congressional Report Faults FBI and CIA Lapses," *New York Times,* Oct. 11, 2001.
"Report of the Joint Inquiry into the Terrorist Attacks of Sep. 11, 2001," Dec. 2002.
Changed America, Catherine Lotrionte, John Hopkins University Press, 2008.

10: Spies Among Us

Betrayal: The Story of Aldrich Ames, An American Spy, Neil Lewis, David Johnston, Tim Weiner, Random House, June 1995.
"Eight of the Most Notorious Spies in History," Harry Sherrin, *History Hit*, Sep. 22, 2021.
"Top Ten Most Damaging Spy Missions in History," Shannon Corbell, *USAA Insurance Publication*, Jan. 3, 2023.
Aldrich Ames, FBI Investigation Report, Feb. 21, 1994.
"An Assessment of the Aldrich Ames Espionage Case," Federation of American Scientists, 1994.
"Security, Lies and Atomic Spies", Aldrich Ames, PBS, 1990.
"How an FBI Sting Took Down KGB Spy Robert Hanssen," *Spyscape*, 1984.
The Spy Next Door: The Extraordinary Secret Life of Robert Hanssen, the Most Dangerous FBI Agent in U.S. History, Elaine Shannon and Ann Blackman, Little, Brown and Company, Dec., 2001.
Advice to War Presidents, Angelo Codeville, Basic Books, March, 2009.
My Life As a Spy: One of America's Most Notorious Spies Finally Tells His Story, John A. Walker, Prometheus Books, Sep. 2008.
Family of Spies: Inside the John Walker Spy Ring, Peter Earley, Bantam Books, Sep. 1988.
"Spy Ring: The Untold Story of the Walker Case," Howard Blum, *New York Times*, June 29, 1986."
Territory of Lies: The Exclusive Story of Jonathan Pollard, Wolf Blitzer, Harper Collins, Dec., 1988.
"Peter Lee Sentenced to Halfway House in Chinese Espionage Case," Daniel Yi, *Los Angeles Times*, March 27, 1998.
The Whistleblower's Tale: How Jeffrey Sterling Took On the CIA—and Lost Everything," Pater Maass, *The Intercept*, June 18, 2015.
"Chelsea Manning Provided Hundreds of Thousands of Military and Diplomatic Records about the Wars in Iraq and Afghanistan to Wikileaks," *NPR*, 10/17/2022.
"NSA Contractor sentenced to nine years in theft of massive amounts of classified material," Dan Morse, *The Washington Post*, June 19, 2019.
The Most Dangerous Man in the World: Julian Assange and WikiLeaks' Fight for Freedom, Andrew Fowler, Skydome Publishing, 2011.
"Putin Grants Citizenship to Edgar Snowden," *New York Times*, Sep. 27, 2022.

11: Ambassador to the Organization of American States

"Rebels Train to Overthrow Somoza," *The Washington Post,* Oct, 15, 1978.
"Nicaragua Junta Assumes Rule in Jubilant Managua," *The Washington Post*, July 21, 1979.
"The Sandinistas held more than 7,000 political prisoners in 1979," U.S. Department of State, February 1980.
"The top leadership of the FSLN held a secret meeting Sep. 26–13, 1979, two months after coming to power," *The Washington Post,* Oct, 10, 1979.
"Sandinista obtained 110 T-55 tanks from the Soviet Union," interview with Sandinosta Army Chief of Staff Joaquin Cuadra, *CBS News*, February 1985.
"Nicaragua is Armed for Trouble," John Guilmartin. *Wall Street Journal*, March 11, 1985.
"After the Guns Were Removed, the Killing Fields Began," J. William Middendorf, *The Daily Signal*, June 16, 2022.

"The Sandinista military build-up would have been impossible without massive assistance from Cuba and the Soviet Union," U.S. Department of Defense publications, Dec. 16, 1983.

Sandinista: Carlos Fonseca and the Nicaraguan Revolution, Matilde Zimmermann, Duke University Press, 2000.

The Challenge to Democracy in Central America, Department of State and Department of Defense, June 1986, Washington, D.C.

Boland Amendment Iran-Contra Affair, Dec. 8, 1982.

"America Dealt With A Nicaraguan Dictator—It Didn't Go As Planned," Nahal Toosi, *Politico*, 3/18/2023.

"Daniel Ortega has become what he fought to destroy," Freedom House, April, 2020.

Inside the National Security Council, Constantine C. Menges, Simon & Schuster, 1998.

"Draft Dodgers Flee Nicaragua for Honduras," *Miami Herald*, Jan.4, 1985.

'Town Battles Military Draft in Nicaragua," *New York Times*, Jan. 2, 1985.

"Sandinista militarism has to be halted before it produces a holocaust in the entire region," *La Nacion*, Oct. 16, 1984.

El Salvador carried out four national elections, Special Report No. 132, U.S. Department of State, Sep. 1985.

"Prolonged war against El Salvador's economy, elections and institutions," U.S. Department of State, Sep. 1985.

"The Soviet-Cuban Connection in Central America and the Caribbean," Departments of State and Defense, Washington. D.C., March 1985.

"The Sandinistas and Middle Eastern Radicals," U.S. Department of State, Aug., 1985.

12: What We Must Learn From the Falklands War

"Argentina invades the Falklands," *The Guardian*, April 3, 1982.

The Falklands War, Martin Middlebrook, Pen and Sword Military, 2012.

The Battle for the Falklands, Max Hastings and Simon Jenkins. W.W. Norton & Company, 1984.

"The Reagan Administration and the Falklands War of 1982," Office of the Historian, 1988.

"Give Maggie Everything She Needs," message during the Falklands Island Crisis, Michael Haskew, *Military Magazine*, March 19, 2022.

"The Improbable Falklands War Still Resonates Decades Later," Kiernan Mulvaney, *National Geographic*, April 1, 2022.

"Short History of the Falklands Conflict," Imperial War Museum, April 2, 2022.

"How Margaret Thatcher's Falklands Gamble Paid Off," Sam Jenkins, *The Guardian*, April 9, 2013.

How to Win A Landslide Without Really Trying: Why the Conservatives Won in 1983, Ivor Crewe, University of Essex, 1984.

Realism, Reagan and Foreign Policy, Alexander Haig, Scribner, 1984.

The Falklands War: Myth and Countermyth, David Monaghan, Macmillan, 1998.

13: Grenada: Operation Urgent Fury: Russia Nearly Gets a Runway

The Crisis Begins, Oct. 12, 1983, Operation Urgent Fury. The Planning and Execution of Joint Operations in Grenada Oct. 12–Nov. 2, 1983, Ronald H. Cole, Joint History Office of the Chairman of the Joint Chiefs of Staff, Washington, DC 1993.

J. William Middendorf, U.S. Permanent Representative, explains to the OAS the reasons for intervention: violence on Grenada endangered the inhabitants, U.S. citizens living there, and the security of neighboring island republics. Article 52 of the UN Charter allowed regional bodies to deal with such disturbances; and

Articles 22 and 28 of the OAS Charter allowed member states to enforce collective security if necessary by inviting joint participation in a peacekeeping force by the United States, Oct. 27, 1983.

Jeane J. Kirkpatrick, U.S. Ambassador to the United Nations, makes a similar case to the Security Council on Oct. 27 and to the General Assembly on Nov. 2, 1983.

Preparations to Neutralize the Threat of a Cuban-Led Insurgency, Operation Urgent Fury, Oct. 21 1983. Final Preparation, Washington and Norfolk, Oct. 27, 1983, Operation Urgent Fury.

Rescue of the Governor-General, the Drive to Grand Anse, and the Push for PSYOPS, Oct. 26, 1983, Operation Urgent Fury.

Final Combat, Evacuation, and Public Affairs, October 27, 1983, Operation Urgent Fury.

The End of Combat Operations, Oct. 29–Nov. 2, 1983, Operation Urgent Fury.

General Vassey appears on *Meet the Press*, Nov. 6 1983.

14: Venezuela's Young Fidel Castro

Hugo Chavez: Oil, Politics and the Challenge to the U.S., Nikolas Kozloff, St. Martin's Press, 2006.

Hugo Chavez, Cristina Marcono, Random House, 2007.

Hugo! The Hugo Chavez Story From Mud Hut to Perpetual Revolution, Brent Jones, Stearforth, 2007.

Comandante: Hugo Chavez's Venezuela, Rory Carroll, Penguin Books, 2014.

"After the Guns Were Removed, the Killing Fields Began," J. William Middendorf, *The Daily Signal*, June 16, 2022.

"A Close Look: Fidel Castro and Hugo Chavez," Jose de Cordoba, *Wall Street Journal*, Mar. 1, 2019.

"Hugo Chavez and Fidel Castro, a father-son bond until death," Agence France, NDTV, Mar. 6, 2013.

"Castro on Chavez: We've lost our best friend," Kristin Deasy, *The World*, Mar. 11, 2013.

"Fidel's Heir," Jon Lee Anderson, *The New Yorker*, June 16, 2008.

"The Fabulous Five: How Foreign Actions Prop up the Maduro Regime in Venezuela," Moises Rendon and Claudia Fernandes, CSIS, Oct. 19, 2020.

15: Ambassador to the European Union

Winston Churchill calls for a United States of Europe, Speech at the University of Zurich, 1946.

"Emphatic 'No' by de Gaulle to UK entry to EU," *The Guardian*, Nov. 28, 1967.

"Clayton Yeutter: Blunt Negotiator of Intricate Trade Deals," *New York Times*, May 8, 2017.

"Highlights of the Airbus-Boeing trade war," *Financial Times*, June 15, 2021.

The EU Hormone Ban, Reuters, 1998.

16: When Russia Nearly Became a Democracy

Opinion Middendorf: *Providence Journal*, May 27, 2021.

"Russian Privatization and Oligarchs," *Facts and Details*, 1995

Kremlin Capitalism: Privatizing the Russian Economy, Joseph Blais, Cornell University Press, Nov. 12, 1996.

"The Logic of Economic Reform in Russia," Jeff Hough, Brookings Institute, April 1, 2001.

"How 'shock therapy' created Russian oligarchs and paved the path for Putin," *NPR*, Mar. 23, 2022.
"Corruption in Russia: No Democracy Without Morality," Barbara Von der Hoydt, The Heritage Foundation, Jan. 21, 1995.
"The Wise Guys of Russia," *U.S. News and World Report*, March 7, 1994.
"Aid to Russia: Yes, But Needs Reform," Heritage Foundation Committee Brief No. 1, February 6, 1995.
The Book of Virtues: A Treasury of Great Moral Stories, William J. Bennett, Simon and Schuster, 1993.
Gorbachev, Glasnost and the Gospel, Michael Bourdeaux, Hodder & Stoughton, 1990.

17: Project Economic Justice: Private vs. Public Ownership of Industry

"Just Economy for Harmonious Civilization," Norman Kurland, Center for Economic and Social Justice, June 19, 2008.
North American Free Trade Agreement, Jan. 1, 1994.
"Russia's Real Aim in Crimea," Carnegie Endowment for International Peace, March 13, 2014.
"Crimea: Six Years after Illegal Annexation," Brookings Institute, May 17, 2020.
"The Nonaligned Movement Crisis," Stewart Patrick, Council of Foreign Relations, Aug. 30, 2012.
"The New Nonaligned Movement is Having a Moment," Andrew Cheatham, U.S. Institute for Peace, May 4, 2023.

18: The Business of Banking

"The 'Post-Olmstead Era, William Jones," *The Washington Post*, May 9, 1977.
"S.E.C. Accuses Lance of Fraud as Banker," *New York Times*, April 27, 1978.
"Bert Lance resigns under fire as Jimmy Carter's budget director," Elizabeth Olson, UPI, March 3, 1981.
"BCCI Scandal: Behind the Bank of Crooks and Criminals," Steven Mufson and Jim McGee, *The Washington Post*, July 28, 1991.
"Lance admits playing key role in BCCI Scandal," Oswald Johnston, *Los Angeles Times,* Oct. 24, 1991.
Agha Hasan Abedi Dies in the Shadow of a Vast Fraud," *The Washington Post*, Aug, 6, 1995.
"File Closes on BCCI Scandal, Simon Bowers," *The Guardian,* May 17, 2012.

19: Advisor to Presidents and a Wanna-Be

The Age of Eisenhower: America and the World in the 1950s, William Hitchcock, Simon & Schuster, March 2019.
Soldier of Democracy, Dwight Eisenhower, Kenneth Davis, Doubleday, 1944.
Richard Nixon, The Life, John Farrell, Doubleday, March 2017. Greene, University Press of Kansas, Nov. 1994.
The Presidency of Gerald R. Ford, John Greene, University Press of Kansas, Nov. 1994.
Time to Heal, Gerald R. Ford, Berkley Publishing Group, May 1986.
Vietnam Evacuation: Operation Frequent Wind, Department of Defense, Sep. 16, 1975.

20: Music, Poetry & Art

Holland Symphony Piano Concerto, J. William Middendorf, Arranged by Somtow Sucharitkul, 1977.
The Lion and the Rose, J. William Middendorf, Recorded by the Cambridge Symphony Orchestra.
"A Man of Many Talents", Robert Higgins, *Standard Times*, Jan. 13, 2001.
"U.S. Philanthropist returns Memling portrait to Bruges," *The Brussels Times*, Sep. 25, 2020.

21: My Life Story

"Middendorf, Hartimo Company," Baltimore, MD, The Historical Society of Hartford County, 1921.
"Remembrance and Recovery," Maryland Civil War Veterans, National Museum of Civil War Medicine, May 30, 1900.
Invasion of Poland, Fall 1939, display at United States Holocaust Museum, New York, 1997.
"First Kamikaze Strike," National Geographic Society, David Stevenson, London School of Enemies & Political Science, 2014.
St. James Palace History by David Ross, British Express, 1986.
University of Southampton Special Collections, 1950.
The Middendorf Foundation, *Maryland Daily Record*, 1960.
Seaboard Air Line Railroad, *Train Magazine*, 1928.
Smart-Hawley Tariff Act, U.S. Congress, June 17, 1930.
World War One and the Short War Illusion, David Stevenson, London School of Economics & Political Science, August 2014.
"Navy Littoral Ship (LCS) Program," Ronald O'Rourke, *Congressional Research Service*, Aug. 24, 2010.
Lord Mount Temple, Wilfred Ashley, London Remembers, 1939.
The Life and Times of Lord Mountbatten, John Terraine, Holt, Rinehart and Winston, 1980.
The King Who Had to Go: Edward VIII, Adrian Phillips, Butobeck Publishing, 2017.
"Admiral Nimitz's Pacific Fleet Confidential Letter on Lessons of Damage in Typhoons," *Naval History and Heritage Command*, Feb. 13, 1945.
USS LCS-102 "Yankee Dollar" Landing Craft Support Museum, Vallejo, CA.
Capitalism, Socialism and Democracy, Joseph Schumpeter, Harper Bothers, 1943.
Marxism Unmasked: From Delusion to Destruction, Ludwig von Mises, Liberty Fund Library, 1944.
Marine Corps Marathon, Nov. 7, 1976, MarathonView.net
"Heroes, Legends Part of Game at Inaugural Hall of Fame Weekend," Bill Francis, National Baseball Hall of Fame, June 12, 1939.
Henley Royal Regatta, 1914 Challenge Cup Final, July 4, 1914.
"Henley Winning 1914 Crew Reassembles Tomorrow," June 2, 1939.

Index

Abedi, Aga Hassan, 228, 230, 233
Abkhazia, 144
Abu Dhabi, 228, 233
Adams, Samuel, 84
Adham, Sheikh Kamal, 231, 232, 233
Aegis, 74–75, 81
Afghanistan, 76, 107, 120, 122, 266, 268
Afghan War, 121–22
Africa, 76, 221, 222, 266. *See also specific countries*
African Americans, 38
Afshar, Amir Khosrow, 102
Agnew, Spiro T., 262
Agnich, Fred, 259
Ahmadinejad, Mahmoud, 106
Airbus, 198, 199, 201
Alabama, 262
Alfa Bank, 204
Alfonsin, Raul, 160
Algeria, 41, 104
Allen, Dick, 219, 265
Aló Presidente, 184–95
al-Qaeda, 120, 122, 223
Altman, Robert, 232, 234
American Bandmasters Association, 271
American Chamber of Commerce, 56
American Enterprise Institute, 240
American Federation of Musicians, 86
American Recolution, 83–84
American Revolution, 87, 89
  Bicentennial of, 83–95
American Stock Exchange, 229
Amerigo Vespucci, 93
Ames, Aldrich, 129, 130–31
Amini, Ali, 97
Amini, Mahsa, 106
Amphibious Commandos Group, 155
Anaya, Jorge, 154
Andes, 216
Andropov, Yuri, 267
Anglican Church, 275
Angola, 177, 268
Ankara, Turkey, 129
Annenberg, Walter, 105
Antigua, 175, 180
Antilles, 166
Apollo 11, 54
appeasement, 124–25

Apra Harbor, Guam, 287
Arab states, 96, 97, 100. *See also specific states*
Arc de Triomphe, 95
Argentina, 14, 36, 40, 46, 141, 152–64, 180, 189, 194
Arias, Oscar, 145
Arizona, 244–45, 251, 252, 257
Arizona Air National Guard, 246
Arkansas, 245
Armed Forces Radio, 110
Army of the Republic of Vietnam, 108
the arts, 270–78
ARVN, 112
Ascension Island, 158
Ashbrook, John, 248
Asia, 219, 221. *See also specific countries*
al-Assad, Bashar, 193
Assange, Julian, 137–38
Associated Press, 54
Association of Southeast Asian Countries, 115
Atcheson, George, Jr., 8–9, 20, 26
Atkinson, Brooks, 16
Austin, Hudson, 169, 170, 179
Australia, 115, 218
"Axis of Evil," 106
Azcona, José, 146
Azerbaijan, 127

Baez, Silvio, 143
Bagley, Worth, 89–90, 91
Bahamas, 105, 180
Bahrain, 107
Bailey, Sidney A., 232
Bakhtiar, Shahpur, 103
Baldwin, Stanely, 279
Baltimore, Maryland, 227, 279, 281–82, 299
Baltimore Museum of Art, 276
banking, business of, 225–34, 279, 295–96
Bank of America, 225, 233
 (BCCI), 228–34
Bank of England, 233
Bank of International Settlement, 54
Bank of Manhattan Company, 295–96
Bank of the South, 189
Barbados, 152, 170, 172–73, 174, 175, 180
Barbados National Radio, 174

Barker Adoption Agency, 300
Baroody, Bill, 240–41, 252, 254–55
Barrett, David, 21
Baseball Hall of Fame, 301
Batista, Fulgencio, 9, 31, 32, 34, 35, 37
Bay of Pigs Invasion, 39
Bazargan, Mehdi, 103, 104
BBC, 8, 101–2
Beagle Channel Islands, 154, 159
Beddow, Jack, 229, 232
Beethoven, Ludwig von, 272
Beijing, China, 212, 222
Beirut, Lebanon, 173
Belarus, 126
Belden, Jack, 26
Belgium, 57, 197, 275
Belize, 29–30, 152, 272–73
Belize Independence March, 272–73
Belmarsh Prison, 137
Ben Bella, Ahmed, 41
Benny, Jack, 65
Benson, Frank, 276
Berlin Wall, fall of, 209
Berryman, Eric, 80–81
Betancourt, Rómulo, 35
Bicentennial, 83–95
  Bicentennial Military Band, 86
  preparations for, 84
Biden, Joseph, 106
  administration of, 194
  Russo-Ukrainian War and, 202–5
Biebel, Fred, 219
Biesheuvel, Barend, 50, 59
Bishop, Maurice, 165–66, 167–69
Black Book of Communism, 15, 212
"Black Friday," 101
Black Sea Fleet, 124
Bleifeld, Stanley, 95
Bloomer, William A., 79
Boeing Aircraft Company, 55, 78, 198, 199, 201
Bogart, Humphrey, 289
Bogota, Colombia, 130
Boland, Edward P., 11, 144
Boland Amendment, 144
Bolivarian Alternative for the Americas (ALBA), 187
"Bolivarian Circles," 186
Bolivarianism, 187
Bolivarian Missions, 188

316   INDEX

Bolivarian Revolution, 188–89
Bolivia, 40, 41, 90, 180, 181, 189, 216
Bolshevik Revolution, 294
Bolton, John, 42
Bon Homme Richard, 87
Borchert, Till-Holger, 276
Borges, Jorge Luis, 160
Boston, Massachusetts, 84, 258, 295, 299, 301
Boston Pops, 271
Bouvier, Jackie, 239
Bouvier, Lee, 239
Boys Club, Harlem Facility of, 300
Boys Club of New York, 300
Boy Scouts of America, 93
Bozell, Brent, 241
Braderman, Gene, 52–53
Brandt, Willy, 51
Brazil, 14, 36, 152, 180, 187, 189, 194
Bristol County House of Corrections, 276–77, 300–301
British Army, 161
British Royal Marines, 155
Brock, Brok, 197
Broder, David, 261
Brooks, Mary, 85
Brown, Harold, 81–82
Brown, J. Carter, 95
Brownell, Herbert, 262, 263
Bruges, Belgium, 275–76
Bruges Museum, 275–76
Brussels, Belgium, 197, 275
Brzezinski, Zbigniew, 10, 102, 104
Buckley, William F., Jr, 7–8, 30, 241
Buckner, Bill, 259
Buffett, Susan, 298
Buffett, Warren, 297–98
Bulgaria, 211
Burch, Dean, 240, 250, 259
Burgundian Court, 276
Burnett, Leo, 251
Burns, Arthur F., 56
Bush, George H.W., 42, 50, 70, 75, 76, 106, 169, 171, 173, 245, 261, 262, 266, 299
Bush, George W., 117, 186, 189, 299
Bush, Prescott, Sr., 46, 299
Business Week, 59
Byrd, Harry, Sr., 281
Byrnes, James, 18

The Caine Mutiny, 289
Cairo, Egypt, 105
Caldera, Rafael, 185
California, 58, 225, 251, 254, 255, 257, 261, 265
Calivigny, Grenada, 171
Cambodia, 52, 264, 268
Cambridge, Massachusetts, 302
Cambridge Symphony Orchestra, 272
Canada, 36, 180, 204, 218, 219
Capitol Hill, 67–70, 71–72, 80, 234
Capriles, Henrique, 190
Caracas, Venezuela, 191, 193, 194
Caribbean, 141–42, 153–54, 165–83, 191. *See also specific countries*
Caribbean Basin Initiative (CBI), 141–42, 153–54
Caribbean Peacekeeping Force (CPF), 174
Carmona, Pedro, 188
Carter, Jimmy, 10, 13, 70, 81, 82, 102, 103, 123, 149, 225, 226, 266
 administration of, 101, 104, 149, 150
 CIA and, 118
 hostage crisis and, 104–5
Casey, William, 118, 168, 265
Castro, Cipriano, 188
Castro, Fidel, 3, 5–6, 11, 13, 25, 26, 28–43, 141, 142, 156, 177, 263
 Chavez and, 184–95
 Grenada and, 166
 the media and, 7–8
Castro, Raul, 42, 43
Catholic Church, 79, 188
Caulfield, Lord, 200
CBS, 172, 265
Center for Advanced Research, Naval War College, 219–20
Central America, 13–14, 141, 142, 149, 150–51, 191. *See also specific countries*
Central Bank, 210
Central Europe, 202–5, 266. *See also specific countries*
Cevat, Daan, 274–75
Chafee, John, 44, 61, 65
Chan, Commodore, 108
Chang Chun, 23
Charles, Eugenia, 181
Charleston, South Carolina, 88
Chase, 45, 225
Chatham, UK, 162
Chavez, Hugo, 3, 5–6, 8, 11, 15, 42, 142, 144, 184–95
Chavistas, 189
Chemical Bank, 45
Cheney, Dick, 135
Chiang Kai-shek, 3, 9, 19–20, 22, 24, 25, 26
Chicago, Illinois, 259
The Chicago Daily News, 247
The Chicago Tribune, 237, 256, 258
Chile, 13, 14, 152, 154, 159, 161, 194, 212
China, 3–9, 18–19, 60, 61, 115, 212, 217, 218, 235, 266, 284–85
 Belt and Road initiative, 151, 222
 Communism and, 4–5, 6, 7, 11, 15, 16–27, 213–14
 Cultural Revolution in, 25
 espionage and, 135–36, 138
 European Union and, 114
 "Great Leap Forward" and, 11, 41
 Japanese invasion of, 248–49
 naval-building spree and, 222–23
 Non-Aligned Movement and, 221–22
 Russia and, 127
 threat from, 120
 United States and, 16–27, 127
 Uyghurs in, 213–14
 Venezuela and, 186, 191, 194–95
Chinese Communist Party (CCP), 4–5, 7, 9, 16–27, 286
Chinese Nationalists, 9, 19, 20–21, 23–24, 26, 286
Christian Democratic Party, 197
Church, Frederic, 273
Churchill, Winston, 162, 197
CIA (Central Intelligence Agency), 10, 13, 37, 39, 41, 45, 47, 76, 101, 103, 168, 231
 9/11 and, 117
 Bay of Pigs Invasion and, 39
 espionage and, 129–40
 Grenada and, 174, 178
 information sharing with other agencies, 117–18
 Iran and, 100, 102
 Operation Frequent Wind and, 112
 role in preventing terrorism, 119
 Snowden and, 137
CIA Transition Team, 117–19, 129
The Cincinnati Enquirer, 256
Citibank, 45
Civil Rights Act of 1957, 246
Civil Rights Act of 1960, 246
Civil Rights Act of 1964, 245–46
Clam Lake, Wisconsin, 77
Clark, Bill, 167–68
Clark, Dale, 297–98
Clarridge, Duane, 169
Claytor, Graham, 82
Clements, Bill, 78–79
Clifford, Clark, 229, 231, 232, 233–34
Clifford, Clark, 229
Clinton, Bill, 42
Clinton, Hillary, 149
Coard, Bernard, 167, 168, 169, 179
Coco River, 146
Codevilla, Angelo, 118, 129, 130
Colby, William, 76
Cold War, 34, 61–62, 66, 70, 76, 152, 200, 212, 221, 235
 "deterrence" strategy and, 73–74
 end of, 207–8
 espionage and, 129–40
 Falklands War and, 162, 163
 Iran and, 98
 Reagan, Ronald W. and, 266–69
Colgate, Austen, 44, 296–97, 299
Colombia, 152, 180, 186, 187, 193
Colorado, 251
Colson, Chuck, 70
Committee for Monetary Research and Economics (CMRE), 220
Committee to Re-Elect the President (CREEP), 61
Communism, 3–5, 15, 16–27, 51, 114, 143, 152, 157, 192, 200,

207–8, 222, 266, 267. *See also specific countries and parties*
China and, 4–5, 6, 7, 11, 15, 16–27, 213–14
crimes of, 212
Cuba and, 11
Czechoslovakia and, 182–83
economic disasters and, 11–15
fall of, 210, 211
five characteristics present in Communist takeovers, 3–15
Grenada and, 141, 165, 168, 169, 182
history of, 16–27, 28–43
media and, 7–8
Venezuela and, 11, 14–15, 184–85
Western media, 7–8, 26–27
wounds of, 220
Communist People's Air Force, 109
Comprehensive and Progressive Agreement for Trans-Pacific Partnership, 115
Concord, Battle of, 83, 84
Concord, Massachusetts, 83, 276
Concord Monitor, 242
Congo-Brazzaville, 41
Congo-Kinshasa, 41
Congressional Budget Office, 219
Connecticut, 69, 262
Conoco Phillips, 6, 187
Conquest, Robert, 213
Continental Navy, 65, 81
Contras, 10–11, 144, 162, 182
Cooney, David M., 84
Cooper, Jackie, 94
Coral Sea, 110
Corbin, Bev, 239
Corcoran Gallery, 276
Cormier, Ralph, 250
Cornwall, Leon, 172, 179
Coronet Magazine, 35
Costa Mendez, Nicanor, 156–57
Costa Rica, 141, 143, 145, 146, 151, 152
Cotton, Norris, 245
Coupe, Jay, 92
Court of St. James, 279
Creedmoor Psychiatric Center, 300
Crimea, 124, 212
Crist, George B., 173–74, 178, 179
Cronkite, Walter, 265–66
Cruz, Donald, 172
Cuba, 3, 6–8, 13, 25, 26, 30, 141, 143, 146, 150, 151, 188, 217, 266
Communism and, 11, 28–43
Falklands War and, 156, 157
Grenada and, 165, 166, 167, 171, 172, 176–77, 178, 183, 268
Ministry of Commerce, 156
Oswald and, 239
in "troika of tyranny," 42
Venezuela and, 189, 191, 192, 193–95
Cuba Democracy Act of 1992, 42
Cuban Communist Party, 41
Cuban Missile Crisis, 40, 141

Cuban Praetorian Guards, 191, 192
Cuéllar, Javier Pérez de, 158–59
Curtis, Laurence, 302
Cussler, Clive, 88
Czechoslovakia, 75, 182–83, 222
Czech Republic, 13, 212

The Daily News, 245
Dam, Kenneth W., 179
Da Nang, Vietnam, 108
Davies, Joseph E., 8, 207
Davis, Shelby, 49, 209
Debasisley, Nicholas, 294
Declaration of Independence, 84
Defense Attaché Office (DAO), Saigon, Vietnam, DAO Compound, 108, 109
Defense Forum Foundation, 220
Defense Intelligence Agency, 119
Defense Security Service, 135
De Gaulle, Charles, 51
De Klerc, Willie, 197
De Koster, Hans, 57
De la Colina, Rafael, 180–81
Delft, 275
Del Toro, Carlos, 81
democracy, 4–6, 8, 149, 150–51, 206–14
Democratic National Committee, 254
Democratic National Convention, 249
Democratic Solidarity Act of 1996, 42
Democrats/Democratic Party, 69, 71–72, 74, 76, 247, 252, 253, 255–56, 258, 260, 281, 298
Denmark, 57, 197, 217
Den Uyl, Joop, 51
DePalma, Anthony, 33
Desert Shield, 76
Desert Storm, 76
d'Estaing, Valery Giscard, 89, 103
Detroit, Michigan, 265
Detroit Symphony Orchestra, 271
Dewey, Frances, 236
Dewey, Thomas E., 235, 236, 237, 298–99
Díaz Canel, Miguel, 43
Diego Garcia, 76
District of Columbia Fine Arts Commission, 85
Dixie Mission, 9, 20, 21
Dole, Bob, 248, 265
Domestic International Sales Corporation (DISC), 56
Dominica, 152, 175, 180, 181
Dominican Republic, 37, 98, 180
Dornan, Dan, 253
Dorticós, Osvaldo, 37
Drees, Willem, 54
Duarté, José Napoleon, 147–48
Dubček, Alexander, 182–83
Duerk, Alene, 63
Dulles, John Foster, 47
Duma, 11, 210, 294
Dũng, General, 112
Duranty, Walter, 7, 206

Dutch and Flemish Masters painting, 275

Eagleburger, Lawrence S., 169, 174
Eastern Europe, 202–5, 211, 266. *See also specific countries*
East Germany, 143, 212
economic disasters, 11–15. *See also* Great Depression
Ecuador, 14, 137, 152, 180, 189, 193, 194
Edgerton, Harold, 88
Edwards, Anne, 15, 213
Edwards, Lee, 15, 213, 251
Edward VIII, 279–80
Egypt, 75–76, 96, 97, 105, 117
Ehrlichman, John, 264
Eibert, William, 85
Eisenhower, Dwight D., 35, 39, 47, 235–58
Eisenhower, John, 47
Elizabeth II, Queen, 83–95
El Salvador, 141, 143, 146, 147–49, 168, 180, 182
Emirates, 223
Employee Stock Ownership Plans (ESOP), 215
Ender, Tom, 29
Enola Gay, 22
Entebbe rescue, 93
Erlichman, John, 70
espionage, 128, 129–40
Estonia, 211, 217, 218, 222
Ethiopia, 177
European Coal and Steel Community (ECSC), 197
European Community (EC), 195, 196–205, 270, 278
"Common Agricultural Policy" (CAP), 198
European Economic Community (EEC), 54, 197
European Parliament, 197
European Union, 114, 124, 126, 128, 197, 201–5, 219. *See also* European Community (EC); *specific countries*
Extraterritorial Income Exclusion (EIE) Act, 56
extremely low frequency (ELF) radio signals, 77–78
Exxon Mobil, 6, 187

Fairbank, John K., 16
Falkland, Viscount, 154
Falkland Islands Defense Force (FIDF), 155
Falklands War, 141, 152–64
Farenkopf, Frank, 219
Fargo, North Dakota, 252
Faribundo Marti National Liberation Front (FMLN), 143
Farley, James A., 257
FBI (Federal Bureau of Investigation), 119, 129, 130, 132–33
9/11 and, 117
Automates Case Support, 132
headquarters of, 132–33

FBI (*continued*)
 information sharing with other agencies, 117–18
 role in preventing terrorism, 119
Federal Reserve, 230–31, 232, 233–34, 293
Feulner, Edward, 24, 113, 208, 209, 211
Feulner, Linda, 113
Fiedler, Arthur, 271
Fieldhouse, John, 156
Financial General Bankshare (F.G.), 225, 226, 227, 229, 230, 231
Finland, 125, 217
First American, 232, 233
Flanigan, Peter, 44, 62
Fogg Museum, 276
Ford, 55
Ford, Gerald R., 70, 73, 76, 83, 92, 111, 263–65
 address at Concord, MA, 83
 Iran and, 100
 Presidential Proclamation 4411, 83
 Vietnam and, 108, 109
Ford, Glenn, 94
Foreign Sales Corporation (FSC), 56
Fort Bragg, 177
Fort Frederick, 177
Fort Rupert, 177
Founding Fathers, 83
France, 24, 196, 197, 198, 199
Franco, Francisco, 46
Franklin, Benjamin, 18, 87
Fredonia, Arizona, 252, 257
free elections, 4–6
Free Trade Area of the Americas, 186–87
Free World, 221, 222
French Navy, 89
Freneau, Bob, 80
Frost, Robert, 272, 300
Fulbright, J. William, 245
Funes, Mauricio, 149

Gairy, Eric, 165
Gallagher, Neil, 132
Galtieri, Leopoldo, 153–54, 156–57, 159, 162
Gantz, Jerry, 297
Gates, Robert, 75
Gaza, 107
Gehrenger, Charlie, 301
General Agreement on Tariffs and Trade (GATT), 199
General Belgrano, 156–57, 159
General Dynamics, 57, 73
General Electric, 255
Georgia (country), 124, 144, 221
Georgia (state), 176, 226, 229
Gerald R. Ford Museum, 112
Gereshchenko, Viktor, 210–11
Germany, 30, 93, 188, 196–97, 199, 201
Gertz, Bill, 60–61

Getman, Nikolai, 213
G.I. Bill, 292, 295
Gill, Fletcher, 296
Gillespie, Charles A., 173
Gingold, Julian, 49
Girl Scouts of America, 93
Givler, Amy Middendorf, 303–4
Givler, Don, 303–4
"Golden Snipe" award, 67
Goldspring, Paul, 137
Goldwater, Barry, 64, 65, 75, 220, 235–58, 283
Gomułka, Władysław, 38
Goodrich, Lloyd, 273
Goodspeed, George, 272
Goose Green, 155
Gorbachev, Mikhail, 161, 208, 269
Gordon, Waxey, 235
Gore, Albert, Sr., 245
Gorman, Paul, 179
Graham, Ben, 298
Graham, Daniel, 122–23
Graham-Newman, 298
Gramma, 31
Granda, Rodrigo, 186
Grand Anse, 176, 177
Grand Challenge Cup, 301
Grand Mal Bay, 178
Grasse, Comte de, 89
Gravely, Sam, 63
Graves Shipyard, 292
Gray, Dwayne, 79
Great Depression, 266, 281–82, 296, 297
"Great Leap Forward," 11, 41
Greece, 197
Green, Dwight H., 235, 298
Green, Hetty, 295
Greenberg, Hank, 301
Green Party, 197
Greenspan, Alan, 265
Greenwich, Connecticut, 299–300
Grenada, 141, 159, 165–83, 268
 People's Revolutionary Army, 172
 Revolutionary Military Council, 169, 170, 172, 173
Grenier, John, 259
Grenville, Grenada, 176
Griffin, Ralph, 55
Griffiths, Gene, 55
Grolier Club, 273
Ground Zero, 121
Grove, Lefty, 301
Guadeloupe, 103
Guaido, Juan, 191, 192, 193, 194
Guam, 68, 287
Guantanamo Bay Naval Base, 40
Guatemala, 141, 143, 146, 149–50, 151, 182
Guevara, Ernesto "Che," 34, 36, 40, 41
Gulags, 15, 206, 212, 213
Guy, Rexford, 8, 207

Hack, Stan, 301
Hadrian, 123

the Hague, 50, 55, 270, 275
Haig, Alexander M., 156, 157, 158, 161, 196
Haldeman, Bob, 70, 264
Haldeman, H. R., 262
Hamilton, Lee, 117
Hammer, Armand, 226, 231, 274
Hanoi, Vietnam, 113–14
Hanoi Hilton prison camp, 115–16
Hanssen, Robert, 131, 132–33
Harrington, Ione, 249
Harris, Brayton, 79, 85, 89–90, 91, 113
Harvard Business School, 295
Harvard University, 15, 212, 276, 282–83, 284, 292–94, 295, 301–2
Hassan II, 105
Havel, Vaclav, 220
Hawaii, 254, 284, 290
Hayek, Friedrich, 299
Hayman, Richard, 271, 272
Hayward, Steven, 267
"Head of the Charles" races, 302
Hebert, F. Edward, 76
Helms-Burton Act, 42
Heritage Foundation, 11, 12, 15, 24, 113, 118, 182, 208, 209, 213, 277–78
 2022 Report of Economic Development, 13
 2023 Economic Development index, 14
 Index of Economic Freedom, 217–19
 Index of Economic Freedom 2022, 145, 192, 218
 Index of Economic Freedom 2023, 217–18
 Index of Economic Freedom 2024, 106, 115
 trip to Russia and, 209–10
Herman, Billy, 301
Hero Sportsman of the Year Gold Medal Award, 302
Herrick, Robert F., 301
Hess, Karl, 240
Hezbollah, 105
Hickenlooper, Bourke, 245
Hi Dee camp team, 301
High Road to Economic Justice report, 216
Hirohito, Emperor, 22
Hiroshima, Japan, 22
Hitler, Adolf, 18, 46, 125, 166, 189
HMS *Britannia*, 83, 84
HMS *Endurance*, 155, 156, 162
HMS *Fearless*, 158
HMS *Serapis*, 87
HMS *Sheffield*, 159
HMS *Spartan*, 156
HMS *Splendid*, 156
Ho Chi Minh City, Vietnam, 114
Hodgson, Thomas, 277, 300–301
Holbrooke, Richard, 114
Holloway, James L. II, 111
Holloway, James L. III, 60, 64, 68, 78, 94, 109, 111, 265, 302–3

Index

Holmes, Kim, 209
Holocaust, 213
Holy Cross College, 283–84, 288, 292, 295
Honduras, 141, 143, 145–47, 148, 151
Hong Kong, 212, 218
Honolulu, Hawaii, 285
Hoover Institution, 294
Hope, Bob, 65
Hopper Edward, 273
Hornet, 79
Howitzers, 125
Hoyo, Joseph, 146
Human Rights Watch, 188, 190
Humphrey, George, 250
Humphrey, Hubert, 252, 262
Humphrey–Kennedy amendment, 162
Hungary, 213
Hunley, 88
Hunt, Rex, 155
Hunter Army Airfield, Georgia, 176
Hurley, Patrick, 9, 21
Hussein, Saddam, 11, 186

IBM, 45, 55
Ibn Khalduun, 215
Ikle, Fred, 169
Illinois, 244, 251, 257
India, 76, 115, 203, 244–45
Indiana, 251
Indian Ocean, 76
Indochina Migration and Refugee Assistance Act, 112
industry, private vs. public ownership of, 215–24
Integrated Revolutionary Organizations (Organizaciones Revolucionarias Integradas—ORI), 39
Inter-American Foundation, 216
Inter-American Treaty of Reciprocal Assistance (the Rio Treaty) (1947), 158
Intermediate-Range Nuclear Forces (INF), 161
International Bank, 226
International Conference of the American States, 141
International Court of Justice, 154
International Covenant on Civil and Political Rights, 154
International Democratic Union (IDU), 159, 219
International Economic Advisory Committee, 265
International Monetary Fund (IMF), 54, 189
International Naval Review, 89–91, 92, 93
International Republican Institute (IRI), 219
Iowa, 244–45, 257
Iran, 3–8, 10, 11, 13, 96–107, 120, 217, 266
  Cold War and, 98
  energy domination and, 223
  Five-Year Military Plan for, 98
  Morality Police in, 106
  National Intelligence Estimate on, 97
  Provisional Government of Iran (PGOI), 105
  Soviet Union and, 101–2
  terrorism and, 105–7
  United Kingdom and, 101–2, 103
  U.S. Congress and, 98–99
  U.S. hostages held in, 104, 266
  Venezuela and, 186, 194–95
  "White Revolution" in, 97, 98
Iran-Contra affair, 105
Iranian Navy, 96, 101
Iraq, 76, 96, 107
Iraq War, 189
Ireland, 73, 197, 217
Iron Curtain, 129
Irvin, Sam, 245
Islam, 3
Islamic code, 106
Islamic Revolution, 3–15, 101–2, 103–4, 105, 106–7, 266
Islamic Revolutionary Guard Corps (IRGC), 103, 105, 106
Israel, 75, 93, 102, 107, 134–35, 139, 180
Italy, 30, 40, 93, 188, 197
Iwo Jima Memorial, 94–95, 303

Jaffee, Henry, 247
Jamaica, 152, 170, 173, 174, 175, 180
Jane's Fighting Ship, 91
Japan, 20, 22, 115, 180, 204, 248–49, 285–86
Japanese Maritime Self Defense force, 291
Jelley, Bob, 55
Jenkins, John, 79
John Paul II, 121, 156
Johnson, Clarence "Kelley," 57
Johnson, Harold K., 225, 226, 227
Johnson, Lyndon B., 70, 97–99, 229, 243, 249, 250, 252, 254, 256, 257, 258, 260
Johnston Island, 285
Joint Chiefs of Staff (JCS), 92, 169, 172, 173, 176–77, 178
Joint Special Operations Command (JSOC), 173, 176, 177
Jones, John Paul, 87–88
Jong, Piet de, 51
Judd, Walter, 248–49
Juglar fixed investment cycle, 293
Juliana, Queen, 48–49, 50, 54, 270

Kabul, Afghanistan, 120, 122
Kahn, Sammy, 266
Kalmbach, Herb, 61
Kansas, 251, 254
Kaufman, James Jack, 86
Kazakhstan, 127
Kean, James, 109
Kean, Thomas, 117
Kelley, Paul X., 179–80
Kennedy, Ben, 55
Kennedy, Jackie, 239
Kennedy, John F., 9, 30, 39, 40, 50, 70, 96–97, 237, 239, 243, 247, 249, 267
  administration of, 96
  Frost and, 273
Kennedy, Robert, 258
Kennedy, Sarah Boone, 279–80
Kent State, shooting at, 52
Kentucky, 244, 251
Kerensky, Aleksandr, 294
KGB, 15, 129, 130, 132, 212, 213, 267
Khomeini, Ayatollah, 3, 5, 10, 96, 100–101, 102–3, 104, 105, 106
Khomeini, Mostafa, 101
Khosrow, Amir, 9–10
Khruschev, Nikita, 38, 39, 40, 97
Kinnear, George, E. R. "Gus," 79
Kirkpatrick, Jeane, 141–42, 153, 156, 157, 180
Kissinger, Henry, 45, 99, 100, 108–9, 200, 263, 264, 265
Kitchel, Denison, 240, 241, 242, 243, 244, 250, 252, 253, 254–55
Kitchin inventory cycle, 293
Kleindienst, Dick, 240
KLM, 47, 273–74
Kondratiev cycle, 293
Korat Air Base, 110
Korea, 23, 65
Korean War, 24–25, 235
Kovac, Frank, 248, 251
Kremlin, 127, 267
Krieble, Bob, 209
Kuomintang (KMG), 20. *See also* Chinese Nationalists
Kurland, Norman, 215
Kuwait, 96

Lage, Carlos, 41
Laird, Melvin, 52, 77
Lake Titicaca, 90
Lance, Bert, 226, 228, 229, 230, 231
Lance aux Epines, 178
Langley, Virginia, 129
La Paz, Bolivia, 216
La Prensa, 155
LaRue, Fred, 259, 262
Latin America, 14, 194, 211, 219, 221, 272. *See also specific countries*
  Project Economic Justice and, 215
Latvia, 211
Lavrov, Sergei, 52, 53, 204
Lawrence, David, 244
Layne, Edward, 179
LCS 53, 284–87, 288–91
Leach, Henry, 156
Lebanon, 105, 107, 117, 169, 173–74
Le Duan, 114
Lee, Peter, 135, 136
Lehman, John, 133–34, 291
Lemmon, Jack, 285
Lenin, Vladimir, 15, 25, 28, 142, 206, 212, 294

Leninism, 10, 144, 208, 267, 269
Lexington, Battle of, 83, 84
Libya, 103, 143
Limerick, Jay, 302
Lincoln Liberty Life Insurance Company, 297, 298
Lippmann, Walter, 247
Lithuania, 211, 222
Little Compton, Rhode Island, 278
Lockheed, 56, 57, 58
Lodge, Henry Cabot, 244
Lodge, John, 46
Loeb, John, 49
Loeb, William, 81
Lois, Jim, 89
The London Daily Herald, 7
Lone Sailor, 95
Los Alamos National Laboratory, 135
Los Angeles, California, 254
The Los Angeles Times, 256
Louisiana, 244–45
The Louisville Courier-Journal, 247
Luciano, Lucky, 235
Lund, Charles, 302
Luns, Joseph, 47, 51–52, 275
Lupton, John M., 236, 248
Luxembourg, 197, 217

MacArthur, Douglas, 3, 8, 20, 27
Macau, 218
MacGregor, Clark, 248
Madura Portland Cement, 281
Maduro, Nicholas, 190, 192, 193, 194–95
Maine, 252
Malaysian Airliner, shooting down of, 124
Malcolm X, 38
Malvinas. *See* Falklands War
Managua, Nicaragua, 147
The Manchester Guardian, 27
Manchuria, 22
Manning, Chelsea, 136
Mao Zedong, 3–7, 9, 15, 16–21, 25, 26, 27, 28, 142, 185, 186
Maracaibo Symphony Orchestra, 272
Marblehead, Massachusetts, 292
Margolis, Laurie, 155
Margriet, Princess, 270
Marshall, George, 3, 18, 19, 20, 21–22, 26, 286, 293
Martin, Dorothy, 111
Martin, Graham, 108, 109, 110, 111
Martin, Harold, 136
Martin, William, 94
Marx, Karl, 215
Marxism, 5, 10, 15, 144, 185, 186, 208, 212–13, 214, 267, 269, 294
Maryland, 225
Maryland Taxpayer's Association, 281
Massachusetts, 67–68, 292, 301
Massachusetts Air National Guard, 139

Massamba-Débat, Alphonse, 41
Massey, Raymond, 252, 253
Masters Sculling, 302
Matthews, Herbert, 8, 28, 30–35, 43, 186
McAdoo, William G., 280
McCain, John, 80, 116
McDonald, Admiral, 174, 178, 179
McDonnell-Douglas, 56, 78
McFarlane, Robert C., 173, 174
McGoff, John, 265
McGrory, Mary, 242
McMahon, John, 112, 169
McNeill, Francis J., 173–74
Mecham, Edwin L., 245
media, 16
  Communism and, 7–8, 26–27
  Iran and, 101–2
  Venezuela and, 185–86
Medwick, Joe, 301
Memling, Hans, 275–76
Menges, Constantine, 168, 169–70, 173
Menuhin, Yehudi, 272
Merrill Lynch, 232
Metcalf, Joseph III, 177–78
Metropolitan Museum of Art, 275
Mexican/American Free Trade Association, 216
Mexico, 14, 30, 105, 141, 180, 181, 194, 216
Meyer, Henry, 98, 302
Meyer, Wayne E., 74
Middendorf, Amy, 303–4
Middendorf, Billy (John William II), 279, 281, 282–83, 301
Middendorf, Colgate, and Company, 49, 299
Middendorf, Frances, 159, 303, 304
Middendorf, Franny, 278
Middendorf, Harry, Jr., 243, 279, 282–83
Middendorf, Harry S., 279–80, 281, 301, 302
Middendorf, Hartman & Co., 281
Middendorf, Isabelle, 53, 59, 216, 271, 272, 275, 296, 298, 299, 300, 304
Middendorf, Jeni, 304
Middendorf, John, 303, 304
Middendorf, John William. *See* Middendorf, J. William II
Middendorf, J. William II, 60, 279, 280. *See also* Middendorf, J. William II, works of
  as advisor to presidents and wanna-be presidents, 235–69
  as ambassador to EC, 196–205, 270, 278
  as ambassador to Netherlands, 44–59, 270, 278
  as ambassador to OAS, 4, 10–11, 141–51, 152–64, 165–83, 184–85, 196, 216, 270, 272, 278
  art and, 273–78

  in banking industry, 225–34, 281, 294–96
  at Bank of Manhattan Company, 295–96
  baseball and, 301
  becomes involved in politics, 298–99
  Caribbean Basin Initiative (CBI) and, 141–42, 153–54
  Castro and, 29
  Center for Advanced Research and, 219–20
  as chair of CMRE, 220
  as chair of Defense Forum Foundation, 220
  as chair of Harlem Facility, Boys Club of New York, 300
  childhood of, 279–82
  children of, 299, 300, 303
  on CIA Transition Team, 117–19, 129
  compared to Theodore Roosevelt, 81
  as composer, 197, 270–72
  in Concord, Massachusetts, 276
  conducts Boston Pops, 271
  confirmation as ambassador to Netherlands, 46
  education of, 282–83, 288, 292–94, 298
  Eisenhower and, 235–58
  family in Germany, 197
  Ford and, 263–65
  in Greenwich, Connecticut, 299–300
  Grenada and, 165–83
  at Harvard, 282–83, 284, 292–94, 295
  at Holy Cross, 283–84, 288, 292, 295
  honors and awards, 59, 76, 160, 271, 272, 278, 302
  at Hoover Institution, 294
  interest in painting, 45
  invited to Soviet Union to help write new constitution, 182
  Iran and, 96–97, 101
  joins U.S. Navy, 301
  as judge for 1960 Rome Olympics, 302
  in kindergarten, 279
  life story of, 279–305
  love of drawing, 276–78
  marriage to Isabelle Paine, 296
  meets Queen Juliana, 48–49, 54, 270
  meets with Hoyo, 146
  at Middlesex School, 276
  music and, 270–72
  Netherlandish business ties and, 44–45
  in the Netherlands, 200–201
  in New York, 294–99
  at New York University, 298
  Nicaragua and, 144
  Nixon and, 258–63
  in NROTC, 283–84, 286

Index

on Olympic selection committees, 302
poetry and, 273
at prep school, 282
as president/CEO of First American, 232
Project Economic Justice and, 215–24
Reagan and, 265–69 (*see also* Reagan, Ronald W.)
as RNC treasurer, 249–50
role in heading off negative OAS vote on Falklands War, 160
rowing and, 301–2
in Russia, 209–10
in Saigon, 108
as secretary of the Navy, 3, 60–82, 83–95, 96–107, 108, 109, 122–23, 264, 270, 277, 300, 302–3
shah of Iran and, 96–97
speech to OAS, 181
sports and, 301–3
teaches art at Bristol County House of Corrections, 296–97, 300–301
testifying on Capitol Hill, 234
as trustee of Heritage Foundation, 220 (*see also* Heritage Foundation)
on U.S. National men's field hockey team, 302
U.S. Navy and, 282–92 (*see also* U.S. Navy)
as U.S. Permanent Representative to OAS, 232
in Vietnam, 108, 115–16
volunteering at, 276–77
welcomes Elizabeth II, 83–95
at Wood, Struthers Company, 296–97, 298
World War II and, 282–92
Middendorf, J. William II, works of
Brazilian Triptych, 272
"European Overture," 197
Fantasia de Marfacaibo, 272
The Great Nightfall, 60–61
High Road to Economic Justice report, 216
"Holland Symphony," 270
Investment Policies of Fire and Casualty Insurance Companies, 297
The Lion and the Rose, 272
Mexican Rhapsody, 272
To Trinidad with Love, 272
Violin Concerto in D minor, 271, 272
Middendorf, Laila, 304
Middendorf, Martha, 303
Middendorf, Rowen, 304
Middendorf, Roxy Paine, 303, 304
Middendorf, Sally, 279
Middendorf, Sofia, 304
Middendorf, William Kennedy Boone, 279

Middendorf & Williams, 281
Middle East, 96–107, 223, 232. *See also specific countries*
Middlesex School, 276
Mikoyan, Anastas, 37
Milbank, Jerry, 236, 239, 241, 248, 259, 261, 262
Military Assistance Advisory Group (MAAG), 56
Miller, Bill, 248, 249
Mills, Wilbur, 56
Minh, Duong Van, 112
Minnesota, 248
Mirage, 56, 57
Miskito Indians, 4, 10, 142
Mobil, 227–28
Moldova, 221
Monge, Luis Alberto, 145
Monroe Doctrine, 182
Morgan, David, 302
Morocco, 105
Morton, Roger C.B., 50
the *Moskva*, 124
Motley, Anthony, 169
Motley, Langhorne A., 169, 174, 178
Mountbatten, Lord, 279
Mousavi, Mirhoseein, 106
Mow, Doug, 79
Moyers, Bill, 256
Mudge, Stern, Baldwin, and Todd, 259
Museum of Fine Arts, Boston, 276
music, 270–78
Muslim fundamentalists, 3, 5. *See also* Islamic Revolution

NAACP, 246
Nagasaki, Japan, 22
National Security Council (NSC), 169
Nakhon Phanom Air Base, 110
Narodnik Populist Movement, 294
Nasser, Gamel Abdel, 38, 96
National Academy of Sciences, 272
National Archives, 94
National Beijing Palace Museum, 23–24
National Democratic Institute (NDI), 219
National Draft Goldwater Committee, 237, 240, 241, 247, 252, 258
National Front, 197
National Gallery, 278
National Review, 241
National Security Agency (NSA), 135, 136, 137
National Security Council, 10
National Security Council (NSC), 45, 103, 158, 168, 170, 173
National Space Agency, 136
National Symphony, 271
NATO, 47, 52, 57–58, 124, 125, 126, 127, 152, 162, 163, 213, 222

Goldwater and, 243
Russo-Ukrainian War and 201–5, 221
NATO-Russia Council meeting, 203
Naval Academy, 265, 283
Naval Advisory Committee, 265
Naval Historical Foundation, 220
Naval History Magazine, 134
Naval Reserve, 94
Naval Reserve Officer Training Corps (NROTC), 283–84, 286
Naval War College, 81
Center for Advanced Research, 219–20
"Navy Jack," 85
Navy League Sea Cadet, 93
"Navy Log," 95
Navy Memorial Foundation, 94
Navy towns, 68–69
NBC, 257
Nebraska, 93, 251
Nehru, Jawaharlal, 38
Netanyahu, Benjamin, 135
Netherlands, 12, 44–59, 196–97, 200–201, 211, 217, 270, 273–74, 278
Nevada, 257
New Deal, 281
New England, 251, 261
New Hampshire, 241–42, 244, 245, 252, 260
New Jersey, 91, 244–45
New Joint Endeavor for Welfare, Education, and Liberation (JEWEL), 165
New Mexico, 245
New Orleans, Louisiana, 256
Newport, Rhode Island, 93, 239
Newsweek, 243, 247–48
New World Chamber Players, 272
New York, 69, 91, 92, 225, 233, 240, 251, 258, 299
New York City, New York, 38, 121, 227, 257, 294, 295, 299
New York Giants, 301
New York Harbor, 90, 92
The New York Post, 247
New York Stock Exchange, 296, 299
The New York Sun, 7
The New York Times, 7–8, 26, 28, 30, 33, 34, 92, 119, 185, 186, 198, 206, 237–38, 247, 257–58, 282
New York University, 298
New Zealand, 115, 217
Nicaragua, 4, 5, 13–14, 39, 142–44, 162, 168, 180–82, 266
Costa Rica and, 145
El Salvador and, 147–48
Honduras and, 146
Nicaraguan Revolution, 7, 8, 10, 11, 141
Reagan and, 268
in "troika of tyranny," 42
Nicolas, Joep, 275
Nimitz, Chester, 289–90

Nixon, Richard M., 35, 44, 47, 49–50, 56, 58, 64–65, 70, 275, 283
  administration of, 264
  Goldwater and, 237–38, 246, 254
  Iran and, 99, 100
  presidential campaign of, 244, 251, 258–63
  Republican nomination and, 262
  SECNAV appointment and, 61–62
  at shah's funeral, 106
NKVD, 213
Non-Aligned Movement, 221
Norfolk, Virginia, 91
Norman, Mike, 155
North Dakota, 251
North Vietnam, 77
North, Oliver, 169, 173
North America Cement, 281
North American Free Trade Act (NAFTA), 216
North Carolina, 245
North Dakota, 244
North Korea, 60, 134, 143, 217, 223, 266
Northrop, 56, 57, 78
North Sea, 162
North Vietnam, 113–14, 260
North Vietnamese, 108
North Vietnamese Army, 108
Norway, 57, 93
Norwegian Air Force, 57
Nott, John, 158
Novak, Bob, 258
NSPG, 173
Nuclear Nonproliferation Treaty of 1968, 100
Nustul, William C., 112–13
Nyugen, Major, 112

Obama, Barck, 42
O'Connor, John, 79
O'Donnell, Peter, 237, 241, 249, 259
Office of the Comptroller of the Currency, 232
Office of the Director of National Intelligence, 136
Officer Candidate School (OCS), 283
Ohio, 244–45, 251, 257
"oil shocks," 100
Okinawa, Japan, 285–86
Oklahoma, 251
Oklahoma Natural Gas, 281
Old North Bridge, 83
Olmsted, George, 225–27
Olmsted & Olmsted, 225, 226, 229
Olympics, 266, 302
O'Neill, Eric, 133
O'Neill, Thomas P. "Tip," 67–68, 179, 267
OPEC (Organization of Petroleum Exporting Countries), 100, 189–90, 263
Operation Corporate, 156

Operation Frequent Wind, 108–16
"Operation Merlin," 136
Operation RYAN, 267
Operation Sail (OPSAIL), 90, 92, 93
"Operation Sail and the International Naval Review," 90
Operation Urgent Fury, 165–83
Opinion Research Corporation (ORC), 251, 253
Organization for Economic Co-operation and Development (OECD), 54
Organization of American States (OAS), 4, 10–11, 141–51, 152–64, 175–76, 184–85, 196, 216, 232, 270, 278
  Charter of, 181
  Council, 156
  Grenada and, 180, 181
  Music Festival, 272
  Permanent Council, 166, 181
  Rio Treaty, 181
  special session on Falklands War, 156
Organization of Eastern Caribbean States (OECS), 166, 170, 172–73, 174, 175, 179
Ortega, Daniel, 5, 8, 10, 14, 142, 143, 144
Ortega, Wilfred, 7
Oswald, Lee Harvey, 239
Otis USANG Base, 139
Ott, Mel, 301

Packard, David, 57
Pahlavi, Mohammad, 3–4, 8, 10, 13, 96, 97–99, 100–102, 103, 104, 105–6
Paine, Isabelle, 296. See also Middendorf, Isabelle
Paine, Roxy Middendorf, 278, 303, 304
Pakistan, 233
Palestine Liberation Organization (PLO), 143
Palestinians, 103, 107
Palo Alto, California, 294
Panama, 105, 180
Pan-American Union., 141
Pan-European Union, 196–97
Paraguay, 152, 189
Paris Peace Accords, 108
Parkinson, Gaylord B., 260
Parsons, Anthony, 101
"Peace through Strength," 122–24, 266–67
Pearl Harbor, Hawaii, 284, 290
Pearls, 171, 172
Pearson, Drew, 247
Pell, Claiborne, 74, 76
Pembroke, UK, 162
Pennsylvania, 68, 251, 257
Pentagon. See U.S. Department of Defense
Pentagon Papers, 52
People's Army, 17

People's Revolutionary Movement, 146–47
Perez, Carlos Andres, 185
Persian Gulf, 3, 100, 101, 107, 223
Peru, 14, 40, 152, 180, 194
Peter Cooper Village, 296
Petrocaribe, 186
Petróleos de Venezuela S.A. (PDVSA), 188, 192
Petrosur, 186
Pham Van Dong, 114
Philadelphia, Pennsylvania, 258
Philip, Prince, 83, 84
Philippines, 113
Philips, 55
Phillips, Howard, 220
Phillips, Ruby, 30
Piedra, Alberto, 156
Piedra, Carlos, 35
Pleasantville, New York, 301
poetry, 270–78
Poindexter, John, 79, 80–81, 169, 173
Point Salines, 171, 172, 176, 177, 178
Poland, 12, 13, 18, 75, 93, 208–9, 211, 212, 222
Polaris/Poseidon missiles, 73–74, 152
Politburo, 112
Pollard, Jonathan, 134–35, 138
Pope, 10, 79
Portland, Oregan, 290
Portsmouth, UK, 162
Port Stanley, 152, 155
Portugal, 197, 199
Prados, John, 134
Prague, Czech Republic, 220
Prague Spring, 182–83
Prescott, Arizona, 252
Price, Melvin, 76
Price Waterhouse, 233
Project Economic Justice, 215–24
Project Sanguine, 77
"Project X," 259
Puerto Rico, 29
Putin, Vladimir, 11, 124, 125, 192, 193, 201, 202, 203, 204, 210, 212, 221

Qaddafi, Muammar, 3, 11, 185, 186
Qom, Iran, 96, 101
Quincy, Abigail, 50
Quincy, John, 50
Quincy Naval Shipyard, 67–68

Radio Havana, 6–7
Raisi, Ebrahim, 106
Ralph's Rules, 255
Ratliff, William E., 34
Reagan, Ronald W., 42, 49, 105, 117, 121, 123, 149–51, 196, 232, 255, 265–69
  1980 presidential campaign and, 265–66
  administration of, 41, 118–19, 133–34, 142, 146, 157, 172
  announcement at OAS, 153–54

INDEX 323

appoints Middendorf as OAS ambassador, 141
bombing of Marine barracks in Beirut and, 173
California Goldwater campaign and, 254
Cold War and, 152, 266–69
election of 1980 and, 258
end of Cold War and, 207–8
Falklands War and, 153–54, 157, 158–59
foreign policy of, 168
Gorbachev and, 161
Grenada and, 166–67, 170–71, 174–76, 179, 183
IDU and, 219
Nixon and, 261
political philosophy of, 260
presidency of, 266–69
presidential campaign of, 168
Project Economic Justice and, 215, 216
"Reagan for President" club, 255
SDI and, 207, 268
Soviet Union and, 267–68
Thatcher and, 277–78
Reagan Doctrine, 208, 268
Red Cross, 121
Red Guards, 25
Red Party, 197
Regional Comprehensive Economic Partnership, 115
Rembrandt, 276
Reports of the Federal Reserve Board, 228
Republican National Committee, 50, 75, 78, 248, 249–50, 260, 265
Republican National Convention, 238, 298
Republican Party, 78, 80, 235–58, 259, 260, 265, 299–300
Republicans, 69, 74, 75, 260
Sea Control Ship (SCS) and, 72
Reston, James, 257–58
Revere, Paul, 83, 84
Revisionism, 222
Revolución Liberal Restauradora, 188
Revolutionary Armed Forces of Colombia (FARC), 186, 193
revolutions, U.S. State Department and, 8–11
Reykjavik, Iceland, 161
RFA *Fort Austin*, 156
Rhode Island, 69, 74, 93
Rice, Condoleezza, 190
Richard the Lionhearted, 272
Rickover, Hyman G., 71–73, 82
Riggs, 225
Rijksmuseum, 275
Rio Treaty, 181
Rippon, Jeffry, 219
Ripton, Vermont, 272
Rockefeller, David, 105
Rockefeller, John D., 273

Rockefeller, Nelson, 92, 100, 237, 242, 244, 258, 260–61, 262, 263, 264–65, 273, 300
Rocky Mountain Rowing Club, 302
Rohter, Larry, 8, 185
Rojas, Francisco de, 276
Romania, 93
Romney, George, 237, 258, 259
Roosevelt, Franklin Delano, 8, 62, 207, 281
administration of, 257
Roosevelt, Theodore, 62, 81, 86
Rowing Regattas, 302
Royal Dockyards, UK, 162
Royal Marines, 155
Royal Navy, 156, 158, 162
Rubinstein, Arturo, 270–71
Rumsfeld, Donald, 87, 135, 189, 263–64
Rusk, Dean, 98
Russia, 11, 12, 120, 151, 165–83, 194–95, 209, 217
annexation of Crimea, 124
China and, 127
democracy and, 206–14
energy domination and, 223
interference in U.S. election, 124
invasion of Georgia, 124
invasion of Ukraine, 124–28, 139, 201–5, 212, 221, 222
Ministry of Agriculture, 211, 212
Ministry of Health, 12
NATO and, 202–5
Non-Aligned Movement and, 221–22
Russo-Ukrainian War and, 124–28, 139, 201–5, 212, 221, 222
Venezuela and, 186, 189, 191, 193, 194–95
Russian-American Business Council, 12–13, 211
Russian Revolution, 28, 206, 294
Russo-Ukrainian War, 124–28, 139, 201–5, 212, 221, 222
Ruth, Babe, 301

Saab, 56
Sadat, Anwar, 76, 105
Sadeghi, Gholam Hossein, 102
Sadr, Abohassan Bani, 105
Saigon, Vietnam, 108, 110, 114, 263, 265
Defense Attaché Office (DAO), 108, 109
U.S. embassy in, 109
Saipan, 287
Salazar Paredes, Fernando, 181
Saltonstall, Leverett, 46, 302
Salvation Army, 121
The San Antonio Light, 261
Sanchez-Sabarots, Guillermo, 155
Sandinistas, 4, 5, 7, 8, 10–11, 142, 143, 145, 147–48, 151, 168, 180, 182

Sand War, 41
San Francisco, California, 254, 290, 299
Santos, Francisco, 195
Saudi Arabia, 76, 107, 117, 207, 223, 231, 232
Saul, Frank, 229–30, 232
Savitore, Henry, 255
Sberbank, 204
Schlesinger, James, 64, 72, 78, 263
Schmeltzer, Norbert, 51
Schmidt, Helmut, 103
Schultz, George, 161
Schumpeter, Joseph, 292–93
Schwartzkopf, Norman, 177–78
Schwarz, John S., 301
Scoon, Paul, 166, 170, 173, 178
Scotland, 73
Scowcroft, Brent, 264
Scranton, Wiliam, 237, 258
Sea-Air Operations Gallery, 94
Seaboard Air Line Railroad, 280
Sea Control Ship (SCS), 71–72
Seaton, Mother, 79
Secret Internet Protocol Router Network (SIPRNet), 137
Securities and Exchange Commission (SEC), 228, 229, 230–31
Serapis, 88
Service, John S., 9, 20–21
Shanghai, China, 18–19, 284–85, 286
Shaw, George Bernard, 207
Shea, Michael J., 113
Shell, 55
Shultz, George, 161, 169, 173, 174, 196, 197
Shumeyko, Vladimir, 209, 211
Sierra Maestra, 31–32
Simpson, Kenneth F., 294
Simpson, Millard L., 245
Simpson, Wallis Warfield, 279–80
Simpson, William Kelly, 294
Sims, Robert, 3, 66, 79, 96
Singapore, 204, 217, 218
60 Minutes, 100
Smedly, Agnes, 17–18, 26–27
Smith, Adam, 215
Smith, Alex, 283
Smith, Debra Evans, 132
Smith, E. I., 9, 35
Smith, Homer, 109–10
Smith, Margaret Chase, 252
Smithsonian Air & Space Museum, 93–94
Smoot-Hawley Act, 281
Snow, Edgar, 7, 17, 27, 186
Snowden, Edward, 137
Snyder, Edwin K. "Ted," 79
Social Democrats (Germany), 51
socialism, 15, 114, 185, 190, 192, 214, 218–19, 267, 294
Socialist League, 190
Socialist Party, 57, 197
Social Security, 255
Socony Vacuum Company, 295–96

324   Index

Solidarity movement, 208
Solzhenitsyn, Aleksandr, 213
Somocismo, 145
Somoza, Anastasia, 4
Somoza, Anastasio, 142, 145, 147
Sonnenfeldt, Helmut, 45
Son Nhut Airbase, 109
South America, 142, 191, 222. *See also specific countries*
South Carolina, 244, 257
South China Sea, 112
South Dakota, 251
Southern Gas Corridor, 128
South Georgia Island, 155, 156, 157–58
South Hampton University, 279
South Korea, 115, 139, 204
South Ossetia, 144
South Vietnam, 108, 109, 113–14
South Vietnamese, 108, 109, 110, 264
South Vietnamese Air Force, 112
South Vietnam Navy, 113
Soviet Union, 6, 17, 22, 24–28, 30, 73, 162, 169, 209–10, 213, 222, 235, 263, 267. *See also* Russia
   Cold War and, 66
   collapse of, 11, 207–8, 209
   Communism in, 15
   Cuba and, 30, 40, 41, 141
   Czechoslovakia and, 182–83
   "deterrence" strategy and, 73–74
   Entebbe rescue and, 93
   espionage and, 129–34, 137
   Falklands War and, 157, 160–61, 163
   Grenada and, 165, 166, 167, 171, 172, 178, 268
   Hungarian revolt against, 213
   Iran and, 96–97, 101–2
   Moscow Olympics and, 266
   Navy of, 70
   Nicaragua and, 143
   Oswald and, 239
   "Peace through Strength" approach and, 123–24
   Reagan and, 267–68
   Stalin and, 206
   United States and, 266–69 (*see also* Cold War)
   Venezuela and, 193
   writing of new constitution in, 182
   Yom Kippur War and, 75
Spain, 154, 197, 199
Spanish Civil War, 30–31
Spanish Empire, 154
Sparrow's Point Shipyard, 280
Spencer, Richard, 81
Spencer, Steve, 239
spies, 129–40
stagflation, 100
Stalin, Joseph, 6, 7, 142, 206, 207, 209, 213, 235
Stans, Maurice, 56, 61
Stennis, John, 64, 76
Sterling, Jeffrey, 136

St. George's, 171, 174, 177, 178
St. George's School of Medicine, 169, 172
Stillwell, Joseph W., 19–20, 26
St. John, Orson, 299
St. Louis Symphony Orchestra, 271
St. Lucia, 175, 180
Stoltenberg, Jens, 203
Stone, William, 65, 79, 81
St. Petersburg, Florida, 252
Strasbourg, France, 197
Strategic Defense Initiative (SDI), 161, 207, 268
Strategic Stability Dialogue (SSD), 202–3
Strong, John, 154
St. Vincent, 175, 180
Suazo Cordoba, Roberto, 146
Sucharitkul, Somtow, 270, 271, 272
Suez Canal, 75
Sullivan, Ambassador, 10
Sullivan, Don, 132
Sullivan, Ed, 8, 28–29, 36–37
Sullivan, William H., 101, 102
Sumulong, Lorenzo, 38
Sweden, 137–38
Switzerland, 217, 218
Symphonic Band of the Belgian Guides, 197
Syria, 75, 96, 193

Taiwan, 23–24, 217, 218, 222
Taliban, 107, 120, 122, 223
Tanguy, Charles, 45
Tan Son Nhut Airport, 109–10
Task Force 121, 177
Taylor, Wesley B., 176
Tehran, Iran, 10, 101, 103–4, 106
Teixeria, Jack, 139
Telesur, 186
Temple, Lord Mount, 279
Ten Boom, Corrie, 53
Tenet, George, 135
Tennessee, 245, 257
terrorism, 105, 106
   in Honduras, 146
   Iran and, 105–7
   terrorist attacks of September 11, 2001, 117–28
Tet offensive, 260
Texas, 244–45, 257, 261
Thailand, 110
Thai Navy, 291
Thames Rowing Club Crew, 302
Thant, U, 40
Thatcher, Margaret, 152, 155–59, 160, 179, 200, 208, 219, 269, 277–78
Thompson, Bill, 86, 94
Three Seas Initiative, 128
Thurmond, Strom, 179, 262
Tiananmen Square, 212, 213
Ticonderoga, 75
El Tiempo de Bogotá, 34
Time magazine, 198, 238, 245, 247, 259

Toronto, Canada, 302
Tortola Comas, Pedro, 177
Tower, John, 64, 239, 245
Towson (Maryland) Normal School, 279
Towson, Maryland, 279, 281–82
Toynbee, Arnold, 293
Trans-Caspian Pipeline, 128
Treischmann, Charles, 113
Trident nuclear missile submarine system, 73–75, 81–82, 123, 136, 152
Trinidad and Tobago, 36, 152, 180, 272
Trobaugh, Edward, 177, 179
Trudeau, Justin, 26
Trudeau, Pierre, 26
Truman, Harry S, 235, 236
Truman, Harry S., 3, 18, 22, 25, 26, 236, 246, 298–99
   administration of, 24
Trump, Donald, 42
   administration of, 42–43, 194
   "America First" foreign policy, 124
   "Peace through Strength" approach and, 124
TRW, Inc., 135–36
Tuck, Lon, 272
Turkey, 40, 97, 129, 194
Turner, Stansfield, 118, 119
Twain, Mark, 272
Tyler, William, 47, 58

U.K. Defense Review, 161
Ukraine, 7, 206, 213
   Russo-Ukrainian War and, 124–28, 139, 201–5, 212, 221, 222
U.K./U.S. Radar Ocean Imaging Program (ROIP), 136
Unilever, 55
Union Boat Club, 301
Union Pacific Pension Fund, 297–98
United Airlines 93, 121
United Arab Emirates, 117
United Kingdom, 24, 29, 180, 197, 199, 204, 218, 267, 279–80
   Cuba and, 188
   espionage and, 136, 137–38
   Falklands War and, 141, 152–64
   Iran and, 101–2, 103
   Ministry of Defense, 155
   National Freight Corporation, 215
United Nations, 40, 104, 114, 141–42, 155, 156, 188, 189
   Charter, 154
   Falklands War and, 152
   General Assembly, 9, 38, 102, 180, 189, 221
   Security Council, 190
United Party of the Cuban Socialist Revolution (PURSC), 39
United Press International (UPI), 7, 26, 27, 181

INDEX   325

United Socialist Party of
    Venezuela, 189
United States, 14, 218, 219. *See also*
    specific branches, agencies,
    and military branches
  anti-shah demonstrations
    in, 100
  Argentina and, 152–64
  China and, 16–27, 127
  Cuba and, 28–43
  EC and, 196–205
  energy security and, 127–28
  espionage and, 129–40
  Falklands War and, 152–64
  farm subsidies and, 198–99
  Grenada and, 165, 166
  Honduras and, 147–48
  Iran and, 96–707
  Lebanon crisis and, 173–74
  Nicaragua and, 143–44
  Russian-Iranian energy
    domination and, 223
  Russo-Ukrainian War and,
    124–28, 202–5
  Soviet Union and, 266–69
    (*see also* Cold War)
  Venezuela and, 184–95
  Vietnam and, 52–53, 98, 99,
    108–16
University of St. Petersburg, 294
University of Virginia, Frost
    Library at, 273
Urban League, 246
Uruguay, 36, 152, 180, 189
U.S. Air Force, 56–58, 75, 76, 78,
    81, 85, 86, 108, 110, 111, 161
U.S. Army, 81, 86, 108, 137, 161,
    282–83
  U.S. Army Observation
    Group, 9
  U.S. Army Reserve, 283
U.S. Commerce Department,
    45, 56
U.S. Commission on Fine Arts,
    95
U.S. Congress, 10–11, 23, 26, 56,
    66, 67–70, 75–77, 80, 147, 216,
    248, 264. *See also* U.S. House
  U.S. Senate Armed Services
    Committee, 86
  Boland Amendment and,
    10–11, 144
  Falklands War and, 158
  Grenada and, 179
  Humphrey-Kennedy
    Amendment, 162
  Iran and, 98–99
  Navy Memorial and, 995
  Nixon and, 65
  Sea Control Ship (SCS) and,
    71–72
  SECNAV appointment and, 67
  shipbuilding bill and, 75
  Trident and, 74
  Vietnam and, 108
  Walesa's address to, 208
U.S. Department of Defense,
    47, 62–67, 79, 86, 87, 99, 109,
    113, 137, 139, 169, 267
  Falklands War and, 158
  Grenada and, 166–67, 177
U.S. Department of Justice, 139
U.S. Department of the Treasury,
    14, 45, 85, 144, 234
U.S. embassy in Lebanon, 169
U.S. embassy in Saigon, 109
U.S. embassy in Tehran, 103–4
U.S. Foreign Corrupt Practices
    Act, 12, 211–12
U.S. House, 80
  Appropriations Committee,
    72, 179–80
  Armed Services Committee,
    72
  Foreign Affairs Committee,
    179
  shipbuilding bill and, 75
USIA, 45
U.S. Intelligence Community,
    117–28
U.S. Marine Corps, 60, 65, 67, 68,
    85, 86, 88, 94, 104, 108, 111,
    112, 123, 173, 264
  Grenada and, 171–72, 178, 180
  U.S. Marine Corps Marathon,
    303
  U.S. Marine Corps Reserves,
    303
U.S. Mint, 85
U.S. National Defense Strategy,
    124
U.S. National Masters Champi-
    onship, 302
U.S. Naval Academy, 64
U.S. Navy, 3, 44, 60–82, 73–77,
    123, 129, 135, 161, 264, 270,
    277, 282–92, 300, 301
  Bicentennial, 83–95
  Commander Task Force 76,
    109
  Grenada and, 170, 171
  in Middle East, 107
  SEALs, 172, 176, 177
  "Twenty Minute Club," 302–3
  U.S. Naval Reserve, 284
  V-12 Officer Training Pro-
    gram, 283
  in Vietnam, 108
  Vietnam and, 108–13
U.S. Olympic Selection Commit-
    tee for field hockey, 302
U.S. Rangers, 171–72, 173, 176, 177
USS *Blue Ridge*, 112
USS *Constitution*, 67, 83–95
USS *Doyen*, 284
USS *Dwight D. Eisenhower*, 265
U.S. Senate, 80, 246
  Appropriations Committee, 72
  Armed Services Committee,
    65, 69–70, 72, 75, 179
  Civil Rights Act of 1964 and,
    245–46
  Commerce Committee, 58
  Foreign Relations Committee,
    46, 147
  Intelligence Committee, 131
  shipbuilding bill and, 75
USS *Enterprise*, 110
USS *Forestal*, 91–92
USS *Guam*, 71, 176, 179
USS *Hancock*, 109
USS *Independence*, 171, 172, 176,
    177
USS *John F. Kennedy*, 91
USS *J. William Middendorf*, 304
USS *Kirk*, 112
U.S. Southern Command, 179
USS *Pueblo*, 134
USS *Ronald Reagan*, 124
USS *Sanctuary*, 63
U.S. State Department, 9, 10, 11,
    13, 20–21, 26, 34, 44–59, 66,
    157, 265, 278
  ambassadorial nominees and,
    44
  Grenada and, 169, 170, 173, 174
  Iran and, 97, 101, 103
  revolutions and, 8–11
  Venezuela and, 186, 189–90,
    193
USS *Wayne E. Meyer*, 75
USTR, 197
U-Tapao Air Base, 110
Uyghurs, 213–14

Vance, Cyrus, 9, 102
Vander Meer, Johnny, 301
Van der Veyden, Rogier, 275–76
Van Waverin Tulip Bulb Com-
    pany, 44
Vatican, 156
Vaughan, Arky, 301
Veliotis, P. Takis, 73
Venezuela, 3, 5–6, 7, 8, 11, 35, 42–
    43, 144, 152, 166, 180, 217, 223
  under Chavez, 184–95
  Communism in, 11, 14–15
  as failed state, 192–93
  in "troika of tyranny," 42
  Venezuelan Armed Forces,
    7, 184
  Venezuelan Congress, 187
  Venezuelan National Assem-
    bly, 188
  Venezuelan National Guard,
    191–92
  Venezuelan Supreme Court,
    187, 190
Vermeer, Johannes, 275
Vessey, John, 169, 170, 171, 172,
    173, 174, 176, 179, 180
Victims of Communism
    Museum, 15, 212–13
Viet Cong, 40, 112
Vietnam, 98, 235, 244, 265, 266
  New Economic Zones (NEZ),
    113–14
  Operation Frequent Wind
    and, 108–16
  Thieu regime, 113
  United States and, 52–53
Vietnamese Communist Party
    (Lao Dong), 114
Vietnam Heroica, 171

Vietnam War, 98, 99, 108, 114, 266
Viguerie, Richard, 251
Villa Colina, Raphael, 160
Virginia, 225, 232
"Visit-USA" program, 55–56
Vitali, Henry, 79
Vollenhoven, Peter, 270
Von Bennekom, Pieter, 181
Von Mises, Ludwig, 293
Voorhees, Harold C., 55

The Wackiest Ship in the Army, 285
Wake Island, 287–88
Walesa, Lech, 12, 208, 211
Walker, John Anthony, 133–34
Wallace, George, 262
Wallace, Mike, 8, 100
The Wall Street Journal, 160, 217
Walters, Vernon, 158
Waner, Lloyd, 301
Warner, John, 61, 64, 65, 72, 84, 85
Warren, Earl, 235
Washington, D.C., 15, 92, 225, 227, 240, 244–45, 276, 300
Washington, George, 123
Washington Navy Yard, 69
The Washington Post, 129, 228, 229–30, 233–34, 242–43, 272
The Washington Star, 238, 244
Watergate, 64, 263, 266
Wayne, John, 255, 261
Wedemeyer, Albert C., 23

Weinberger, Caspar, 133, 156, 157, 158, 169, 173–74, 179–80
Welch, Robert, 247
Weldon, Felix de, 94
Wells, H.G., 206–7
West Germany, 51, 180
Westminster Magistrates' Court, 137
West Virginia, 252
White, F. Clifton, 236, 241, 242, 243, 244, 245, 253–54, 261
White, Theodore H., 16, 242, 257–58
Whitney Museum, 273
Whitworth, Jerry, 133
Wickham, John A., Jr., 178
Wignall, Sydney, 88
Wikileaks, 137
William of Orange delft, 275
Williams, Dessima, 166, 180, 181
Williams, John S., 280
Willkie, Wendell Lewis, 237
Wilson, Louis (Lew), 68
Wilson, Woodrow, 293
Winston-Salem, Norht Carolina, 252
Wisconsin, 244, 257
Wood, Struthers Company (Wood & Struthers), 296–97, 298, 299
Woods, Rose Mary, 262
Woods, Rosemary, 262
World Bank, 189

World Championships of Men's Field Hockey, 302
World Masters Rowing Championship, 302
World Masters Rowing Championship Globe, 302
World Trade Organization (WTO), 201
World War I, 280, 283
World War II, 65, 68, 70, 88, 139, 166, 235, 246, 280, 282–92, 300
Wouk, Herman, 289
W.R. Grace Company, 29
Wyeth, Andrew, 273
Wyoming, 245, 251, 257

Xuan Loc, 109

Yeltsin, Boris, 11, 209, 210
Yemen, 107
Yeutter, Clayton, 197–98
Yom Kippur War, 75–76, 100
Youth Employment Act of 1963, 246
Yunan, China, 9

al-Zawahri, Ayman, 120
Zelenskyy, Volodymyr, 204
Zhivkov, Todor, 38
Zhou Enlai, 9, 20, 21
Zimbabwe, 180
Zumwalt, Elmo, Jr., 62–63, 64, 71, 72, 113